Narrative Ethics

Narrative Ethics

Adam Zachary Newton

HARVARD UNIVERSITY PRESS

Cambridge, Massachusetts
London, England

First Harvard University Press paperback edition, 1997

LIBRARY OF CONGRESS CATALOGING-IN-PUBLICATION DATA
Newton, Adam Zachary.
Narrative ethics / Adam Zachary Newton.
p. cm.
Includes bibliographical references and index.
ISBN 0-674-60087-8 (cloth)
ISBN 0-674-60088-6 (pbk.)
1. Ethics in literature. 2. Fiction—Moral and ethical aspects.
3. Philosophy, Modern—20th century. 4. Ethics, Modern—20th century.
5. Narration (Rhetoric). 6. American fiction—History and criticism—Theory, etc.
7. English literature—History and criticism—Theory, etc.
PN49.N52   1995
809.3′9353—dc20
94-19710

To my mother and my father

שְׁלֹשָׁה שׁוּתָּפִין הֵן בָּאָדָם: הַקָּדוֹשׁ בָּרוּךְ הוּא וְאָבִיו וְאִמּוֹ.
בִּזְמַן שָׁאָדָם מְכַבֵּד אֶת אָבִיו וְאֶת אִמּוֹ -- אָמַר הַקָּדוֹשׁ בָּרוּךְ הוּא:
מַעֲלֶה אֲנִי עֲלֵיהֶם כְּאִילּוּ דַרְתִּי בֵּינֵיהֶם וְכִבְּדוּנִי.

Kiddushin 30b

וַיָּשָׁב יִצְחָק וַיַּחְפֹּר אֶת בְּאֵרֹת הַמַּיִם
אֲשֶׁר חָפְרוּ בִּימֵי אַבְרָהָם אָבִיו.

Genesis 26:18

Contents

Acknowledgments   ix

Abbreviations   xiii

1. Narrative as Ethics   1

2. Toward a Narrative Ethics   35

3. We Die in a Last Word: Conrad's *Lord Jim* and
   Anderson's *Winesburg, Ohio*   71

4. Lessons of (for) the Master: Short Fiction by
   Henry James   125

5. Creating the Uncreated Features of His Face: Monstration
   in Crane, Melville, and Wright   175

6. Telling Others: Secrecy and Recognition in Dickens,
   Barnes, and Ishiguro   241

   Conclusion   287

   Notes   295

   Index   331

Acknowledgments

A parable about parables is associated with the Dubner Maggid, the most masterly folk preacher in eighteenth-century Poland. His great admirer the Vilna Gaon, the supreme Torah authority of his time and an ethicist rather than a storyteller, once asked the Maggid about his uncanny talent for crafting *meshalim* (parables) to gloss any scriptural verse. The Maggid explained that his system was identical to that used by a village marksman who, when asked to explain his own proficiency, pointed to the bull's-eye and said, "I merely shoot at the wall, and then outline the hole with circles."

It is an ideal image for the coefficient relation between narrative fiction and ethics which I explore in the following pages—the ripple effect of story, its necessary entailments and consequences—except that prose fiction, unlike the *meshal*, remains an open and unfinalized form, and ethics, in the sense I employ it, does not neatly reduce to a simple matter of apologue or moral example. And if a more modern parable about parables is to be believed, even the simplest narratives can bind just as easily as they can loose; thus, as Kafka wrote, one may "win in reality" while already having "lost in parable."

Still, the Maggid's very name ("teller") betrays a linguistic connection between the Hebrew words for narrative and declaration, a performative dynamic which lies at the heart of narrative ethics as both theory and practice—hence, I must admit, the gravitational force for me in an image of story banded by ever-widening ethical circles. Nevertheless, as befits that part of a book devoted to registering one's debts and one's thanks, and whose very burden—acknowledgment—names a concept which plays an integral role in the analyses to follow, I would like to apply the Maggid's parable in a different way.

Thus if I have hit my mark in these pages, it is due as much to points already marked for me which I have merely encircled as to any I may have selected myself. For their guidance—sometimes a matter of intent, sometimes not—I acknowledge first my parents, to whom and before whom I say *hineni*—here am I. Most of the wells I have dug in my life my brother Scott has dug before me, or led me to; fraternal Abraham to my Isaac, fellow Ishmael (or Bulkington) with back to leeward land, he is perhaps this book's most understanding reader. I thank also my brother Fredric for his generosity and for his pivotal suggestion that I be a teacher, and Laura Newton for early modeling in the discipline. As always, the steadfastness and loyalty of Buster Newton were a tonic.

I am grateful for grants from Harvard University that enabled me to begin this project, and for support from the Woodrow Wilson Foundation that allowed me to finish it. At every stage, Jo Keroes has exemplified Roland Barthes's observation that friendship essentially works out to be a matter of acoustics: the greater the sonority, the better the friend. Shlomith Rimmon-Kenan has my deep gratitude for her solicitude and advice, both free-flowing in Cambridge as well as in Jerusalem. I thank Philip Fisher, Martha Nussbaum, and Werner Sollors for their willingness to read these chapters as they were taking shape on one coast, and Rosemary Patton and Bill Robinson for getting me started while I resided on the other. I am grateful to Stanley Cavell for giving the finished manuscript his blessing.

A special thanks to Irene Kacandes and Paul Panadero, wonderful colleagues both, for their kindness, availability, and shared interest in this work. Richard Cohen, Robert Gibbs, Sandor Goodhart, and Stephane Moses all helped me in the always-to-be-accomplished task which is reading Emmanuel Levinas. My editors at Harvard University Press, Lindsay Waters, Alison Kent, and—invaluably—Nancy Clemente, facilitated the almost-as-elusive task of bringing this work from manuscript to print. Rabbis Harry Sinoff and Ben-Zion Gold gave that task the shape of redemptive conversation when I found myself, while revising, in need of Wedding Guests.

In that same capacity as Ancient Mariner, finally, I acknowledge the interlocutors of my life—above all, Doris Sommer—for life lessons in narrative ethics. In one's own story, too, may lie a "not yet" (as Emmanuel Levinas has put it) "more distant than any future." For life-stories, mariners know, are where we build a ship and a harbor at the same time, and complete the harbor long after the ship has gone down.

How, then, to keep/stop narrating? There is no more exigent a feat, except perhaps the striking home, which (in the spirit of Mikhail Bakhtin) is the art of answerability.

Mention of Bakhtin and Levinas returns me full circle to the Maggid's parable, and to its obligingly generative metaphor. Although one strives in a work like this for marksmanship that is as personalized as it is precise—one prefers, that is, to call one's own shots—a set of mimetic circles orbiting a centripetal hub quite aptly describes my methodology in this book. The textual analyses which compose Chapters 3–6 can be seen as pivoting out from and around a common core, itself coaxial: the allied intersubjective projects of Emmanuel Levinas, Mikhail Bakhtin, and Stanley Cavell. Any philosophical claims I put forward in this book, therefore, are meant less than programmatically; here too, my deployment of bull's-eyes should be construed Maggid-like, in the spirit of thematic extension—of throwing (to adapt Cavell's formulation) philosophy's voice.

Abbreviations

AA   Mikhail Bakhtin, *Art and Answerability: Early Philosophical Essays*, ed. Michael Holquist and Vladimir Liapunov (Austin: University of Texas Press, 1990)

AN   Henry James, *The Art of the Novel* (New York: Scribner's, 1934)

BI   Paul de Man, *Blindness and Insight: Essays in the Rhetoric of Contemporary Criticism* (Minneapolis: University of Minnesota Press, 1983)

CWK   Wayne Booth, *The Company We Keep: An Ethics of Fiction* (Berkeley: University of California Press, 1988)

DI   Mikhail Bakhtin, *The Dialogic Imagination*, ed. Caryl Emerson and Michael Holquist (Austin: University of Texas Press, 1981)

ED   Simon Critchley, *The Ethics of Deconstruction: Derrida and Levinas* (Oxford: Blackwell, 1992)

ER   J. Hillis Miller, *The Ethics of Reading: Kant, de Man, Eliot, Trollope, James, and Benjamin* (New York: Columbia University Press, 1987)

HH   J. Hillis Miller, *Hawthorne and History: Defacing It* (Oxford: Blackwell, 1991)

LK   Martha Nussbaum, *Love's Knowledge: Essays on Philosophy and Literature* (Berkeley: University of California Press, 1991)

MWM   Stanley Cavell, *Must We Mean What We Say? A Book of Essays* (Cambridge: Cambridge University Press, 1976)

NDR   Gérard Genette, *Narrative Discourse Revisited: An Essay in Method*, trans. J. E. Lewin (Ithaca: Cornell University Press, 1988)

OTB   Emmanuel Levinas, *Otherwise Than Being, or beyond Essence* (The Hague: Martinus Nijhoff, 1981)

RB   *Rethinking Bakhtin: Extensions and Challenges*, ed. Gary S. Morton and Caryl Emerson (Evanston: Northwestern University Press, 1989)

RT   Paul de Man, *The Resistance to Theory* (Minneapolis: University of Minnesota Press, 1986)

SS   Ross Chambers, *Story and Situation: Narrative Seduction and the Power of Fiction* (Minneapolis: University of Minnesota Press, 1984)

TI   Emmanuel Levinas, *Totality and Infinity: An Essay on Exteriority*, trans. Alphonso Lingis (Pittsburgh: Duquesne University Press, 1969)

Narrative Ethics

1

Narrative as Ethics

"Say quick," quoth he, "I bid thee say—
What manner of man art thou?"

Forthwith this frame of mine was wrenched
With a woeful agony,
Which forced me to begin my tale;
And then it left me free.

Since then, at an uncertain hour,
That agony returns:
And till my ghastly tale is told,
The heart within me burns.

Samuel Taylor Coleridge,
The Rime of the Ancient Mariner

And as he spoke, I was thinking, the kind of stories that people turn life into, the kind of lives that people turn stories into.

Philip Roth, *The Counterlife*

1

Opening Story

THE ANCIENT MARINER'S narrative begins, once again. But it is doubtful that a story as such is even expected. What's bidden is merely a short answer—"Say quick"—a point of information—"What manner of man art thou?" And yet, what the Wedding Guest elicits far, far exceeds what he could have predicted, or even wanted. Instead of an answer, he gets a narrative; instead of plain fact, he's given, or rather subjected to, gesture, performance, *relation*, whose energy and effect quite overflow the interrogative cupped hand held out for response's small coin. Like Descartes's "idea of Infinity" the story surpasses the thought measured to think it.

Perhaps it's the fault of the imperative. The Wedding Guest bids, "say!" And the Mariner willingly complies; he does so not by stating a proposition, a "Said," but rather by staging a performance, a "Saying," a proposing and exposing of the self. He does not answer; he "stories"—not a noun but a verb both transitive and reflexive, since the Mariner's is not the only life here (to echo Philip Roth's Nathan Zuckerman in *The Counterlife*) that could be said to have turned into story. Odd as the conjunction of my two epigraphs may at first seem, they are indeed meant as a pair. And even if pairing them this way does set the stage for more perhaps unlikely combinations of texts in the chapters to follow, that is not my primary aim.

Rather, glossing Coleridge with Philip Roth allows me to call attention to a common, though sometimes overlooked, fact about narrative: that the story it frequently tells is a story of storytelling. Narrative, as participatory act, is part "Said" (to refer again to terms employed by Emmanuel Levinas) and part "Saying," the latter—the level of inter-subjective relation—being the site of surplus, of the unforeseen, of self-exposure. And while it is true that each level has its own way of

3

turning life into story, and story into life, "Saying," as Coleridge's poem so memorably illustrates, tends to exact the profounder price of such communicative alchemy—from speaker, from hearer, and from text.

What "kind" of life, what "kind" of story, then, do we find in Coleridge's poem? And what price(s) paid? (The answer to the latter, more pressing question, follows naturally from the first.) Both life and story, we discover, are much like the "rime" of the poem's title: hostages to reiteration, the eternal return of chill, thaw, and chill again. Not the poem as touchstone, but rather the tale it tells as hoarstone— the rime of repetitive rhyming, the self-referencing of narrative frost. Additionally, both life and story (or rather their union as "life-into-story") suggest a performative analogue to the character the poem calls "Life-in-Death," the entity who "thicks man's blood with cold." Mariner, tale, and, finally, listener all remain suspended—animated but numbed—in the grip of narrative compulsion. It is the paradox of seizure *as* paralysis.

Is this immobilization, this Medusa effect, the sort of thing, then, I have in mind when I say that narrative exacts a "price"? It is, and more. Which is to say that beyond the moral thematics of Coleridge's poem is a realm of ethical confrontation. The price, in other words, is higher even than the skeptical dead end that the Mariner discovers in his striving after authenticity, the kind of blockage which Stanley Cavell locates as the poem's moral in a brilliant essay on Romantic poetry. That essay tracks the Mariner's journey as an allegory of skepticism, interpreting the Mariner's crossing of the "Line" (identified by Coleridge's gloss as the Equator) as an attempt to pierce the Kantian screen separating noumena from phenomena.[1]

Like some intrepid phenomenologist, the Mariner sets sail in order to recover "the things themselves," while at the same time seeking to reach uncharted linguistic shores, leaving behind his expressive connection with others (his "attunement") precisely so that he may rediscover and thus revivify it. Skepticism, in the form of the Mariner's travails of language and sojourn, is the price one pays for wishing to be on intimate and authentic terms with human discourse.

Hence the Mariner's predicament and the price of his telling passion: striving for immediacy puts him on a course full of skeptical detours. To appreciate what is found, as well as what is lost, along these detours, to acknowledge, in words borrowed from Emmanuel Levinas, a price exacted "otherwise and beyond" skepticism, I should make clear that my reading will have to exceed or veer away from the philosophical logic that drives Cavell's interpretation and leads him to "the Mariner's" moral.

By following the premises and strictures laid out by the text, Cavell reads the poem as philosophy. And this critical speculativeness does indeed nicely parallel the poem's own speculations, in the form of the seriousness, the "religiosity," of the skeptical attitude as personified by the Mariner.[2] Thus, Cavell will speak of needing to "imitate" the Mariner in the form of "responding to" and "answering for" a certain claim enjoined by the text, drawing from it, in a word, its moral.

And yet while the talk of morality here accords with Cavell's own subtle inquiry into the claims of intersubjectivity against the claims of reason (the very tension between knowing and acknowledging which will surface again and again in this book), its thematic orientation to the price paid for "overcoming" language does not explicitly engage the sense of ethics I'm after here.[3] A fuller price is reckoned by the text. And it requires that we leave the dimension of the poem's "Said" for its "Saying."

A finer attunement to the Mariner means that to "imitate" or "respond to" the Mariner even further, goes beyond and across the traditional hierarchical "line" which divides form from content, or "Saying" from "Said," and makes the one subserve the other. Let us, then, pursue the Mariner otherwise and beyond (Levinas' vocabulary again) the "Line" which "drawing a moral" marks out.

One way to do that (as the Mariner perhaps anticipates) is to disrupt the conventionally understood synonymy of the words *moral* and *ethical*. Coleridge's *Rime of the Ancient Mariner* already enacts that disruption itself in the distinction it makes between moral propositionality, or the realm of the "Said," and ethical performance, the domain of "Saying." Thus, as exemplum, the poem does indeed invite readers to "draw a moral," a paraphrase of the poem's own prescriptive intent. "He prayeth best who loveth best all creatures great and small" expresses the Mariner's atonement for an unwarranted violation; that atonement generates attunement all around, as readers then apply the "moral" in whichever way most persuades them. "Drawing" a moral, like "applying" it, is thus a conscious and external act of *imitatio*.

But as *story* the poem opens out onto a quite different realm: that territory inside the poem shared by Mariner and Wedding Guest in their communicative, interlocutionary relation—in their immediate claim on each other—and that territory outside the text marked out by the claims it makes upon readers (though, as I will make clear, the question of textual "inside" versus "outside" is neither simple nor self-evident). It is in this domain or at this level that we can more fully address what I mean by a price of "saying" in text or story.

"Saying" in Coleridge's poem is unmistakably contaminating. Any doubt we may have had about the potency and exigency of the Mariner's speech fades in the face of the paralytic effect it has on his listeners. "If someone talks without stopping," writes Maurice Blanchot, "he is locked up in the end," which implies for me more than simply literal incarceration.[4] Being locked up by voice, for instance, by the headlong rush of story, is a fate which the Mariner must suffer, but always in company with an unwitting listener.

I have already suggested that the mechanical repetition of his tale, despite the urgency it produces, keeps the Mariner in an expressively de-animated state. As he "stops," that is, narratively suspends, Wedding Guest, Hermit, and each interlocutor in turn—"Now wherefore stoppest thou me?"—he transmits to them some measure of his own predicament. What produces merely a temporary release from living his story—retelling it—not only returns him to death-in-life, but similarly sentences every person whose ear (and destiny) he bends. As he is gripped by compulsive storytelling, so he grips and compels others in turn: he "bends them to his will"; they "cannot but obey."

As a communicative act, then, the Mariner's narrating could be said ultimately to repudiate more than revivify. And as Cavell has pointed out, if the Mariner initiates conversation with others, he does so merely to use them to catalyze his own storytelling, to force him to his tale, while forcing them to listen. Thus like all good father-confessors, the Hermit in effect functions to beget or engender narrative; likewise the Wedding Guest first stimulates, then incubates the story, to be left more affected than instructed, contaminated rather than genuinely transfigured.

But such seemingly fecund effects belie the stillborn aspect of language in the poem. As in Mary Shelley's *Frankenstein*, storytelling culminates here in polar desolation; or, to cite another sibling text of Romanticism, E. T. A. Hoffmann's "The Sandman," the distinctively uncanny property of language in Coleridge's poem is *penetration*, its capacity to leave a lasting and irrational mark or impression.

Among the various allegorical personae traditionally imputed to the Mariner—mystic catalyst, redemptive scapegoat, teacher, sage, apostle, or, as in Cavell's reading, skeptic—the one which undergirds and enables all other possibilities is, simply, that of narrator. All allegorical translations of the poem's meaning to an order external to it—allegories of salvation, of skepticism, of the Fall, of Romanticism—rest upon on a more basic allegory internal to the text: narrative structure and form as ethical relation.

Independent of any external moral brought to bear upon it (or of those it may aphorize for itself), Coleridge's poem is built around an armature of intersubjective relation accomplished through story. That armature is what I will call *ethics*: narrative as relationship and human connectivity, as Saying over and above Said, or as Said called to account in Saying; narrative as claim, as risk, as responsibility, as gift, as price. Above all, as an ethics, narrative is performance or act—purgative, as in Turgenev's "The Country Doctor," malignant, as in Camus's *La chute*, historically recuperative, as in A. B. Yehoshua's *Mr. Mani*, erotic and redemptive as in *The Thousand and One Nights*, obsessive and coercive, as in Coleridge's *Rime of the Ancient Mariner*.

To juxtapose just the last two: In the *Arabian Nights' Entertainments*, narrative, through coercion, ultimately enables marriage; in Coleridge's poem, a similar process disables it. In one, the procreative capacity of narrative serves to model relations of friendship and conjugal love—teller, listener, and witness become bound to one another through the liberating force of story; in the other, storytelling fastens on to its participants only to sever them from the world—driven out or emptied out, they remain forlornly yoked to one another only through involuntary and baleful narrative enchainment.

Both these as well as the other permutations I list above represent certain models of narrative as an ethics, paradigms which in turn imply fundamental ethical questions about what it means to generate and transmit narratives, and to implicate, transform, or force the persons who participate in them. I have already gestured toward such ethical questions through the link between the Ancient Mariner's inauguration of his "ghastly tale" and Nathan Zuckerman's lucubrations on it as the reciprocal transformation of life and story.

The Mariner supplies but the first of three textual instances I will adduce in this introduction. Together, they prepare the way for the more extensive readings which make up the rest of this book, each of which to one degree or another touches on aspects of both narration and representation, vicissitudes of the narrative act, on the one hand, and of the fictionalization of person into literary character, on the other. But Roth and Zuckerman, whether they would own up to it or not, stake a profounder claim: they announce both a theory and a moral inquiry (into a reciprocity between life and fiction), and in so doing articulate the thrust and scope of what I have named narrative ethics.

The Sense of Narrative Ethics

Why this phrase? Each of the two elements of "narrative ethics" calls up a welter of implications. And their linkage within a single phrase might therefore threaten to swell a register already inundated with like constructions—"rhetorical hermeneutics," "masculinist semiotics," "tropological politics," and so on. But this book's title is intended to connote a logic which binds its two parts intrinsically and necessarily. The fact that narrative ethics can be construed in two directions at once—on the one hand, as attributing to narrative discourse some kind of ethical status, and on the other, as referring to the way ethical discourse often depends on narrative structures—makes this reciprocity between narrative and ethics appear even more essential, more grammatical, so to speak, and less the accident of coinage.

In this book I will argue for such a relation as a defining property of prose fiction, of particular import in nineteenth- and later twentieth-century texts. The cultural and periodic delimitations I have chosen reflect developments within specific and complex literary histories; but an implicitly general claim remains for other traditions of fiction, as well as certain kinds of narrative poetry.[5]

The simpler term in my title to explain is "narrative," a term obviously familiar to literary criticism and usefully formulated in Gérard Genette's triadic model: (1) the story, or signified content, (2) the narrative, the signifier or narrative text, and (3) narrating, the narrative act. It is primarily this third element, what I have previously identified as the level of "Saying," that I discuss in the following chapters, building upon it my own three-part structure of narrational, representational, and hermeneutic levels. Genette awards *narrating* logical pride of place in fictional discourse, explaining that "the true order is . . . something like narrating/story/narrative, with the narrative act initiating (inventing) *both* the story and its narrative, which are then completely indissociable."[6] But since I believe that this act initiates responsibilities alongside forms, it receives far greater attention here than Genette or other narratologists have allowed.[7]

To define the particular sense in which I employ the concept of "ethics," however, I will begin by saying what it does *not* mean, by turning to the practical, problem-solving role it has usually been forced to assume in literary criticism.[8] Traditionally, that role has been central. To take the obvious example, as exemplum again, ethics closely informed the novel's early development as a discourse both accessory (Samuel Johnson) and internal (Richardson, Fielding) to narrative texts. Novels trained ethical sensibility. On the one hand, in texts like *Tom Jones*, and later and with greater sophistication, *Pride and Prejudice* and *Middlemarch*, narrators schooled their readership in the correct evaluation of and response to character and moral situation. This tradition culminated, with Henry James's novels and critical prefaces, in an inquiry into moral language and the way words shape and deform social relations.

More overtly sentimental fiction like *Pamela*, *Uncle Tom's Cabin*, or *Dombey and Son*, on the other hand, instructed response by inducing identificatory states of compassion and pity; a novelistic practice that anticipates the Geneva School's reader-response theory of borrowed consciousness, such texts predicated their moral effects on a Humean or Rousseauistic model of sympathy as contamination, prose fiction being the occasion for lending out states of experience. In both cases, however, ethics operates in interpolated fashion, bolstering the authoritarian character of the novel with deontic and legislative weight. It exercised this influence both autonomously and hand in hand with epistemological, sociological, and political frameworks which the novel inculcated from its outset.[9]

From this perspective, one speaks of ethics as a "defining property of the novel" in terms of "authorial responsibility," or of literary characters' "moral imagination," or of the "exemplariness" of theme and topic; narrative form functions as a vehicle for substantive ethical "content." Into this closed system of moral exemplification enters the self-adequating ethos of the critic, who, with Arnoldian flair and Aristotelian probity, matches form to content, and content to conduct. Ethical criticism, in this wise, unproblematically translates literary discourse into moral recourse.[10]

Despite the formal innovations of literary modernism, "ethics" (with some qualifications) until very recently signified just this kind of approach to textual interpretation, its relevance for narrative theory undermined only by the advent of formalist and poststructuralist approaches and their sustained repudiation of normative, extra-linguistic categories. (The cottage industry which has formed around moral philosophy's interest in a text such as James's *The Golden Bowl* illustrates this—sophisticated though still parasitical—relation between ethics and literary analysis.)

In 1957 Northrop Frye correlated ethics and criticism under the aegis of liberal humanism as "not a rhetorical comparison of social facts to predetermined values, but . . . the consciousness of the presence of society."[11] A position attacked for its outmoded liberal humanism by theorists as different as Frank Lentricchia, Hans Robert Jauss, and Tzvetan Todorov, Frye's stance makes ethics essentially synonymous with critical pluralism.[12] Perhaps not incidentally, the working definitions of ethics in two recent books, J. Hillis Miller's *The Ethics of Reading* and Wayne Booth's *The Company We Keep: An Ethics of Fiction*, despite enormous differences from Frye's, suggest at least a family resemblance to it.

In their parallel determinations to "submit" to the effects of fiction Miller and Booth both espouse what they might want to call a narrative ethics. Their purposes are nevertheless very different from each other's and from my own. While Miller subscribes to an ethic of unreadability, a linguistic imperative from which readers cannot exempt themselves, and Booth constructs a theory of textual ethos in terms of ratios of friendship, each operates essentially within a formalist and Kantian framework. Literary texts demand judgment from their interpreters; so all that remains at issue is to distinguish kinds of ethical criticism from one another according to the degree to which such judgment rests upon criteria either bound or free. (Ethics as freedom, ethics as duty: the ambiguity attaching to the word was never so clear.)

Hence the curious fact that while Booth and Miller stand poles apart in critical approach, they can be legitimately described as two kinds of ethical critics, principally invested, like Frye, in the distinctive quality of ethical/critical judgment, of its rightness as textual commentary. Accordingly, each prises apart the more conjunctive dynamic between narrative and ethics I wish to pursue here. "The ethics of reading"/"the ethics of fiction"/"the ethics of criticism": all such formulations sit precariously on an ambiguous genitive. By purposeful contrast, my proposal of a narrative ethics implies simply narrative *as* ethics: the ethical consequences of narrating story and fictionalizing person, and the reciprocal claims binding teller, listener, witness, and reader in that process.

To cite the case of Coleridge again, the difference lies between readings which allegorize the poem's events to a second-order story of translated meaning and those I will develop in ensuing chapters which attend exclusively to the shape, the drama, and the circumstances of the poem's own story, its strictly narrative details, since that story already reads, or allegorizes, itself. It is the difference, to put it another way, between a deontology and a phenomenology—between a reading which attempts to evaluate or even solve a text's problems and one which engages them in their concrete, formal, narrative particularity. One faces a text as one might face a person, having to confront the claims raised by that very immediacy, an immediacy of contact, not of meaning. (Like the sense of "claim" intended by Cavell's *The Claim of Reason*, my use of the word here yokes together "a claim staked" by fiction for its own seriousness and "a claim exerted" by it, as with Mariner and Wedding Guest, on readers and critics.)

And in the field of intersubjectivity demarcated by such claims one can discern the more authentic provenance for "ethics" as I understand the term. Jürgen Habermas has called intersubjectivity the road not taken by the "discourse of modernity," that line of thought which stretches from Hegel through poststructuralism. In analytic philosophy, the intersubjective became either a strictly epistemological question (the problem of "other minds") or a casualty of the fact/value split (meta-ethics versus ethical praxis). And while it did become an explicit topic for phenomenology, continental philosophers also tended to ramify it in the customary terms of subject/object relations. Ironically, this anemic sort of life granted to the ethical in philosophical discourse merely parallels the phenomenological thinness it has had to endure in literary criticism.

The concept and term have taken root nevertheless. Thus while intersubjectivity (or "the question of the Other") has quite rapidly become the focus of post-Heideggerean social ontology, hermeneutics, and communicative ethics (as well as of a rejuvenated moral philosophy in Britain and the United States), so "alterity" as the common issue in difference criticisms (gender, cultural, and post-Marxist) has come to saturate the discourse of contemporary literary and cultural theory.[13]

Literature and philosophy now often intersect along just these lines, most accessibly, for instance, in the case of Mikhail Bakhtin's "dialogism."

"Ethics," in this alternative sense, signifies recursive, contingent, and interactive dramas of encounter and recognition, the sort which prose fiction both crystallizes and recirculates in acts of interpretive engagement. Traditionally, when philosophers proceed from ontology to ethics, they replace a model of theoretical necessity with a model of human freedom. But as Emmanuel Levinas and Mikhail Bakhtin have argued (two thinkers whose work I braid together with Stanley Cavell's in the pages to follow), moral philosophy remains under the shadow of the totalizing pretensions of ontology as *prima philosophia*, even and especially when it concerns itself with questions of freedom.

Ethical theorists have traditionally defined freely determined action according to a law of rationality from which they can derive criteria for moral behavior at once universalizable and intrinsically intelligible. Ethos, in effect, borrows from logos a normative account of human action which subsumes particular and contingent facts under a general and totalizing order. In Aristotle, Kant, Hume, and more recently Habermas, ethics is expressed in terms of obligation and autonomy, both attributes determined by reference to universal and self-evident laws of reason.

By contrast, in the special, but by no means unusual, sense I intend it and provisionally describe above, "ethics" refers to the radicality and uniqueness of the moral situation itself, a binding claim exercised upon the self by a concrete and singular other whose moral appeal precedes both decision and understanding. As Fabio Ciaramelli puts it, the ethical subject is *"assigned to morality* by the appeal of the other."[14]

Reversing the conventional logic of moral philosophers (indeed repudiating it *as* logic), Levinas, for instance, argues that consciousness and even subjectivity follow from, are legitimated by, the ethical summons which proceeds from intersubjective encounter. Subjectivity arrives, so to speak, in the form of a responsibility toward an Other which no one else can undertake; if, from this perspective, selfhood always remains in some way incomplete, it is because ethical responsibility continually outstrips one's capacity to assume it. For Levinas, "ethics" describes neither ontic nor deontic categories, which generalize theories of reality from subjective experience; ethics, rather, originates from the opposite direction—from the other to me, in the sensible experience of the *face* which he or she presents to me. "The approach to the face is the most basic mode of responsibility. As such, the face of the other is verticality and uprightness; it spells a relation of rectitude. The face is not in front of me but above me . . . In the relation to the face I am exposed as a usurper of the place of the other."[15]

One of my claims here is that certain kinds of textuality parallel this description of ethical encounter in several obvious ways. Cutting athwart the mediatory role of reason, narrative situations create an immediacy and force, framing relations of provocation, call, and response that bind narrator and listener, author and character, or reader and text. Again, these relations will often precede decision and understanding, with consciousness arriving late, after the assumption or imposition of intersubjective ties. In this sense, prose fiction translates the interactive problematic of ethics into literary forms. Stories, like persons, originate alogically. As ethical performance, in Levinas' sense, they are concussive: they shock and linger as "traumatisms of astonishment."

The "logic" which binds narrative and ethics, then, is really a pragmatics, implying an interactive rather than a legislative order,[16] a diachrony across the temporal world of the text and the real time of reading. Since the vicissitudes of narrative situations do not easily submit to prescriptive or procedural norms of rationality (they take place as the stories which produce them unfold), "ethics" in this book will therefore not signify a set of meta-theoretical ideas or preexisting moral norms.[17]

Instead, it will mean, as Mikhail Bakhtin puts it, "the historical concreteness of the individual fact, and not the theoretical truth of a proposition," a moral discourse which derives from a more primordial "groundwork." As a problematic, then, it finds for me its most satisfying correlations in the respective philosophical projects of Emmanuel Levinas, Mikhail Bakhtin, and Stanley Cavell.

And since my methodology focuses upon prose fiction, I turn now to the second of three textual instances I invoke in this chapter. A short story by Sherwood Anderson will let me flesh out some of the ideas introduced through Coleridge's poem in order to introduce a vocabulary and set of concepts.

In this short reading and the one I call "true story," which comes later in the chapter, one can trace the common thread of blurred boundaries between reading people and reading plots, between the separate domains of life and story.

Pure Story

Like *The Rime of the Ancient Mariner*, Sherwood Anderson's *Winesburg, Ohio* stands as representative of a certain cultural moment in literary history.[18] Its topic, form, and closeness to Anderson's own personal circumstances together herald a shift toward American modernism, toward an aesthetic of the fragment, toward a kind of anti-Romantic Romanticism. But, as I have also maintained about Coleridge's poem, one can also see the stories which make up Anderson's novel as telling an internal story: of storytelling and of narrative form. As case studies, they form a kind of Krafft-Ebing of narrative dynamics; a repetitive lesson in the price exacted by storytelling, they demonstrate what one might call an American Chamber of Narrative Horrors.[19] The brevity of these stories merely calls attention to, or grotesquely highlights, the stripped-down dialogics of narrative exposure.

The novel collects these stories under the rubric "The Tales and the Persons." Almost all feature an isolated protagonist forced up against a rather blank interlocutor; tale and person metonymize each other in a way we recognize from Coleridge, as lives turn into stories and stories fold back again into lives.

Anderson calls his narrators "grotesques" not merely because of their disfigured sociality, but because, like the Mariner's, their lives collapse to those rare moments in which they can narrate the story of a collapsed life. "Loneliness," one of these, is described by the governing narrator as "the story of a room almost more than it is the story of a man."[20] This formulation is important, since it effectively reduces person not just to the confines of a tale, but, more, to the narrative space within.

The story, we discover—and I mean that in the two senses of "finding out" and "exposing"—reflexively examines the dynamics of authorship, in particular autobiographical narration. It lays bare the grotesque implications of a life and self transformed into narrative fiction in such a way that being recognized or understood become tantamount to being deciphered or read. Perhaps most important, the story uniquely dramatizes the risk, both discursive and existential, of telling one's "life-story." Not coincidentally, all these matters describe the motivations of the storyteller, Enoch Robinson, for they embody the very things he implicitly wishes his audience, George Willard, to comprehend. "'You'll understand if you try hard enough,' he said conclusively. 'I have looked at you when you went past me on the street and I think you understand. It isn't hard. All you have to do is believe what I say, just listen and believe, that's all there is to it'" (175).

But eliciting comprehension here means forcing it—the paradox of narrative "seizure." Now an old man, Enoch (the Hebrew meaning of *hanoch*, "teacher," being quite apposite here) introduces a highly charged narrative formula in his instructions, since for the first time in the sequence of *Winesburg*'s stories, the listener is drawn to minister to the storyteller (rather than the other way around) by the laying on of hands: "He wanted to put his arms around the little old man. In the half darkness the man talked and the boy listened, filled with sadness" (175). Before this moment, though, George—a faded figure for the reader—acts "the young reporter." Enoch represents for him merely another curiosity, another exposé, one more of Winesburg's grotesques.

Until this point a narrator outside the story's diegesis has disclosed the salient features of Enoch's tale, in particular the fact that as a young man he had escaped the confines of Winesburg and moved to New York. Although ostensibly freed from Winesburg's weird narrative bale, and despite the advent of artistic friendships, marriage, and fatherhood, Enoch nevertheless gives himself over to the imaginative production of character, to "making up people."[21] "He wanted most of all the people of his own mind, people with whom he could really talk, people he could harangue and scold by the hour, servants, you see, to his fancy. . . . He was like a writer busy among the figures of his brain, a kind of tiny blue-eyed king he was, in a six-dollar room facing Washington Square in the city of New York" (178). Merely to come from Winesburg, it seems, provides sufficient cause to disfigure one's personhood, and twist lived experience to the dimensions of literary figuration.

Ultimately, Enoch leaves wife and children and sequesters himself in the room which he peoples with his fictions (as did Anderson himself, famously forsaking his own domestic circumstances in Elyria, Ohio, for the freedom of Cleveland). And it is in this collapsed space that, as a kind of allegory of autobiography, the story models its own internal narrative conditions.[22]

At a crucial moment in the story, the narrator allows Enoch to take over the narration of his own story, a meaningful transition since it sets in motion a series of metonymic transfers of authorial responsibility. The story now reduces to one particular and summary incident, what Enoch gnomically refers to as "the thing that happened." Enoch proceeds to speak of his room, his "people," a woman next door to whom he unwisely confessed one night, his ambivalence about being understood, and of the incompatibility of all these things.

For unlike Coleridge's Mariner, Enoch finds risk, not intermittent (and illusory) release, in narrative unburdening. The risk in telling his story means that he will find himself caught in language, a phrase which cuts two ways: either he will make himself understood, and thus be "caught," or he will speak and not be understood, thus "catching himself up." How does one, the story asks, tell oneself without losing oneself: as though the tellability of one's story were a finite, measurable thing, a volume capable of being diminished, like air in a room. As Edmond Jabès writes, "To tell a story, in my opinion, is to lose it. If I tell you about my life in detail, it escapes in the details I have chosen to recount."[23]

In his essay on Henry James, Joseph Conrad notes, "I doubt the heroism of my readers," suggesting that they might not be equal to the interpretive tasks he poses for them. For Enoch it could well be said that he "fears the hearing of his hearers," since for him storytelling depends on the acoustic space in which it occurs, its success being a function of the listeners' capacity for sonority, for resonance; in not keeping his words to himself (as the common expression says of *hands*), Enoch fears he will lose them in the dead air of deficient response. When, in a scene uncannily reminiscent of Dostoevsky's *Notes from Underground* (another text about the hazards of self-fictionalizing and narrative exigency), the lure of narrative having become too irresistible a force, Enoch speaks; not surprisingly, things go "to smash":

> I became mad to make her understand me and to know what a big thing I was in that room. I wanted her to see how important I was. I told her over and over. When she tried to go away, I ran and locked the door. I followed her about. I talked and talked and then all of a sudden things went to smash. A look came into her eyes and I knew

she did understand. Maybe she had understood all the time. I was furious. I couldn't stand it. I wanted her to understand but, don't you see, I couldn't let her understand. I felt that then she would know everything, that I would be submerged, drowned out, you see. That's how it is. I don't know why. (177)

It is at precisely this point in the story that the frame breaks, and Enoch performs outside the story exactly what he relates had occurred inside it, the same ambivalence, the same retraction, the identical conflict. That is, the narrative pressure which he describes as having driven away the woman in his story—a matter of description—repeats itself, is enacted, in his effect on George, whom he drives away. The story is, to paraphrase Stanley Fish, a self-contaminating artifact. George (Wedding Guest now turned Mariner) forces the storyteller, coaxing and browbeating him for the "story," and ultimately confirming Enoch's fears by failing to grasp what's happening.

The story counts on its readers, however, for more sophistication. The phrase "the story of a room" really means the narrative contours of the story Enoch needs to tell at every point. The "room" is the story he tells the woman next door, as it is also the story that he tells George, as it is the story he tells us. And in each successive frame but one, the same volume diminishes, the same life goes out of the room.

The one frame provisionally exempted remains the one that governs the reader's interpretive response. Thus the narrative logic here requires that after Enoch finishes the story and explains that "she took all my people away. They went out through the door after her," George must respond similarly. He "gets" the story—but only as a reporter would, not a genuine interlocutor. What remains, once the life has gone out of the room, finally disclosed and stripped of all fictional appurtenances, is all there ever was: narrative voice marooned in narrative space. Its readers now remain its only hearers; and it is their acoustical sensitivity which stands at issue.

Ethical Self-Situating

The story is its own lesson. As an allegory of narration which follows from the *internal* framework of the text, it compactly outlines the triadic structure of narrative ethics which I merely hinted at in my reading of Coleridge and which I can spell out now. The triad comprises: (1) a narrational ethics (in this case, signifying the exigent conditions and consequences of the narrative act itself); (2) a representational ethics (the costs incurred in fictionalizing oneself or others by exchanging "person" for "character"); and (3) a hermeneutic ethics (the ethico-critical accountability which acts of reading hold their readers to).

These three categories will form the conceptual core of the readings in the following chapters. Since it is at the outset one of the grounding assumptions of this project that character and narration, like theme and form, presuppose each other, both in turn inflected by hermeneutic demands, these lines of inquiry should be understood as interlaced, though I separate them for clarity's sake.

To recall, the first category refers to what narratologists call "narrative situation" or "narrative act," and what I have referred to, following Levinas, as "Saying"—the dialogic system of exchanges at work among tellers, listeners, and witnesses, and the intersubjective responsibilities and claims which follow from acts of storytelling. The word "relational," in fact, quite neatly captures the two qualities, interpersonal and discursive, which combine here in the domain of narration proper—in Coleridgean terms, the selecting out, stopping, and holding "one of three."

The second category, as the concept of "life-turned-into-story" implies, denotes the small but still momentous distance that lies between person and character, or character and caricature, the gains, losses, and risks taken up when selves represent or are represented by others. Emmanuel Levinas has described the dialectic here in terms of the dis-enchanting nudity of "the face," on the one hand, and the forms or manifestations which clothe and mystify it, on the other:

> Here is a person who is what he is; but he does not make us forget, does not absorb, cover over entirely the objects he holds and the way he holds them, his gestures, limbs, gaze, thought, skin, which escape from under the identity of his substance, which like a torn sack is unable to contain them. Thus a person bears on his own face, alongside of its being with which he coincides, its own caricature, its own picturesqueness. . . . There is then a duality in this person, this thing, a duality in its being. It is what it is and it is a stranger to itself, and there is a relationship between these two moments. We will say the thing is itself and is its image. And that this relationship between the thing and its image is resemblance. . . . The whole of reality bears on its face its own allegory, outside of its revelation and its truth. In utilizing images art not only reflects, but brings about this allegory.

In art allegory is introduced into the world, as truth is accomplished in cognition.[24]

This idea of an essential doubling of reality—that, in the case of Anderson's story, people can be both fashioned out of thin air as well as bleached of their own humanness—ties acts of representation to responsibilities in a way which parallels the claim I make for the underlying conditions of actually telling stories. However, the epistemological parallel which Levinas draws between allegory and cognition suggests not only that fiction can operate as a kind of "knowing," but also that fiction's modus vivendi—its power to represent—at some level gives way before the more severe and plenary power of ethical responsibility.

The last category, "hermeneutic ethics," suggests why an alternate title for this book could have been *Performing the Text*, since textual interpretation comprises both private responsibilities incurred in each singular act of reading and public responsibilities that follow from discussing and teaching works of fiction.[25] Reading, in effect, contaminates, just as storytelling in Anderson's text communicates its burden in both senses of the word. "You are perfectly free," as Sartre says, to leave that book on the table. "But if you open it, you assume responsibility for it."[26] Responsibility for what exactly? For simply opening the book? For reading it? For responding to it? For putting it back?

The responsibility is twofold. In part it means learning the paradoxical lesson that "getting" someone else's story is also a way of losing the person as "real," as "what he is"; it is a way of appropriating or allegorizing that endangers both intimacy and ethical duty. At the same time, however, one's responsibility consists of responding to just this paradox. To illustrate the first point—the price of getting a story—consider for a moment Anderson's tale in contrast to Joseph Conrad's *Lord Jim* (which I discuss in detail in Chapter 3). For one thing, the story "Loneliness" is its own lesson; it reads itself, in advance of any "moral paraphrase." When readers turn to *Lord Jim*, by contrast, they find a conventional and perhaps deliberately banal sense of an ending.

If Jim remains unclear to Marlowe, he has at least provided the satisfaction of storybook closure, a "heroic" death at yarn's end, so to speak. "He was not—if I may say so—clear to me," says Marlow. "He was not clear. And there is a suspicion he was not clear to himself either." A complaint J. Hillis Miller extends to observe that "interpreting his story is a ceaseless movement toward a light which always remains hidden."[27]

I will have occasion to take this position up again, but here I wish to suggest that the process Miller alludes to, inside the text as well as "outside" it, needs to be recast in ethical terms (indeed, Miller's final words remind one of Levinas) if only to clarify the easy dialectic of inside/outside here. There is another sort of price to be reckoned beyond opacity, a price which Anderson's story, we could say, makes quite transparent. In "Loneliness," the cost of the process Miller describes for *Lord Jim* shows more dearly; the closer readers approach the light, the dimmer it becomes—not because of any internal self-occlusion, but as a response to the readers' proximity.

To "get" someone's story in this regard—as George Willard uncritically does—is analogous to the belief in certain cultures that photographing a person's image in some way absconds with it. As is often the case in classical tragedy, recognition here exacts the price of a disappearance, an abscess caused by knowledge. That is, it is our staring, our looking for enlightenment, and our witnessing of Enoch which the story "knows" beforehand, and will hold us accountable for (in much the same way as a Jamesian puzzle story forces upon its readers the perturbations of hermeneutic self-consciousness).

And for a text like this, perturbation, not privilege, and accountability, as opposed to free access, define the conditions of reader response. Reading this story takes the form of a constant drawing-nearer; and yet, paradoxically, the closer we approach the text, the farther away from it we get, and the more exorbitant our responsibility toward it consequently becomes—an infinite movement.

Now the "task to be discharged" (in Sartre's phrase) which follows from the ethical constraint against fixing or fictionalizing a life story is, as I have said, a kind of negative capability of response. Consider in this light another document of self-reflexivity more famous than Anderson's "Loneliness": Velásquez's *Las Meninas*. In a brilliant analysis, Michel Foucault interprets Velásquez's painting as an allegory of subjectivity.[28] Velásquez himself sits at the apex of a representational triangle ("Le regard souverain commande un triangle virtuel"), invisible as such, but twice reproduced through mirror effects; simultaneously in the picture and outside of it, he commands its dialectic of representation. All of what we see is circumscribed by, leads to, and follows from, his totalizing gaze. To look at the painting means granting its painter legislative mastery, since his positionality wholly constrains the field of representation.

While Foucault himself admits the dangers in moving between different orders of representation, in his case, from the visual to the literary, in mine, from Spanish painting to American short story, the works share certain effects in common. For instance, both implicate their respective audiences; ironically, they force responsibility outward. But the difference lies in this: where Velásquez fetishizes vision as a source of knowledge, Anderson depicts listening as an ethical act, response as responsibility.

Where painter manipulates his own subjectivity's play of presence and absence, always answerable to his dictates, the story's narrator (here, admittedly, the formal analogy ceases to be precise) gives the story's progressive transfer of authority to the reader as his or her problem, so that "answerability" resides—taken up or refused—outside the story's representational and aesthetic limits. What readers answer for, as Cavell has put it, is their separateness before another's helplessness—in this case, the helplessness of literary character per se—derelict and stripped bare. *Loneliness*, we could say, implies not merely a circumstantial property but a textual one, the loneliness of an exposed, synthetic construct. True, we shut our eyes, and we shut out Velásquez; but the ethical drama of Anderson's story happens as we read. We never question Velásquez's hegemony while we subject ourselves to his painting, to his sly subjectivity. But in subjecting ourselves to the story we witness its authority change hands, and, ultimately, fall into our own.[29]

One might object: nothing "falls into" anything here, and such a phenomenalist vocabulary merely reveals a basic misunderstanding of purely textual procedures. But "Loneliness" exactly concerns the desolation which attaches to the "purely" textual or acoustical (sound signifying a kind of notation). A literary character's voice imitates the intonation of spoken language, as Theodor Adorno once wrote of punctuation, but at the same time it confirms that no one is really "speaking." As "each carefully avoided mark is a sign of reverence shown by writing toward the sound that it suffocates,"[30] so the slow, deliberate distancing of Enoch signifies the "suffocation" of the pleas for help it simultaneously inscribes. "I felt that I would be submerged, drowned out, you see."[31]

Anticipating the formulations of theorists like Genette or Lucien

Dällenbach, Anderson the *storyteller* understands quite well the ease
with which readers tend to conflate authorial and narrative audiences,
transgress diegetic levels, or reverse *énoncé* for *énonciation*, especially in
self-consciously "addressive" texts like "Loneliness." Indeed, I want
here to highlight the fact that such texts exactly call for mimetic,
performative acts from readers, in spite of the ontological and
epistemic borders between fiction and reality. As ethical burdens, such
acts represent, in Sartre's words, their "task to be discharged." Like a
great deal of American short fiction, Hawthorne's, Twain's, or even
Ring Lardner's, for instance, Anderson's text unapologetically invites
the very ideological "confusion" which Paul de Man has identified as
(linguistic) "reference" blurring into "phenomenalism."[32]

(At the extradiegetic, authorial level, Anderson, of course, presides
over the seeming *mise-en-abyme* of embedded actions. But this is not to
say that he, or even the implied author, stands at one end of the story's
traffic of responsibilities, with the implied reader, then, at the other.
The story works because it just does transfer those responsibilities
through successive frames. Anderson's "role" as governing narrator
remains essentially empty; his "function," in contrast, activates the
autonomous workings of the text. In terms of children's games, one
might make the analogy to the initial hander-off in "Hot Potato,"
rather than, say, the message sender in "Telephone.")

Just as the "other" in Levinas assigns the self to obligation before it
is willingly chosen, so Anderson's story teaches or commands some
readerly transfiguration before the book is put aside and the mind has
a chance to catch up. Like persons, texts present and expose themselves;
the claim they make on me does not begin with dedicating myself to
them, but rather precedes my discovery of the claim.[33] One can call
this the imperative aspect of literature—the sort commonly exercised
by conversion narratives like Augustine's or Thoreau's, or which Sartre
generalizes to all literature in his essay "Why Write?"

More than mere autonomous textuality is at work here then, I am
arguing. Unlike the ritual communality which a theatrical performance
can generate, "Loneliness," as its title also suggests, burdens each
individual reader with both his own singularity, his own separateness,
and the responsibility for the character's as well. Witnessing, overhearing, even reading, all involve a kind of passive culpability. If the story
traces a sequence of exits at each diegetic level, it places ultimately, as
I say, in readers' hands its recurrent problem of "live-exiting."[34]

Whereas theater provides a group confirmation of others' presentness, solitary reading—and especially the reading of narrative fiction, where voices are routinely lent out and impersonated—involves no such dispensation, since it leaves all differences intact between the reader and possible but invisible others.

Indeed, perhaps the profoundest ethical dilemma which reading fiction poses *is just* the fact of solitude, that it is accomplished alone, forcing one's own single self against and into the world(s) of fictional others. Paradoxically, the situations it discloses for the most part remain intersubjective, yet the witnessing of them, so to speak, reduces to an audience of one, the single reader.[35] In the ethical dramas it rehearses—human separateness and the claims of recognition—every reading, we could say, stages a "command performance," the legislative power here belonging not to author or to text but to the critical and responsive act. The very act of reading, in other words, like prayer or casual looking, permits things to happen.[36]

The Sartrean argument for "responsibility" which I quote above dialectically links the correlative responsibilities of reading and writing, of "invention" and "disclosure," and grounds them in the obligation to be engaged, invested in somehow hooking literature up with the world; from this standpoint, one actively resists Kantian disinterest. Sartre's claim also recalls and clarifies the distinction I made earlier between a narrative ethics whose thrust is phenomenological and a deontological ethics of criticism.

That responsibility introduces the question of critical allegiances (something I address below). By invoking the "ethical Sartre" I incur the risk of making my position sound suspiciously normative, perhaps not terribly far removed from the very brand of morally inflected literary theory which I claimed to distinguish myself from earlier. In a post-traditional world, traditions like this do not fare well.[37] My own formulation is introduced here after one final "textual" instance—from life—of the vexed relations among persons, their lives, and the stories they create.

True Story

In an early essay, Mikhail Bakhtin remarks, "It is only when my life is set forth for another that I myself become its hero."[38] Bakhtin is using "hero" in a very particular sense here: as the burden assumed in constructing one's life as a story for others.[39] For this entails more than merely an aesthetic challenge, and stands apart from conventional associations of outsize performance or larger than life "heroics." Elsewhere in the same essay, Bakhtin makes the related point that, because of their unique vantage point, others are more commonly the heroes of my own life than I am, able as they are to render me with an aesthetic generosity I myself am incapable of; to be narrated by others taps into a play of ethical-discursive forces.

An uncanny literalization of these ideas can be found in A. R. Luria's *The Man with a Shattered World*, the painstakingly assembled narrative of a soldier nearly incapacitated by a severe brain wound. (The book is one of two discursive experiments in what Luria called "Romantic Science," or, as Oliver Sacks perhaps more aptly puts it, the "neurological novel.") The labor Luria's patient undertakes to construct himself through narrative, while extreme, does mark a universal passage from lived to told lives. It becomes, moreover, a collaborative effort through Luria's own interpolated analysis and empathetic, "novelized" commentary.

In Bakhtin's terms, the victim, Zasetsky, reclaims his life with the greatest difficulty in the very process of telling it (indeed, only by narrating himself can he be said to possess himself); similarly, Luria, in the reciprocally creative role of co-authoring listener, bestows upon Zasetsky the gift of a narrative purchase on his life, to be gained only from outside it by a responsibly "authoring" other. Storytelling, again, lays claims upon all its participants, those circumscribed within the narrative as well as those Luria-like witnesses and ethical co-creators from without—its readers.

A Defense of Narrative Ethics

I am aware of the dangers in collapsing the difference between the world of the text and the world which this final example of life-turned-into-story raises, but I think it is fairly well established that narrative literature shares structures and assumptions with other forms of social understanding. The strong mimeticist position argues that narrative fiction is continuous with common structures of everyday experience. "The novel does not invent its structures," this position argues, "but heightens, isolates, and proceeds to analyze the narrative forms, methods, and motions of [everyday] perception and communication; sometimes explicitly, always implicitly, the novel is concerned to analyze the narrative forms of ordinary life."[40]

One need not dismiss this as so much naive reflectionism, since it merely suggests a continuous relationship between everyday narrative forms and those of literary texts. The question is, however, *how* to conceive of such a relationship. Is it unilinear and hierarchical? Or instead, interactive and reciprocal? Does it simply replicate at another level the dictates of ideology? Or does it resist and read against them? The questions are important and familiar, but the ones I pose here veer away from both ideological and deconstructive approaches.

I argue simply that narrative prose fiction (particularly in texts leading up to and away from modernism), like real-world discourse, is subject to an "ethics." One of the discursive worlds it inhabits is an ethical one, manifesting certain characteristics which resemble features of everyday communicative experience. In the order they appear in my analysis, those characteristics are: first, the formal design of the storytelling act, the distribution of relations among teller, tale, and person(s) told (narrational ethics); second, a standing problematic of recognition, an anagnorisis that extends beyond the dynamics of plot to the exigent and collaborative unfolding of character, the sea change wrought when selves become either narrating or narrated (representational ethics); and last, "hermeneutics," as both a topic within the text and a field of action outside it, that is, a narrative inquiry into the extent and limits of intersubjective knowledge in persons' reading of each other, and the ethical price exacted from readers by texts (hermeneutic ethics).

I claim an ethical status for such features because I believe they underscore an ethical mandate built into language use: vocative, interpellative, or dative impulses in utterance, we might say, which take narrative shape as address, command, plea, gift, and trust (or simply as "telling one's life story," depicted so compellingly in the example of Luria's Zasetsky), and which in the light of an alternate narrative counter-text of secrecy, gossip, coercion, or control become even more palpable.

To mark how profound a "negative" confirmation of the ethical can be, it is enough to remember Miss Havisham's "authorial" influence on Pip's narrative self-understanding in Dickens' *Great Expectations*; or the various kinds of defective narration which conscript or deform their agents in Faulkner's *Absalom, Absalom!* or Kate and Densher's insertion of Milly Theale as "character-function" into their jointly composed

"plot" in James's *The Wings of the Dove;* or the contaminant quality of
human relations through confession or accidental language which supplies the moral fiber so unmistakable in the fiction of George Eliot and
Thomas Hardy.

For this book, however, I have chosen another set of textual instances: the magic effect of personality in Conrad's *Lord Jim* and Anderson's *Winesburg, Ohio;* the shrinkage of personhood to sign in
certain texts by James, Crane, and Melville, and, *mutatis mutandis,* its
re-amplification through the delicately encrypted acts of autobiography
of J. S. Mill or the narrator in Kazuo Ishiguro's *The Remains of the Day;*
the pulse of recognition hindered or achieved in Dickens' *Bleak House.*
These will constitute the facets of the variegated model of narrative
ethics which I develop in this book.

I must emphasize, however, that the structure of fiction, that is, its
status as both artifact and instrumentality, is not the structure of personal encounter; fiction justifies itself in part "by differentiating the
practices of the world from the practices of representing it."[41] Each of
my readings will show that to ask phenomenologically, how is reading
characters in a book like reading persons in life? or conversely, how is
"facing" outside fiction like its counterpart within?—should not beg
the implied question of isomorphism, but rather set before us two
separate modes of intersubjective access, which is either solicited or
denied.

The limits bounding the ethics of fiction, in other words, are ones
posed by reading and responding to fiction—to be reckoned as one
performs and interprets a text—and not facilely breached in order to
apply "lessons for life." The profoundest meaning of narrative ethics,
then, may be just this sheer fact of limit, of separateness, of boundary.
It engages us, it places claims upon us, not exactly as life and persons
do, but similarly, and with similar ethical consequences. If, as the
narrator of Julian Barnes's *Flaubert's Parrot* remarks, "truths about
writing can be framed before you've published a word; truths about life
can be framed only when it's too late to make any difference," then
reading is an act which, in some way, does make a difference.

Ethics assumes in this book the proportions of what in German is
called *das Stumme Wissen,* "tacit knowledge," an integral though not
always systematized or articulated given in a common field of actions
and purposes. As practical wisdom, such tacit knowledge assumes that
naming and negotiating the world occur not (or not ultimately) as

functions of obedience to invisible sites of "power," but through representational frames held in common, socially and cognitively fundamental. In what therefore might be called a chastened or self-aware essentialism, my analysis assumes that consciously or not we hold these "ethical truths" to be inalienable, if not always self-evident. Thus the most far-reaching claims for narrative ethics (like its outermost boundaries) are metaphysical.

While some recent attempts to conflate ethics with politics seek to establish for ethics a greater status by default (a kind of borrowed credibility), I am insisting instead on its own critical legitimacy.[42] Political and historical contexts often write large the intersubjective details of narrative encounter (as I take pains to illustrate in Chapter 5), and thus the ethical need not be consigned to a realm lying outside history and politics.[43] Circumstances of narrative disclosure, their motives and their consequences, conduce, as I have said, to a set of ethical questions. These, however, remain distinct from (without supplanting) economic, cultural, or erotic power relations as analyzed, for example, by Roland Barthes, Fredric Jameson, Ross Chambers, and others. Again, I propose that as specifically ethical claims exacted by narrative relationships, these terms are less contractual than immanent/transcendental: the limiting intersubjective conditions of the narrative imagination.

Let me then briefly situate such ambitious claims against three alternative positions which I take up in the next chapter, but here enumerate specifically in terms of the relative weight each is willing to cede to ethics.

Deconstruction

The deconstructive refutation of such claims remains on its own terms irrefutable. I am incorporating its critique into this book not because I expect to contest its validity, but to draw out an important difference between two distinct ways of reading. That difference does not lie between two contrastive instrumentalities, methods, or viewpoints, two different kinds of cameras, so to speak, focused on the identical object. Rather, it lies in respective commitments to "facing": where deconstruction persists in immodestly "looking at" its textual objects (an attitude justified by recourse to its "scrupulosity" toward texts), narrative ethics calls into question that very performativity, that self-privi-

leging staring at texts conveniently legitimized by the fact that of
deconstruction it should be said, "Ça se deconstruit" ("it deconstructs
itself").[44] Narrative ethics asks about the impulse behind such staring—
whether it is after all so very different from a similar impulse to stare
at people. It is what Stanley Cavell calls "a specific response to the
claim [people] make upon us, a specific form of acknowledgment; for
example, rejection" (*MWM*, 331).

Like Levinas' philosophy of ethical alterity, Cavell's concept of acknowledgment as the necessary response to an intersubjective claim
assigns ethical action and language to a plane which is not primarily
epistemological or ontological; such a plane lies transverse to or, as
Levinas puts it, "otherwise than" the dimensions of being or knowing
whose common project of adequation—the grasp after persons—it cuts
across and interrupts.

In discursive terms, the complementary relationship can be traced in
the immediacy of a fictional text's representational and narrative acts,
the varieties of narrative "capture": from the transfixing and hectoring
of *The Rime of the Ancient Mariner* or "Loneliness" to the dialogic
surplus and redemption of *The Man with a Shattered World*. Extending
Cavell, we could call these claims ethics' challenge to the claim of
reason: "the claim of the other" or "the claim of narrative relations."
This divergence in claim between ethics and epistemology is the difference between the genuine surprise which is to experience what is
other and a refusal, as the philosopher Richard Cohen has put it, "to
be taken by surprise."[45]

To return to deconstruction, Paul de Man would argue that literature "knows" its own unreadability before criticism points it out, as I
remarked earlier of Anderson's story that it "knows" the culpability, so
to speak, incurred by reading. Practically speaking, of course, literary
"knowledge" still requires exegesis, which, in de Man's case, plays out
in rigorously epistemological fashion. De Man's enterprise (until the
mention of ethics in the passage from Cohen) might seem to be predicated upon the same urge to subvert and demystify the "project of
knowing," to expose, that Jacques Derrida has said underlies Levinas'
work—philosophy as ideology.

Nevertheless, for all the severity of *its* conditions, de Man's project
can be understood as occurring on exactly the same epistemological
plane as that other project it wishes to deconstruct. It is, in a word, an
economy (indeed, de Man speaks of all systems, including the parallax

of rhetorical criticism, as closed systems). Only by participating in the will to knowledge can deconstruction make its objections. The pathos of deconstruction is that it remains continuous with, not transverse to, the tyranny of self-knowing. The bad faith of deconstruction is that it cannot admit this.

Narratology

If deconstruction countervails the role of ethics in literary theory, narrative poetics has done worse by ignoring it altogether. Fortunately, if one cannot fully "contest" deconstruction, one can, however, redress formalist indifference, and to accomplish that is one of this book's primary aims. Narrative theory—the attempt to construct a comprehensive model for the *differentia specifica* of narrative form—has yet to account, adequately or fully, for the ethical in the narrative process as either a formal property (on the order of fictional patterns and structures) or a constitutive force (relations which bind tellers, listeners, and witnesses). I argue for just this formal and constitutive value for ethics in any accounting of the way narrative works.

Neo-Humanism

Best understood perhaps as a response to the deconstructive position, neo-humanism (though superficially akin to my own) significantly misses what I take to be the main point. Neo-humanism centers on the vexed issue of "representation," maintaining that common notions of it are matters of nonarbitrary social practice.[46] After Kant, mimetic theories of literary character, in the ascendant through the early nineteenth century, come to seem less and less convincing; once literary texts become fully autonomous, representation becomes an extremely troubled concept.

But instead of taking the extreme turn of substituting a linguistic pluralism for Kant's anthropology, neo-humanism reinterprets socioculturally the indeterminate but general harmony of faculties that, according to Kant, the aesthetic enjoys. Shifted thus into the phenomenal world, the world of selves tangled with selves and selves tangled with images, the moral value of art means exchanging aesthetic disinterest for social interest: aesthetics becomes a social performative, not simply a "how to do things with art" but a "how art does things with (and to) persons."

Although neo-humanism seeks to escape the charges leveled by Marxist critics at the liberal-humanist notion of the self, it still assumes a margin of individual interiority that remains opaque to theoretical analysis, since social typification also serves to protect individual privacy. But I see that margin as probably always subject to a shadow cast on it by the other: the self, as Bakhtin, G. H. Mead, and others have said, is a dialogue, inside and out.

Thus, in my view, the delicate balance to which the neo-humanist position aspires does not entirely succeed. One result is an underestimation of the "price" at stake in textual engagement. To the solitary Kantian self, neo-humanists counterpose an overly generalized and impersonal process of social embedding for both literary character and person. Though meaning to claim for literature a valid continuousness with lived experience, they seem too willing to construe oppositionality in terms of Self and Culture, obscuring the challenge of alterity posed by a unique and concrete other.[47]

Narrative fiction, I will argue, makes that challenge particularly keen, since confronting a text in its particularity both resembles and differs from the acts of human encounter which the story itself narrates, that is, the relation between subjects and what (or those whom) they objectify. Bakhtin uses the term "axiological" to describe this parallel dynamic between persons on the one hand and person and text on the other, a dynamic he locates in an individual's own singular, responsive, and historically concrete act of affirming value and conferring it upon reality.

As an ethical imperative, this act exchanges epistemological abstractions for a participatory consciousness bound to a condition of "answerability" for cognitive and aesthetic choices alike; in other words, we "sign" what we re-present to ourselves—artworks or persons. Here, the interfusion of narrational, representational, and hermeneutic ethics which I spoke of above becomes clearest, the third category filling out and deepening the other two.

Textual Choices

The thrust of my analysis, obviously, is not meticulously historicist, yet it seeks nevertheless to interpret and be accountable to the double mediation in art specified by Theodor Adorno: once by general history, and again by the history of its forms. My vehicle is an ethical lens, an optic underutilized by critical theory. Thus although I make what may seem perhaps surprising leaps within and between chapters in my choice of texts, I see them as all related texts of narrative ethics.

I focus on work which both anticipates and follows from literary modernism, British and American fiction from the nineteenth and twentieth centuries. The literary history I fashion here is driven by a hybrid of contextualist and immanentist assumptions, as I explain below.[48] Secure in the knowledge that any literary history is in part a restrospective in(ter)vention, I stand by the legitimacy of the organizing logic which informs my choice of texts here.

It has become commonplace to typify modernity as both intrinsically "sociological" and reflexive, and to cite literary modernism's self-consciousness as one of its direct results.[49] I want to go beyond claiming a simple reflexive connection between modernity and modern fiction, however, to argue that formal innovations in the novel dovetail with an increased anxiety about what it means, simply, to render oneself, and to affect others, narratively; what does it mean to assume (or defy) the responsibilities which storytelling perforce assigns?

Hence I have chosen a set of texts in which a kind of genealogy for such anxiety can be tracked: from novels and short fiction of the mid to late nineteenth century, in which the expressivist prerogatives of Romanticism undergo a pressure from within; through modernism's challenges to the stable narrative categories assumed by realist authors; to contemporary fiction, wherein the dynamics of telling a story, or of telling one's own story, becomes a topic in its own right, an intersubjective dilemma. Just as, for example, Defoe's *Robinson Crusoe* has been read in terms of empiricist concepts of mind and eighteenth-century notions of the self as property, so the texts I have assembled here can be similarly historicized according to the intersubjective paradigm of narrative ethics.

For many critics, however, it is the rise of the modern city or the invention of abstract labor by a market-driven economy or the legal and philosophical redefinition of personhood which underpins the transition from nineteenth- to twentieth-century styles of fiction. For example, Vincent Pecora has argued that the realist novel provides for the autonomous self a peculiar sort of home: no longer free-standing, Quixote-like, the individual continues to pursue an idealism it recognizes as no longer tenable, positing an immanent "return to itself" in a world permeated by metaphysical homelessness. In contrast, modernist fiction disembeds the self entirely and, by abandoning the tempered irony which enables the self to be deployed as fictive construction in the first place, breaks faith "with the only home the novel has ever known."[50]

Yet Pecora's thesis, in common with otherwise very different arguments by critics such as D. A. Miller and Richard Eldridge, suspends form between the twin poles of self and instrumentalizing societal power.[51] This operation, I believe, renders superfluous any third term such as "intersubjectivity," assimilating it to either one side or the other. But could we not say that narrative fiction, viewed intersubjectively, above all treats the circumstances and effects of human relations against the standing fact of heteronomy—tellers and listeners within, a multiplicity of readers without?

And doesn't such messy entailment contest the great curve of autonomous selfhood which is so often construed to be the modern novel's prevailing "plot"? This is the quality of narrative relation which George Eliot, at the end of *Middlemarch*, terms "incalculably diffusive," the interstices between selves where, to borrow from Eliot again, "the lights and shadows must always fall with a certain difference."

An alternative perspective on the complex shifts from realism to modernism to postmodernism, then, will see the increasing internal pressures on narration and representation within the novel as forcing into attention its fundamentally addressive or performative nature—the telling of stories *about* the self and others, *to* the self and others. From this perspective, concepts of "home" or "homelessness" are first oriented by reference to concrete and singular moral others, not the equivalently abstract categories of subjectivity or "ideology." This is perhaps one way of construing George Eliot's phrase the "home epic" as a description for the intersubjective claim of fiction.

But perhaps the most important point to convey about the particular texts I have selected is that I do not confine myself to works which openly declare their ethical import, or which stake out a recognizably "ethical" terrain. The readings cover texts by Sherwood Anderson, Richard Wright, and Kazuo Ishiguro as well as those by Conrad, Dickens, and James.

A theory of narrative ethics need not be determined by, nor does it necessarily arise out of, considerations about novels' or their authors' moral or moralizing intentions. As I have said, it is concerned with the intersubjective dynamics of narrative, and their ethical implications, independent of the "moral paraphrases" which they may invite or which can be ascribed to them. Such dynamics are often governed by an immanent ethical-textual principle, as I demonstrate in detail in Chapter 4. (In this intrinsic sense, one might also speak of a pedagogical ethics, or a therapeutic ethics, features peculiar to a certain kind of communicative situation or discourse.)

As for narrative ethics, the connection between the two terms will be defended in the next chapter against positions which deem it ideologically suspect or methodologically naive (poststructuralist and postmodern theory); superfluous (structuralist narratology); and a function of "judgment" and moral value affixed to content (Anglo-American rhetorical criticism and moral philosophy). I treat these positions extensively not merely to situate my own concerns, but also to draw out the very real ethical consequences of holding certain critical positions, indeed, of holding any critical position at all; in the deciphering of dreams also begin responsibilities. By linking the ethical consequences of criticism to ethical patterns and forms in literary texts, I hope to invest ethics with the kind of interpretive force exercised by the sharpest of contemporary ideological modes of literary analysis. But at the very least, even as regards the study of literature, we should resolve ourselves to the importance, as Levinas puts it, of knowing whether or not we are duped by morality (*TI*, 21).

2

Toward a Narrative Ethics

Someone said, "Our right hand is in the book. But the left has the privilege of opening and closing. Thus both hands preside over the morrow of the book."

Edmond Jabès, *The Book of Dialogue*

You read. You tie yourself to what comes untied—to what unties you within your ties. You are a knot of correspondence . . . a knot of innocence, craftiness, of things likely and unlikely, of infinite faithfulness.

Edmond Jabès, *The Book of Questions*

A book is interrupted discourse catching up with its own breaks. But books have their fate; they belong to a world they do not include, but recognize by being printed, and by being prefaced and getting themselves preceded with forewords. They are interrupted, and call for other books and in the end are interpreted in a saying distinct from the said.

Emmanuel Levinas, *Totality and Infinity*

Evasions of the existence of others may take the form of smothering a person, or a text, with seemingly scrupulous questions.

Michael Fischer, "Stanley Cavell's Wittgenstein"

Kafka wanted to know at which moments and how often, with eight people sitting within the horizon of a conversation, you have to speak up in order not to pass for taciturn.

Maurice Blanchot, "Interruptions"

The Deconstructive Critique

To JUSTIFY MY observations about ethical confrontations in any practical sense, to make myself answerable to the dynamics of writing and reading, is to engage dialogically with contemporary criticism. I want to confront some of its most interesting faces, not so much to win an argument as to follow through on ethics' own discursive modus operandi. If the confrontation is to remain alive and in tension—not unlike the process of reading fiction—its anti-dialectic character is one lesson to be learned and cherished from deconstruction, the first and surprisingly the most fruitful interlocutor for a narrative ethics.

The tête-à-tête seems unlikely at first glance: ethics apparently imposes a responsibility to the world and the word, whereas deconstruction—especially the brand perfected by Paul de Man—seems to abjure such responsibility. But that easy opposition trivializes the tension in each term. And before I insist on the way they part company, I want to show the company they keep. Ethical answerability here is not a flattened prescription for action; it is not a moral recipe book. Nor is deconstruction an indifference to answerability; it is at its best a scrupulous hesitation, an extreme care occasioned by the treachery of words and the danger of easy answers.

To predict where the dialogue between narrative ethics and deconstruction will lead, it is safe to say that the former exerts most pressure precisely at the point of a text's hesitations and interruptions, its caution before smothering interrogation. For ethics pauses before the impulse to flatten and rectify (a kind of fictionalizing), just as de Man's deconstruction stops before interpreting away the textual tension at hand. From a scrupled ethical perspective, of course, de Man stops woefully short himself, and his hermetic or paralytic precautions look like a kind of cowardice.

37

In terms de Man himself develops in an essay on Kleist, deconstruction takes place in the gap between *schwer* and *antitgrav*, between falling and rising—a paradox of continuous movement as stasis, of grammar as trap *(Fälle)*. This is the "trick" which deconstruction plays and replays ad infinitum. And that is to say only that deconstruction thrives on, and casts itself in the image of, "suspended" discourse. By contrast, the epigraph from Levinas to this chapter speaks rather of "interrupted discourse." I will now investigate what that may imply within an ethical frame of reference.

In staging this dialogue with deconstruction (as well as the antiphonal encounters which make up the next two sections of this chapter), I ask forbearance while I seem to "interrupt" the exposition I began in Chapter 1. It is precisely through such apparent interruption that a theory of narrative ethics catches up with its own breaks, so to speak, and consolidates its own voice: through the call for others' "Saying." I want readers to hear a polyphony of voices alongside my orchestration of them. I try, in any event, to steer a middle path between smothering critique (as the epigraph from Michael Fischer frames it) and anxious taciturnity (as described by Maurice Blanchot) by cleaving to what Jabès calls the "knot" of correspondences.

What, then, could "interrupted discourse" mean? Levinas intends, it is safe to assume, both a certain (characteristic) dubiety about writing—a fear that it impedes or defers the ethical immediacy of human speech—and a certain gratitude for the interventive nature of rational discourse—the fact that another's Saying *(le Dire)* will always interrupt and "unsay" the finitude of the Said *(le Dit)*. In an essay appropriately entitled "Interruptions," Maurice Blanchot makes a similar point: "Discontinuity assures continuity of understanding . . . To stop in order to understand, to understand in order to speak."[1] Speech, through interruption, unifies and connects.

And yet, continues Blanchot, one can think of interruption in another way—language itself as nondialectical, as separation, cleft, gap: not "the pause that permits exchange, but [rather] the waiting that measures an infinite distance." Interruption, in this sense, means severance, incommensurability of horizons—in a word, writing: a relation with alterity not in Levinas' interpersonal sense of ethical encounter, but rather as the very structure of discourse, of inscription. Here language, through interruption, unsays itself.

While I quote Levinas above because the fate of interruption he describes stands over the texts I read in this chapter (as well as my own book), "interrupted discourse" in this other sense enables me to broach the topic I treat in this section: the status ascribed to language and human relations by deconstruction. It is a concept not easily dismissed, not least because of its potential for ethical seriousness. Sympathetic or not, one therefore needs to exercise a little caution about hastily "summing up" deconstruction, or trivializing the nature of its "Said." Deconstruction, moreover, is not a monolith: it has its styles and its permutations.

Thus if one is prompted to think of synonyms for "interruption," the first that comes to mind will probably not be "dissemination"—the language of textuality that never stops—but rather something closer to "disarticulation"—the language of expression broken up or voided from within. To tip my hand, one will discover (a word still meant in its double sense of "expose" and "find") the vocabulary of Paul de Man, not that of Derrida.

And it is with de Man that the following dialogue with deconstruction takes place.[2] In the first place, any ethically charged argument for linguistic communication must take up the gauntlet thrown down by a proclamation such as this: "[since] language is not made by us as historical beings, it is perhaps not even made by humans at all, [not] in any sense human" (*RT*, 87). As both a theory of language and a moral position, this attitude simply demands a reckoning, especially since it contests the very position I wish to hold.

In the second place, de Man is least convincing as a theorist of narrative fiction. As I observe below, his domain is Romantic and modernist epiphany, not narrative duration, up to and including the narrative "moments" which he selects from novelists like Proust. De Manian deconstruction, I submit, simply misconceives the uses of fiction; it is a blindness without any redeeming insight. (In this regard the essays on prose fiction which de Man wrote for *Le Soir* are simply anterior to the theoretical apparatus he was to elaborate later on, and therefore of less relevance to my purposes here.)

Finally, in letting Blanchot serve as a kind of bridge over interruption between de Man and Levinas, I have indulged, I must admit, an ulterior purpose. Levinas and de Man share certain perhaps not altogether surprising resemblances (call them unelective affinities)—a severity, a prophetic kind of tone and conviction, and finally a shared skepticism about graven images that, given the cultural gulf that separates them, has some potentially fascinating implications. In other respects, of course, they stand worlds apart,[3] but their parallel scrupulosity about human discourse presents a valuable point of contact. While I actually depend on Bakhtin and Cavell in this section more than I do Levinas, a facing (or face-off) between his work and de Man's seems quite natural to me.

On a purely performative level, I have to say that I continue to find de Man's orthodoxy compelling, especially in the light of less uncompromising critics' pastiches or critiques. I am tempted to trace this effect to a (for me) unmistakable pathos lying at the core of de Man's project and motivating or standing behind its austerity—limned as all his work is now by its author's own posthumous, unwilled confrontation with, if I may put it this way, a narrative ethics. (I am wary, nevertheless, of using de Man's critical theory as a skeleton key for repressed features of his life.)

It is the "resistance to theory" that de Man's ideas intrinsically pose to my own that warrants my attention (even though critical bias has now tilted away from such inhospitable altitudes toward more oxygen-rich climes). While de Manian deconstruction calls into question all three of the narrative categories I introduced in the previous chapter—narrational, representational, and hermeneutic—its primary target is the last, because of hopelessly divergent notions of interpretive sovereignty on the one hand and interpretive answerability (Bakhtin's phrase) on the other.

In his essay "The Resistance to Theory," Paul de Man takes pains to explicate once again his view that texts refer neither to readers nor to readers' worlds, but only to themselves. He does not deny the referential function of language (a common misconception about his semiology); he denies only "its authority as a model for natural and phenomenal cognition" (RT, 15).

> This may seem obvious enough on the level of light and sound, but it is less so with regard to the more general phenomenality of space, time, or especially the self; no one in his right mind will try to grow grapes by the luminosity of the word "day," but it is very difficult not to conceive the pattern of one's past and future existence as in accordance with temporal and spatial schemes that belong to fictional narratives and not to the world. . . . What we call ideology is precisely the confusion of linguistic with natural reality, of reference with phenomenalism. (RT, 11)

In its asceticism regarding narrativity, expressed as the necessary distinction between two narrative "kinds" (textual versus real, or referential—that is, linguistic versus phenomenal), de Man's assertion implicitly drives a wedge between the very two concepts this book's title yokes together. It diagnoses, moreover, a certain confusion I seem to have about the correct ranking of discourses.[4]

De Man elsewhere calls ethics a "category, not a value . . . a discursive mode among others"[5]—in that sense, no different from any other mode or category where linguistic articulation remains discontinuous with both things and ideas (that is, as they might exist apart from language). For once things and ideas pass into language, they answer to its special laws of *dis*articulation. Of course, they are always already "in" language, and that's the rub. As philosophical discourse, however, ethics is mocked by its very pretensions to be meta-linguistic.

Already "fallen" into linguistic unreliability, ethics proves its rank bad faith by asserting its claim to authority through somehow self-sufficient, legislative "values." And if ethics itself suffers from such structural errancy, then its entanglement with literature (narrative fiction, for example, which is ethically charged, structured, or self-situated) produces—with all the negative valence this word can carry for de Man—a "mixed" (that is, ideologically confused) mode par excellence.

De Man contemns mixture. Metaphor, symbol, dialectic—all become prey to an almost puritanical bias, especially fervent in his later essays. (And correlatively, he sees literature's primary duty as that of fictionalizing into tropes its reading subjects.) Scrupulously, de Man will expose as category errors blurrings of linguistic and phenomenal orders of perception which invoke some false symbolic unity or dialectical synthesis. "Aesthetic ideology" is the favorite culprit here: Hegel's aesthetics, or Schiller's suspect and misappropriated Kantianism, the general belief that art can reconcile concepts and sensuous intuitions.[6]

For de Man, the very notion of a narrative ethics would seem hopelessly confounded, since the flagrant linkage of narrative and ethics merely amplifies and doubly obscures the deep epistemological difficulties attaching to each as separate discursive modes. In his essay on Bakhtin, for instance, de Man nullifies the hope "that by starting out . . . in a poetics of novelistic discourse one may gain access to the power of a hermeneutics" (*RT*, 113). Indeed, any poetics worth its salt will "disarticulate" such hermeneutics. And in his analyses of Rousseau (the closest he comes, I think, to addressing specifically narrative structures) de Man argues that language exhibits the greatest degree of ideological sophistication when it drives a wedge between subjectivity and language, when it demonstrates their absolute incompatibility.

Implicitly, like the other nondialectical oppositions in de Man's work that remain intact even after deconstruction, "narrativity" in its two senses lives a prince and pauper kind of life. Either it applies to lived experience *or* it designates language (just as "ethics" can mean matters of practical performance or some meta-theoretical enterprise); but for each pair, the descriptive term refers to both alternatives at once only at its epistemological peril. Indeed, like analytical philosophers, we should probably make a practical distinction between "narrativity" and "narrativity'," or "ethics 1" and "ethics 2," depending on whether it was life or language we wished to refer to.

But then in each case, the latter of the two alternatives—the "linguistic"—gives the lie to the ostensibly free-standing status of the former; or, as de Man puts it, "Morality is a version of the same language aporia that gave rise to such concepts as 'man' or 'love' or 'self,' and not the cause or consequence of such concepts."[7] We are more "duped by morality" than we even knew.

(Stanley Cavell would probably cast this whole matter of choosing between alternatives like "narrativity" and "narrativity'" in the same terms as he analyzes the Mariner's contestation of "the claims of knowledge": a venture to be staked perhaps but ultimately surpassed and left behind. "Not all the pointing in the world . . . will distinguish the one . . . from the other. The trouble can be put two ways; you can't point to the one without pointing to the other; and you can't point to both at the same time. Which just means that *pointing* here has become an incoherent activity" [*MWM*, 320].[8] Levinas, too, makes the identical point about skepticism's necessary complicity in the very knowing it rejects.)

Although an interpretive stance such as de Man's carries persuasively, I think, for analyses of lyric poetry (hence de Man's critical preferences for the works of Yeats, Hölderlin, Wordsworth, and Rilke or for overtly figural narration like Proust's or Rousseau's), its descriptive power diminishes when forced to account for how we read and experience drama or prose fiction. The never-ending debate over the ontological status and referentiality of fiction merely footnotes de Man's much larger claim that literary language (itself metonymic of "language") *disfigures* the humanity that bestows meaning upon it. As he is quoted as saying, "if you want to talk about men, you are in the wrong field. We can only talk about letters."[9]

Consider, in contrast, Stanley Cavell's trenchant analysis of the country yokel's confusion of reference with phenomenalism when he leaps on stage to prevent Othello's murder of Desdemona. Like some neo-Aesopian fool, he does seem to believe it possible to "grow grapes by the luminosity of the word, 'day'." By simply deriding such an impulse, however, one misses not only its poignancy, but exactly the thing it seems to account for: that linguistic structures *do* have worldly consequence, that art, so to speak, gives off light, that phenomenalism spills over into reference.

Citing Samuel Johnson's commonsense pronouncement that theatrical events are neither to be credited nor discredited, Cavell underscores its failure to take seriously the fact that an audience subjects itself or is subjected to the theatrical events staged for it; theater happens to us, we witness it, and our immobilization as spectators may therefore have something important to teach us about what it means merely to watch and do nothing.[10]

Almost as if in rebuttal to de Man, Cavell remarks that "the empirical and the transcendental are not as clearly separate as, so to speak, we thought they were" (*MWM*, 318). In contrast to the sort of confusion de Man finds, Cavell will argue that "tragedy [rather] arises from the confusion of *these* states": (1) acknowledging the separateness of others, and thus admitting a certain helplessness before them, and (2) failing to overcome the need to "know" and thereby assimilate their separateness. That failure, that knowledge, means not being "emptied of help, but [rather] withholding it" (*MWM*, 319; my emphasis).

The title of Cavell's collected essays on Shakespeare places the problem squarely: *Disowning Knowledge*. Since that problem does not properly fit the contours of epistemology, after a certain point epistemological concerns must cede priority. Knowing, in Cavell's terms, gives way to acknowledging.[11] Such a renunciation in de Man's view would disguise a failure of cognitive nerve. Indeed, it cannot even be a critical possibility, since in drawing a limit to what we can know, we blithely ignore a limit already drawn for us by language; there is no such thing as nonlinguistic knowledge anyway.

But contrariwise for Cavell, de Man's linguistic/natural opposition as it applies either to a split self or to a language itself divided does no more than name a problem. And the question here is whether a pedagogical or critical imperative for reading—call it "naming" unreadability—supersedes an intersubjective one. The question, in other words, is whether one names a problem, or substitutes for it the undertaking or assuming or enacting of one.

Now, though such enactment precisely describes de Manian deconstruction's métier—at its best ethically rigorous in reading unreadability—what it enacts is simply the ethic of nondecision.[12] Thus the "problem" Cavell would like to transcend remains for de Man nontranscendable. Cavell's desire to do so, moreover, discloses his deep investment in "ideology," a temptation obviously "difficult" for him to resist. But what's "difficult" in Cavell's terms is not resisting unwarranted analogies between life and art, but rather resisting that resistance. Like the Mariner's skepticism, de Man's "rhetorical correctness" (if I may so put it) is a thing to be owned then disowned, exercised if only to be ex*or*cised.

Another way I might put this is in terms of the "price" exacted by engagement with persons or texts. For de Man, I suggest, pays a price over and above that which his epistemological ethic demands: namely, the loss of a text's continuous presentness before him, as something to be either confronted or "interrupted," taken up or refused, acknowledged or merely, with all the negative valence Cavell attaches to the word, "known."

De Man's crucial statement denying analogies between life and art (left atypically open), "The hermeneutics of reading and the hermeneutics of experience are not necessarily compatible" (*RT*, 62), assumes that one analogizes from empirical to linguistic structures (and back again). Any theories about literature which depend on such analogies betray themselves with the very disfiguring features of language they need to discount. Cavell's example of the yokel, on the contrary, goes in the opposite direction: it asks the question "How is human encounter like witnessing a theatrical performance?" or rather "What does our ontological separateness from aesthetic events have to teach us about the facts of separateness depicted there as well as those which constrain our daily interpersonal engagements?"

Raskolnikov's waiting, in Sartre's astute phrase, "is *my* waiting which I lend him,"[13] but it is at the same time *only* his, a fact of separateness, of difference I can but acknowledge (or withhold—a withholding which unlike ignorance, negatively confirms the acknowledgment I avoid).

Literary texts—in their material self-sufficiency, in their matter-of-fact repudiation of whatever we wish out of them (they speak to us, after all, through our own acts of ventriloquism), allegorize the crevasse dividing person from person, as well as the techniques they invent (for seeming) to traverse it.

My phrase "material self-sufficiency" may sound uncomfortably de Manian, but materiality here refers to a text's otherness on the analogy with a person, not to the dis-articulating properties of language. Construed this way, reading as ethical relation is the experience of exteriority.[14] Or as Edmond Jabès memorably puts it, "The book never actually surrenders."

But Raskolnikov is not a person, one wants to reply to Sartre; he is a literary character: to think of him as or as like a person subscribes to the error de Man calls "ideology." As should be clear by now, however, the issue I want to draw out here is not the ontological status of the literary character, but rather the special nonontological and ethical claims Raskolnikov, for example, makes on readers.[15] Those claims belong to the realm of performance, not of speculation. To read a text like Anderson's "Loneliness," for example, means bearing some burden of responsibility, believing oneself addressed, and thus answerable—to the text itself, or to one's reading of it.

De Man's deconstruction moots such answerability. Whether it is the represented character or the representing reader he makes the more fictitious entity, the site of a more negative insight about human subjectivity, subjectivity suffers evacuation—"a void [whose] persistent naming we call literature."[16] How to respond to such an exorbitant notion? With the even more exorbitant demands of immediacy and exposure before the Other. If de Man views textual vigilance as resulting in interpretive *vertige* and the deconstruction of the reading subject, the radically ethical position sees it as justifying subjectivity in the first place. The task of selfhood is proposed, called into being, from outside the self as answerability. Textual understanding, according to Levinas, "all happens as though the multiplicity of persons . . . were the condition for the fullness of 'absolute truth,' as though each person, through his uniqueness, ensured the revelation of a unique aspect of the truth, and that certain sides of it would never reveal themselves if certain people were missing from mankind."[17]

In his early essays, Mikhail Bakhtin makes a similar point: "What can be accomplished by me cannot be accomplished by anyone else, ever."[18] Selves are constituted in, or by, their answerability before others; they acquire meaning only through intersubjective horizons, horizons which surround textual as well as human encounter. In my triangulation of Levinas-Cavell-Bakhtin, it is Bakhtin who explicitly links these insights with narrativity. Toward that goal, he sees one's physical singularity in time/space (one's ir-re-place-ability, as Michael Holquist puts it) as standing for one's axiological uniqueness. That singularity enjoins responsibilities both aesthetic and ethical, the two not easily prised apart as they converge "in the unity of my answerability" (*AA*, 2).

I want now to pivot this dialogue with deconstruction toward Bakhtin, because he directly challenges the de Manian split between poetics and hermeneutics. Indeed, such differences as mark their respective theories of language and hermeneutic responsibility seem to follow naturally from wholly divergent vocabularies. Bakhtin's writing is swollen with "phenomenalist" metaphors of sight, voice, and above all personhood ("I-for-myself," "the others-for-me," the "mask of selfhood"); like Levinas, he conceives identity as an entirely sensible phenomenon: "After all, it is only the other who can be embraced, clasped all around, it is only the other's boundaries that can be touched and felt lovingly. . . . Only the other's lips can be touched with our own, only on the other can we lay our hands, rise actively above the other and 'overshadow' all of him totally" (*AA*, 41). Myriad small *narratives* about selves in relation to others complicate and soften the analytical thrust of these essays; technical nomenclature and style constantly give way (as they do in Levinas) to a kind of rhapsodic ethics about human interaction.[19]

De Man's writing, by contrast, again and again exploits the language of melodrama and violent crime—"disfigurement," "de-facement," or most ghoulishly, in a passage about derivative, secondary languages in his essay on Benjamin: "They kill the original, by discovering that the original was already dead."[20] If the word "intersubjective" has a referential value for de Man, it consists of two equally dismaying possibilities: either the condition of a split self (the Heideggerian doubling of the self into two empirical and ontological entities) or the mutual deconstruction of author and reader: "Both parties tend to fuse into a single subject as the original difference between them disappears" (*BI*, 10). De Man exerts relentless pressure to crack open the self from within, to see it fissured, permanently alienated, made *de trop* by language.

Bakhtin, conversely, conceives of intersubjectivity as linguistic salvation—the liberation of dialogism.[21] The self's inner division is a sign of life, not estrangement, since it records the presence of others, the saving heterogeneity of consciousness: "[considered singly] consciousness is more terrifying than any unconscious complexes" (quoted in *RB*, 198). An epistemological gain surfaces here. In an individual's "answerability," which forms a link between cognition and the objects it invests with meaning and value, mind and world discover a certain harmony.

As in Kantian philosophy, formal analogies between the cognitive, ethical, and aesthetic create an architectonics. Bakhtin avoids the "theoretism" of Kant's faculty psychology, however, by refining those analogies into a "philosophy of the act," the singular deed of evaluation which, though self-responsible—*signed* by me (as it were)—can never be limited to or identical with the self because of exteriority's gravitational force—selves aim outwards toward others.[22]

But the crucial divergence between de Man and Bakhtin takes place on a plane other than cognition. Bakhtin would find simply incoherent de Man's Heideggerian drive inward into some inalienable authenticity (or authentic alienation) or his later obsession with wholesale "disarticulation." "A human being experiencing life in the category of his own *I* is incapable of gathering himself by himself into an outward whole that would be even relatively finished" (*AA*, 35).

Bakhtinian ethics exposes the de Manian self's need to subtract from without as it fissures from within, exposes the fact that truth, for de Man, works by expropriation: truth is "always something that must always first be *wrested* from entities," as Heidegger put it in *Being and Time*.[23] As I argued for Anderson's story in Chapter 1, narrative fiction and the resistance (and vulnerability) it can offer to the imperious reader dramatize the cost of such (de)privation, of the drive toward knowing at the expense of acknowledging. Instead of "an unveiling which destroys the secret," interpretation should mean, as Benjamin wrote, "the revelation which does it justice."[24]

Bakhtin conceives one's relation to meaning, rather, on the level of exigency, bestowal, gift. Immediately after his example of the "naive spectator" (which I cite in my note to the identical case in Cavell), he says:

An ultimate issue out of itself is not *immanent* to a lived life: it descends upon a life-lived-from-within as a gift from the self-activity of another—from a self-activity that *comes to meet* my life from *outside* its bounds. . . . The organizing power in all aesthetic forms is the axiological category of the *other*. . . . [When I abandon the futured vision of my unfinalizability] the only thing left for me to do is to find a refuge in the *other* and to assemble—out of the *other*—the scattered pieces of my own givenness. ("Author and Hero in Aesthetic Activity," in *AA*, 79–81)

Or as a character in Toni Morrison's *Beloved* puts it from the opposite perspective, "The pieces that I am, she gather them and give them back to me in all the right order." These co-efficient grants of meaning take place "on the border of two consciousnesses"—in time and space and in story form. Thus in its orientation to others and in the irreducible difference between itself and another, the self suggests not merely a dialogic but a "novelistic" entity—defined by some necessary sort of narrative orientation to others. And it is, of course, precisely this awareness of the novel which de Man's work lacks—the genre most saturated by, as Bakhtin puts it, "the living word."

Recall, for a moment, the two orders of interruption I began with. What we find in Bakhtin is interruption on the level of the Saying: a call for stories which are themselves interrupted in turn. "Every word is directed toward an *answer* and cannot escape the profound influence of the answering word it anticipates" (*DI*, 280). Not interruption as if on a Riemann surface[25]—broken up and hollowed from within—but rather interruption as exchange: "Now wherefore stoppest thou me?"—to stop in order to understand.

Since the very fact of alterity obliges a constant interplay across the borders of self and other, each held mutually hostage by a constant exchange of surpluses of meaning accessible only from outside, a narrative *is* ethics in the sense of the mediating and authorial role each takes up toward another's story. The "gift-giving, consummating potential" (as Bakhtin puts it) that one bears another is most meaningfully bestowed narratively—across time, and through a call of/for stories.

De Man, in his essay on Bakhtin (based on a reading of "Dialogue and the Novel"), seizes on the incompatibility of poetics and hermeneutics as they collide in Bakhtin's work in order to "interrupt," as it were, dialogism from inside. De Man reads Bakhtin carelessly, however.[26] After isolating the incriminating presence of a phenomenalist vocabulary in a certain passage, and censuring the "illegitimate" modulation from dialogism to a hermeneutics of question and answer shortly thereafter, de Man concludes, "The ideologies of otherness and of hermeneutic understanding are not compatible, and therefore their relationship is not a dialogical but merely a contradictory one" (*RT*, 111).

But the talk of incompatibility is familiar, since de Man merely suspends the otherness of Bakhtin's text by refusing to engage it, in Maurice Blanchot's phrase, "under the sign of the neutral."[27] The recurrent "evidence checkpoint" in de Man's criticism illustrates not only its circularity but, more important, its unsatisfiable demand for more knowledge, and the narcissism and privation such knowledge endlessly rehearses. An intolerance of exteriority, a moralist's zeal for disclosure—de Man's incessant probing and wresting make language into a house of detention, and convert readers into its jailer-detainees.

Let me be clear about this. The profoundly anti-ethical thrust of de Man's deconstruction does *not* stem from its need to champion "undecidability" or "polysemy," or from any other threat to the literary or social fabric. That argument, I believe, is a strategic error made by liberal and conservative critics alike attesting to the weak (pluralist or authoritarian) model of ethics they hold in common. Rather, ethics finds no place in de Man's theory because of his absolute reification of epistemology. Ethics is nullified beforehand: meaning not just simply disclosed "in the full light" (Levinas' phrase), but pre-understood—totalized, digested, "precisely thought."[28] Bakhtin perhaps best deflates the hyperbole and hubris of such a project, no less "fruitless" in its intent than wanting to "grow grapes by the luminosity of the word 'day'": "All attempts to overcome the dualism of cognition and life, of thought and singular concrete reality *from inside theoretical cognition* are absolutely hopeless . . . [tantamount to the attempt] to lift oneself up by one's own hair" (quoted in *RB*, 8).

The point here is precisely not to pose an epistemological rejoinder to deconstruction; John Searle's fate of literal incorporation and disfiguration (into SARL, as Derrida cuttingly dubbed him) by the very discourse he thought to debunk should prove at least instructive.[29] What's warranted instead is an oppositionality in the Levinasian sense: interruption, or the over-going by the Saying of the Said.

That is why I have enlisted the aid of Levinas, Bakhtin, and Cavell: to "interrupt," as it were, de Man's hypostasis of "interrupted discourse." What interrupted discourse really amounts to is a peculiar kind of post-Kantian version of autonomy. And in a post-Kantian world, concepts of autonomy and freedom tend, de rigueur, to be linked to "language" without any reference to the human attributes or ideals they may (erroneously) symbolize. As Tobin Siebers puts it, this "shift ends by radically altering Kant's idea of pluralism, robbing it of its human context and transforming it into an issue of language . . . [that is, that language] does not permit judgments, that it defers differences."[30]

But linguistic pluralism seems to me untenable without some sort of philosophical anthropology to undergird it. If the Kantian framework is to be linguistically reinterpreted, Bakhtin's concepts of signature and tone (the concrete and particular meanings individual language uses "underwrite") or Cavell's morally democratized and communal acknowledgment would seem far better suited to maintain a Kantian bridge between ethics and aesthetics, while opening that bridge up to a genuine heteronomy of ends.[31]

I bring this dialogue with deconstruction to a close with a final dialogic "interruption": de Man's essay on Kant. De Man uses the *Critique of Pure Judgment* to illustrate how its letter, despite its spirit, carries on an (as it were) autonomous and immanent critique of aesthetic ideology. Aesthetic judgment, the metaphor-laden and duplicitous structure which bridges a priori knowledge and empirical experience, ends up arrogating to itself the mental concepts and practical interest it should by rights eschew. That Kant's language betrays his philosophical intentions, that a resistance can be detected between his text's "materiality" and its lapses into a "phenomenalist" register, that his text exposes the cleavage between faculties which aesthetic judgments falsely reconcile—all this secures the text's permanent value for de Man as a model of self-deconstruction, particularly because it is philosophy, not literature.

De Man's reading, though brilliant, remains perverse. It enters the interiority of Kant's text, in Levinas' words, "as if by burglary" (*TI*, 67) and leaves the "disfiguring" imprint of an alien presence. The term Levinas applies to such invasive "occupation" is "totality": the drama which casts its roles in advance, whose actors cannot be its authors, and whose outcome another knows beforehand—the very "inverse of langauge" (*TI*, 79).

De Man's essay does, however, serve as an important bridge to my discussion of narrative poetics because of the contrast it draws between Kantian aesthetics on the one hand and post-Kantian ideologies that blindly champion their "confusion" on the other. Latter-day formalisms, as Christopher Norris has observed in *Paul de Man, Deconstruction, and the Critique of Aesthetic Ideology*, operate in exactly this same spirit, being the lineal descendants of their organicist precursors.

If, finally, de Man's rhetorical criticism profoundly misunderstands the experience of reading fiction, it nevertheless expertly assesses the often totalizing pretensions of literary theory. Since formalist theories of narrative account for a goodly number of these, in particular the claim to have left the "ideological confusion" of ethics behind, I turn to them next.

Formalisms Critical and Ethical: A Short Story

While Paul de Man was bearing witness to the incommensurability of poetics and hermeneutics, poetics by itself—in the form of structuralist narratology—was industriously honing its techniques, its analytic precision, and its specialized nomenclature. It wanted very much to don the mantle of "pilot science" of literary studies. Since the story of narratology is a Bildungsroman, urbanity, maturity, and the advent of new fashions speedily generated embarrassment, if not outright contempt, for jejune tastes since outgrown. And so a trunkful of such items—"theme," "reliable narrator," "moral imagination"—was consigned to village oblivion, poked around in occasionally by passers-by or those "versed," as Robert Frost put it, "in country things," but for the most part happily forgotten.

After a short while under city lights, some of this outmoded attire was discovered to possess a vintage modishness heretofore unsuspected, for instance, "point of view," which was revamped to a more contemporary cut—"focalization"—and trimmed of any telltale signs from its more arrière-garde youth. Unfortunately, as the conventions of this genre dictate, a "dressing down" could not be far off. Thus was narratology put in its place by those more versed in city things—like poststructuralist couture. And thus, its wardrobe not a little threadworn, does narratology languish even now, in the comeuppance that is Bildung. It has not, Stephen Daedalus–like, forged the uncreated conscience of its field. Nor has it felt the need to return to the forge like Pip. But it has, like Lord Jim, "missed its chance"; its aspirations for any "pilot's" mantle which says sartorially, "I am unimpeachable," have, regrettably been laid aside.

I have described the fortunes of narrative poetics as a story for a reason. Its "dressing down" at deconstruction's hands made of it "a tragic critical practice—tragic because at once inescapable and doomed to alternate, without the possibility of totalization, between its dependent constituents."[32] Those constituents are story and discourse, the plot "as it happened in time" and the plot "as it is told," the former, of course, being logically prior to the latter. Or is it?

Could it not be said that in telling a story of chastened ambition and dashed expectations, I was merely bending the "events" of narratology's deconstruction to the will of purely discursive and generic decisions? And don't these criteria make of the story "a story" as much as the real-time sequence of events that "really happened"? Whichever option you prefer, the deconstructive "sequel" to narratology's "story" demonstrated that emphasizing only one of its dependent constituents—story, for instance—forces the other one—discourse, in this example—to become, as Wlad Godzich put it, "a perturbatory element rather than a resolving one."

But this is by now an old story. Deconstruction's dismantling of the *histoire/récit* or *fabula/sujet* distinction now perhaps appears no less reductive than narratology's fond hopes, which deconstruction so eagerly subverted. Like the supplement that it is, deconstructive criticism simultaneously "interrupts" and prolongs structuralist prejudices (something Gérard Genette himself admits in *Narrative Discourse Revisited*). Deconstruction's more damaging accusation—that narrative discourse is, like any other, prey to tropological forces it cannot control—narratology need not bear alone; all criticism devoted to analyzing stable linguistic structures assumes the same "tragic burden." Again, for all its acuity, deconstruction merely "names a problem," it seems to me. De Man, for instance, criticizes formalist reductions of figure to grammar, but only because "rhetoric" supersedes, by exercising power over, both.

Fortunately, however, all grammars leak (as Edward Sapir once observed), even rhetorical grammars. And in the past decade narrative theory has greatly enlarged its own sense of grammar: "perspective," "voice," "consciousness," and "situation" have all generated important critical work. Indeed, since Gérard Genette, Mieke Bal, and Gerald Prince began to systematize categories other than the relation of events to their discursive presentation, narrative theory much less comfortably fits the pinched contours of the satire I sketched above.

But in another sense, it remains still very much dual. The old "ideological" schism between form and content is hard to shake. In Genette's words: "Apparently, there is room for two narratologies, one thematic in the broad sense (analysis of the story or the narrative content), the other formal or, rather, modal (analysis of narrative as a mode of 'representation' of stories, contrast to the non-narrative modes like the dramatic and, no doubt, some others outside literature)" (*NDR,* 17).

Like any good binary opposition, this one subordinates while it opposes—Genette assigns methodological rigor to modal, not thematic analysis. It also begs for and deserves to be deconstructed: into the content of form and the form of content.[33] But even *sans* deconstruction, the narrative movement from deep syntax to textual surface, to choose an example from Algirdas Greimas, needs to be explained in terms of messages as well as codes. "Operations" of practical reason, the "field" of social relations and values, play as fundamental a role in narrative structure as the logical operations of contrariety, contradiction, and supposition, or the field of actantial permutations.[34]

Consider, for example, that "theme" or "topic" can be interpreted narratively (what or how the story tells), discursively (what or how subjects tell), or figurally (what or how grammar, syntax, and lexis tell); "content" suddenly appears a far weightier analytic matter.[35] "Voice" possesses both a form and a content; "point of view" involves an interdependence of percepts and concepts.[36] Structural entanglements of teller and listener defy analyses which privilege their independent roles. (Genette's clarifying distinction between "who speaks?" and "who sees?" still resolutely avoids filling out the truncated predicate in each case, because the subject's positionality presides for him over intersubjective relations.) Whereas deconstruction cannot allow the ethical category status, narratology tends to deny it formal consideration.

But excising the "price" of encounter, the "mark" left by Saying, ignores the extent to which strictly figurative properties such as metaphor become experiential, the way characters, as in Hawthorne and James, can become inculcated figures of speech. It leaves to characters and text the fate of Poe's M. Valdemar, who was immobilized yet still alive, and prompts Levinas' observation that "a novel shuts beings up in a fate despite their freedom . . . [a fate] like being buried alive."[37]

Moreover, confining ethical analysis to the abstract realm of "values" simply duplicates the identical, now discredited strategy of meta-ethical theorists in philosophy. To broach such concepts as temporality, point of view, or agency while confining them entirely to thin descriptions of autonomous narrative structures to my mind bears out de Man's anxiety about reified aesthetic formalisms.[38] Methodological rigor need not exclude "perturbatory" links between clearly related domains, which is another way of talking about literature's selective "resistance to theory." (This straitjacketing of ethics can be at least partially attributed to traditional ethical criticism, whose own essentialist moves merely encouraged bloodless formalist correctives.)

But perhaps most important, like deconstruction's decisions, narratology's determination to delimit narrative analysis this way have an extraordinarily ironic consequence: willy-nilly, formalist/structuralist theories of narrative incur an ethical responsibility precisely because they eschew it. To recall Godzich once more, it is ethics which in this case becomes the "pertubatory" element rather than the "resolving" one. ("Perturbatory," in this context, signifies for me narrative ethics's critical vigor.) To truncate narrative discourse by fitting it to a scientific model it overreaches is to impoverish it narratively as well as ethically.

Narration and representation cannot be explained without reference to ethical considerations of agency; "functions" and "roles" liquidate the substantial self. Since I have reintroduced here two of the three axes upon which my own study is based—narration and representation—I want now to examine more carefully how each has fared in narrative poetics, and suggest how they can be more thickly described.

Representation

Like it or not, some version of "reflection" has to describe the mediation of text by life and life by text. For instance, one can speak of a rough homology between the world as "always already" experienced through a set of frames and representations and fiction as a second-order, correlative system of signification. As Theodor Adorno and others have argued, however, the "order of mimesis" cannot simply duplicate the authoritarian order of the real, that is, it cannot command or order, because it necessarily disorders what it finds.[39] Indeed, it is often quite violent in the transpositions it effects, exposing the fictiveness (and violence) of real-world categories like homogeneity or readability. "Homogeneity" constitutes not a brute fact of the world, but a template through which cultures regulate experience.

But if we grant that literary texts *in some way* reflect states of reality, does such reflectionism need to be taken as naive? Barthes's distinction between writerly and readerly texts, for instance, insists that it is the former which corrects for the latter's "nauseating" closure and reduplication of ideological constraints; thus, Balzac's short story "Sarrasine" represents a borderline text in which subversive forces can be seen rapidly encroaching upon the blandly bourgeois status quo. But this distinction rests on a selective idea of the forces of subversion: erotic desire, in this instance. But persons are routinely subverted in all sorts of nonerotic ways: by projections of "character" upon them, for example, or the indiscreet effacement of discrete selves through typification.

Allegory is a fate literary characters are often consigned to—by their authors as well as one another. Hawthorne's *Scarlet Letter*, an obvious case, shows how allegorical modes of perception can imprison social relations far more effectively than any stocks. No wonder Hester's Pearl seems unreal; she is in effect the child of allegory. To recall Levinas' words, "the whole of reality bears on its face its own allegory, outside of its revelation and its truth." Literary fiction, then, simply echoes a self-fictionalizion already intact as a possibility for ordinary human interaction.[40]

The power of representation over personhood casts a peculiar light on formalism's tendency to blanch those very features of representation which the process of narrative fiction makes apparent. As it is for so many kinds of reading, Mary Shelley's *Frankenstein* serves as the classic cautionary tale here. Formalist theorists devise theoretical constructs to substitute for fictional "instantiations" of them, when in doing so they reenact the (often monstrous) exchange of substitutions between character and person that texts already depict. Might we not think of such models as unconsciously "deforming" persons in ways that literature either avoids or knowingly exploits? (Shlomith Rimmon-Kenan makes the pertinent observation, for instance, that in dissolving person into "character," and character into text, semioticians are only following the lead of modernist writers such as Woolf, Stein, and Kafka.)[41]

And yet I must draw a crucial distinction here: as Ricoeur and Adorno in different ways observe, narrative fiction puts its readers in the dock by requiring them to refigure what it configures: to witness it, to let the text happen to them in such a way that they are, in Ricoeur's phrase, "produced in front of it." Conversely, formalist criticism avoids this recurrent question of answerability by locating its judgments behind the workings of the text, limiting its role merely to matching objective description with textual fact.

As in my critique of the deconstructive position, I am interested here in pursuing the degree to which ethics exerts a negative pressure exactly within a "scientific" practice which had tried to dismiss it; the relation between ethical and literary form is not so fungible. When one takes ethics to imply didacticism or subservience for literature, one finds an impoverished notion of ethics. Concomitantly, when one takes what Roman Jakobson called the poetic function to represent the totality of a work's signification, so that "psychological" or "evaluative" structures are deemed invasive and unscientific, one is working with an unhealthily reified notion of literature.

The mobile drama of the individual person, whether as subject or intersubject, is refractory to systems which try to digest or eviscerate it. The variety of terms which designate a single human entity—self, character, individual, person, agent, figure, protagonist, soul—attests to the stubborn historicity of each, which resists the false recuperations of diachronic and intercultural comparisons that flatten persons out. And each one of these terms, in turn, signifies certain extensional properties: character and characteristics, person and choice, self and property, individual and right. A full account of narrative representation needs to provide for the differentiated picture these terms suggest.[42]

At bottom, however, one still needs to reckon with the brute fact of the obstinate mimeticism of readers and texts. Both not only grow, but pick, eat, and seem to enjoy their linguistic grapes, de Man notwithstanding. Need we understand this obstinacy solely in terms of the ideologically manipulative norms of "common sense"? (In mimeticism's "scandalous" refusal to disappear, one is reminded also of the pertinacity Levinas and Cavell both ascribe to skepticism.)[43] Should "resisting novels" or "reading (the) oppositional (in) narrative"[44] exhaust our repertoire of postmodern strategies designed to compensate for earlier "confusion" and malaise?

Perhaps, in fact, we overcompensate. Consider that we miss the point of "mimetic illusion." It was (and still is) always on some level just that: a knowing deformation of the real. Consider, moreover, that such illusionism in literature apes a similar phenomenon in real life and, further, that certain texts actively measure, analyze, and critique it. This is literature as a kind of biotechnology—the purposeful cross-mixing of reference and phenomenalism. Since literary texts thematize illusionism—which can be rephrased as "a certain resistance to the claims of otherness"—on at least some level, one needs to suspend *Ideologiekritik*, to actively resist one's own resistance. (The most sensitive readings of Aristotle's *Poetics* in fact isolate just this critical sense of mimesis.)[45]

To make my position clear: one of the "functions of criticism," as I see it, is to follow the lead of literary texts by mediating their mediations. Thus I do not at all demur from criticism's need to resist the truth-claims of bourgeois normativity, its legitimation of powers that be. (Take the verb in this end phrase as active, and you arrive at Levinas' critique of ontology: powers that *be*.) I do, however, want to call attention to the role which the hermeneutics of suspicion already plays in lived experience well before it becomes a critical strategy. That is something, as I said earlier, which texts like Anderson's short story "know beforehand"; they know that they are being read, in other words.

As an analogy to what one could call the hard Levinasian kernel of alterity at the bottom of every mediated encounter (in world or text), one might cite the Lacanian thesis about the real—that behind the mask of everyday appearances there lies a surplus, a remainder of reality which cannot be assimilated to "illusionism," but which is still only accessible through that same play of mirrors.[46] But the important point here is the dialectical relation between fictional world and real world—the play of representation "across the borders" between them. (The self is already borderline, anyway, always "half someone else's," as Bakhtin puts it.)

Fictional narratives do not just offer us a "laboratory" in which to study this overdetermination of otherness within intersubjective horizons—how characters and authors construct others in order to escape a certain deadlock of/in subjectivity. More important, perhaps, they elicit this very same process in the performance of reading. To "resist" this textual elicitation means balking at an ethical demand to "undergo" a book by reading it.

I develop a theory of such "representational ethics" over the course of chapters 4 and 5, and apply it in various contexts in the remaining chapters. What the texts I assemble have to "say," I argue, initiates a chain of critical responsibilities. To read a text such as Henry James's "The Real Thing" as simply "exemplary," already misrecognizes it since it enacts a critique of "illustrativeness" per se. If Dickens' *Bleak House* politicizes representation as "a matter for the police" (Christopher Prendergast's apt phrase),[47] Stephen Crane's story *The Monster*, transforms that politicization into cultural decisions about what will constitute recognition and who will count as recognizable in the first place. The common theme shared by all these texts is recognition—an extension of the trope of anagnorisis beyond the restrictive contours of emplotment, detection, or subjective identity.

Narration

Since the readings of Coleridge and Anderson in Chapter 1 anticipate much of what I have to say here, I shall move quickly. The topic of narration has recently fared better than representation in narrative theory, one must say, almost certainly because of its "transactional and contractual" nature, which draws particular attention to the shaping of power relations in, and by, literary texts. At the same time, this healthy attention to the performative function of storytelling frequently serves to demonstrate the power of representation, since narrators dictate conditions and, in so doing, reify their authority. (One sees how, even methodologically, representation and narration do not easily separate.) Thus the authority increasingly inscribed in literary texts themselves gradually compensates for the decrease in the storyteller's authority, which Walter Benjamin chronicles in his essay of the same name. (The most self-aware of such texts in turn inscribe an awareness if not critique of that very "inscription.")

At least four directions for these implications now limn the critical landscape: Marxist, psychoanalytic, semiotic-performative, and political-ideological.[48] All four perspectives share a common concern with narration's contextual conditions, the situational features which mobilize social relations and, in Ross Chambers' words, give "force and point to . . . storytelling" (*SS*, 6). Structuralist narratology made a point, as I have noted, of eschewing "point" in its attempt to theorize the invariant components of narrative structure, reducing it to the superfluity of "theme," and narrowly confining situational conditions to perceptual details: point of view or focalization.

Each of the four perspectives I list above, by contrast, convincingly rehabilitates point, "to focus attention onto the need, not simply to read texts in situation (which is inevitable) but also to read, in the texts, the situation that they *produce* as giving them their 'point'" (*SS*, 4). Prose fiction, in other words, models its own storytelling circumstances. Whether overtly, as in Henry James's "The Figure in the Carpet," or indirectly, as in Conrad's *Lord Jim*, narrative fiction can stage its own transactional procedures within the text.

Unfortunately, each of these same four perspectives tends to limit this important observation to only certain lines of argument. Chambers' description of the narrative act as "seduction," for example, unduly generalizes the erotic component in narrative (and in reading) to the act itself. Storytelling becomes a contract relation fueled by desire and desire alone—desire enacted, transposed, or refused; even the desire for closure figures a sublimation of erotic desire. Any narrative act in this view is necessarily an act of seduction.[49]

Any narrative act can be, of course, but whether it must be (and this does seem to be Chambers' "point") seems to me an instance of definitional aggrandizement. To be fair, Chambers explains that the nineteenth-century texts he studies all exemplify narrative seduction because "seduction" marks their historicity in the development of the novel—a tradition in place, one notes, since Cervantes, Richardson, and Laclos. Chambers' methodology—in particular, the principle of textual reflexivity through self-situating—provides quite valuable tools for analysis.[50] But the underlying assumptions are insufficient, as I want to underscore by turning again to Shakespeare's *Othello*, to compare Chambers' comments on Othello's wooing of consort and court with the same example as treated by Stanley Cavell.

At the end of *The Claim of Reason*, in a section titled "The Stake of the Other," Cavell adverts to Othello's murder of Desdemona as the quintessentially violent admission/denial of the claim which her separateness makes upon Othello. Cavell's analysis shows that narrative acts can commit discursive violence not exclusively because of their power to seduce. In making Desdemona enamored of him through narrating his exploits, Othello also compels from her a certain kind of recognition, just as Iago twists that need by fabricating a story in which recognition degenerates into detection. Contract relations (as Cavell explains elsewhere) proceed from instrumental purposes for exchanges of goods, services, and terms.

But narrative situations do not necessarily conform to this model; rather, they often work quite differently—to express an "acceptance of human relatedness" which requires "the acceptance of repetition." Othello cannot accept either, and thus what a "contract model" (for marriage as well as for narrative) illustrates is Othello's failure to approximate a norm for relationships not based on a contract.[51]

Chambers focuses entirely on the naked instrumentality of Othello's seducing through story in Act 1, scene 1. (Contract models instrumentalize even good conduct, since one gets satisfaction and "good feeling" in exchange for doing good.) To be sure, *Othello* registers the deep enmeshment of human discourse and desire, but it also shows the mutual complicity of desire and knowledge in dampening the claims of acknowledgment. (Othello's skepticism reverberates politically, of course, but not, I would argue, in Chambers' sense of authoritarian and oppositional practice. What Levinas calls logic's alliance with politics already overcodes Othello's erotic *liaisons* with Venetian society, and does not, in my view, reduce to them.)

Although Chambers limits his treatment of narrative situation to texts which exemplify seduction and contractual relation, he implies too narrowly that such conditions represent a norm for all narrative (and one presumes, nonnarrative) relationship. Yet in the closing paragraph of *Story and Situation,* Chambers unexpectedly enlarges his scope to assert that narrative "point" is indistinguishable from the "point" of human relationships—one might as well say (for humans as communicating creatures) "the point of existence" (*SS,* 221). The point I have been arguing thus far is that the point, if you will, at which this "point of human existence" gets called into question in fact points beyond power relations; it points to the ethical relation.

If I argued against a false opposition between poetics and a hermeneutic approach to fiction in the first section of this chapter, here I have decried an undertheorized connection between the two instead. In titling this section "Formalisms: Critical and Ethical," I wanted to convey the fallout of such a mésalliance: the reductively formalist conceptualization of ethics which results when literary theory champions linguistic formalism as its regnant value.[52] In a strange reversal of the Platonic story, philosophers are shown the door in order to accommodate both poets and their critical entourage. In the rest of this chapter, I explore how certain of those philosophers—thus *fuori le mura*—have described the vexed relation between ethics and aesthetics and how (or indeed whether) their insights might correlate with a theory of narrative ethics.

Literature and Philosophy: A Somewhat Longer Story

To speak of literature and philosophy together incurs a variety of critical risks, choices, and consequences. Without being facetious, by merely reversing the order of terms as I stated them above—"philosophy and literature"—I disclose the hidden pressure of syntactic bias. So I shall proceed carefully. But first, to define my terms: "literature" signifies prose fiction, "philosophy" denotes ethics.

Martha Nussbaum titles a section of her Introduction to essays on this subject, *Love's Knowledge*, "the ancient quarrel." One assumes this phrase must refer to the historical connection between literature and philosophy. But before its reference becomes clear, Nussbaum proceeds to detail her own dual encounters with philosophy and literature—by telling a story. She relates the institutional obstacles she faced in attempting to combine her joint interest in what were regarded as two separate sets of questions, texts, and disciplines.

Her original narrative, which she now rejoins, becomes folded inside her own, as she tells a story of the deep imbrication of ethics and literature within philosophical thought in classical Greece. Thus the "ancient quarrel," it turns out, lies not between philosophy and literature but rather between "forms of discourse and views of life" (*LK*, 20)—both situated within a common field of inquiry, an inquiry presided over by the omnipresent discourse of ethics.

But in few places outside Nussbaum's story do "literature and philosophy" now remain so linked and so safely embedded. Not only sundered from each other but disembedded from any larger narrative except historical memory, each now commonly resides in a separate discipline of its own, and each prompts a separate set of questions. Traffic between the two tends to be rare and unsatisfying.

Thus similar nostalgic "stories" about ethics and literature are narrated severally by Charles Taylor, Tobin Siebers, and Wayne Booth, and their conclusions echo Nussbaum's: contemporary literary study requires an infusion of the very things it once depended on but has since expelled. (One is reminded of Wlad Godzich's point about would-be resolutions which become perturbatory.) All these authors believe that criticism functions at any time to mediate between life and

art, to bridge, as Habermas puts it, the everyday world and the specialized culture of literature.[53] All concur that aesthetic judgment depends
on cognitive and practical values alike.

One can, of course, rebut by invoking a postmodern demurrer like
Lyotard to explain how descriptive accounts such as these—stories, in
fact—follow smoothly and imperceptibly from normative and prescriptive assumptions. From within the confines of moral philosophy, Bernard Williams has detailed that very process in action, insisting that
the disposition to accept ethical statements does not then necessarily
prove their truth.[54] Still, however, one must grant that it is possible for
normativity to follow simply from a more or less accurate set of descriptions.

Take Nussbaum's own Aristotelian framework, for example. Flexible
and recursive, it specifies the noncommensurability of qualitatively
different goods; the conflicted nature of obligations—the embedded
character of our loyalties, the importance of particular persons, the
intervention of the unforeseen—and the consequent need to discern
differences and make judgments; and the cognitive/ethical value of
emotions. Lyotard's and Williams' critiques work only if the circularity
of the life/ethics/literature argument fails accurately to describe (in the
geometrical sense) a relation which is in fact healthily circular. If prescription does surface in Nussbaum's account, it does so only with
respect to the acuity and fullness of critical judgment, the musician's
skill she calls being "richly aware and finely responsible."

Nevertheless, Lyotard need not even be invoked in order to point
out that the models for such perceptual discernment in Nussbaum's
account—the Ververs in Henry James's *The Golden Bowl*—display an
assured, aristocratic quality in the articulacy of their judgments which
in its very taken-for-grantedness can seem remote and too easy. The
Ververs seem to dispense their morals, along with their other posses-
sions, with imperial largess.[55]

Clearly, articulacy is the whole point here, since the capacity to say
things in a certain *juste* way demarks more finely tuned judgments from
those blunter and more crude. It also symbolizes the virtue of literary
texts as expressions of moral problems which philosophical discourse
could not render with the same subtlety. Nussbaum makes the most
extensive argument for this claim. But phrases such as "getting the tone
right," "obtuseness is a moral failing," and "an achievement of the
precisely right description, the correct nuance of tone" (*LK*, 156) imply

a kind of chill perfectionism, impatient with lapses not in intent, but in performance—as though one had a single chance of "getting it right" (which, admittedly, one often does—not necessarily a virtue but simply a fact of life). More often than not, ordinary persons do not share the Ververs' rich moral attunement, "the delicate communication of alert beings who stand separated by 'an exquisite tissue' through which they alertly hear each other breathing" (*LK*, 153).

Thus the metaphor of a jazz musician which Nussbaum uses in her Introduction to describe the improvisatory quality of ethical discernment I see as possibly going in two alternative directions. In "real time" as it were, improvisatory aggrandizement can lead to simple performative tyranny—when Miles Davis walks off stage to show contempt for his fellow musicians and the audience, or when Charlie Mingus physically assaults players who do not "get the tone right," whose obtuse musicianship proves a "moral failure," one man's attunement becomes another's egoism. Or conversely, in "story time," that same gift can suggest an ethical unfinalizability, such as we see thematized in stories like James Baldwin's "Sonny's Blues" or Julio Cortazar's "The Pursuer."

"The Pursuer," for instance (which I referred to in an earlier note), is a brilliant riff on the dissonance-cum-polyphony of aesthetic freedom in dialogue with the ethics of storytelling. In this story, however, getting the tone "right" means deadening it. How to keep/stop playing? How to keep/stop narrating? These questions involve an ethic of "articulacy" wholly different from the one Nussbaum's moral perfectionism can address. Indeed, Cortazar's story is allergic to the very idea of "perfectionism." (Nussbaum's discussions of Dickens, Proust, and Beckett do show an alternative possibility, however, one less concerned with "legislative" than with "interactive" pressures.)

In the same spirit, I lay claim to my own preference for texts which exemplify "an ethics of inarticulacy"[56] or a-not-so-always "lucid bewilderment." Such texts thematize the need for a sufficiently capacious and generous narrative which forgives a broken movement toward "getting the tone right." More often than not in life, one needs the expanse of an entire life and life story to encompass the work of knowing, to develop "an ability to miss less, to be responsible to more" (*LK*, 189). (This is the reason perhaps that one feels about novels like Eliot's *Middlemarch* that they should go on and on, and not capitulate to the formal pressures of quiescence, of the "nonnarratability" of everyday life.)[57] In his preface to *The Golden Bowl*, James says the following about life's narratability:

> We are condemned, in other words, whether we will it or no, to abandon and outlive, to forget and disown and hand over to desolation, many vital or social performances. . . . We give them up even when we wouldn't—it is not a question of choice. Not so on the other hand our really "done" things of [a] superior and more appreciable order—which leave us indeed all license of disconnexion and disavowal, but positively impose upon us no such necessity. Our relation to them is essentially traceable, and in that fact abides, we feel, the incomparable luxury of the artist.

Thus do we find the desolation depicted in Anderson's "Loneliness," where narrative ethics conduces to a botched instance of aesthetic judgment, where life and art imperfectly align.

Even with the qualifications I am registering here, "imperfect alignment" probably wouldn't leap to mind as a description of the way in which my own project stands relative to Nussbaum's or the others' I list above. From the double meaning Wayne Booth, for instance, locates in ethos as betokening both character and judgment to the link Charles Taylor draws between narrative and moral space, we all seem to be proceeding in the same spirit. And yet my purpose here is precisely to distance myself from that spirit and its normative set of arguments and critical choices.

To show what I mean, I want briefly to take up a point which Booth makes in *The Company We Keep*. He argues that the primary index of a generalizable moral consciousness is the capacity for "second-order valuings," which are discriminations about the judgments we make. He suggests that narrative fiction in particular requires an initial act of assent and surrender, asking readers "to follow story . . . to accept and pursue a pattern of desires imposed by an other" (*CWK*, 13). He calls this Burkean view of aesthetic response "hypocrisy upwards," that is, an active rhetoric by which readers try on roles and "desire better desires" (*CWK*, 17).

A sound, if ego-psychological approach, very similar to Charles Altieri's, Booth's still structures itself in terms of author-reader relations. Even if readers imagine stand-ins like "implied author" or "extradiegetic narratee," they still remain busy imagining ethical relations with authors. This is why for Booth reading a text can be thought of in terms of friendship; for ultimately it is the author—whether free-standing or represented by his text—who will turn out to be a better or worse friend for us.[58]

But acts of assent, surrender, seduction, coercion, and bestowal all occur inside fictional texts; we must be a party to these, before we construe literary texts as messages sent from authors to readers. The "trying on of roles" *within* the text exactly demands our second-order reflections about those actions that we imitate as readers. In other words, we are witnesses or even interlocutors before we deflect risk and find security in the role of "readers."

As Levinas says of interpersonal contact, the self is better thought of as skin rather than mind, because its relation to others precedes rational decision and choice—it is first *felt* as exposure. To read is to be vulnerable. Booth would perhaps agree, and even object that his sense of surrender implies or logically entails these discriminations. But his continuing attention to fictional rhetoric—now weighted by an ethics—shows how dedicated he is to a mostly unidirectional and static model of literary discourse: from author through text to reader.

I have used Booth as an example to suggest that the philosophical deficits of narratological analysis which I noted in the last section to a degree correspond to narratological lacunae in "philosophical" criticism like Nussbaum's or Booth's. His otherwise excellent approach seems to me not to go far enough either in thinking through a certain set of concerns—knowing versus acknowledging, separateness and substitution, recognition and alterity—or in sufficiently formalizing their ramifications as narrative ethics. But why is this so?

Literature as Example

Tolstoy wrote, "The activity of art is based on the fact that a man receiving through his sense of hearing or sight another man's expression of feeling is capable of experiencing the emotion which moved the man who expressed it. . . . *Art is a human activity consisting in this, that one man consciously by means of certain external signs, hands on to others feelings he has lived through, and that others are infected by those feelings and also experience them.*"[59] Tolstoy's theory of art as *infection* remains the most potent theory of aesthetic exemplification since Plato. If expressive kinds of art are, to use T. E. Hulme's famous phrase, so much "spilt religion," then the art which Tolstoy values most highly, by comparison, amounts to religion "transfused," so minimal is the aesthetic prophylaxis needed for self-protection; call it "unsafe art." (Indeed, improbably or not in this connection, Tolstoy's aesthetic veers quite close to Antonin Artaud's theory of art as plague.)

Perhaps just as improbably, Tolstoy believed *Uncle Tom's Cabin* was a greater work of art than *King Lear*. Harriet Beecher Stowe's novel actively works to generate results by example, to set into motion a chain of mimetic and performative substitutions which its readers are meant to imitate and inculcate. *King Lear*, conversely, as Cavell reads it, stands as a monument to distances of every kind: to the extent that it stands over against the power of exemplification, the play legislates unmediated acknowledgment.

No doubt it has its lesson, invites drawing all kinds of morals (as Cavell says, "it could not happen without us"). But, as I explained in my own reading of *The Rime of the Ancient Mariner*, seeing the play as exemplary in some way misses the fact that it is meant first to be *confronted:* an audience stands before such a play, stands before its characters' brute separateness—not to contemplate them as "examples" but to acknowledge them as being, standing, and suffering apart.

Obviously, "exemplarity" in *Lear* can mean the represention of a general truth, the sharing of its clarifying insights.[60] But the concept has a far more performative reach: the play installs us, so to speak, as its executors—not only its "legal witnesses," but its capital punishers. In Cavell's words, "It shows that we are responsible for the death of others even when we have not murdered them" (*MWM*, 318).[61] In other words, a performance of *Lear* places us in the presence and the present of others, while it simultaneously repudiates our own presence, insofar as the acknowledgment we owe Lear, Cordelia, Edgar, and Gloucester cannot be completed.

One of the things that artworks do, then, is to send us away from them: they permit us access, but at the price of a resistance—not ours, but theirs to us. In the first two sections of this chapter, I argued that a certain resistance to texts should itself be deferred in acknowledgment, as it were, of epistemology's limits. Now I am suggesting that artworks also formally, materially chasten a too hasty temptation to extract, or to be overwhelmed by, their "moral" value. Yet most well-intentioned use made of literary texts by moral philosophers makes exactly such appropriative moves: "wresting" truth for truth's sake.

The fourth epigraph to this chapter speaks of smothering persons and texts, smothering being a fate similar to the "suffocation" I find in Anderson's "Loneliness." In this regard, philosophers—even ethical philosophers—can err along with textualists and formalists. As the philosopher Richard Brudney puts it, "Even when a philosopher provides a genuine reading of a text, use of that text to defend or refute a general theory [even 'expressive idealism'] may inhibit recognition of its real philosophical interest."[62] Construing aesthetic form in terms of ethical (practical) exemplarity as a way out of the content-as-morality bind seems to me to result in a somewhat errant notion of form, because it generalizes the power of example without paying sufficient attention to formal particulars.[63]

But in "performing the text" (as I called it in Chapter 1), don't readers merely carry out the actions/messages which the text frames as examples? Doesn't "textual power" reduce ultimately to the force of the example? Only, I would answer, if one is dedicated to a strong pedagogical imperative—a bias which together unites such disparate positions as Charles Altieri's, Hillis Miller's, and Wayne Booth's. And as my reference to Tolstoy above implies, literary fiction—because it plugs into the "strong ethics" of narrative relations—"infects" better than it "teaches." And even if we want our prose fiction Brechtian rather than Artaudian, *it* knows that despite the clarifying *Verfremdung* of cigarette smoke for aesthetic distance (Brecht wanted his audience to send up its own intrusive curtain of haze), smoke still gets in your eyes.

So how should philosophy "use" literature? Or rather, how should it respond to it? In his article on *The Golden Bowl*, Richard Brudney enumerates three options: the literary text can serve as an extended philosophical example; the literary text can be seen as a kind of moral training or, relatedly, as a proof of the practical impossibility of certain positions, moral relativism, for example; and the literary text can extend and develop a philosophical problem by placing it in a new light. This last possibility describes the philosophical intent of my book.

Brudney's own analysis bears out the significance of doing so in the twin distinctions he goes on to elaborate for reading fiction like *The Golden Bowl*—one outside of James's text, one within it; one, a sense-making procedure of exemplification, the other, a way in which *The Golden Bowl* seems to understand itself. This pair of distinctions we can see as roughly corresponding to the one I introduced above in reference to *King Lear*. (James's mention of "fear and pity" at the end of the novel, and Maggie's double move of hiding/acknowledging in the Prince's arms, make the analogy with *Lear*, I think, uncannily apt.)

The first distinction opposes evaluating an action to fashioning one;

in Brudney's terms, this is the difference between, on the one hand, circling around conduct in order to name it and, on the other, opening action up from within through ethical praxis. Whereas the first is "more like a critic's ability to appraise accurately," the second "seems analogous to an artist's ability to create" (423). In a nuanced reading of Nussbaum's reading, Brudney concludes that James's novel complements moral philosophy's work through its depiction of moral deliberation as a craft, rather than a reflection on the nature of moral rules.

The discussion of ethical fashioning leads, in turn, to the second of Brudney's distinctions, which contrasts the novel's own performativity with the sort of philosophical approach that gets at literature through paraphrase and exemplification. As Brudney puts it simply, "philosophical force may sometimes reside in the words of the literary text itself" (426). (This distinction, moreover, seems analogous to me to one within Brudney's academic field, between meta-ethical theory and more experiential, embedded models like communicative ethics.)

But along with a Tolstoyan capacity to be moved by philosophical force—to perform its performances, as it were—one also needs the counter-gesture of textual acknowledgment, a matter of interpretive tact. And of tact, in reference to Maggie Verver's tactful silences, Brudney wisely observes: "Here, tact involves a willingness to accept 'otherness,' where this means not to seek *an account* of what makes the other other, to accept the sheer fact of difference. . . . Maintaining the surface can be a way to keep from knowing another's personal quantity or a way to express your knowledge" (433, 432).

The point of this final section has been to suggest that ethically poised philosophy probably serves literature best when it opts for such tact—when it allows texts first to speak, to tell their whole stories, before it responds. Such a response needs tactfully to mediate between knowledge and silence, between bestowing a critical surplus that literature cannot provide itself and simply registering the fact of literature's alterity, its repudiation of categories which attempt to appropriate and "theorize" it—at its best, an equilibrium of call and response, not blindness and insight. In this also, ethical theory keeps company with literary theory.

In the readings which follow, I will be adapting the thought of Stanley Cavell, Mikhail Bakhtin, and Emmanuel Levinas in order to apply their insights about the claims of intersubjectivity to my own theory of narrative ethics. It seems to me methodologically sounder to unfold those insights alongside the details of the texts for which they are relevant, rather than to indulge in any more propaedeutics.

In terms of "unfolding," however, it needs to be made clear what this book does and does not do. It does not systematically "read" Bakhtin's, Cavell's, or Levinas' philosophical projects. Rather, it applies Levinasian, Cavellian, and Bakhtinian themes to literary texts. In doing so, it tries to exercise the same caution about "instrumentalizing" philosophy that it argued for in literature's behalf; it does not wish to bend the content of ideas to the whims of critical *bricolage*.

I appeal to the recurrent analogies each writer makes to literary examples (many, in Levinas' case, drawn from prose fiction) as something of a sanction for the engagements I rehearse here. I appeal also to Levinas' implications for his own writing when he says, "Labor remains economic; it comes from the home and returns to it, a movement of Odyssey where the adventure pursued in the world is but the accident of a return. . . . Works have a destiny independent of the I, are integrated in an ensemble of works" (*TI*, 176). Fittingly, the *literary* image Levinas uses to underscore that idea—Abraham's movement away from home in contrast to Odysseus' circular return—is drawn from narrative—sacred narrative.

Of the three, Levinas, one must say, poses the same hard challenge to/for literary theory that he does with respect to philosophy. More than even philosophical tact is at stake here, since Levinas' philosophy questions not the quality of one's critical assumptions, but rather the right even to hold them—the *conatus essendi*, as he would say, the "I can" of discursive autonomy. In this way, Levinas' ethical project seeks even from itself a critical accounting, its own answerability.

In the critical duties it owes to text and to interpretation, literary theory, as Levinas says of Judaism, practices a difficult freedom. And that is why it requires interruption, a Saying distinct from the Said. In the chapters which follow, the texts I discuss know such necessity beforehand; to recall my epigraph from Jabès, together, they tie a knot of correspondences which unties the act of reading within its ties.

3

We Die in a Last Word: Conrad's *Lord Jim* and Anderson's *Winesburg, Ohio*

[A dream:] This is my sister here, with some identifiable friends and many other people. They are all listening to me and it is this very story that I am telling: the whistle of three notes, the hard bed, the neighbor whom I would like to move, but whom I am afraid to wake as he is stronger than me. I also speak diffusely of our hunger and of the lice-control, and of the Kapo who hit me on the nose and then sent me to wash myself as I was bleeding. It is an intense pleasure, physical, inexpressible, to be at home, among friendly people and to have so many things to recount: but I cannot help noticing that my listeners do not follow me. In fact, they are completely indifferent; they speak confusedly of other things among themselves, as if I was not there. My sister looks at me, gets up, and goes away without a word. . . . My dream stands in front of me, still warm, and although awake I am still full of its anguish: and then I remember that it is not a haphazard dream, but that I dreamed it not once but many times since I arrived here, with hardly any variations of environment or details. I am now quite awake and I remember that I have recounted it to Alberto and that he confided to me, to my amazement, that it is also his dream and the dream of many others, perhaps of everyone. Why does it happen? Why is the pain of every day translated so constantly into our dreams, in the ever-repeated scene of the unlistened-to story?

Primo Levi, *Survival in Auschwitz*

Are not our lives too short for that full utterance which through all our stammerings is of course our only abiding intention? I have given up expecting those last words, whose ring, if they could only be pronounced, would shake both heaven and earth. There is never time to say our last word— the last word of our love, of our desire, faith, remorse, submission, revolt.

Joseph Conrad, *Lord Jim*

We die in a last word.
Edmond Jabès,
The Book of Questions

I N THIS CHAPTER I focus on two novels written within fifteen years of each other. "Mariner texts" we can call them in a number of important respects, *Lord Jim* and *Winesburg, Ohio* together chart a course which modernist fiction was to navigate from both sides of the Atlantic. Antirealist for different reasons, both texts turn inward to explore the constitutive features of storytelling itself and the iconic relationship between the novel and the everyday narrating of lives. Speaking anthropologically (each novel does have the effect of "spying on" its chosen alien world), one could say that Jim, Marlow, and their interlocutors inhabit the same Coleridgean space of storytelling ritual and role as George Willard and the landlocked Ancients of Winesburg.

Conrad's ambivalence about cultural or national loyalties, on the one hand, and Anderson's sense of artistic singularity, on the other, inform their novels' obsession with exile and solitude, with identity and culture at the fin de siècle. Both texts explore a problematics of narration in extreme circumstances, the loneliness of long- and short-distance narrators alike. Each novel, finally, could be described as a narrative of moments: Jim's intermittent leaps into individuation and story in Conrad's tale, the bursts and flashes of narrative self-revelation which both disclose and produce grotesque identity in Anderson's stories.

In Chapter 1, I used the phrase "caught by language" to suggest how the mechanics of narrative discourse in a fundamental sense already implies an ethics; I reinvoke it here, not only because it provides a convenient point of contact between Conrad's and Anderson's texts, but also to show why I think they serve as paradigms for narrative ethics. In chapter 20 of *Lord Jim*, after recounting the story of capturing a rare specimen, and just prior to Marlow's story about his own such specimen—Jim—old man Stein quotes from *Faust:* "So halt' ich's endlich denn in meinem Händen / Und nenn' es in gewissem Sinne mein" ("For when I hold it finally in my hands, I take it in a certain

sense as mine").[1] The quotation's literariness—not least its being left
in German—perhaps draws readers back to the epigraph from Novalis
which begins the novel, "It is certain my conviction gains infinitely the
moment another soul will believe it." The one epigraph seems to fulfill,
even answer the other.

For Marlow within the text, however, the *Faust* quotation stands for
the hermeneutic challenge that Jim poses for him, and that Marlow's
story poses in turn for its interlocutors. The "grasping" calls to mind
not only Jim's need for recognition (his telling as a means for counting,
as Stanley Cavell might say), but Marlow's reciprocal desire to capture
Jim and his story by more than just a "glimpse through a rent in the
mist" (11:100). And it also implies the complicity of the listeners in
such a capture, their arrogation of its meaning. "Frankly," as Marlow
pauses to say to them, "it is not my words that I distrust but your
minds" (21:172). At the same time, it should give *these listeners* pause,
by forcing awareness of the evaluative process required to sort through
just these multiple valences which collect around the idea of "capture."

This almost incidental scene from *Lord Jim* strikes a subtle rhythm
between apprehension and comprehension. Although Stein refers to
his experience as a purely individual epiphany, we can read it intersubjectively as a certain pulse of narrative language: in the act of narrating,
storytellers lay their hands on those they address, possibly to minister
to them, possibly to do them violence (if only verbal). And those
addressed, in the ways they construe or respond, perform answering
actions in turn.

(Hence the luxury of deontological judgment, which eschews such
"close contact," a vantage point occupied in the novel by its designated
narratee, the recipient of Marlow's written notes. An unnamed moralist
who comes by his familiarity with "ethical progress" wholly untested—
"cleverly, without singeing [his] wings" (36:255)—this reader simply
pronounces judgment; his task is merely juridical: to fit case to gener-
alization like the officers at Jim's inquest.)

Stein, evidently, finds consolation in the temporary, ineffable quality
of his illumination. *In gewissem Sinne* ("in a certain sense") can be taken
as the positive counterpart to de Man's "not necessarily" in his argument that hermeneutic understanding in life and in literature are "*not
necessarily* compatible." Stein seems to suggest that the conditionality
life and art share—the pathos of encounter—is what unifies ethical and
aesthetic response, binding reference to phenomenalism. The lines

from Goethe—as an image for narration—describe a swaying between reference and phenomenalism, perception and possession, which grounds the novel throughout.

How might this be seen as an ethical moment in the text? Stein speaks of catching sight of the butterfly while "looking over" one of the men he has just shot: "And as I looked at his face for some sign of life I observed something like a faint shadow pass over his forehead" (20:160). Forcing a strict imagistic logic, we can correlate this small incident with the fact that all the while Stein relates it, he meaningfully directs his attention toward or away from Marlow—he "withdrew his eyes from my face . . . looked again at me significantly . . . his thoughtful placid face twitched once" (161).

I want to call attention here to the important role assigned to the human face, how it functions from one scene to the next as both cipher and decoder, text and commentary, object and means of recognition, a presence behind shadows or clouds and the force that shines through them. This image, too, pervades the text; to a great degree, face, or its metonym, vision, forms the topic of *Lord Jim*.

Stein, for example, senses an affinity between himself and Jim, the "visionary" or dreamy sensibility they both share—"To follow the dream, and again to follow the dream" (164). But vision more typically functions in the text (as it does in the scene above) as the material sense itself—"seeing" as reading or interpreting or recognizing (accurately or not), "sight" as something to be focused or narrowed or viewed against a background.

Ethically speaking, the directed quality of vision, the fact that sight takes hold of and commands the objects it views or selects out, makes it estrange what it thereby domesticates. We correct for this "ethos of alienation"[2] latent in any act of seeing only by acknowledging the special character and demands of intersubjective encounter—when faces look out onto other faces which return their gaze. As Levinas puts it, "Vision moves into grasp. Vision opens upon a perspective, upon a horizon, and describes a traversable distance, invites the hand to movement and to contact, and ensures them. . . . [Light] makes possible the signification of objects that border one another. It does not enable one to approach them face to face" (*TI*, 191). But obviously, "face" also means speech. And as "speech cuts across vision" according to Levinas, just so optics and dialogue, impression and expression, will clash in *Lord Jim* as competing modes of encounter. But more important for my analysis of this scene, the first word of expression that Levinas ascribes to the face—its transcendental signification before any words are even spoken—is, "You shall not kill!" Such a command contests the murderous reduction and assimilation that looking tacitly promises—the violence that, as Levinas says, "aims only at a face."

The force of Stein's anecdote, then, and of its staging in the text (innocuous as they may seem), is just this theme of force and perceptual aggrandizement. Stein catches sight of the butterfly, holds it in his hand and "takes" it as his own, and at the same time surveys the face of the man he has just killed. What is the shadow he sees? And why does he look at Marlow while narrating this? And how does Marlow look in turn, we should ask ourselves, when he retells this same story to *his* audience? Thus begins a chain of contaminated looking which at every point enjoins an ethical complicity—if, that is, listeners "grasp," or mediate—the significance of their very grasping, their comprehension.

In his preface to *The Nigger of the "Narcissus,"* Conrad famously and paradoxically remarks, "My task which I am trying to achieve is, by the power of the written word to make you hear, to make you feel—it is, before all, to make you *see*." Over and above the complex synesthesia at play here, Conrad yokes together art and authorial power and plainly specifies their connection: he makes readers aware of the force behind aesthetic perception. Extending Conrad's observation, we can say that narrative relations depend in part on a kind of perceptual violence: on the producing end, for good or for ill, force ("to make you see"), and on the receiving end, denied or not, recognition ("Yes, I see" or "No, I do not see"). As vision appropriates, so language fixes and holds fast, narrative discourse doing so in its own distinctive ways.

Sherwood Anderson explores this identical dilemma of catching and being caught in language in *Winesburg, Ohio.* In a short piece not included in the novel, he addresses directly the peculiar symbiosis which Conrad locates between representation and narration, between seeing and saying, transforming a hermeneutic dilemma into an ethical one.

Did you ever have a notion of this kind—there is an orange, say an apple, lying on the table before you. You put out your hand to take it. Perhaps you eat it, make it a part of your physical life. Have you touched? Have you eaten? That's what I wonder about. The whole

subject's important to me because I want the apple. . . . For a long
time I thought only of eating the apple. Then later its fragrance
became something of importance too. The fragrance stole out
through my room, through a window and into the streets. . . . The
point is that after the form of the apple began to take my eye I often
found myself unable to touch at all. My hands went toward the object
of my desire and then came back. There I sat, in the room with the
apple before me, and hours passed. I had pushed myself off into a
world where nothing has any existence. Had I done that, or had I
merely stepped, for the moment, out of the world of darkness into
the light? It may be that my eyes are blind and that I cannot see. It
may be I am deaf. My hands are nervous and tremble. How much do
they tremble? Now, alas, I am absorbed in looking at my own hands.
With these nervous and uncertain hands may I really feel for the form
of things concealed in the darkness?   ("The Form of Things Concealed")[3]

In addition to the coincidence of the light/dark imagery which forms
so much of the symbolic background for *Lord Jim*, Anderson's and
Conrad's texts correspond in more interesting ways. But Anderson's
narrator refracts Stein's insight through a harsher and perhaps more
distorting prism. His story traces a minor nightmare of defamiliariza-
tion, beginning in a desire like Stein's to possess what it perceives, and
ending in a grasping as unsure of its own power as of that no longer
visible thing for which it continues to reach. Most frightening of all is
the state of arrest it describes: perceiving subject suddenly finds himself
in bondage to the object of his gaze, his predicament suddenly that of
perceiving subject *as* perceived object. The eye sees, the hands reach,
the eyes become riveted to the sight of trembling hands, the hands
falter.

Again, like Stein's anecdote, Anderson's implies a purely personal
and perceptual dilemma, the tension between aesthetic vision and self-
consciousness; Anderson's narrator shares with *Lord Jim*'s Captain Brierly the dangerous interpretive flaw of autonomic empathy. Similarly,
the passage's final question works much like Brierly's abandoned chro-
nometer, found on the rail off which he has jumped to his death—a
riddle which lacks an answer. "With these nervous and uncertain hands
may I really feel . . .?" What does it mean? Which of two linguistic
possibilities—a rhetorical question or a real question—does it imply?
Does the chain of unsettled points of reference terminate with uncer-

tain hands feeling around in the darkness? Or, as a sequence of narrated events, each more attenuated than the one before, does it thereby implicate readers by drawing them inside its own circle?

The last "event," in the form of a question, seems to solicit a possible response. Are readers thus being solicited? Does an aesthetic problem shade into an ethical problematic when it invites readers to participate in its solution? If so, then the function of this final question would roughly parallel that of the contrapuntal theatrical gestures—lowered voice, twitching face, match struck, match blown out—which Conrad assigns to Stein as he talks to Marlow. (This sort of imagery—contracting listeners to individually sensate body parts—accompanies a variety of conversational encounters in *Lord Jim*, and draws attention, I would argue, to our presence as real, though silent, eavesdroppers.)

Each of these small prose poems of recognition, of encounter narrates an allegory of perception and recognition—the perceptual and epistemological issues at work on the broadest level in Conrad's and Anderson's texts. These become ethical issues, however, when perception folds into narration and subject/object relations become intersubjective.

The excerpt from *Lord Jim* shows how complexly hermeneutic, representational, and narrational ethics intersect. While Conrad may intend this scene to be read simply as a sign of Marlow and Stein's sententiousness—a trite dose of "moralism"—I think it demands a wider field of vision: indeed, by encompassing Stein's and Marlow's own visual and discursive fields, readers "take into" their own—assimilate and become responsible for—the acts of seeing and narrating which they read.

The Anderson passage likewise traces a nexus of ethical responsibilities. A subtle piece of mimesis, it lands, like the story called "Loneliness," in readers' hands—but without the benefit of Marlovian interposition. It designates readers as active witnesses, "author-creators," as Bakhtin would say, and not simply "author-perceivers."

Each text sets before the reader an ethical structure simultaneously descriptive and performative. Each suggests a model for interpretive response: in Conrad, perception which becomes a state of possessing or "catching" and, in Anderson, perception as a state of being possessed or "being caught." Each employs confessional narrative, as do *Lord Jim* and *Winesburg, Ohio* as a whole. Each text, finally, analogizes aesthetic looking and human relation, showing the close relation between aesthetic perception and an ethics of Saying and Said.

"How the *other* looks from my position," in Bakhtin's phrase (*AA*, 124), is the larger dilemma—a transitive as well as intransitive task—which *Lord Jim* and *Winesburg, Ohio* both examine. How to convert perception into language through consummating acts of "live-entering" (Bakhtin's coinage) is the novels' common inquiry—in short, how to "author": "In this sense, one can speak of the absolute aesthetic need of one person for another, for the seeing, remembering, gathering, and unifying activity of the other" (*AA*, 98).

Anderson confines his explorations to the shortest of modern narrative forms by mirroring in its brevity the shrinkage of narrators' lives to the moments they get to narrate their stories. His narrators, however, lack the luxury of Marlow's expansive and well-honed performative expertise, and readers accordingly must evaluate and respond within the foreshortened space of one-time disclosures of self. If *Lord Jim* encloses face-to-face encounter within the processual dynamics of interpretation, *Winesburg* makes it contingent on jagged and obsessive bursts of speech. Since Anderson generously minimizes any hermeneutic uncertainty about his stories' "meaning," the ethical drama unfolds almost exclusively on this narrational plane—the plane of use, the atavistic manner in which stories get told and the calculated or incalculable effects they have on listeners.

It is in *Lord Jim*, however, that we find a definitive illustration of hermeneutic ethics, that set of exegetical demands which the text models and propels outward toward readers. The formulaic genre of "adventure yarn" gives way to a complex web of narrative relations, of dialogic weave and counterweave. The temporal dislocations which result, at the most fundamental level of *mythos*, of narrative *energia*, suggest nothing less than the lure as well as the threat of the "last word," the Penelope's shroud of stories' endings as well as the Odyssean scar of their beginnings.

That is, in part, what Marlow intimates when he asks the question I quote as an epigraph to this chapter—"Are not our lives too short for that full utterance," that is, a finished story? But such narrative desire ineluctably shades into, is overtaken by, what Levinas calls "metaphysical desire": the reaching out and liberating of an other, while exposing and making answerable the self.

Lord Jim
Living Aesthetically

Lord Jim installs a critique of perception even before its story actually commences. Conrad's prefatory "author's note," a corrective to some common misconceptions about the novel when it was first published, paraphrases it as "the acute consciousness of lost honour." The note records a glimpse of Jim in passing and the instant and profound effect he has on Conrad's narrative imagination, and ends with a preliminary statement of the novel's grand fugal theme: "One sunny morning in the commonplace surroundings of an Eastern roadstead, I saw [Jim's] form pass by—'appealing—significant—under a cloud—perfectly silent.' Which is as it should be. It was for me, with all the sympathy of which I was capable, to seek fit words for his meaning. He was 'one of us'" (8). "Form" joined to a series of empty descriptions, sensuous perception linked to a discontinuous process of making sense, sympathy folded into the challenge of expression—these represent the set of "problems" which the novel explores as a whole.

The novel's first chapter, however, starts with Jim positioned in space before readers; not merely does he advance, but with "dogged self-assertion" he "advances straight *at you*" (1:9). Conrad positions him according to height as well, describing him as falling just short of heroic stature—"an inch, perhaps two, under six feet." Attitude and altitude, one could say, combine throughout this text to select Jim out, forcing him on readers' attention as an object of scrutiny arrayed against a changing set of backgrounds. *Lord Jim* tells of perceptual possibility—of angle and depth of focus, of looks, gazes, glances, and contemplations. But as a simultaneous critique of such a possibility, the novel subjects this same scrutiny to one of its own, as readers of Jim are, so to speak, "caught looking." In this way, perceptual judgment becomes deliberative and acquires moral force.

The novel counterbalances Jim's deliberateness, however, with an equivalent propensity for immobilization; his will is held in suspension, his senses are oddly detached: "He stood still. It seemed to him he was whirled around. . . . A push made him stagger. . . . A yelling voice reached him faintly . . . Jim felt his shoulder gripped firmly" (1:12). Of his most famous lapse, his non-Kierkegaardian leap, which Marlow not unfairly calls "his abstention," Jim explains, "I jumped . . . it seems. . . . I knew nothing about it till I looked up" (9:88). Linguistic deautomizing exposes cognitive automatization. (The ideational gaps even echo the orthographic spacing of adjectives in Conrad's prefatory note.) This self-forgetfulness contrasts sharply with Jim's "original position" of dogged self-assertion, and yet it reveals a similar animal simplicity; it is not surprising, then, that Jim's reflex when meeting Marlow is to force an imagined association between himself and a dog.

At moments like these, perception becomes merely sensory, unthinking, a possibility always available in the novel even under the social pressures of dialogue or face-to-face encounter; from the inquest at the novel's beginning to readers' awareness of their own silent and continual staring at the fates of others, *Lord Jim* places empty seeing on trial. As in Coleridge, such gazing involves a fateful narrative peril when faces interlock; one speaks, the other keeps silent, the narcosis of Saying is reflected in a listener's glazed eyes as well as in those which "glitter." Jim falls under such a spell even after he has reclaimed the chance for heroism he had previously "missed," when facing and fatefully misrecognizing Gentleman Brown: "Have we met," says Brown, "to tell each other the story of our lives?" (41:288).

> To me the conversation of these two across the creek appears now as the deadliest kind of duel on which Fate looked on with her cold-eyed knowledge of the end. . . . At last Brown threw himself down full length and watched Jim out of the corners of his eyes. Jim on his side of the creek stood thinking and switching his leg. The houses in view were silent, as if a pestilence had swept them clean of every breath of life; but many invisible eyes were turned, from within, upon the two men with the creek between them. (42:291)

Here all actors, including Fate, become spectators, and all action reduces to accuracy of perception: cold-eyed, wide-eyed, or snake-eyed. Where Gentleman Brown's sight employs dead-on empirical reduction, Jim's aims at a reduction in the "transcendental," most phenomenologically benighted, sense.

Indeed, Conrad renders Jim's perceptual attitude in the novel's first four chapter with almost Husserlian evocativeness. But rather than distill consciousness to some eidetic substrate, Jim brackets the contents of ordinary reality so as to let himself dream. "The hazy splendour of the sea in the distance, and the hope of a stirring life in adventure" (1:11), "these dreams and the success of his imaginary achievements" (3:21), together make up the preeminently movable horizon for Jim's defect of consciousness. "Jim on the bridge was penetrated by the great certitude of unbounded safety and peace that could be read on the silent aspect of nature like the certitude of fostering love upon the placid tenderness of a mother's face" (3:19).

But read by whom? By Jim or by anyone? At first, one might take it to be a generalized description. As such—consciousness screened away from its ego, and against a background of the everyday—it does rather closely approximate Edmund Husserl's description of "the natural standpoint" in *Ideas:*

> I am aware of a world, spread out in space endlessly, and in time becoming and become, without end. I am aware of it, that means, first of all, I discover it immediately, intuitively, I experience it. What is actually perceived, and what is more or less clearly co-present and determinate (to some extent at least), is partly pervaded, partly girt about with a *dimly apprehended depth or fringe of indeterminate reality* . . . an empty mist of determinacy gets studded over with intuitive possibilities or presumptions, and only the "form" of the world as "world" is foretokened. Moreover, the zone of indeterminacy is infinite. The misty horizon that can never be completely outlined remains necessarily there.[4]

In Jim's case, however, a horizon of mist circumscribes his entire perceptual apparatus. (A similar outline frames him in the eyes of others, particularly Marlow.) It limns his own natural standpoint, blanking the horizon which lies "out there." But as his subsequent encounter with Gentleman Brown shows, Jim's "exquisite sensibility" involves more than mere dreaming; it derives from projective egoism and a fatally sympathetic imagination: an "imaginative beggar," Marlow aptly calls him (7:68).

We see this ironic contrast immediately: on the one hand, dreams of being "always an example of devotion to duty, and as unflinching as a hero in a book," and on the other—a mere four lines later—paralysis in the face of imminent danger ("he stood still—as if confounded") (1:11). Bakhtin calls this sort of cataleptic narcissism "living aesthetically," a defective form of self-forgetfulness whose only "surplus," paradoxically, consists in self-inflation. "It is really only other people living and not me, a lovingly perceptualized past life of other people . . . I will not find myself in that life, but only my double pretender . . . a hollow fictitious product that *clouds the optical purity of being. . . . a soul without a place of its own is created, a participant without a name and without a role—something absolutely extrahistorical"* (*AA*, 32; my emphasis).

Here, Bakhtin critiques not the aesthetic attitude, but only its misapplication to oneself. Through a refusal of boundedness, of a *point d'appui* outside subjectivity from which to pierce the mists of interior sortilege and rectify its weak assimilation to surrounding others, one commits "optical forgery." Indeed, as Marlow later realizes, Stein's famous defense of that attitude—"the way is to the destructive element submit yourself, and with the exertions of your hands and feet in the water make the deep, deep sea hold you up" (20:163)—can be no more reliably depended on than can Jim's own clouded visions.

Narrating Reliably

Jim's dreaminess represents but the first of several faulty models of reading which the text assembles for our study. The most important of these in the first four chapters belongs not to Jim, however, but to the narrator himself. If Jim rails at the weather's unfairness at "taking him unaware," but becomes tractable in the face of its mildness—"then fine weather returned, and he thought no more about it" (2:15)—the narrator plays the identical game of pathetic fallacy. He describes the sunshine as having "killed all thought, oppressed the heart," and the ship "as if scorched by a flame flicked at her from a heaven without pity" (1:19). The last sentence of the chapter—"The nights descended on her like a benediction"—commences a riot of simile in the chapter which follows: "The new moon . . . was like a slender shaving thrown up from a bar of gold . . . the propeller turned without a check, as though its beat had been part of the scheme of a safe universe. . . . Jim paced athwart, and his footsteps in the vast silence were loud to his own ears, as if echoed by the watchful stars" (3:20–21).

Does Jim hear this "echo" or does the narrator? Compare Marlow at his most deflationary: "The sea hissed 'like twenty thousand kettles.' That's his simile, not mine" (10:89). Despite Conrad's penchant for "supernatural naturalism," here, where one would expect the narrator's point of view to offset Jim's romanticism unequivocally, it actually seems to endorse it through similar impressionistic excess.[5] In fact, having rather slyly mocked Jim up to this point, the narrator gradually negates that critical distance, and surrenders to his own imaginative projection.

The virtuoso moment of convergence appears just before the *Patna's* convergence with its unidentified "hurt": the undersea collision which damages but does not scuttle the ship. As Jim glances at the navigation chart, he translates symbol seamlessly into referent. The chart's surface becomes the ocean, the pencil line, the path of the pilgrims' souls, and the pencil, "a naked ship's spar floating in the pool of a sheltered dock" (3:21). Luxuriating in his natural standpoint, Jim discovers again in dreaming his life's "secret truth, its hidden reality"; when he comes to, glancing now at the ocean's surface, he sees "the white streak of the wake drawn as straight by the ship's keel upon the sea as the black line drawn by the pencil upon the chart" (3:22). Tenor and vehicle have imperceptibly changed places.

But a more interesting problem suggests itself: to what to ascribe the relativity and instability of description? The implied free indirect style only underscores the collusion here between the narrator and Jim. In a novel which places such a premium on narratorial trust, Conrad seems intentionally to exploit the affinity between a traditional form of literary empathy through images and Jim's distinctive brand of "living aesthetically," in order to pose just this question about the moral sense which resides within subjective impression.

The immediate discursive transition to the inquest and the swiftness with which the narrator describes its proceedings in chapter 4 suggests that systematized models of interpretation and judgment cannot sufficiently tackle such a question. Conventional morality, "as instructive as the tapping with a hammer on an iron box" (5:48), does not possess the imagination needed to contextualize mere fact. In describing Jim's trial for abandoning ship, the narrator again links imaginative subtlety to optics, but this time in terms of dearth rather than excess: "the audience seemed composed of staring shadows. They wanted facts. Facts! They demanded facts from him, as if facts could explain anything!" (4:27).

The narrator exposes the thinness of legal concepts of "fact" and the bankruptcy of public, judicial discourse when one needs to fathom what Bakhtin calls "the man in man." The question of his probity still pending, however, the narrator nevertheless makes it clear that the story needs to be told in a different way; indeed, it needs to be told *as* a story—orally. Hence the tie between sight and mesmeric narration: "from below many eyes were looking out at [Jim] out of dark faces, out of red faces, out of faces attentive, spellbound, as if all these people sitting in orderly rows upon narrow benches had been enslaved by the fascination of his voice. It was very loud, it rang startling in his own ears, it was the only sound in the world" (4:27).

Certainly, legal ethics involves a form of narrative ethics, since defense, prosecution, and judgment all depend on ordinary acts of narration and witnessing. Contrariwise, extortional motives and a covert imperialism of question and answer may just as easily lie behind simple storytelling, as they may influence the trying of legal cases in court. As Stanley Cavell has aptly observed, narratives in both the first and the third person can withhold more than they divulge.[6] Having thus exhibited both the defects of a restricted notion of testimony and the unreliability of two kinds of unrestricted fictionalizing—Jim's first-person fantasizing and the original narrator's third-person arabesques—Conrad now turns to face-to-face models of narrative encounter for the duration of the novel.

Vzhivanie; or Live-Entering

The novel now encloses second-order hermeneutic consultations within the enframing structure of the "yarn." With the interpretive dependability of one narrator in doubt, readers are, as it were, passed along with Jim to another; the story requires a storyteller, and the novel must now masquerade as spoken language. Marlow descants before a group of "staring shadows." Jim's desires for language—"he had come round to the view that only a meticulous precision of statement would bring out the true horror behind the appalling face of things" (4:29)— have proved over-optimistic: "the sound of his own truthful statements confirmed his deliberate opinion that speech was of no use to him any longer" (4:31). Marlow must therefore act as Jim's father-confessor. But he bears the additional burden of having to transmit Jim's laying down of his own burden through the laminae of *vzhivanie*, "or live-entering," to use Bakhtin's term; since Marlow must "consummate" Jim's suffering through language, live-entering must now acquire a live voice.

Though perhaps closest in literal meaning to "incarnation", *vzhivanie* translates for practical purposes as "live-entering," and means, simply, a mode of active engagement with the other which mediates between identification or empathy on the one hand, and objective respect at a distance on the other. I must put myself in another's place and "fill in" his horizon with the surplus of perspective outside him. An aesthetic as well as an ethical act, *vzhivanie* represents the sort of transferable property between the hermeneutics of reading and of experience that poses most immediately the issue of what de Man calls their "compatability." A suffering person, for instance, in Bakhtin's evocative description, "does not see the agonizing tension of his own muscles, does not see the entire, plastically consummated posture of his own body or the expression of suffering on his own face. He does not see the clear blue sky against the background of which his suffering outward image is delineated for me. . . . I must put myself in his place and then, after returning to my own place, 'fill in' his horizon through that excess of seeing which opens out from this, my own, place outside him" (*AA*, 25).

But I must also "return to myself" after such projective forays, and refer what I have experienced back to the other. (Contrast this delimiting of boundaries with a romantic elision—indeed, a doffing of them—like Walt Whitman's: "Agonies are one of my changes of garments./I do not ask the wounded person how he feels, I myself became the wounded person.") The double sense of "return" which follows this lending out of understanding and identity to others is "an obligatory condition," in Bakhtin's words. It functions precisely as what enables any hermeneutic endeavor, since it avoids the disabling and obstructive threat of "infection" by texts as well as by persons. (In his theory of otherness, one must say, however, Bakhtin is more concerned with preserving subjectivity than exposing it, as Levinas would prefer; "consummation" is thus the other side of what Levinas calls another's "infinition" in and through me.)

To return to the text, Marlow's perception of Jim, like the narrator's and Jim's own, remains far from unobstructed, and thus does not necessarily supply the most unalloyed "excess of seeing." Jim—his real name never disclosed—always appears against a background of indeterminacy, of Husserlian mist: "To watch his face was like watching a darkening sky before a clap of thunder, shade upon shade imperceptibly coming on" (6:59). "Face," in Levinas' sense of immediate revelation, merely mystifies here, being the external correlate to Jim's oneiric self-reading. Deciphering a human face, a hallmark of Marlow's encounters with Jim, becomes simply another kind of occluded interpretation, as the novel now starts placing the greatest pressure on narrative revelation.

Mediation; or Dialectical Speech

"Eyes seeking the response of eyes / Bring out the stars, bring out the flowers" is how Robert Frost describes one happy consequence of unmediated vision in the fittingly titled poem "All Revelation." But the kind of productive opposition needed in *Lord Jim* is vocal—"original response," in a phrase from another poem by Frost. Conrad stresses both its necessity and its difficulty by stringing a set of face-to-face encounters across a spectrum at whose middle sits Marlow's ongoing dialogue with Jim. All these encounters—with Stein, Jones, the French Captain, Brierly, and Jim himself—are flawed in one way or another, not simply because each necessarily amounts to partial testimony, but rather because each ethically misfires. The two bedridden figures—the hospitalized mate at the story's beginning and Gentleman Brown at its end—thus form a kind of frame around this collective narrative infirmity.

The former, while prey to his "batrachian" delirium, exclaims, "I tell you there are no such eyes as mine this side of the Persian Gulf" (5:45). At the same time, however, he dehumanizes the *Patna*'s pilgrims by hallucinating them as so many pink toads; he eventually lapses into "an interminable and sustained howl." Gentleman Brown comes off similarly. After he relates his own optical seizing of Jim, "I could see directly I set my eyes on him what sort of fool he was" (37:25), Marlow describes him as having "said all these things in profound gasps, staring at me with his yellow eyes out of a long, ravaged brown face."

We can, then, take Marlow's earlier remark—"I am trying to interpret for you into slow speech the instantaneous effect of visual impression" (42)—as a sort of cautionary note about such "invalid" vantage points, and the extra pressure consequently needed to translate between different orders of communication. "Invalid," in short, cuts two ways: "ill" and "null." In the cases of Brown and the mate, discourse and vision degenerate, or else cancel each other out, in particularly crude instances of a general malady afflicting the entire text.

Thus discursive mettle as well as perceptual judgment lies under a cloud in this text. And therefore Jim—the focus for both—needs to be "cleared" in more senses than one. The failure of judicial procedures early in the novel merely confirms (if negatively) how deeply speech and vision become matters of *justice*, in this case a capacity to delineate boundaries—to outline, to frame, to discern, to "interrupt," in an ethical sense. And marking boundaries between persons—discursively and perceptually—is a fundamental principle, this text tells us, of narrative ethics.[7]

Levinas describes two ways in which intersubjective boundaries become obscured: by knowledge as object-cognition and by vision *stricto sensu*. Both reduce to conditions of disclosure rather than to expression or revelation, vision being a means of adequating another, and knowledge a means of enclosing him or her within a "theme." Together, these two orientations exercise a kind of sorcery, screening as through mist, disclosing "as if by burglary." "Absolute experience is not disclosure; to disclose, on the basis of a subjective horizon, is already to miss the noumenon. The interlocutor alone is the term of pure experience, where the Other enters into relation . . . where he expresses himself without our having to disclose him from a 'point of view,' in a borrowed light" (*TI*, 67).

Marlow himself captures some of the spellbinding quality of mediated encounter when he invokes the figure of the moon, a defining image for Patusan and for "haunted" persons and their converse: "it is to our sunshine, which—say what you like—is all we have to live by, what the echo is to the sound: misleading and confusing whether the note be mocking or sad. It robs all forms of matter—which, after all, is our domain—of their substance, and gives a sinister reality to shadows alone" (24:187). "Discourse," by contrast, "is rupture and commencement—prose" (*TI*, 203) (very like Bakhtin's notion of unfinalizability).

> A relation between terms that resist totalization, that absolve themselves from the relation or that specify it, is only possible as language. The resistance of one term to the other is not due to the obscure and hostile residue of alterity, but, on the contrary, to the inexhaustible surplus of attention which speech, ever teaching, brings me. For speech is always a taking up again of what was a simple sign cast forth by it, an ever renewed promise to clarify what was obscure in the utterance. (*TI*, 97)

Each time Marlow retells Jim's story, each time he threads it through its various approximations, he renews that promise narratively.

Thus Marlow freely acknowledges that it is *his* narration which has disclosed Jim to us, Jim's story bookended by Marlow's repeated tellings of it: "He existed for me, and after all it is only through me that he exists for you. I've led him out by the hand and paraded him before you" (21:171). Aside from the paternalistic tone such a statement conveys (a consistent feature of Marlow's friendship with Jim), we may detect an almost punitive quality. Being paraded means being caught and exhibited, like Stein's specimens or Jim at the mercy of the inquest's legal machinery.

But spectacle enjoins accountability. Thus in leading Jim out before his interlocutors, Marlow implicates them not in a complicity of mere watching, but in a certain custodial function; his listeners now become "keepers" of Jim's story. Though Marlow expresses distrust at the intradiegetic level—"Frankly, it is not my words I mistrust but your minds" (172)—even so, he extends stewardship outward, where it passes into *critical* scrutiny: "You may be able to tell better, since the proverb has it that the onlookers see most of the game" (171).

Marlow's admissions, like other models of reading in the novel, attest to the dialectic of expression and disclosure which becomes Conrad's special concern in *Lord Jim*. The primacy of ethical principles in Levinas forbids any such dialectic. In turn, it demands an absolutism that Conrad's impressionism simply cannot afford. Levinas speaks of the Other as one whose presence dispels the anarchic sorcery of facts, as someone "who has broken through the screen of phenomena and has associated me with himself" (*TI*, 99). In *Lord Jim*, however, while Jim and Marlow join each other in reciprocal contemplation, screens and mists prevail between them as two of the novel's regnant values.

Indeed, personality is itself already screened; experience, as Conrad's contemporary Walter Pater phrased it, is "ringed round for each one of us by that thick wall of personality through which no real voice has ever pierced on its way to us, or from us to that which we can only conjecture to be without." But if speech does in fact "cut across" vision, as Levinas insists, then Marlow nevertheless speaks for a certain collusion between tongue and eye—the naked appeal persons make alongside their often thwarted speech: "'I am here—still here' . . . and what more can the eye of the most forsaken of human beings say?" (12:106).

Precisely because it is literature and not ethical philosophy, a represented reality rather than actual or "absolute" experience, *Lord Jim* can only work in terms of successive mediations, partial disclosures, syncretisms of vision and expression, always on the way perhaps to an irreducible face to face.[8] Mediation, in this sense, is the novel's very topic, in theme and in structure: "the expectation of some essential *disclosure* as to the strength, the power, the horror, of human emotions" (6:48).

But as the novel's premise seems also to rest on Jim's ultimate unfathomability or, rather, on the ceaselessness of the interpretation he invites, we still need to weigh the merits of Marlow's method and motive. If perhaps not fully "Levinasian," they do, I believe, remain ethically sound within the novel's own impressionistic categories, a matter of shadows as well as light: "Perhaps this is the real cause of my interest in his fate. I don't know whether it was exactly fair to him to remember the incident which had given a new direction to his life, but at that very moment I remembered very distinctly. It was like a shadow in the light" (27:201).

Disclosure; or Solipsistic Speech

But what of the novel's other readers and storytellers? Captain Brierly, for example, stands (or more accurately, falls) as a monument to projective identification. He is a very poor reader of Conrad's Jim. Or, as the mate puts it, "We never know what a man is made of" (6:50). What we may thus take for the nihilistic heart of the novel casts a painfully ironic light on Brierly's brand of empathy, its solipsism and self-regard. To his onlookers, Brierly seems to possess "a surface as hard as granite" (6:49). But Marlow comes to realize otherwise: "he was probably holding silent inquiry into his own case" (6:49). Besides dogs and doggedness, Brierly and Jim share a good deal in common; each recapitulates the other's narcissistic excess, each prefers mirrored reflection to "the seeing, remembering, gathering, and unifying activity of the other."

Bakhtin writes at length on the peculiar identity relation which self-reflection involves. In a mirror, for instance, "we see the *reflection* of our exterior but not ourselves in terms of our exterior." "Indeed, our position before a mirror is always somewhat spurious, for since we lack any approach to ourselves from outside, we project ourselves into a peculiarly indeterminate possible other, with whose help we then try to find an axiological relation to ourselves. . . . Whence that distinctive and unnatural expression of our face which we see on it in the mirror, but which we never have in real life" (*AA*, 33).

Mirrored reflection, a variant of "living aesthetically," describes both Jim's and Brierly's orientation to others and to themselves, a commonality Conrad has Marlow focalize at the inquest, "now [that] I had them both under my eyes . . . one attitude might not have been truer than the other" (6:57). Brierly leaps offship to his death, unable to distance himself from Jim's own fall from heroic neverland into the prosaic.

And somewhere between Jim's natural standpoint of mists and haze and Brierly's seeming granite, the two meet and merge. Each, as Bakhtin puts it, becomes "fictitious[:] is possessed by another's soul." Each in his own way has lingered in the chambers of the sea; each, awakened by human voices, drowns. Stein implies as much: "A man that is born falls into a dream like a man who falls into the sea" (20:163).

Mergers of this kind simply replace mirrors with persons. "What would I have to gain if another were to *fuse* with me?" Bakhtin writes. "He would see and know only what I already see and know, he would only repeat in himself the inescapable closed circle of my own life; let him rather remain outside me" (*AA*, 96). Brierly fuses with Jim just as Jim repeatedly fuses with his own "fictitious other"; each, fatally, finds only himself. Marlow says of Brierly, "at bottom poor Brierly must have been thinking of himself" (6:55); he says of Jim, "He was not speaking to me, he was only speaking before me, in a dispute with an invisible personality, an antagonistic and inseparable partner of his existence— another possessor of his soul" (8:75).

Like Brierly, Jim also can be said to have committed suicide because of mirror effects. The projective encounter with Brown in Patusan which precipitates his death merely justifies Marlow's earlier assessment: "the youth on the brink, looking with shining eyes upon that glitter of a vast surface which is only a reflection of his own glances full of fire" (11:101).

"To purify the expression of the reflected face" (*AA*, 34) describes Marlow's odyssey thereafter in this novel. In hope of such purification, and like a more sophisticated but perhaps more impressionable Alice, Marlow passes Jim, readers, and himself through one distorted intersubjective lookinglass after another. Hillis Miller claims that the novel itself dashes such hope, as it must if it is to convey fully the meaning and effect of endless semiosis.[9]

But, as I have argued, if the novel features "mediation" as its topic, it nevertheless disables inquiry or "interpretation" as modes of approach to Jim. Marlow comes to realize that the significance of Jim's story lies simply in its acts of telling—by and about Jim. The degree to which Jim is made a hero in others' lives (that is, a character to author, shape, and consummate, and not merely to make sense of) measures the governing force of narrative ethics in the novel—over and above relativity of perspective.

Thus to choose a second obvious example, the French Captain awards Jim no narrative credence at all: Jim's story, in itself, possesses simply cautionary significance—it is a lesson, an example. "One truth the more ought not to make life impossible . . . But the honour—the honour, Monsieur! . . . The honour . . . that is real, that is! And what life may be worth when . . . the honour is gone—*ah ça! par exemple*—I can offer no opinion. I can offer no opinion, Monsieur, because I know nothing of it" (13:115). Marlow frames the Captain's pronouncement with a discomfort at thematization worthy of Levinas; he even speaks of "disclosure" when setting the scene of their meeting: "He drew up his heavy eyelids. Drew up, I say—no other expression can describe the steady deliberation of the act—and at last was completely *disclosed* to me" (13:115). Of course, it is Jim who becomes completely disclosed (in Levinas' sense) to the Captain, whose able sea- and see-manship place him at the opposite extreme from both Jim and Brierly.

The Captain is a lofty, unflappable, one could say almost de Manian reader, and his utterly dispassionate reading of Jim allows for no live-entering at all. Indeed, Marlow finds the Captain's judgments lifeless and inert: "His own country's pronouncement was uttered in passion-less and definite phraseology a machine would use if machines could speak" (14:123).

While Brierly merely hides behind a granite surface only to succumb to imagination, the Frenchman, his brow "half hidden by the paper," defends "like alabaster" against imagination and the flow of attach-ments. Whereas the bubble of narcissistic exceptionalism bursts for Brierly, it remains intact for the French Captain, granting him there-fore the impunity to go on pricking others'. In a novel packed with imagery of health, sickness, and diagnosis, he represents the ultimate clinician, initially earning Marlow's respect: "And suddenly I began to admire the discrimination of the man. He had made out the point at once; he did get hold of the only thing I cared about. I felt as though I were taking a professional opinion on the case. His imperturbable and mature calmness was that of an expert in possession of the facts, and to whom one's perplexities were mere child's-play" (13:113).

But despite his admiration, Marlow's remarks expose the ethical cost of becoming "the mouthpiece for an abstract wisdom" (13:113). The Captain's brand of Gallic hermeneutics knows only transcendence—

not the immanence of live-entering. Of this fortress of comprehension, Marlow says, "Indeed his torpid demeanor concealed nothing: it had that mysterious, almost miraculous power of producing striking effects by means impossible of detection which is the last word of the highest art" (12:110). One senses not only the coercive quality of such an understanding, its universal applicability to particular circumstances, but also its rejection of the positive sort of authoring—"the gift-giving, resolving, and communicating potential"—which storying demands. The Frenchman's bloodless and abstract ethical code, like all such theoretisms, "far from strengthening a moral or evaluative position and making it more authoritative, merely discredit[s] and devaluate[s it]" (*RB*, 153).[10]

This is one reason perhaps why the novel gives him no other name than "the Frenchman." As with the *Patna*'s oafish German skipper, its Asian owner and Arab lessee, culture or nation in *Lord Jim* functions as the lowest common sorter for identity. And that is only fitting, given that (for colonial powers particularly) substitutions of *volkisch* for personal identity make for the crudest of narrative schemas. To be French, in this respect, means one is immediately knowable; to be knowable, in turn, means that one is effectively "solved," one's story is secured.[11] The status of Jim's Britishness—his "membership"—forms a common burden for Marlow, Brierly, Chester, and even Cornelius and Gentleman Brown.

It remains for Stein, however (a non-Britisher graced by Conrad with a surname), to move Jim into a different, perhaps less reductive field of typifications: "I understand very well. He is romantic" (19:162). But since that assessment proves to be only a more subtle form of cultural imperialism and projection—"Even Stein could say no more than that he was romantic" (20:17)—we must turn finally to Marlow and his efforts through narrative "to grapple with another man's intimate need" (16:138).

Conversation; or Therapeutic Speech

The examples of Brierly and the French Captain above, and of Stein and Gentleman Brown later in the novel, show Marlow conversing *about* Jim. In chapters 6–12 and 21–23, in contrast, he speaks *with* Jim (21:169). In recalling Jim as either second person or third person, memory presents no obstacles. The flexibility with which Marlow ma-

nipulates complex anachronies across thirty-one chapters of narrated
time means that the question of memory has been carefully hedged to
throw maximum weight upon the immediacy of encounter. If Conrad
means Marlow to be more than a structural vessel of consciousness for
innovations in form, Marlow's dislocations of time must appear in the
same light as Conrad's—quite intentional.

Another dialogic context which structurally integrates the problem
of memory, of course, is psychotherapy, for which the Malabar House
"session," the longest and most intense in the novel, appears a remarkably prescient prototype. Indeed, Marlow's very first encounter in the
novel—with the hospitalized second mate whose "case" so fascinates
the resident physician[11]—throws a diagnostic cast over all the others
that succeed it. All Marlow's partners in talk become either physicians
or patients; they all "see things," to one degree or another—pink toads,
butterflies, "things as they are" (as Chester absurdly claims), mirror
images, occluded perceptions. The analogy extends to the interpretive
level, too, as readers will see or be made to see images or truths through
fiction.

But a world of difference divides hallucinatory cowardice—the
mate's ravings about "pink toads"—from racist invective—the German
skipper's description of his Muslim pilgrims as "dese cattle." Even more
does it separate both these crudities from Marlow's discriminating and
revisable observations. Marlow's job, in short, involves keeping pink
toads and butterflies taxonomically distinct—a responsibility he shares
with his interlocutors and his readers. He implies as much at one of
the two places in the first part of the novel where Conrad acknowledges
the presence of listeners: "I could be eloquent were I not afraid you
fellows have starved your imaginations to feed your bodies. I do not
mean to be offensive; it is respectable to have no illusions—and safe—
and profitable—and dull. Yet you too in your time must have known
the intensity of life, that life of glamour created in the shock of trifles,
as amazing as the glow of sparks struck from a cold stone—and as
short-lived, alas" (21:171).

"Our neuroses are our rhetoric about ourselves," says Anatole
Broyard. "There is something paradoxically esthetic about suffering
and failure, and perhaps analysis needs to develop an esthetic to answer
them."[13] Marlow knows that Jim's great character flaw is a surplus of
aesthetic vision: "He was a finished artist in that peculiar way, he was
a gifted poor devil with the faculty of swift and forestalling vision"

(8:77). Marlow himself is animated by the sheer hypnotic pleasure of telling stories—"and with the first word uttered Marlow's body . . . would become very still, as though his spirit had winged its way back into the lapse of time and were speaking through his lips from the past" (4:31).

And yet he establishes at the outset his relations with other men as something other than purely aesthetic. A sort of confessor cum lay analyst, a bedeviled Wedding Guest to life's Mariners, he consistently intercepts their stories: "[A familiar devil] is there right enough, and, being malicious, he lets me in for that kind of thing. What kind of thing, you ask? . . . the kind of thing that by devious, unexpected, truly diabolical ways causes me to run up against men with soft spots, with hard spots, with hidden plague spots, by Jove! and loosens their tongues at the sight of me for their infernal confidences" (5:31).

Now although Marlow cannot answer his own somewhat disingenuous questions about the mystery of his being cast into such a role—the sometime physician forced to "see spots"—he stores them up and transmits them narratively. Alternately plied, and flowing, with talk, he develops an informal expertise for judging the compatibility of different sorts of hermeneutics: on the one hand, trying to make sense of one's story while living it, and on the other, conducting a similar inquiry at an "aesthetic" distance. Plainly, Marlow exercises different functions when he listens to others' observations of Jim and when he delivers them himself. Conversations about and conversations with answer to different methodological and ethical constraints. "The truth about a man in the mouths of others, not directed at him dialogically and therefore a second-hand truth, becomes a lie degrading and deadening him, if it touches upon his holy of holies, that is, 'the man in man.' Truth is unjust when it concerns the depths of someone else's personality."[14]

Or, as Levinas formulates approaching someone else, "The condition for theoretical truth and error is the word of the other, his expression, which every lie presupposes . . . in which at each instant he overflows the idea a thought would carry away from it" (*TI*, 51). Marlow, then, "approaches" and draws near to Jim by means of two dialogic modes: live-entering and the penetrative word, in Bakhtin's formulation "a word capable of actively and confidently interfering in the interior dialogue of the other person, helping him to find his own voice."[15] This latter can instructively deflate as well as enable.

In his superb book on Conradian dialogics, Aaron Fogel notes how Conrad typically muffles characters' verbal "detonations" through interlocutors' "de-tonating" responses.[16] Marlow does this several times to Jim—Jim: "I had jumped. . . . It seems." Marlow: "Looks like it" (9:88); "'It was like cheating the dead,' he stammered. 'And there were no dead,' I said" (12:104).

Before his international collective of readers, Marlow, in effect, learns or develops a hermeneutic ethics—how to listen skillfully, how to respond, how finally to "live into" Jim's situation without surrendering his own vantage outside it. And as I note above, because this process unfolds *narratively*—as a question of how best to judge, participate in, and transmit Jim's *story*—Marlow passes from strictly hermeneutic to therapeutic obligations.

But in this regard, do Marlow's obligations to Jim demand *vzhivanie*, or rather a scrupulously maintained objectivity—to understand without extending sympathy, that is, merely to understand? How good an interactive therapist is Marlow, really? If we think of therapy as the "de-novelization of people's lives," even if that means shifting the patient "from one novel to another—from a gothic romance, say, to a domestic comedy"[17]—then Marlow probably falls short of therapy's first rank because he merely shifts Jim from tragic novel to adventure romance.

Proximity; or Narrational Ethics

Although great therapists and great readers often coincide, "therapist," I think, less aptly describes Marlow in *Lord Jim* than "reader." For, at the very least, therapy may involve narratives but it cannot, in good conscience, transmit them publicly. The discourse of therapy, moreover, may "de-novelize" lives, but it nevertheless depends on thematizing them—comprehension, to paraphrase Maurice Blanchot, under the sign of the clinical. Finally, the limits of the therapeutic as an "ethics" consist in this: the narrowly construed sense of ethics as professional responsibility (what is the "right" thing to do here? respond? intervene? interrupt?).

Therapy reigns in its performative effects with deontological caution and, like courtroom fact-finding, justifies itself ultimately through probitive method.[18] Conversely, as Bakhtin argues, the novel represents the unfinalizable genre, a realm of posited, not given values. As a narrator, thus, Marlow must tell the story of Jim's story; that is his largest "professional" duty, situating him "beyond therapy" as guide and custodian for specifically storial effects.

Thus the accidental nature of Marlow's encounter with Jim; the extraordinary quality of an event that "did not happen"; the unexpected significance that Marlow finds in it—"as if the obscure truth were momentous enough to affect mankind's conception of itself": precisely this synchronicity of unrepeatable features makes any theoretism—legal, psychoanalytic, deontological—inadequate to the task of narratively engaging Jim.

Were a "method" available to or practiced by Marlow, the "doubt" in the "doubt of the sovereign power enthroned in a fixed standard of conduct" (5:44) would not exercise the power in the novel which it does. Jim's story would not have to be recalled, Stein and Brierly would be demystified, the French officer would be the story's hermeneutic hero, and the entire ethical problematic of live-entering, of the constraints upon recognition, would vaporize. If the border-structure of intersubjectivity—the "outsideness" which frames personhood—deflects an essential fidelity to the persons themselves (to paraphrase the phenomenologists), then trying to "make them out," "reading" them, assumes even more ethical force.

Only charged moments of recognition grace experience, Conrad suggests, but any "fixed standard of conduct," any science that attempts to systematize them, like the inquest on the *Patna* incident, comes too late, and can only substitute *Methode* for *Wahrheit*; it forces rather than establishes their compatibility. Instead of such ethical formalism, the text substitutes what Levinas calls "proximity"—an ethics of approach, of immediacy, of nearness.

Hence, Marlow progresses from an initial self-interest when finding himself discovered by Jim's eyes in the courtroom—"Was it for my sake that I wished to find some shadow of an excuse for that young fellow?" (5:44)—to something more general, more federated—"it seemed to me that the less I understood the more I was bound to him in the name of that doubt which was an inseparable part of our knowledge" (21:169). While disclaiming the credentials of a super-reader in the following crucial passage, Marlow fails to disguise the "certain impact" Jim's story has had upon him, the reason for its compelling transformation into ritualized narrative:

"One has no business really to get interested. It's a weakness of mine. His was of another kind. My weakness consists in not having a discriminating eye for the incidental—for the externals—no eye for the hod of the rag picker or the fine linen of the next man. Next man— that's it. I have met so many men," *he pursued with momentary sadness*—"met them too with a certain—certain—impact, let us say; like this fellow, for instance—and in each case all I could see was merely the human being. A confounded democratic quality of vision which may be better than total blindness, but has been of no advantage to me, I can assure you . . . and then comes a soft evening; a lot of men indolent for whist—and a story." (8:75–76)

Perhaps that also explains why Conrad disturbs the fictional surface of storytelling at this moment, first when Marlow pauses "to put new life in his expiring cheroot," next in the italicized description above, and then again after the word *story:* "He paused again to wait for an encouraging remark perhaps but nobody spoke; only the host, as if reluctantly performing a duty, murmured, 'You are so subtle, Marlow.'" As in the first four chapters, Conrad throws readers on their own devices in order to question whether they too might justifiably accuse themselves of a "confounded democratic quality of vision" (8:76).

Of course, when positioned face to face with others, Marlow discriminates incidentals with anything but leveling democratism, with an almost aristocratic care. Chapters 7–11 (which cover the first part of the Malabar House conversation) describe a marvel of close reading. The discoveries that Marlow makes about Jim and those Jim lets slip about himself; the different plays on recognition (visual deciphering, for instance, or the archery contest of dialogue containing Marlow's "perfidious shafts"); the effect Jim's story has upon Marlow's hermeneutic model; and most of all the "interpretive charity" with which Marlow receives Jim—all of this tracks a continuously self-revising ethics of proximity, of drawing ever nearer. "In the responsibility we have for one another, I have always one more response to give," writes Levinas (*OTB*, 84). Implicitly, having himself been "made to see," Marlow, in his capacity as Mariner, likewise elicits that additional response, that "one step more," from readers too.

Recognition; or Hermeneutic Ethics

In *Reading for the Plot*, Peter Brooks points to a certain cross-diegetic process in *Heart of Darkness*. Juxtaposing dialogue and "summing up" as two different but related modes of understanding, Brooks suggests that the multiplied deferrals of any final pronouncement of meaning—from Kurtz to Marlow to his interlocutors and finally to Conrad's readers—parallel a self-reproducing chain of transmitted dialogue, "a dynamics of transference in which the reader is solicited not only to understand the story but to complete it: to make it fuller, richer, more powerfully ordered, and therefore more hermeneutic."[19] I do not see this analysis carrying over to *Lord Jim*, however, despite features common to both works.[20] If it does describe operations at work in the novel, Brooks's model of "transference" makes better sense in terms of a two-tiered structure of recognition, where the first level gradually becomes canceled out and superseded by the second.

Thus the maritime inquest at the beginning of the text follows the logic of classical anagnorisis in its drive to unmask the threat of imposture through a recovery of missing knowledge.[21] As "narrative desire," such juridical recognition has a proairetic rather than hermeneutic function.[22] And like the tribunal (but specifically in terms of a dynamics of reading), it too fails to satisfy "the expectation of some essential disclosure as to the strength, the power, the horror, of human emotions" (5:46).

As I have suggested all along, narrative ethics and metaphysical desire can more meaningfully describe the workings of *Lord Jim* than can the dynamics of transference and narrative desire. And thus a second level of recognition—the interactive structures of encounter in vision and speech—is needed to redirect the energies summoned by the first, baldly factitious one.

Terence Cave notes that in one of the flexible redefinitions of anagnorisis by Renaissance critics, the trope came to signify a heuristic principle; recognition scenes, in effect, teach inferencing skills. Recognition in *Lord Jim*, I am arguing, functions similarly, though its heuristic value should be thought of as ethical rather than logical. And thus "transference" across textual boundaries means a summoning of recognition from readers as a debt owed to (self)-allegorized literary character. This second level of anagnorisis cuts across all three ethical dimensions of the text: narrational, hermeneutic, and representational.

Authoring; or Representational Ethics

The novel does in fact represent Jim in a number of competing ways. The first belongs to Conrad. Plainly, Conrad resists the fatherly benevolence that Marlow lavishes on Jim; indeed, he comes closer to what Roland Barthes and Jacques Lacan call the hypostasized or hidden father—the disposer of plot.[23] The thematic juxtapositions early in the novel (Jim's incident with the "yellow dog" being the most telling); the cramped interior spaces of courtroom, Malabar House, lifeboat, and canoe; the jerking from port to port and job to job—all these authorial decisions shrink Jim and enframe him within those same ironic proportions which first disclose him to us in the novel's first paragraph. In an especially telling passage, the preliminary narrator tells us that after his injury aboard ship, Jim sequestered himself in the cabin below and "lay there *battened down in the midst of a small devastation*" (1:16; emphasis mine). Doublings and mirrorings within the text reduce his stature further to almost fun-house distortion.

Moreover, from his initial dreaminess through his halting speech and injury from a falling spar to his Gulliver-like apotheosis in Patusan, Jim is subjected to a consistent parody of damaged heroism—a boy's life in an adult novel. "He was becoming irrelevant; a question to the point cut short his speech, like a pang of pain, and he felt extremely discouraged and weary" (4:29). Lamed, dumbed, and foreshortened by the plot, Jim appeals to Marlow as if helplessly imprisoned by the text—"held hostage," as Levinas says of certain characters in Poe's stories.

Marlow's representational palette is more extensive than the implied author's; aside from dignifying Jim's pathos or inscrutability, Marlow can also treat Jim with simple condescension; he leads him out by the hand and parades him. He frequently describes him in less than complimentary terms: "he was outwardly so typical of that good, stupid kind we like to feel marching right and left of us in life, of the kind that is not disturbed by the vagaries of intelligence" (5:39).

At the very least, Marlow exploits Jim's yellow badge of cowardice by commodifying him: "He looked as genuine as a new sovereign, but there was some infernal alloy in his metal" (40). Conrad clearly puns here on both Jim's mettle and his adequacy to a "sovereign power in a fixed standard of conduct," running motifs in the text. Even the tragedifying which Marlow later indulges in has the partial effect of making Jim appear more ludicrous by outsizing him. And in the following passage, Marlow places the miniature and the gigantic side by side: "an incident as completely devoid of importance as the flooding of an ant heap, and yet the mystery of [Jim's] attitude got hold of me as though he had been an individual in the forefront of his kind, as if the obscure truth involved were momentous enough to affect mankind's conception of himself" (8:75). Yet Marlow grants Jim a freedom that Conrad does not: "From the way he narrated that part I was at liberty to infer he was partly stunned by the discovery he had made—the discovery about himself—and no doubt was at work trying to explain it away to the only man who was capable of appreciating all its tremendous magnitude. You must understand he did not try to minimize its importance. Of that I am sure; and therein lies his distinction" (7:67).

This is an enormously important passage. It voices what for me are essential principles of narrative ethics at work in the novel. First, it links both parties through connective heteronomy: Jim, to narrate, and Marlow, to interpret. Second, it distributes ratios of magnitude—Jim's refusal to minimize, and Marlow's sensitivity to the largeness of Jim's discovery—according to their felt proportions. (The grandiosity of Jim's self-discovery need not be understood ironically here.) Third, it expresses Marlow's certainty. If the novel does trace a hermeneutic circle, then it travels around the fixed point of Marlow's determined instincts for recognition. Finally, the passage summons readers and exercises a claim upon them: "You must understand."

Thus rather than miniaturizing Jim in the way I have ascribed to Conrad, Marlow enlarges, in effect creates, Jim. He provides him with the "sonority" which justifies the acoustic space which *is* intersubjectivity. *Lord Jim*'s peculiar "dynamics of transference" require that Conrad in effect give over authorial care and imaginativeness to Marlow, whose stance before Jim readers are then invited to imitate and participate in for themselves.[24] As the critic James Phelan put it, Marlow fills out mimetically a mostly synthetic character; and to correlate Phelan with Levinas, Marlow (and the novel's readers) accordingly keep Jim from mere thematic disclosure.[25] Where Jim's excess of imagination causes him to miscalculate his leaps at sea, the surplus of vision he receives from Marlow and readers buoys him through successive calentures of story.

Reading; or the Ethics of Inarticulacy

When Marlow observes Jim after the inquest "scanning my features as though looking for a place where he would plant his fist" (6:61), one recalls other occasions—in the *Patna*'s lifeboat, for example—when

threatened violence lapses into "strange passivity"; Jim "looked generally fit to demolish a wall" (59), but more often than not only threatens
demolition. How fitting that as Jim stands paralyzed before Marlow
here, the case going on behind their backs involves assault and battery!
With its relative clause—"a place where he would plant his fist"—thus
neutralized, the sentence above likewise diminishes in syntactic force:
Jim, we can say, scans Marlow's features just looking for a place.

Marlow sums up the yellow dog episode by observing that "a single
word" had stripped Jim and incapacitated him: "He made an inarticulate noise in his throat like a man perfectly stunned by a blow on the
head" (62). Indeed, Jim's inarticulacy, his inexpressiveness Cavell would
call it, when emotion chokes him, de-tonates graphically throughout
the text in clipped phrases, dashes, and ellipses: "'Thank you, though—
your room—jolly convenient—for a chap—badly hipped' . . . The rain
pattered outside and swished in the garden; a water pipe (it must have
had a hole in it) performed just outside the window a parody of the
blubbering woe with funny sobs and gurgling lamentations, interrupted
by jerky spasms of silence . . . 'A bit of shelter,' he mumbled and
ceased" (16:137).

Even Jim's writing fails: "The pen had spluttered, and that time he
gave it up" (36:256). Perhaps more tellingly, upon departure for
Patusan, Jim exclaims, "You—shall—hear—of—me" (23:184). The
dashes and staccato delivery call up Conrad's string of adjectives in the
author's note to which I referred at the beginning of my reading. More
important, Marlow's gloss—"Of me, or from me, I don't know which.
I think it must have been *of* me"—suggests that the rest of Jim's story
will be conveyed not by Jim but by others. Hence perhaps the significance of Jim's final gesture: he places his hand over his lips.

"Yet after all this," Marlow says, "was a kind of recognition"
(34:245). Marlow ends his oral narrative on the veranda. His listeners
drift off like so many Wedding Guests, bereft of response. Marlow and
Conrad, vocal and textual voices, finally converge, as Marlow cedes the
rest of Jim's story enclosed within his to the story of its telling—in
Levinas' words, "the ever renewed promise to clarify what was obscure"—to text. In that promise, literary text enlivens rather than
imprisons character, bringing voice, vision, and face into some merciful
repose: "No more horizons as boundless as hope, no more twilights
within the forests as solemn as temples . . . but the opened packet
under the lamp brought back the sounds, the visions, the very savior

of the past—a multitude of fading faces, a tumult of dying voices, dying away upon the shores of distant seas under a passionate and unconsoling sunshine. He sighed and sat down to read" (36:254). Although the last sentence refers to the one man privileged "to hear the last word of the story," I would suggest that this sentence be taken as a figure for the solitary reader, as Jabès puts it, "presiding over the morrow of the book." Marlow's narration sustains Jim throughout the novel in a communicative alembic (though his acts of *vzhivanie* and bestowals of perceptual surplus may remain clouded at times). "It is impossible to see him clearly—especially as it is through the eyes of others that we take our last look at him" (255). But the important point here is that Marlow delegates this stewardship, hands it off, to readers as Conrad has already done with him. Thus, exploiting the pronoun's function as shifter, we can read the "we" in the sentence just quoted as the text's own self-reference. "Others," then, designates *us*, its readers—the hands in mutual clasp with the text.

That Marlow does not gain final clarity, that he remains "strangely un-enlightened" attests to a felicitous resistance; even literary characters' holy of holies—their "man in man"—resists full disclosure. If *Lord Jim* "interprets itself," then, it knows how readers are implicated in its problematic of answerability, its narrative ethics. In Jim's stammerings ("I want—want—tobacco," "I would have tried to—to . . .," "No better than a vagabond now . . . without a single—single—. . . and yet . . ."), in Marlow's eloquent attempts to get him "caught in language," and in the figure of Jim seen "through the eyes of others," Conrad articulates the hinge between narratorial, hermeneutic, and representational ethics: the redemptiveness of inarticulacy, the ethical claim of the unfinalized text. And just so, in these closing observations by Marlow, Conrad also provides a transition to another distant but related fictional world—a transition from the obscured jungles of Malaya to the darkened streets of Winesburg, Ohio.

I found out how difficult it may be sometimes to make a sound. There is a weird power in a spoken word. And why the devil not? (15:134)

But it was I, too, who a moment ago had been so sure of the power of words, and now was afraid to speak, in the same way one dares not move for fear of losing a slippery hold. It is when we try to grapple with another man's intimate need that we perceive how incomprehensible, wavering, and misty are the beings that share with us the sight of the stars and the warmth of the sun. It is as if loneliness were a hard and absolute condition of existence; the envelope of flesh and blood on which our eyes are fixed melts before the outstretched hand, and there remains only the capricious, unconsolable, and elusive spirit that no eye can follow, no hand can grasp. It was the fear of losing him that kept me silent, for it was borne upon me suddenly that should I let him slip away into the darkness, I would never forgive myself. (16:138)

Winesburg, Ohio

More than mere geography separates these two novels, to be sure. But if one grants them both a parallel interest in the anthropology of exile or shipwreck within the world at large, then more than geography connects them as well. They share, for instance, a common Bildungsroman structure, however attenuated it may be in *Lord Jim* or promissory in *Winesburg, Ohio*. The "heroes" of the texts resemble each other in their shared adolescent blankness. The interview structure of *Winesburg* and the inquiry structure of *Lord Jim* represent two not dissimilar modes of gathering and evaluating material. Both novels seem to cast a clinician's eye and take a case-history approach to the mystery of personality and fragmented existence. Both, finally, tie ethical gains and losses to the structure of narrative.

And yet they remain very different texts. Bakhtin's concept of *vzhivanie* offers us as good a means of differentiation here as any, since the intersubjective stakes each novel poses differ significantly from each other. Live-entering in *Winesburg* is not the slow, cumulative process it is in Conrad's novel; at best partial and haphazard, it brings to the fore the question of the *fragment*. If we recall the debate between de Man and Bakhtin which I traced in Chapter 2, for Bakhtin, authoring in life and authoring in literature differ to the degree that only in fiction can authors fully realize their characters. In life, however, as authors of their own fragments, persons can only recognize one another through glimpse and approximation; they wait on the charity of narrative amplitude.

In her novel *Middlemarch*, George Eliot observes, "For the fragment of a life, however typical, is not the sample of an even web: promises may not be kept, and an ardent outset may be followed by declension; latent powers may find their long-awaited opportunity; a past error may urge a grand retrieval."[26] *Lord Jim* makes this a structural as well as a thematic possibility. *Winesburg*, by contrast, suspends it.

Anderson's novel proposes as its central fact the fragment: a set of mostly unrelated stories told by or about "grotesques" whose life urgency gets "caught" within extraordinary and fragmentary moments of narration. If perception acquires ethical force by being sedimented over time in Conrad's novel, narrative acts acquire ethical force in Anderson's novel because of their brevity and, for the most part, unrepeatability. Aestheticizing Bakhtin's notion of non literary authorship, Winesburg's grotesques author their own fragments in charged moments of storytelling, moments at once liberating and entrapping, celebratory and pathetic. In effect, they give form to themselves by narrating themselves.

The ethical force of such discourse lies in its sheer self-thematizing exorbitancy, "in the risky uncovering of oneself, in sincerity, the breaking up of inwardness and the abandon of all shelter, exposure to traumas, vulnerability," as Levinas puts it (*OTB*, 48). George Willard's wan reportorial attempts to capture his subjects' stories notwithstanding, the narrators of Winesburg defy being made thus to "signify," by violently and primordially signifying first. In Levinasian terms, they reveal rather than disclose; they announce their exteriority, they affirm self-presence before interpretation.

It is exactly here, of course, that one may object to my use of Levinas, since the "force" of the ethical relation would seem to militate against narrative unfolding. True, Levinas sees a temporal dislocation in intersubjective contact, but only because the Other's approach is always out of phase with the "I" in the present: it derives from an immemorial past or an unencompassable future. "Narrative," by contrast, interrupts the interruption which is otherness. Stories, by definition, traffic in theme and plot, devices of curtailment and constraint.

In the brakes it puts on ethical immediacy, therefore, narrative might be seen to seriously compromise the mechanics of Levinasian encounter, the pure shock of alterity. And yet, in his later work, Levinas entirely recasts the terms of his phenomenological ethics: there the ontological critique cedes its place to a sensuous poetics of encounter, "height" giving way to "nearness." The most important of these reformulations is surely the distinction between Saying and Said—ethical performance over against theme or content. And it is here, I think, that Levinas' schema has specifically narrative implications; we understand storytelling in *Winesburg* as verb not noun—small epics or tableaux of Saying, of self-exposure.

A Levinasian Underside

Anderson's novel diverges sharply from *Lord Jim* in the way it minimizes intercession. A single word strips Jim of his discretion but thereby admits him into Marlow's language world. In triggering conversation in *Winesburg, Ohio,* however, a single word can dramatically alienate and isolate dialogic partners in the frightening immediacy of their encounter; such contact is always a "traumatism of astonishment." If Conrad explores the pathos of the long journey to "the final utterance," Anderson investigates its abbreviation—the pathos of epiphany. Marlow's fleeting observation about Jim—"this is, I suppose, what people mean by the tongue cleaving to the roof of the mouth"—and Jim's concise corroboration—"too dry" (7:69)—describe the permanent conditions for storytelling in *Winesburg, Ohio.*

Why should such a state of affairs be understood as an ethics, however? Quite simply, because narrative serves as the primary vehicle for intersubjective exposure and reciprocity in these stories. To narrate in *Winesburg* is to give; to listen is to redeem. Almost. For these stories are always on the way to bestowal, to redemption, but never quite arrive. That is why Levinas provides such a helpful gloss on this text, because *Winesburg* depicts a primitive and partial, let us say pre-Levinasian world, a world of ethical risk and encounter without the transcendence or succor which Levinas also describes. Such a world is an ethics, in effect, unformed and void: a *tovu vavohu*—originary chaos—before the beneficent clarity, the grace, of another's *interruption.* Neighbors are approached in *Winesburg,* but in these encounters instead of the commanding resistance, the positive cleft in encounter which Levinas insists on, hands are aggressively laid on, and faces searched and scanned in the desperation which is this novel's version of alterity.

That said, however, the world of narration (or authorship) in Winesburg is a teeming one, where storytelling may take a variety of different forms. It can be lyrical, spontaneous, and unheard, as in the story "Drink":

> Tom left his room on Duane Street just as the young night began to make itself felt. First he walked through the streets, going softly and quietly along, thinking thoughts that he tried to put into words. He said that Helen White was a flame dancing in the air and that he was a little tree without leaves standing out sharply against the sky. Then he said that she was a wind, a strong terrible wind, coming out of the darkness of a stormy sea and that he was a boat left on the shore of the sea by a fisherman. (216)

Or it can be compensatory: in the absence of occasions for live-entering in life, one authors characters, as does Enoch Robinson in "Loneliness": "With quick imagination he began to invent his own people to whom he could really talk and to whom he explained the things he had been unable to explain to living people. . . . Among these people, he was always confident and bold. They might talk, to be sure, and even have opinions of their own, but always he talked last and best" (171).

Or storytelling may reduce to an unwilled and grotesque fragment which, Kafka-like, "sentences" its utterer to the queerness of his life, as in "Queer": "Elmer tried to explain. He wet his lips with his tongue and looked at the train that had begun to groan and get under way. 'Well, you see,' he began, and then lost control of the tongue, 'I'll be washed and ironed. I'll be washed and ironed and starched,' he muttered half incoherently" (200). Sometimes, however, the miraculous happens: "The woman's voice began to quiver with excitement. To Doctor Reefy, who without realizing what was happening had begun to love her, there came an odd illusion. He thought that as she talked the woman's body was changing, that she was becoming younger, straighter, stronger. When he could not shake off the illusion his mind gave it a professional twist. 'It is good for both her body and her mind, this talking,' he muttered" ("Death," 226).

Or, finally, storytelling may take the form of epiphanic release. Words long withheld become liberated, but only for the moment of utterance; thereafter they remain incommunicable: "'There was no promise made,' he cried into the empty spaces that lay about him. 'I didn't promise my Minnie anything and Hal hasn't made any promise to Nell.' . . . 'They are the accidents of life, Hal,' he cried. 'They are not mine or yours.' . . . When he came to the fence at the edge of the road . . . he could not have told what he thought or what he wanted" ("The Untold Lie," 207–208).

The narrating of life stories in these fictions, like more obvious kinds of rhetoric, exposes at once the permeability of language and the impermeability of human difference; it forces into consciousness the very limits of intersubjectivity and the stubborn fact of borders, of "outsideness." "Force" being the operative word in this text, one confronts the profound slippage of language into violence, the force, in other words, behind illocutionary force. Just as *vzhivanie* (or rather the attempt at it) can often misfire in *Winesburg*, so the "penetrative word" can penetrate destructively, revealing coercive possibilities of narrative discourse in the midst of language's "weird power," in Marlow's phrase.

As in Conrad's novel, however, intradiegetic effects force into consciousness the obtrusive presence of readers, their vulnerability or safety outside the book. Each narrative level signals certain ethical pressures peculiar to it—for the grotesques, the question of telling or withholding and the demands made on response; for readers, a complicity in overhearing. Much as the bleeding through of one overheard conversation into another in Conrad's novel makes readers self-aware, Anderson's stories address their audience, fixing them in narrative space.

Words Carry with Them the Places They Have Been

In "The Book of the Grotesque," the prelude to the novel, the narrator explains that it would be "absurd to try to tell what was inside" (22) its writer-protagonist because what he was thinking was far more important and accessible—accessible only because the narrator uses him as a mouthpiece. In the rest of the stories, the problem of "other minds" becomes, simply, the problem of other mouths; spoken words or their substitutes—hands or balled-up pieces of paper, for example—bring people flat up against the "thick wall of personality" and no further. Words may carry with them the places they have been, as Barthes memorably puts it, but in *Winesburg, Ohio* they also mark frontiers, dead ends.

Thus in "The Teacher," when Kate Swift tells George, "The thing to learn is to know what people are thinking about, not what they say" (163), she implies that writing will make alienable the inalienable, set free the tongue by forcing its silence. But this is a possibility only if one leaves the confines of town and text. While one is in Winesburg, however, expression drives a wedge between persons, and inscribes differences, gaps, traces. It interrupts. But it does not unify. The novel returns Derridean categories to their original intersubjective horizons; as a function of narrative relation, *différance* describes ethical limits on encounter before it defines facts of language.

But how can this be when, as "grotesques," persons have already been converted into facts of language, when like Alice Hineman in "Adventure," they have only words to go on. In *Totality and Infinity*, Levinas ascribes transcendental power to language, removing it categorically from other intrinsically profane kinds of expression. Language stands over against the currency of works, signs, and symbols, which "comes from the home and returns to it, a movement of Odyssey where the adventure pursued in the world is but an accident of return" (*TI*, 176). "Saying is communication, to be sure, but as a condition for all communication, as exposure" (*OTB*, 48).

But in *Winesburg* language reflects the fate of its speakers, and thus exists in a state of exile, making merely external people's abyss of interiority; it does not, however, mediate it. It does not abolish the inalienable property of enjoyment, or make the world common, as in Levinas; rather, language becomes a kind of private property in these stories. Even when left unspoken, words leave behind a legacy of unspent potential, like the $800 George's mother fails to tell him about, money known only and always to readers of *Winesburg, Ohio*, but never to the town's citizens. Far from being a "burglary," however, the appropriation of such knowledge comes to readers as the novel's bequest. It is a hope for expressive continuity outside the novel's own terms, which preclude an unencumbered residence, a homestead, within them.

In the same story, "Death," an accidental substitute for speech—a bang in the hallway—robs Mrs. Willard of the chance to speak. The words being lost, "the thing that had come to life in her as she talked to her one friend, died suddenly" (228). In "Sophistication," Anderson deliberately reverses this polarity. What George and Helen could not express to each other signals their participation in the "mature life of the modern world," a realm thoroughly at odds with the discursive autism which is Winesburg. But surely this cements rather than abolishes the "inalienable property of enjoyment." That one of the only moments of benign live-entering in the novel involves its two flattest characters, and that in terms of narrative ethics the moment reduces to aesthetic epiphany only, confirms for me the defective conditions under which language must operate in this text.

In addition to words unspent, we discover those that remain simply uncashable. "The story of Wing Biddlebaum is a story of hands" (23), says the narrator, and hands being Wing's linguistic medium, his story is also a story of speech. As the "piston rods of his machinery of expression," Wing's hands are fired by a kind of nervous internal combustion. They are ignited, however, by the rare occasions for sympathy or influence "for which the hands were but the fluttering pennants of promise" (31). (Wing's nickname, of course, connotes the kind of hands used in flight.) He tells George, "You have inclinations to be alone and to dream and you are afraid of dreams. You want to be like others in town here. You hear them talk and you try to imitate them" (31).

He proceeds to dream in George's presence and on his behalf, envisioning a pastoral of seemingly gentle but forceful teaching, a dream figure for Wing's own buried life. The hands begin to talk as well, caressing until they're withdrawn in horror. If the near homophony of "coerce" and "caress" in language is accidental, their convergence in Wing's hands and speech is not. In the same way that the old man in Wing's dream roars exhortatively, "you must shut your ears to the roaring voices," Wing unconsciously lays on hands, shading caressing into coercion: "In a way the voice and the hands, the stroking of the shoulders and the touching of the hair were part of the schoolmaster's effort to *carry a dream into the young minds.* . . . Under the caress of his hands doubt and disbelief went out of the minds of the boys and they also began to dream" (31).

The other in Levinas looks *down* at me from a height, a sign of our incommensurability, and that is what defines the other primoridally as teacher. But here Wing literally descends on his pupils; he cannot keep his hands off them. In their eroticized expressiveness, those hands both grasp and lose grip: they telegraph messages which cannot be sent, which cannot "create commonplaces," in Levinas' phrase. ("The hand," Levinas elsewhere observes, "takes and comprehends [*prend et comprend*]; it recognizes the being of the existent, seizing upon the substance and not the shadow; and at the same time it suspends that being, since being is its possession" [*TI*, 161].)

For perhaps this most tragic of Winesburg's grotesques, the very act of narration—in its religious fervor—becomes self-damning; Wing is driven out of town under a cloud of suspicion, forever blighted. Wing's story, finally, becomes the story of preternaturally expressive hands that must be silenced into beating fists, of electric desires to inspirit dreams—to lay on hands—stifled, for all their religiosity, into a profane and frenetic darting for breadcrumbs: "A few stray white bread crumbs lay on the cleanly washed floor by a table; putting the lamp upon a low stool, he began to pick up the crumbs, carrying them to his mouth one by one with unbelievable rapidity. In the dense blotch of light beneath the table the kneeling figure looked like a priest engaged in some service of his church" (35).

Me Voici

As the first real story in the novel, "Hands" sends themes and images like semaphores through the rest of the novel; and its religious sensibility—its choked or muffled *ekstasis*—stands over the entire text. Language in *Winesburg*, as in Levinas, is religion, but only in a presocial, anchoritic sense. Many of the stories, the four-part "Godliness" in particular, treat religious language in the absence of religion; precursors to some of Faulkner's or Flannery O'Connor's fiction, these stories focus on the deformation which comes from evangelical need untethered to the ballast of communal narrative. *In-spiration*, in effect, becomes these stories' alternative to live-entering.

For Bakhtin, Christ's incarnation stands as an archetype of *vzhivanie*, the capacity to enter inside yet remain outside, enfleshment being both a defense against abstraction and a token of willed participation. In *Winesburg*, where images of fire or flame occur repeatedly, it is rather the descent of the Paraclete, with its transformation of language into tongues of fire, that more fittingly symbolizes live-entering. But no comfort awaits those possessed, since the hypertrophy of religious discourse here marks merely how attenuated real expression—ordinary dialogue and narrative—has become.

"Godliness," for example, transforms the benign excitation of lullaby ("Tandy") or dream ("Hands") into hostile narrative takeover. For his son David's sake, a latter-day Jesse looks into scripture and wrenches the story of Abraham and Isaac into twentieth-century Ohio. Here again, *Winesburg, Ohio* instructively offsets Levinas, since it skeletalizes the sort of covenantal force which Levinas attributes to speech, and skews it in the direction of parental perversity; in this story, storytelling is child abuse. But as a crazed form of narrative ethics, such violent thematizing precisely exploits the *binding* quality of storytelling (never more graphic than in the story of Abraham's near sacrifice of Isaac); it forces Said through histrionic Saying.

In Genesis, what is called the *akedah* counterpoises three sorts of binding: the binding and subsequent loosing of Isaac, the compensatory binding of community to cultural narrative, and the binding nature of obligatory response. The last is the most important for my purposes here; it takes the form of a formula, a sign and countersign: "Abraham," the Lord's vocative address, and "Here am I" (repeated twice by Abraham, once by Isaac), the gesture of human answerability and exposure.[27] Some form of that structure—mandate, response, dispensation—undergirds even ordinary narrative give-and-take, I would argue; it certainly does so with a vengeance in *Winesburg*, whatever the mode of solicitation, whatever the nature of response.

And yet the story of the *akedah* transcendentalizes at the same time as it ritualizes covenant. It inaugurates a permanent narrative relationship between divinity and man; to be in this story is to walk with G-d. Moreover, such narrative summons endless interpretation from its reader-participants. In *Winesburg*, however, narrative covenants are neither permanent nor illimitable. They strip bare rather than simplify, demand finite acknowledgment instead of infinite exegesis.

In *Lord Jim* Marlow became the accidental legatee of a covenant binding him to Jim, since an act of overhearing, of misaddressed language, brings them together; readers overhear and become bound in a similar way through a second-order contract. But in "Godliness" and in *Winesburg* generally, binding—part Coleridgean, part Abrahamic—works more primitively. Narrative forcibly yokes together lives and stories without, so to speak, G-d's blessing. It may take the form of an impulse to plunge oneself, as with Jesse Bentley or Curtis Hartman, into an established narrative; or it may require plunging one's story into arrested interlocutors, as Wing Biddlebaum or Kate Swift attempt to do.

In "The Teacher," for instance, the anarchic form of *vzhivanie* I describe above, along with its telltale fire imagery, overcomes Kate Smith: "Kate Smith's mind was ablaze with thoughts of George Willard. In something he had written she thought she had recognized the spark of genius and wanted to blow on the spark. . . . 'You will have to know life,' she declared, and her voice trembled with earnestness. She took hold of George Willard's shoulders and turned him about so that she could look into his eyes. . . . A passionate desire to have him understand the import of life, to learn to interpret it truly and honestly swept over her" (163). A familiar chain of exigent linguistic events, from language to physicality to violence, quickly follows:

> The impulse that had driven her out into the snow poured itself out into talk. She became *inspired* as she sometimes did in the presence of the children in school . . . So strong was her passion that it became something physical . . . When [George] came and put a hand on her shoulder she turned and let her body fall heavily against him. For George Willard the confusion was immediately increased. For a moment he held the body of the woman tightly against his body and then it stiffened. *Two sharp little fists began to beat on his face.* (162–165)

As in "Mother," "Hands," "Queer," and "Godliness," speech and violence clash together with perverse logic. In "Queer," Elmer Cowley rains blows down on George Willard's breast, neck, and mouth to express frustration over his own traitorous organs of speech. Language simply falls short of accommodating experience. For Kate Swift also, fists fare as badly as words: says George, "I have missed something. I have missed something Kate Swift was trying to tell me" (166).

"Mother" recapitulates the familial pathology of "Godliness," what one might call its generational narrative tyranny; it depicts the compulsion to force one's story not simply onto someone but into them as well. Elizabeth Willard bases a "deep unexpressed *bond* of sympathy" with her son on a "girlhood dream that had died long ago" (40). Her husband, Tom, though markedly unsympathetic, similarly attaches himself to George through the medium of unfulfilled ambitions.

Each of his parents could be said to be living "through" rather than "into" George, drawing from him compensation for their mutual loss. In fact, each wants George to "express something for us both," and though his mother silently prays for him to dream, and his father exhorts him to wake up, together they not only tell him separate stories, but craft them for him too. In the promise they hold for emplotment, children, as in Dickens' *Great Expectations*, serve as their parents' compensation.

While Tom swaggers and "dramatizes" (50) himself, Elizabeth interprets an ongoing tableau between a baker and a cat in the alley "as a rehearsal of her own life, terrible in its vividness" (41). With the help of an old theater make-up box, she hopes to act out a revenge fantasy of murdering her husband; making her melodramatic entrance, she "would be silent . . . coming out of the shadows" (47). Each parent thus inculcates essentially similar versions of self-projection, of "living aesthetically."

Refusing the amplification and critique possible from another's vantage point, the parents can author only fragments, and condemn themselves to a compensatory literariness instead. Tom Willard's attempt to coerce George to speak—"What you say clears things up"—and Elizabeth Willard's violently Oedipal fantasy of punishing the speech-forcer both depend on the press of speech, words either imposed or drawn out. Both parents trap George, and remain themselves entrapped, through language.

Force Is Ethics

In *Coercion to Speak*, Aaron Fogel speculates that the prototype for dialogue derives not from some "ideal speech situation," but in fact from a scene, as in Sophocles' *Oedipus Tyrannus*, of speech-forcing, "a sort of broken forced catechism—of persons making other persons speak but without being able to determine the words spoken."[28] For dialogue to take place, in other words, someone must force it into existence.

Winesburg, Ohio provides little place for dialogue, its scenes of storytelling being so many instances of noninterrupted speech. As Edmond Jabès remarks, "Any dialogue is two condemned monologues facing each other. Fraternal violence."[29] But where Fogel's model derives from ritual drama, its counterpart in *Winesburg* depends on the sort of ritualized telling and listening I have already pointed out in narrative contexts like *The Rime of the Ancient Mariner*.

Narrative ethics in these cases conforms to a strict physics of force and counterforce. Although one may appeal to pragmatics to find empirical support for ethical behavior in discourse, turn-taking procedures, for instance, or maxims for conversation, narrative ethics construes force in a more metaphysical sense, the "Abraham," one might say, to "Here am I." As coercion, as desperation, as interruption, as pained speech or hearing, "force" *is* ethics in *Winesburg, Ohio*. It is, in Levinas' terms, the "nakedness of the face": "This gaze that supplicates and demands, that can supplicate only because it demands, deprived of everything because entitled to everything—this gaze is precisely the epiphany of the face as a face. The nakedness of the face is destituteness" (*TI*, 75).

As narrative, as telling one's story, such ethical immediacy shocks, and possesses the power to transform both self and other. In "Death" Elizabeth Willard achieves an apotheosis through the generous eyes of Dr. Reefy in a casual moment of recollection; narration lets fall the grace of moments in one of the few beneficent instances in the novel. In "Respectability," by contrast, the narrator mercilessly cages Wash Williams within the text by describing him as grotesquely as possible—zoologically: "If you have lived in cities and have walked in the park on a summer afternoon, you have perhaps seen, blinking in a corner of his iron cage, a huge, grotesque kind of monkey, a creature with ugly, sagging, hairless skin below his eyes and a bright purple underbody. This monkey is a true monster. In the completeness of his ugliness he achieved a kind of perverted beauty" (121). (The last sentence of this passage prefigures a later description of Wash's only naturally unsullied feature: his hands. Wash's hands, his ironic nickname, and his status as telegrapher all recall the character of Wing Biddlebaum, who in respect to the caressing/coercing force of language is very much the analogous figure.) As Wash sits together with George across railroad ties, the very site of transport, he proceeds then to relate his version of "laying on of hands": "'It is because I saw you kissing the lips of that Belle Carpenter that I tell you my story,' he said. 'What happened to me may next happen to you. I want to put you on your guard. Already you may be having dreams in your head. I want to destroy them'" (125).

As a desideratum for language, the caress may never arrive. It does not in Wash's story, a tale of bitter and disappointed love: "The longer I waited the more raw and tender I became. I thought that if she came in and touched me with her hand I would perhaps faint away" (127). The story, for George, has a remarkable effect. Having heard it, "The young reporter felt ill and weak. In imagination, he also became old and shapeless" (127); his mother, by contrast, in *telling* hers becomes young and beautiful.

In "Hands" George resists inquiring about Wing's story after a dream has been fondled into him; it remains for the narrator-"poet" to tell us, because George is but a cubnarratee as well as a cub reporter. But in "Respectability" (as in "Loneliness"), George presses for the story. And in the process a dream perhaps is wrenched away from the storyteller. Reporting, Anderson implies—the drive toward theme—is linguistic violence; just listening can also disclose or reveal.

Between revelation and disclosure, the impulses to caress and coerce, hands which minister and hands which take hold through language, resides an ethics of narration. Like its hermeneutic counterpart in *Lord Jim*, ethics here does not mean a systematic arrangement of checks and balances; rather it means the performance of the singular claims narrative acts elicit. These claims establish their authority and their meaning in such performances, just as the ethical relation in Levinas installs itself and exercises power only in its being undergone.

While several of the novel's stories do link these claims, as in Conrad and Coleridge, to the threat of death, they neither emphasize nor cultivate a "being toward death" as a guarantor of narrative authenticity. For the most part *Winesburg* prefers entropy to full stops, winding down to the resolutions of closure. We find compelling formulations in Walter Benjamin and Bakhtin of narrative's thanatos principle, the satisfaction and sense of an ending that only the knowledge of death can provide. For Benjamin, for example, "Death is the sanction of everything that the storyteller can tell."[30] Bakhtin regards death as the "ultimate aesthetic act," because, in freeing me from the authorship of fragments, it enables the other's gift of wholeness, of a finally legitimate "aesthetic shaping of my personality" (*AA*, 89).

Winesburg's stories, on the contrary, show a preoccupation with death in life—the buried life, the life not lived, and the compression of the fragmentary life lived into fragments of story told. Plot or symbol—the twin functions of death in narrative—cede priority to strictly narrational tensions. The scene at the end of many of the stories may often provide a dramatic coda, but it restates the story's "problem" rather than resolves it. Similarly, Anderson all but tells the reader what certain representative images "mean." Ultimately, his text forces into consciousness narrative ethics simply as narrated force. Because exigency lies behind occasions for storytelling in this novel, the stories of *Winesburg, Ohio* perform a narrative ethics.

Sometimes this means that a story simply cannot be told. In "Queer," for instance, another father narratively deforms his son. When Ebenezer Cowley acquires from a half-wit a peculiar sort of penetrative *phrase*—"I'll be washed and ironed and starched"—what should function simply as another portable "Well, I'll be" variant bleeds pathos as the seven-word summing up of a life. The narrator says of Ebenezer, "Still, he existed"; and minimally he does, as he stands around in his grease-spotted Prince Albert coat, the second-hand phrase in his mouth not only ludicrously inappropriate, but emblematic of the freshly laundered life not lived. But, when uttered by Ebenezer's son, Elmer, the phrase adapts itself once again, this time even more pathetically: it stanches Elmer's desperate desires for speech, and bleaches him dry.

"I will not be queer—one to be looked at and listened to" (194), he exclaims, defying baleful influences of nature and culture. He develops a particular antipathy to George Willard, who as a reporter represents public opinion, that is, impersonal looking and listening. "And had not public opinion," the text affirms, "sentenced the Cowleys to queerness?" In point of fact, the Cowleys "sentence" themselves; the cruel "play of differences" in Winesburg oversees Elmer's displaced rage just as it does the "floating signifier" that gags his expression. Wandering aimlessly, he walks into the countryside, the site of temporary and illusory respite in many of these stories, and stops at his boyhood home to speak with Mook, the original, half-witted author of the Cowley family fragment: "'[George] don't know but I know,' he shouted, stopping to gaze down into the dumb, unresponsive face of the half-wit. . . . 'Do you know why I came clear out here afoot? I had to tell someone and you were the only one I could tell. I hunted out another queer one, you see. I ran away, that's what I did. I couldn't stand up to someone like that George Willard. I had to come to you'" (197).

Mook responds predictably: "I'll be washed, ironed, and starched." Just so, when it becomes time to confront George, does Elmer. Only afterward does he renounce expression altogether, beating George about the breast, the neck, and the mouth. Language and narrative turn in on themselves. Elmer, pathetically, seeks only conversation, but finds it only with an uncomprehending half-wit who indirectly hobbled Elmer's speech in the first place. He desires to "create commonplaces"; banal clichés trip him up instead. Stories and phrases may, disease-like, be communicated in Winesburg but they do not themselves have to communicate. And once again, perceiving that sadness is entrusted to readers, left in their hands.

What? What Say?

In "The Buried Life" Matthew Arnold writes, "Long we try in vain to speak and act / Our hidden self, and what we say and do / Is eloquent, is well—but 'tis not true." *Winesburg*'s narrators usually lack even eloquence, and live a life while trying vainly to squeeze out its story. In "Adventure," for example, Alice Hineman utters words which never stop resonating for her, although they fail to deliver what they promise. She tells her lover, "'We will have to stick to each other now.' The words echoed and re-echoed through the mind of the maturing woman" (116). In fact, only the words stick, standing reminders of broken troth, like Miss Havisham's stopped clock.

Again, the overdetermined moment of expression dies on the wing. Running naked through the rain, Alice sees someone and, defying shame, calls to him, "'Wait! Don't go away. Whoever you are, you must wait.' The man on the sidewalk stopped and stood listening. He was an old man and somewhat deaf. Putting his hand to his mouth, he shouted, 'What? What say?'" (120). His fateful question leaves Alice more naked and exposed than she was before. The eerie closeness to, and at the same time telling distance from, Levinas' sensuous vocabulary of human encounter, its erotic plenitude, is never more piquant than here:

> The subject in saying approaches a neighbor in expressing itself, in being expelled, in the literal sense of the term, out of any locus, no longer *dwelling*, not stomping any ground. Saying uncovers, beyond nudity, what dissimulation there may be under the exposedness of a skin laid bare. It is the very *respiration* of this skin prior to any intention. The subject is not *in itself*, at home with itself, such that it would dissimulate itself in itself or dissimulate itself in its wounds or its exile, understood as *acts* of wounding or exiling itself. Its bending back upon itself is a turning inside out. Its being "turned to another" is this being turned inside out. A concave without a convex. The subject of saying does not give signs, it becomes a sign, turns into an allegiance. (*OTB*, 49)

"What? What say?" Saying falls on deaf ears.[31]

It Is Face

In "The Philospher," the companion piece to "Loneliness," *Winesburg, Ohio* explores perhaps its most complex instance of twisted communication as narrative ethics. Dr. Parcival, like his fellow physician, Dr. Reefy, is a writer; he has also worked as a reporter, and as his name suggests, he fits the lineaments of storyteller as well. The story marks Parcival in the metonymic manner so common to this text; he is afflicted with a twitching left eye. But signs and emblems mark everyone in this story: Will Henderson, another monologuist—distinguished by a red birthmark; the doctor's brother—"covered with the nasty colored orange paint"; his mother in an apron—"covered with soap suds"; his father—housed in an insane asylum. George is marked too, we could say, insofar as Parcival seeks him out, ostensibly, to have him listen to long tales about his life.

It becomes clear, however, that Parcival's stories work much like his twitching left eyelid: narrative windowshades, they advance and turn back upon themselves, alternating fact and fiction as though someone were playing with the cord. "The tales Doctor Parcival told George Willard began nowhere and ended nowhere. Sometimes the boy thought they must all be inventions, a pack of lies. And then again he was convinced that they contained the very essence of truth" (51).

The stories baffle; tales of petty crimes confessed to and murders alleged to have been committed, tales of insanity, death, and sibling jealousy, they track evidently significant moments in Dr. Parcival's life in erratic switches of revelation and concealment. Small phrases of pathos occasionally leak out: "I have a desire to make you admire me, that's a fact" (50); "My mother loved my brother much more than she did me. You have no idea with what contempt he looked upon mother and me" (53). Finally, though, Parcival interrupts his own storytelling to explain his motives: "I want to warn you and keep on warning you. . . . I want to fill you with hatred and contempt so that you will be a superior being" (55).

But Parcival's unchivalrous behavior has little effect on George or the rest of the town. After noting the doctor's diffidence about assisting at the scene of an accident, the narrator says, "The useless cruelty of his refusal had passed unnoticed. Indeed, the man who came up the stairway to summon him had hurried away without hearing the refusal" (56).

The tale hints at tragic possibilities. As the story which immediately follows "Mother," "The Philosopher" recycles the motif of hoarded money as frustrated expression. That Parcival might have stolen large or small sums of money fits the erratic tenor of his talk: he speaks with fugitive abandon, as social conversation again mirrors deviant behavior. But truth value is not really what's valuable about these stories. Rather, it is their performative effect; Parcival's tales draw George in through their vividness as specimens of the "real," of *vraisemblance*, not of truth as disclosure.

Although the hint of criminality suggests there might be a hermeneutic at work like that in detective fiction, where readers' *vraisemblable* proves inferior to and dependent on the text's own, Dr. Parcival finds as little use for facts as does the initial narrator in *Lord Jim*. Restive with epistemology as well as with moral reasoning, "The Philosopher" gravitates instead toward the uncanniness of narrative ethics—the force of "shadowy personality" (27) and "elusive individuality" (28). Like the devices of delayed decoding and deciphering in *Lord Jim*, Parcival's narrative "cord-pulling," outside the norms of social conversation and narrative logic, solicits a certain kind of recognition; to accommodate the special features of his face, one has to see past it as well as look at it.

In Levinas' terms, Parcival neither dispels the anarchic sorcery of facts nor attends to his own manifestation by breaking through form; he neither reveals nor discloses. He need not mask his face, since it already conspicuously hides itself. Parcival explains it best himself, with Levinasian suggestiveness: "It is not face. It lies in fact in my character, which has, if you think about it, many strange turns" (50). Like "Loneliness" the story invites readers to follow such turns, not because they can or should be puzzled out, the stuff of classical anagnorisis, but because only in that way do they ever become traversed, undergone; in merely following Parcival's story, readers bind themselves to him in an ethics of narrative.

Yet obviously, the story *does* reduce to face, although not to the unvarnished role it plays in Levinas' model of unmediated ethical relation. As *Winesburg*'s homegrown equivalent to the Mariner's glittering eye, Parcival's ocular windowshade commands attention whether it goes up or down. It doesn't compel so much as entice—like a fisherman's lure. In his refusal or inability to supply a narrative logic and reliability, Parcival nevertheless infuses a kind of grace into his fragmentary and elliptical stories by asking merely that they be followed.

As John Ruskin once commented on a verse in Milton's *Lycidas*: "I pause again, for this is a strange expression; a broken metaphor, one might think, careless and unscholarly. Not so: its very audacity and pithiness are intended to make us look close at the phrase and remember it."[32] "The Philosopher," in its audacity and pithiness, works in just this way.

Then at what audience does the story aim? Nominally, of course, at George, but he remains typically blank for its duration. Since, as Levinas points out, the self is potentially answerable only insofar as it is separate in the first place, it is perfectly fitting that George be so *chez soi* in most of these stories; moreover, as a mostly inconsequential subject, he can be said to keep his subject position empty precisely so as to make way for readers.

Thus we discover only that to George "the tales were very real and full of meaning. . . . Sometimes he thought they must all be inventions, a pack of lies. And then again he was convinced that they contained the essence of truth" (5). At no point in the tales that "began nowhere and ended nowhere," however, does George register a response, not even to Parcival's pleading at the end. His transparency calls even more attention to the wild chromaticism of the doctor's storytelling.

The plea with which the story concludes, "You must pay attention to me" (57) recalls Enoch Robinson's desperation at being muffled by his own text. In Dr. Parcival's case, however, it gestures toward the structure of Coleridge's *Rime of the Ancient Mariner* by visually arresting an audience through a grotesque or uncanny mark.[33] In this way, it threatens to mark the one element in the story so far left uninscribed within it—its readership. And as I have argued earlier, Anderson's novel depends on the kindness of strangers, the presiding *hands* for which it centripetally aims.

In this respect, the gulf between *heim* and *unheimlich* which we see in this story records two kinds of displacement: persons displaced from one another and stories displaced from lives. Both of these, the text says, are conditions of ethical emergency.

Live-Exiting

When displacement follows displacement, there can be no words of exile. Words only tend to break the exile. There is only the exile of an unutterable word amid our countless words without echo. Languages tend secretly toward articulating that word, toward discovering its limits. Toward somehow turning the unutterable infinite into a legible and audible finite.

Edmond Jabès, "The Question of Displacement into Lawfulness," *The Sin of the Book*

> What translation does, by reference to the fiction or hypothesis of a pure language devoid of the burden of meaning, is that it implies—in bringing to light what Benjamin calls *die Wehen des eigenen*—the suffering of what one thinks as one's own—the suffering of the original language. We think we are at ease in language, we feel a coziness, a familiarity, a shelter in the language we call our own, in which we think we are not alienated. What the translation reveals is that this alienation is strongest in our relation to our own language, that the original language within which we are engaged is disarticulated in a way which imposes a particular alienation, a particular suffering. . . . This movement of the original is a wandering, an *errance*, a kind of permanent exile if you wish, but it is not really an exile, for there is no homeland, nothing from which one has been exiled.
>
> Paul de Man, *The Resistance to Theory*

Winesburg, Ohio and *Lord Jim* are texts of exile. Characters, language, meaning—all seek different orders of return. Each novel, solicits from readers at the very least a corresponding exile in the sense of an acknowledgment that cannot be completed. Jabès' words suggest that exile somehow redeems precisely because it *cannot* be completed; a necessary and universal phenomenon, exile frees man from G-d as it frees up speech; both become subject to dynamisms of the uncanny. But at the same time it requires that words and men attempt a constant journey back home.

In Lurianic Kabbalah (as Jabès knows) exile creates the circumstances for redemption; in what is called the *shevirah*, or rupture, the receptacles designed to receive the divine light of creation shatter, and from that point on, all creation contains a flaw and awaits mending.[34] In a parallel process, exile produces *narrative*—either "the way back" itself or a narrated story about it.

In either case, making the journey enables one to encounter all those others whose separate exiles crisscross one's own. As the narrator says in Toni Morrison's *Beloved:* "Silent except for social courtesies, when they met one another they neither described nor asked about the sorrow that drove them from one place to another."[35] At its beginning as well as at its consummation, a narrative of ingathering can take shape simply as distilled acknowledgment—as proximity. Acts of narration, in other words, forge intersubjective ties which bind subjects in exile, mending, as it were, their singularity.

At the opposite pole from Jabès, de Man seizes on exile as figure, not story. In "Benjamin's 'The Task of the Translator,'" he takes the same image of the breaking of the vessels as a sign of unredeemable exile and fragmentation in discourse. Translation merely demonstrates the interior exile, the immanent homelessness (to paraphrase Georg Lukács) at the heart of language. In selecting the sentence in Benjamin's essay in which the image appears—"the fragments of a vessel, in order to be articulated together must *follow* one another in the smallest detail"—de Man emphasizes that the word "follow" implies a metonymic rather than metaphoric pattern. Shouldn't this by rights suggest the organizing force of narrative? No, de Man says, since the vessel was never whole in the first place; the succession of its fragments can produce nothing more than a random and therefore narratively incoherent order.

Benjamin's own image bears out this incoherence, because, as Hillis Miller points out in his own essay on Benjamin in *The Ethics of Reading*, it simply does not succeed as a metaphor, and consequently cannot adequately carry its own meaning—exactly like a broken vessel. The critical bias here reads exile as a linguistic phenomenon first, conditioning all other instances—religious, psychological, social. All these must, then, "follow."[36]

Yet *Lord Jim* and *Winesburg, Ohio* understand exile only as their own precondition, a call requiring response. In emphasizing the one-time or ever-circulating bonds between teller, listener, and tale as acts of testimony over against impersonal judgment, they stand as emblems of restoration and return. Such acts can indeed arrest history, but only to make it less impersonal, more human. As Levinas writes, "the judgment of history is always pronounced in absentia. The will's absence from this judgment lies in the fact that it is present there only in the third person" (*TI*, 23). Refusing (or unable) to lend their lips to the "anonymous utterance of history," Jim, Marlow, and the Winesburg grotesques speak—however brokenly—for themselves, to others.

The epigraph to this chapter drawn from Primo Levi's *Survival in Auschwitz* testifies not only to the unforeseen miracle of an actual reprieve, but to the specific claims on personal judgment and restoration which such texts place on their legatees. The fear of a possible

passivity, indifference, or evasion—of nonsonorous response—Levi
perfectly renders as the dream of the unlistened-to story, cast back into
exile. Given the implications of such a nightmare of narrative ethics, I
think it is no accident that for his final book, *The Drowned and the Saved*,
Levi chose for his epigraph the identical stanzas from Coleridge's *Rime
of the Ancient Mariner* which stand at the head of this book. Even for
texts of exile, there is interruption: to stop in order to understand, to
understand in order to speak.

The listened-to story means a homecoming. It performs a narrative
tikkun—a restoration—where the finding, gathering, and restoring of
the scattered sparks of divine light takes the shape of Bakhtin's "seeing,
remembering, gathering, and unifying activity" of watchers, listeners,
and readers. For simple acknowledgment's sake, answerability thus
participates in states of exile, and in so doing, heals them a little.

Still, in the particularity of its texts, its characters, its narrators, and
its readers, literature like life teaches the perils and the impossibility of
a fusion. Thus the fragments, broken vessels, wedding guests and mariners of *Lord Jim* and *Winesburg, Ohio* remain in exile despite the acts
of recognition, of *vzhivanie*, which they summon from readers. For
them, if a Promised Land of return and restoration remains forever
pending, a livable Diaspora of narrative ethics transmits their stories.
Readers live into these as from one state of exile to another. In this
sense, narratives take on a life of their own, over and above the impulses
of narrators and readers alike, in order to defend against the threat of
death, of the last word. "And how," wrote Melville, "can a man get a
Voice out of Silence?"

4

Lessons of (for) the Master: Short Fiction by Henry James

He who looks from the outside through an open window never sees as many things as he who looks at a closed window. There is no object deeper, more mysterious, more fruitful, more shadowy, more dazzling than a window lit by a candle. What one can see in the sunshine is always less interesting than what goes on behind a pane of glass. In this black or lighted hole life lives, life dreams, life suffers.

Beyond waves of roofs I perceive a mature woman, already wrinkled, poor, always bent over something, who never goes out. With her face, with her clothes, with her gestures, with almost nothing, I have rewritten the story of this woman, or perhaps her legend, and sometimes I retell it to myself with tears.

If it had been a poor old man, I should have rewritten his story just as easily. And I go to bed, proud of having lived and suffered in others than myself.

Perhaps you will say to me, "Are you sure that this legend is a true one?" What does it matter what the reality which exists outside myself may be, if it has helped me to live, to feel that I am and what I am?

Charles Baudelaire, "Windows"

The house of fiction has in short not one window but a million. . . . They are but windows at the best, mere holes in a dead wall, disconnected, perched aloft; they are not hinged doors opening straight upon life. But they have this mark of their own that at each of them stands a figure with a pair of eyes, or at least with a fieldglass, which forms, again and again, for observation a unique instrument, ensuring to the person making use of it an impression distinct from every other . . . There is fortunately no saying on what, for the particular pair of eyes, the window may not open; "fortunately" by reason precisely of the incalculability of range. . . . Tell me what the artist is, and I will tell you of what he has been conscious. Thereby I shall express to you at once his boundless freedom and his "moral" reference.

Henry James, *The Portrait of a Lady*

. . . But as through the monotony we ran,
We came to where there was a living man.
His great gaunt figure filled his cabin door,
And had he fallen on the floor
He must have measured to the further wall
But we who passed were not to see him fall.
The miles and miles he lived from anywhere
Were evidently something he could bear. . . .
Nor did he lack for common entertainment.
That I assume was what our passing train meant.
He could look at us in our diner eating,
And if so moved uncurl a hand in greeting.

Robert Frost, "Figure in a Doorway"

I N THE PREVIOUS chapter I dealt primarily with constraints on acts of narrating and interpretation. In building an argument for narrative ethics, I showed how stories reveal an ethics not through exemplification but rather through the force with which they are ex-pressed, propelled outward. I also described concomitant acts of reception and interpretation as acts of responsible authoring.

The epigraphs which begin this chapter ask a related but different set of questions. What limits exist for the authoring, that is, the imaginative filling in, of persons? How does a doorway or a moving vantage point frame figures for our portraiture? How do such figures or such framing attract or repel our fictionalizing acts? Where, in short, does person end and (literary) character begin?

The excerpts from Frost, Baudelaire, and James all ascribe a certain proprietary attitude, a lèse majesté, to acts of representation. In all three, physical spaces frame or permit the objectification of persons, not of things. Dwellings (the very place of the human) seem to justify, in several senses, the making up of others—a kind of sovereignty which Levinas (on the model of Husserl's theory of intentionality) calls a "movement . . . with no searchlight preceding it," an "absolute" projection which invents its own goal and "discovers, properly speaking, nothing before itself" (*TI*, 125).

As another philosopher puts it, "if philosophy is a struggle over pronouns, and moral philosophy an engagement over persons, then literature is the strife over irrealities."[1] The stories by Henry James which I explore in this chapter make that strife their common topic as the commerce between different orders of representation—semiotic, economic, and aesthetic. Together, these stories elaborate a theory of selfhood across the boundary of literary text.

In Chapter 2, I discussed how both structuralist and postmodern theories of character prefer to speak in terms of sets of predicates or proper names rather than of mimetic or ethical values; such theories eschew thematic and mimetic dimensions for the synthetic. Subjects of enunciation—real, single, self-identical—collapse into subjects of utterance—split, plural, absent.[2] I argued that inalienable facets of literary character, and their link to nonliterary discourses about personhood, fall needlessly by the wayside in this kind of analysis.[3]

In the previous chapter, I spoke of the distribution of narrational roles and responsibilities as emblematic of the moral separateness of persons. Narrators, listeners, and witnesses assume the responsibilities of ethical relation in discharging their "roles" and "functions." In the present chapter, I concentrate on specifically representational contexts for the boundaries separating, and transgressed by, persons within a field of narrative ethics. Rather than analyzing the force of exigent acts of narration, here I will look at the force of representation itself, the power of images and the shadows they can cast.

From time to time, aesthetic theory focuses on the redemptive and humanizing aspects of such power; Crocean aesthetics and Maurice Merleau-Ponty's essays on Cézanne are two examples. But images can also hold sway far less benignly—they project (or absorb) raw emotional power, they loom eerily beyond their own aesthetic borders, they thrust themselves into space and consciousness. Consider, for example, the slashing by the suffragist Mary Richardson of Velásquez's *Rokeby Venus*. In its raw assertiveness, that act testifies to a kind of sovereignty nowhere in sight in Foucault's discussion of a painting by the same artist; *Las Meninas* may command attention, but the *Rokeby Venus* incites physical assault—behind the backs, as it were, of both Venus and Velásquez.[4]

Or consider that the Nazis saw German modernist art as "aesthetic aggression," and responded out of all proportion with the anti-exhibition of "degenerate art" in 1937. Indeed, the National Socialist counter-aesthetic stands as a monument to the power of representation, a "triumph of the image" over and above any Triumph of the Will. It shows how, in Jay Cantor's words, an "image overwhelms the imaginative faculty, that sense, redolent with instinctual involvement, that we collaborate in making the world through our shaping violence and our love."[5]

On the surface, representation in prose fiction would seem exempt from such consequences because it finally arrives so highly mediated. Yet whatever power fiction does wield comes about only through the "collaborative" assistance of readers' mediations. Thus Cavell insists that regarding fiction as simply a limit case for epistemological and intersubjective dilemmas we experience in life misunderstands the purpose of fiction. Fiction does not demarcate art from life by announcing: this close but no closer—in fiction we stand as spectators but life is where we participate. Rather, it offers up for encounter—not simply for contemplation—hard facts of distance, separation, and alterity which seem familiar as "facts of life," but which gain extra pathos and piquancy when framed by the special boundaries of art—a proscenium arch, the rootedness of painting and sculpture, the closed covers of a book.

In this chapter, I explore one facet of this double mediation: how slippage between mimetic, synthetic, and thematic aspects of character can actually *de-realize* the person in the text. I focus on the permeability of literary character, how its "outsideness" typically undergoes a breach across several textual levels, and finally on what all this may have to say about texts' and persons' "standing" in the everyday.

The text I turn to first, "The Real Thing," confronts all these issues in a study of the troubling marriage of sovereign representation and domestic life. The way the married couple is treated within the text directly raises questions about other salient kinds of relationship: namely, text to reader and author to text. Indeed, the fact that the Monarchs (the couple's name) have been overthrown by textual fiat before the story even gives them a chance implies a ruthless "sovereignty" that James as well as readers must reckon with—a certain, shall we say, totalitarianism. Hence this chapter's title: a rebuke of the exercise of authorial "lordship" which sentences characters to textual "bondage."

When James remarks in the preface to *Roderick Hudson*, "Really, universally, relations stop nowhere, and the exquisite problem of the artist is eternally but to draw, by a geometry of his own, the circle within which they happily *appear* to do so," metaphors of circumscription collude with those of visual representation, and hint at a possible tyranny desired by both. "The Real Thing" depicts the effect of such collusion, as "happily *appear*" ceases to be an innocuous figure of speech and becomes cruel and ironic commentary instead.

"The Real Thing"
Dem Bones

A commonplace in James's view of "life and art" holds that in being alternately enriched, corrected for, and sharpened, life best finds itself *in* art, particularly that of imaginatively and precisely conceived fiction. In the preface to *The Spoils of Poynton*, James says,

> Life persistently blunders and deviates, loses herself in the sand. The reason is of course that life has no direct sense whatever for the subject and is capable, luckily for us, of nothing but splendid waste. Hence the opportunity for the sublime economy of art, which rescues, which saves, and hoards and "banks," investing and reinvesting these fruits of toil in wondrous useful "works" and thus making up for us, desperate spendthrifts that we all naturally are, the most princely of incomes. (*AN*, 120)

The economic metaphor is unmistakable (especially tantalizing in light of the Monarchs' financial predicament in the story), but for me it merely subserves the more interesting theme of artistic value, a central concern in "The Real Thing."

In personifying "life" as it does, the passage above seems to efface the presence of persons in it. That is, fiction for James provides the vantage point from which to view life as life and not, most immediately and consequentially, as "other people." "Life, being all inclusion and confusion, and art being all discrimination and selection, the latter, in search of the hard latent *value*, with which it is alone concerned, sniffs around the mass as instinctively and unerringly as a dog suspicious of some buried bone" (*AN*, 120).

Despite a subsequent distinction James draws between artist and dog (the dog destroys his bone, but the artist cherishes his "nugget"), this statement implies that it is life which first denudes and buries material value; only then does art dis-cover and return it to us, purified. Art "invents the goal," in Levinas' words, for which acquisitive hands will later grope. Yet in the materiality, as de Man would put it, of James's metaphor, *hard value* remains skeletal, a bone: life reduced to body and body reduced to lifelessness. Indeed, the terms of James's proposition beg deconstruction; art is just as much confusion as discrimination, and thus borrows from life more than it might allow. And like some dogs, it even forgets from time to time where it has buried its bones.[6]

Further, life and art quite frequently conspire to strip, conceal, and otherwise transform the material world. But as I have said before, actions of stripping, concealing, and transforming do not lie innocently in the abstract; rather they lie in the hands—often quite literally—of agents, that is to say, of persons. "The Real Thing" is the first of three instances in this chapter which disclose the handprints, so to speak, of unethical and unwarranted acts of representation. Its artist-narrator (who is and is not a figure for James) parades his character-subjects before us, ruthlessly exposing their utter lack of representational value. The hands that are supposed to render (that is, re-create) them *render* (that is, *de*-create, "bone") them instead. This I take for an allegory of authorial privilege and authorial culpability, notwithstanding James's own Velásquez-like self-awareness, which mediates the text; such *kynicism*, in other words, should not itself escape critique.[7]

"The Real Thing," in particular, bears out Levinas' claim about the transformative capacity of hands, their ability to turn fact into artifact, body into figure, and figure into the figural. It tells a story, in James's phrase, of the "economy of art." In representing reality either an artist circulates its free values intact, and in doing so reveals the ordinarily unseen; or he commodifies, transvalues, and converts these values into artistic capital, a law of diminishing returns which Levinas calls "the descent into merchandise." And in "The Real Thing" artistic value stands fairly obviously for social and personal value made manifest through representation.

James's fiction, especially the late novels, reflects a powerful investment in language's ability to represent states of mind and being, "language being . . . the stamped and authorized coinage which expresses the value of thought."[8] In its often frequent extravagance, Jamesian metaphor connotes a deep belief in words as authentic carriers of experience; even when the experiences attenuate, language preserves them. As a fact of language, "dead metaphor" nevertheless flourishes as a very live and pregnant term. But figuration, as Levinas and de Man differently propose, can powerfully disfigure reality as well—not "life," "experience," "relation," or other Jamesian intangibles, but concrete persons, reduced to, in Levinas' phrase, a play of forms.

Thus "The Real Thing," as the crux of my reading will show, also tells of the descent of person into type, in a double sense of the word: general class and merely *graphic* character. The story's artist-narrator remarks of his subjects, "in the pictorial sense, I had immediately *seen* them. I had seized their type."[9] In that "seizing," we note the fate which looms over every literary character—a shrinkage of person within representational space parallel to Enoch Robinson's within the space of narration. In this respect, the story does not oppose individual persons to collective forms, as the later novels commonly do; instead it opposes them to the specifically *aesthetic* forms which give them textual life— and efface their personhood.

The Adventure of Allegory

In "The Real Thing," the stamp of authenticity that makes persons representable—the real thing—is a matter of thing not person. Like the unnamed article produced at Woolett in *The Ambassadors* or a Poynton spoil, "thing" resides in "the abstract class of highly concrete entities—typical singularities and generic particulars."[10] Exactly what the word refers to may in fact be multiple; the question remains whether the will to classify that the term "real thing" implies belongs by rights to the Monarchs, to the narrator, or to James himself. In a sense not immediately obvious, however, "the real thing" comes to mean "the textual thing," which means that story has turned into allegory.

All three texts by James in this chapter can be read as allegories of a particular kind. "The Real Thing," however, treats what Tzvetan Todorov has called "the adventure of allegory itself."[11] Not merely an apologue, but rather a story about how apologues become constructed, it sketches the danger of representing person, and losing surface, through type or theme. It allegorizes the different possibilities by which literary character can be represented. Because it is the most "lifelike" of these possibilities, the "mimetic" component of character offers the least resistance to being absorbed into theme or synthetic artifice. This is especially true when fiction explores the adventures of allegory.

"In the sense of signing characters up to do a job and placing them . . . at the service of a power beyond themselves,"[12] apologue serves as, so to speak, the employment agency for agency. In the same way, James's story introduces the Monarchs in the process of looking for work; and however they may fare as artistic models, they do successfully hire on as synthetic constructs. As the story opens, however, the Monarchs (yet to be named by the story) are mistaken by the never-to-be-named artist-narrator for certain social types his business routinely

brings him into contact with: "I had, as I often had in those days . . .
an immediate vision of sitters. Sitters my visitors in this case proved to
be; but not in the sense I should have preferred" (110). In fact, upper
class though no longer moneyed, the couple have come to sit not for
their portraits (for which they would naturally pay), but as *models* for
illustrations (for which they expect to be paid). The Monarchs serve as
the means for art to work its magic, rather than the end for which it
might be expected to serve. The story begins, then, with a case of
mistaken identity.

In this first of the story's surface-level and thematic inversions, representation precedes the "real thing"; the Monarchs appear to the artist
first in his imagination—"I had as I often had in those days, *for the wish
was father to the thought*, an immediate vision of sitters"—and only
subsequently in his studio. We could say that along with these two
characters a "theme" has been introduced: the functioning and foregrounding of mimesis before a story's events actually occur.

Representation quickly descends to the level of reality, however, and
the narrator's expectations lower accordingly, for he discovers that he
has to accept a job rather than a commission. When confronted with
the paradox of his social "betters" asking to pose for hire, the artist
experiences a subtle but definite rise in station. His "standing" increases
as the couple change from one sort of "sitters" to another, falling
precipitously from clients to breadwinners. (To be a sitter means either
to sit for one's own portrait or to serve as the model for illustrations
which assure anonymity.) Economically speaking, consumers find
themselves sublated—both preserved and overcome—by the forces of
production. Semiotically speaking, the phenomenal image takes prece-
dence over its substance. On both levels the "real thing" now signifies
the capacity for representability, or "mimetic illusionism."

The Standing of Sitters

The particular kind of represented image one sits for in an artist's
studio—portrait or illustration—fixes the social position one assumes;
portraits, as the narrator declares, are "honorable," but illustrations are
merely "potboilers." Each gives social value concrete form through a
differentially valued artistic medium. Semiotic and economic axes together plot coordinates of value.

Portraits signify a fixed value in one of two ways. Either they preside

over private residences, as reference points within a closed and specialized sign system; or they extend their ambit to the public sphere—gal-
leries and museums—where they bathe in contemplative gazes which
carry them away. As variable capital, in Marx's terms, a portrait's
ideological values circulate undiminished, benefiting sitter and artist
alike.[13] Illustrations, by contrast, perform a subsidiary function as both
sign and money, usually accompanying a more important (textual) medium. James, in fact, explains this point in his preface to *The Golden
Bowl:* The "question of the general acceptability of illustration comes
up sooner or later, in these days, for the author of any text putting
forward illustrative claims (that is, producing an effect of illustration)
by its own intrinsic virtue and finding itself elbowed, on another
ground, by another and a competitive process" (*AN*, 331).[14] Endless
reproduction causes the anonymous quality of illustrations to increase
at the same time as it diminishes their intrinsic worth. And yet the same
dynamic is at work in this story between two competitive processes of
expression: ordinary (that is, experiential) and artistic (that is, representational).

As Hillis Miller has said in reference to Trollope's fiction, character
in its capacity as moral exemplar betokens "the free circulation of
regnant social values" (*ER*, 86).[15] But in "The Real Thing" it is rather
the *un*free circulation of values—itself morally suspect—which defines
"character" and "exemplarity," commodifying representability at the
expense of personal and social worth. Distinction, or "the real thing"
(as the Monarchs refer to themselves), becomes a kind of floating image
capital. How exactly, then, does "the real thing" express its owners?
What becomes of "the real thing" when its social, economic, artistic,
and semiotic values all fall prey to the same deflationary process?
Needless to say, all these questions involve something like the phenomenon which Marx called commodity fetishism, where "a relation
between men assumes the form of a relation between things."

Marx, one may recall, invokes Hegel's reflex category of (mis)recog-
nition to explain how for men as well as commodities what are in fact
structural effects in a network of relations appear on the contrary to be
natural properties. The analogy Marx uses is highly appropriate to
James's story: "For instance, one man is king only because other men
stand in the relation of subjects to him; they on the contrary imagine
they are subjects because he is king." For the Monarchs, however, this
process has shifted back into the terms of commodity fetishism: the

couple imagine that they are "real" because they are "the Monarchs," when in fact both the surplus value known as "the real thing" and their own "natural standing" possess value only insofar as they can be marketed.

In "The Real Thing," the normally defetishized nature of human relations in capitalism has exactly been refetishized, as though it were taken for granted that a relation between persons has assumed not only the form but the look of a relation between things; thus the Monarchs give themselves over to bondage before a master in the very midst of free market exchange. As a simple equation, selling here means exposing means losing. But then, all this seeming detour into economic theory really does not take us far from the narrator's studio at all, nor redirect us away from his own observations.

Thus, for the narrator, observing means "letting me take them in" (107), a phrase whose instrumentality can cut two ways: measurement or dupery. In fact, the vocabulary the narrator uses to describe his professional and semi-therapeutic relation to the Monarchs involves, at different times, "seizing," "drawing out," and "seeing"; all are used uncharitably. "In the pictorial sense I had already *seen* them. I had seized their type—I had already settled what I would do with it" (109). "Seizing on" the artistic and eschewing the nonartistic is an artist's privilege, the analogue to social privilege, which moneyed sitters exploit and make public.

The artist notes the Monarchs "professionally—[meaning not] as a barber or yet as a tailor"—and lights on what he calls their "frontage," that is, their visible distinction, a word one might apply to the conspicuous acreage fronting a stately home. But in "The Real Thing," "frontage," a word the narrator uses in passing, advertises rather one's bodily self—the front one shows to the world. It also, quite appropriately, recalls Levinas' analysis of the falsifying property of self-representation which I quoted in Chapter 1, "the caricature, allegory, or picturesque element which a person bears on his own face."[16]

In that respect, the Monarchs' substantiality as literary persons bows to the pressure of figuration. They represent characters in the strict sense of the term, *figures* rather than selves, persons, or individuals. The husband's title, "Major Monarch," appears doubly ludicrous, since he neither rules nor controls anything; the calling card which he makes a point of exhibiting perfectly captures the couple's reality—being reduced to pure sign. They are types of reduction—on the one hand, the upper classes reduced to job hunting and, on the other, persons reduced to figures.

As a keen observer of surface, the narrator quickly discerns the real state of the Monarchs' pictorial values in real life. He establishes for himself the Monarchs' "points"—their compositional values: "[Their] advantages struck me as preponderantly social; such as would help to make a drawing-room look well . . . 'Oh, I can fancy scenes in which you'd be quite natural.' And indeed I could see the slipshod rearrangements of stale properties—the stories I tried to produce pictures for without the exasperation of reading them—whose sandy tracts the good lady might help to people" (110, 115).

"The stories I tried to produce pictures for without the exasperation of reading them": such is the dialectic of life and story as rendered by "The Real Thing." Hence the narrator asks Mrs. Monarch to don a costume—used clothing—in order to conceal "the real thing" which her own outfits radiate below the neck. Mr. Monarch wonders out loud about the costume's general use, and the narrator remarks, "I had to confess that they were [used], and I mentioned further that some of them (I had a lot of genuine, greasy, last-century things) had served their times, a hundred years ago, on living, world-stained men and women" (115). Mr. Monarch replies, "We'll put on anything that *fits.*" And the narrator says in turn: "Oh, I arrange that—they fit in the pictures" (115). Of course by playing on the word "fit," he willfully doubles Monarch's meaning here (just as he does with the couple representationally). Monarch swallows his pride and accepts doffing his world-stained reality for that which has sheathed others—as long as the clothing fits his person; but the narrator in turn subtracts the person, and construes "fit" to signify merely a match of clothing to scene.

Think of the problem of *fit* as marking a transition between evolving stages of what Amelie Rorty calls the "person concept" from, say, "character" to "individual"—except that here the movement is retrograde: from individual back to character: "I was vexed at [Monarch's not having] read with me the moral of our fruitless collaboration, the lesson that, in the deceptive atmosphere of art, even the highest respectability may fail of being plastic" (131).

They had bowed their heads in bewilderment to the perverse and cruel law in virtue of which the real thing could be so much less precious than the unreal. "Somehow, with all their perfections I didn't easily believe in them. After all they were amateurs, and the ruling passion of my life was the detestation of the amateur. Combined with this was another perversity—an innate preference for the represented subject over the real one: the defect of the real one was so apt to be a lack of representation. I liked things that appeared; then one was sure" (113–114).

Allowing for modifications in voice and tone, such sentiments coincide exactly with James's own in his prefaces. "Character," in the sense of fixed dispositions, habits, and traits—stable indices of value over time—looks back to a Victorian sensibility: characteristics "stand for" ultimate principles which guide choices. The artist, in contrast, stresses staple modernist principles, the kind which literary modernism was pledged to and which nineteenth-century fiction simply could not have imagined.

Thus, in repudiating the Monarchs, the narrator perhaps passes judgment on the obsolescence of Victorian character. Perhaps "The Real Thing" allegorizes just this transition from a class-restrictive notion of characters who answer to a governing moral typology to one more mobile, more "plastic." The Monarchs encapsulate the perfect emptied type of a type—class abstraction manifested as exemplars of an abstract class. Perhaps in this story James critiques his own devotion to typification and "the stability of immaterial forms."[17]

But even if it may seem to read against the grain of James's own self-aware aesthetic (or rather precisely because it might), I would prefer to interpret the story's attenuation of character and its artist-narrator's hand in "seizing" and "drawing out" his subjects as an allegory of narrative ethics and, in particular, of "aesthetic" responsibility. Aesthetic boundaries extend beyond the limit of technical problems to encompass choices about the delicate and potentially harmful relationship of "author" to "hero."

The Sense of the Creatures Themselves

But hasn't James already beaten me to this point? Like much of James's fiction, doesn't "The Real Thing" simply moot questions about aesthetic responsibility because of its purposeful fudging of boundaries between narrator, "implied narrator," and author? If "The Real Thing" replaces the longer novels' systematic inquiry into intersubjective knowledge and the relation between personality and aesthetic form with an exploration of more local and immediate problems of representation, it also significantly shifts the dynamics of textual relations.[18] Thus whatever allegory of character James intends, or whatever aesthetic philosophy he promotes, the story has its own to tell.

The title of Bakhtin's early essay "Author and Hero in Aesthetic Activity" names both that allegory and that philosophy in short form. As I have mentioned in earlier references to it, the essay details the ethical constraints on acts of artistic representation. In contrast the following is what James might have understood by the phrase "representational ethics":

> [The fictive picture] began for [Turgenev] almost always with the vision of some person or persons, who hovered before him, soliciting him, as the active or passive figure, interesting him and appealing to him as they were and by what they were. He saw them, in that fashion, as *disponibles*, saw them subject to the chances, the complications of existence, and saw them vividly, but then had to find for them the right relations, those that would most bring them out; to imagine, to invent and select and piece together the situations most favourable to the sense of the creatures themselves, the complications they would be most likely to produce and to feel. (*AN*, 42–43)

Obviously, the little scene which this passage rehearses describes the identical circumstances facing the artist-narrator at the outset of "The Real Thing." Although James's formalist inclinations predominate, his "philosophy" here folds aesthetic and ethical concerns together, specifying an artist's twin duties as "boundless freedom and 'moral' reference." But "The Real Thing" suggests that philosophy's natural extension. The artist-narrator does not scruple to find the "right relations" which best minister to artistic values instead of to the persons who represent them. Indeed, it is the very "sense of the creatures themselves," together with their solicitations, which obstruct imagination and, from the artist's perspective, neutralize his entirely self-interested live-entering. His appraisals of the Monarchs remain just that—reductive, indelicate, remorselessly aesthetic.

When Monarch ventures, "We thought that if you ever have to do people like us, we might be something like it. *She*, particularly—for a lady in a book, you know," the narrator thinks to himself: "I was so amused by them that, *to get more of it, I did my best to take their point of view*; and though it was an embarrassment to find myself appraising physically, as if they were animals on hire or useful blacks, a pair whom I should have expected to meet only in one of the relations in which criticism is tacit, I looked at Mrs. Monarch judicially enough to be able to exclaim, after a moment, with conviction: 'Oh yes, a lady in a book!' She was singularly like a bad illustration" (110; my emphasis). Major Monarch receives his stamp of disapproval in this way: "The case was worse with the Major—nothing I could do would keep *him* down, so that he became useful only for the representation of brawny giants. I adored variety and range, I cherished human accidents, the illustrative note; I wanted to characterize closely, and the thing in the world I most hated was the danger of being ridden by a type" (120).

In point of fact, the last sentence reverses customary interpersonal behavior in real life, or rather pictorializes it; all of us hang suspended between the individual and the type, requiring a careful balancing of the competing demands on recognition of each. What distresses the narrator so greatly is the Monarchs' surplus of character, what Lacan named the *objet petit à*, their signal inability to be anything but what they reliably are. (Indeed, Lacan defines "the real thing" as just this: the remainder of the Real within appearance, Reality, we could say, as supplementary irritant.) What the narrator denies them as a consequence is his ethical surplus, his constructive live-entering, the renewable promise of a nonarbitary point of support outside them.

He values in his subjects only their mimetic potential for synthetic transformation, the capacity to imitate life by suppressing self-identity. In a real sense, the Monarchs come to him, as I have implied, already "characterized"—like bad illustrations, creatures of one dimension, stock characters from an Edwardian novel—this, one must say, is their own fault, their own fetishized and self-debasing investment in "frontage." (Properly speaking, then, the story rehearses a pragmatic ethics in a very basic sense, which means simply that both the Monarchs and the artist are culpable, each in different ways.) The narrator receives them, in turn, with authorial contempt, not unlike the derision James reserves for illustrations in his preface to *The Golden Bowl*.

Frontage Capital

The narrator reintroduces the economy of representation and its connection with character when he notes explicitly of the Monarchs that "their good looks had been their capital, and they had good-humouredly made the most of the career that this resource marked out for them" (112). In assessing them, he decides that such capital would best be invested in commercial advertisements, the lowest rung on the ladder of mimesis. First portraiture, then sketchbook illustrations, and, finally, an advertisement for soap, with "we always use it" pinned on the Monarchs' bosoms—thus does their value as persons become fully commodified. But as the narrator escorts them downward through the division of labor, the Monarchs make known their past expertise in an allied technology of painting, that of photography; and this new venue for "frontage capital" introduces a new angle on the specific conditions of pictorial/textual representation.

In this case, of course, photography does not signify the unself-conscious depiction of identity, the catching people unawares one sees, for instance, in Walker Evans' famous "Subway Portraits." It means posing and class privilege. Mrs. Monarch explains that she and her husband have been photographed "*immensely*," that photographers have always pursued them for snapshots, without their ever having to pay. Photographs function for them as tokens of nonreciprocal exchange, a relationship exactly reversed in the artist's studio.

Although on the surface photographs seem a vulgar and cheap commodity, the Monarchs retain some control over their circulation in public: though they can "be got in the shops," their autographs accompany their images. Thus notarized, such photographs, in effect, act as portable portraits, a debased but still privatized medium for representation. While it is true that "the real thing" has considerably fallen in value since their photographic heyday, the Monarchs remain on intimate terms with being viewed, captured, "seen." Major Monarch inadvertently stokes the fires of irony when he relates of his wife, "when I married her, she was known as the Beautiful Statue" (112).

For frontage's sake, the Monarchs sacrifice their value through a downward spiral of servitude: as illustrations for "stale properties," as models for an artist who takes their measure and finds it wanting, and finally and most pitiably, as his actual domestic servants—failures at representability, but willing to take any part they can get. Nor do they remain oblivious to the debasement in value: "Naturally it's more for *the figure* that we thought of going in," says the Major, disclosing his wish to preserve their anonymity, behind added-on physiognomies.

Face-currency, even if circulated, returns undiminished in value in the form of portraits; figure-currency, the reduction of persons literally to their bodies, circulates unowned and unidentified, never returned. Their persons already given over to the abstraction of type, the Monarchs accept surrender to, quite literally, "the play of forms."

But the Monarchs are not the only players here. The narrator, like James, also accepts a role in a market economy; he (and implicitly James as well) stands not outside the system of representation personified by the Monarchs, but rather within it. If the story sketches more than an allegory of debased personhood, as I am arguing, then the narrator remains hardly unaffected.

The deflationary introduction of "the real thing" into the narrator's work gradually begins to diminish his market-value as well. A friend of the artist derides the work in which the Monarchs appear (with an irony which escapes them), as looking like "a photograph or a copy of a photograph" which contains "a big hole" in the form of Major and Mrs. Monarch themselves. "Material culture incorporates into itself the frailties of sentience" (in Elaine Scarry's useful observation).[19] The artist's representational economy absorbs the perceptual flaws of narrator and couple alike.

The narrator merely dramatizes a process that precedes and includes him, placing in wider circulation values that have reached him in an already debased form. The Monarchs remain all along nonplused by his treatment of them, and by his preferences for his lower-class models and part-time servants. Why "make" Miss Churm into a lady, when Mrs. Monarch is a lady "who's already made?" (117). Why fabricate and fictionalize when all the time "the real thing" stands at the ready? The answers elude the Monarchs because they fail to understand the unmooring of sign—the real thing—from its referent: their intrinsic worth, at least as it is externally perceived, depends on their representability, which possesses little or no intrinsic value of its own—soup-bones at best, we might say.

Similarly, the narrator's customary Cockney model Miss Churm, "so little in herself, and yet so much in others" (116), and Oronte the unemployed Italian model, "a bankrupt orange-monger, but a treasure" (124), produce a high representational yield because they are social ciphers, in the narrator's classist estimation—intrinsically empty, valuable only insofar as they "carry off" mimetic transfer. Miss Churm bears "no positive stamp" (120) (even her name "pronounces" affected charm), and can therefore bear the impress of artifice—permutable, plastic, synthetic character—sooner than the loss of which, the narrator notes, "everything was to be sacrificed."

In the artist's eyes, every attitude Oronte strikes, even genuine supplication, suggests a pose, a picture; his representational value is secure precisely because of his ability to present even real need "pictorially."

This ability to lose oneself in others—call it "the fictive thing"—possesses far greater value than any reality these models might possess in themselves. The Monarchs, contrariwise, "the real thing, but always the same thing" (119), live their value unsuccessfully, condemned, even in the midst of real need, to being real, thus unrepresentable.

With the introduction of Miss Churm and Oronte, the sequence of inversions with which the story begins comes to an end. The servants pose for royalty, and the Monarchs, unwittingly, model for menials. In a bitterly ironic final touch, resigned to their unrepresentability, the Monarchs become, not merely play the part of, servants. "If my servants were my models, my models might be my servants. They would reverse the parts—the others would sit for the ladies and gentlemen, and *they* would do the work" (132).[20]

Face Capital

"There is a fictional existence with a vengeance," says Stanley Cavell. "The Real Thing" displays it in no uncertain terms. It shows how intricately webs of exchange and signification substitute for webs of interlocution, how quickly they follow in the wake of the actual world's bending to the force of artifice. As if to fill in the gap left by demands on recognition and acknowledgment no longer exercised, sign and economic values circulate viciously. If characters signify to one another in this story, they do so entirely *as* signs, recyclable like Miss Churm or in-significant like the Monarchs. The thin membrane between persons, as James calls it elsewhere, yields easily through substitution: the narrator substitutes thing for thing, fictional for the real—the servants host alien selves, the sitters confuse their surface value with their ostensibly primary value as individuals, Monarchs and servants trade places. In each case, substitution mystifies intersubjective encounter, rather than acting as its guarantor, the placing oneself in hostage-for-another which Levinas in his later work describes as an intersubjective norm.

In a famous parable by one of James's American contemporaries, class reversal partakes of equal parts live-entering and substitution, as prince and pauper learn about, by "becoming," the other. In "The Real Thing," by contrast, Monarchs and servants—sign-functions rather than mimetic entities—learn little about the price of fiction. In Levinasian terms, the story allows no third term outside of sign and theme; it illustrates the aesthetic slippage which takes place in the absence of a countervailing expressive discourse. The Monarchs, already self-the-matized, so to speak, by the enchantment of form, supply the artist with merely the first in a chain of representational screens which serve as his customary métier.

(Not unimportantly, expression ill serves both parties. The Mon-archs seem perpetually bedeviled on the plane of language; their awk-wardness in correcting the narrator's initial mistake simply abets his confusion as to the reason for their visit; thus he must "draw them" out, something he must do continually. For his part, the narrator also falters at crucial moments: "'Ah, you're—you're—a—?' I began, as soon as I had mastered my surprise. I couldn't bring out the dingy word 'models': it seemed to fit the case so little" (109).[21] Moreover, when he does not trap the couple for his amusement in word play, the narrator stonewalls their inarticulate entreaties: "I was not obliged to answer these remarks—I was only obliged to place my sitters" (126)—a hard fact of technologies of representation, perhaps, but also a transparent indictment of authorial attitude.)

What's wanted here, as I noted in connection with *Lord Jim*, is *signification* in its Levinasian sense, "the signification of the face break-ing through all form" (*TI*, 75). But except for the Monarchs as husband and wife, all the story's characters fail decisively in facing each other in this sense—an ironically fitting touch, perhaps, in the context of modeling and portraiture, the very place where faces are stared at for hours on end. (The Major's lodgings are untenable to him without his wife's presence, as opposed to the narrator's "compositional" brand of interior space, which is to be "filled out" or "peopled.")

If the face for Levinas *is* signification, the bedrock upon which communication can then go forward, the Monarchs' frontage in itself merits little attention: either they sit for colossal figures minus the head, or they ruin the drawings in which their faces appear—"I had not the least desire that my models should be discoverable in my picture" (126). In the *regard* of others which is mere vision, not sym-pathy, the Monarchs neither live nor breathe, but they do, sadly, have their being.

Author and Hero

Just as face for Levinas signifies the impossibility of slipping away and being replaced by someone else, the authority of *here am I*, so clan-destinity introduces a gap in discourse—the impunity of Gyges, for whom, unseen, the world becomes a spectacle: "Thus silence is not a simple absence of speech; speech lies in the depths of silence like a laughter perfidiously held back. It is the inverse of language: the interlocutor has given a sign, but has declined every interpretation; this is the silence that terrifies" (*TI*, 91).

Stanley Cavell, too, insists that to remain hidden before another converts him or her "into a character." But as I have claimed, the story's self-situating extends beyond the allegorical frame of textual representation as such, which it shares with other tales by James as well as with much modernist fiction. Indeed, this story looks back perhaps ultimately to Hawthorne, where "anxiety of influence" means something closer to an author's nervousness over peopling his fictions rather than a reaction-formation to literary competition.[22]

Obviously, the several diegetic levels in this story interconnect. And as I have implied all along, willy-nilly Henry James himself falls under the deflationary "Fall" this story records. Indeed, my reading of "The Real Thing" as ethical deconstruction leads finally to a question one wants to put to James himself, "How much of the *I* who shapes the characters is in fact an *I* who has been shaped by characters?"[23] For my purposes in this study, then, the "adventure of allegory itself" at the level of character ultimately bows to its counterpart at the level where narrator and implied author converge, where representational ethics *governs* (à la Velásquez), and not simply resides in, text.

James would identify the story as an example of the genre he calls in his prefaces "the concise anecdote." Although it is not the "ideal" form of the nouvelle[24] illustrated by the other texts in this chapter, *The Aspern Papers* and *In The Cage*, and although James's own few words about it in his preface give no hint of the importance which I ascribe to it, "The Real Thing" in my view subsumes within a minor work a major function—a small model of narrative ethics, a lesson of and for the Master.

As much as James distances himself from the story's first-person narrator (as he does from that narrator's counterparts in *The Aspern Papers* and *The Sacred Fount*), a disturbing continuity in their roles persists. (It is tempting to imagine James's tongue planted resolutely in cheek in the following sentence from the story's beginning: "Perhaps [the Monarchs] wished to be done together—in which case they ought to have brought a *third person* to break the news"; 167, my emphasis.) At an extremely simplistic level, of course, James preserves the clandestinity of authorial silence; his is a world behind appearances, as

Levinas describes it, an-archic. In "The Art of Fiction," James describes the artistic and moral senses as meeting at one crucial point: "that is in light of the very obvious truth that the deepest quality of a work of art will always be the mind of the producer."[25] But in this essay as elsewhere, James's frequent analogies between pictorial representation and the novel only compound the blurring of authorial and narratorial levels so evident in "The Real Thing."

Bakhtin suggests the stakes in keeping such levels distinct (except in cases, of course, when the author knowingly ambiguates):

> Before the countenance of the hero finally takes place as a stable and necessary whole, the hero is going to exhibit a great many grimaces, random masks, wrong gestures, and unexpected actions, depending on those emotional-volitional reactions and personal whims of the author, through the chaos of which he is compelled to work his way in order to reach an authentic valuational attitude. In order to see one we apparently know well—think how many masking layers must first be removed from his face, layers that were sedimented upon his face by our own fortuitous reactions and attitudes. (*AA*, 6)

James's prefaces to his novels testify to the elaborateness with which he wrestled his fiction into form—their "geometry" and "composition," single and multiple centers of consciousness, *données* and middles. So "The Real Thing," I would argue, reveals the armature upon which that consummated form rests, the manikins, so to speak, who lie beneath the stable and whole countenances of the entities who "people" his fiction. The story depicts an artist already faced with the necessity of deconstructing the real masks before him in order to construct more aesthetically perfect ones of his own.

The last sentence in the passage from Bakhtin goes to the heart of the matter, since it stresses the composition, the making up of other people, which "seizing their type" imposes; formulated, pinned, and wriggling on the wall, the Monarchs share Prufrock's fate. They stand before the narrator as James's characters stand before him; indeed, like the perspectival lines in *Las Meninas*, an angle of vision connects character, narrator, and author in hierarchical formation, the author, behind his *regard souverain*, being the true "Monarch," or to echo James himself, the "muffled majesty" of the piece. A direct line passes from author to narrator and makes them coincide across levels of text.

In exposing that line, "The Real Thing" proposes a representational ethics behind and below both James's technical considerations and his stated moral purpose: "the perfect dependence of the 'moral' sense of a work of art on the amount of felt life concerned in producing it" (*AN*, 31). The story, in other words, uncovers a formal ethics behind a morality of form and, in this sense (analogous to Mary Richardson's behind-the-back "undercutting" of Venus and Velásquez),[26] speaks over the head of narrator and author alike.

This is one sense in which I intended my observation at the end of the previous chapter that a text can take on a life of its own, an ethical autonomy which speaks against the grain of the text. And it is also how one might read the story's "accidental," almost Levinasian turn at its end, when it conveys a glimpse of submerged expression momentarily overturning sign. As the Monarchs transform themselves into servants, the narrator betrays the trace of acknowledgment fleetingly but negatively present when he says, "When it came over me, *the latent eloquence* of what they were doing, I confess that my drawing was blurred for a moment—the picture swam" (132).

The value of an admittedly curious text like "The Real Thing" lies in its almost casual delineation of narrative ethics, as its narrator draws the faces of his subjects, and as James draws through them some moral of his own. "Viewers," observes Jay Cantor, "need not quite acknowledge that they too imagine the world in the image and so participate in what it represents; rather one pretends that one *sees* it."[27]

Rather than having taken a longer and more important work like *The Portrait of a Lady* or *The Wings of the Dove* to show how this process works across the length of a novel, I have lavished attention on a minor work to explore the implications *there on view* that authors can be thought of as viewers of a very specialized and elusive sort. As Hawthorne knew, authors' houses of fiction are sometimes more Baudelairean than Jamesian; even when it comes to James's own, writers of fiction often play host to tenants they themselves may remain unaware of. The following transitional interlude features a text for which this question of host and guest becomes an issue in itself; we are shown into a house where thresholds are transgressed, not merely viewed, and where the "bones" of authorial de-realization become so many skeletons in the closet.

The Aspern Papers: A Bridge about Borders

Although the title *The Aspern Papers* implies for the story's narrator a merely literary history, the double figure it conceals—property versus propriety—opens out to encompass both text and person. However, the conventional moral question that figure raises—which has priority: the ethics of social relations on the one hand or loyalty to a valuable aesthetic good on the other?—too blithely uncouples the interrelated senses of "proper" and "property" which the story's depth structure of ethics keeps entangled.

I propose an alternative figure for reading the text: habitation/in-habitation, which focuses particular attention on the story's mapping of author's, readers', and characters' respective domains and on the transgression of boundaries between them. Additionally, it has the virtue of canvassing the many figures of lodging, lodgers, possession(s), and borders which pervade the story. Borders, to select just one of these, remain at issue throughout. A border separates real and fictional worlds; the border between the author and his work provokes the narrator's desire. Residential and domestic borders challenge his passage into the world of the villa; homonymy makes him a boarder; and finally, of course, there are the Bordereaus (like Marcher, May, or Monarch, a classic Jamesean cognomen).

Just as the story does not casually link the Bordereau household to concepts of the domestic (from L. *domus*, house) and economic (from Greek *oikonomikos*, house-management), so these different senses of "border" do not fortuitously intersect. Think of them as different denominations within a common currency. And indeed, for this story as well as the last, economics bounds the terrain through which the story's characters and its meanings travel.[28]

Once again, James's prefaces illuminate his fiction's thematic and linguistic structures by suggesting one additional mode of crossing borders. I quote from the preface to *The Aspern Papers:* "I delight in a palpable imaginable *visitable* past—in the nearer distances and the clearer mysteries, the marks and signs of a world we may reach over to as by making a long arm we grasp an object at the other end of our own table" (*AN*, 164). The proprietary and cavalier manner (Levinas' "movement without a searchlight") in which James takes possession of the past closely parallels his narrator's ability to step into Jeffrey Aspern's past by taking up residence in the Bordereaus' present. The story eventually questions such easy access, and poses a parallel between the bar on reclamation which memory imposes and the constraints on untroubled passage into others' lives.

Before I discuss that parallel, however, I want briefly to survey some of the story's inflections on borders and border-crossings, and get the lay of its land. "Intimacy" and "inhabitation," we could say, serve as the terms of Bakhtinian *vzhivanie* which *The Aspern Papers* expresses as modes of parasitism. Bakhtin developed his concept, as I have said, to counter an uncritical notion of empathy by insisting upon the integrity of relational borders; respect for persons' "outsideness" is a sine qua non. In the narrator's hands, however, live-entering acquires the sinister overtone of infiltrating others' confidence, of occupying their premises—residential and cognitive—on false pretences. And in this story, premises are first and foremost matters of property.[29]

"Confidence" becomes the means by which the narrator insinuates himself all through the story; its first sentence—"I had taken Mrs Prest into my confidence"[30]—sets into motion a lubricious circuit as the word then moves from person to person, context to context. Its two sides—trust and trickery—are this story's way to say *heim* and *unheimlich*. And indeed, the narrator takes up residence in the confidence Tita Bordereau extends him, as surely as he takes lodgings in her aunt's house. This initial colloquy rehearses one lengthy confidence game, itself merely a prelude to the longer one with Tita's aunt, Juliana.

Each of these successive encounters involves a transgression of both borders and Bordereaus, and together with the narrator's uncanny communion with the "spirit" of Jeffrey Aspern, they constitute what passes for live-entering in the text. Where Bakhtin's intersubjective principles aim at enriching the boundary between two facing consciousnesses, however, the narrator's aim at effacing it. If he can be said to "live into" others' particular set of circumstances, it is only to wrest something away from them.

A precedent for such parasitism can be found in the narrator's already extreme and somewhat pathetic adulation of Jeffrey Aspern. When Tita reports to him that her aunt thought Aspern "a god," he takes it as "direct testimony" (52) of what he himself had always felt: "One doesn't defend one's god: one's god is in himself a defence" (12). Of course, like other gods before his, the narrator's has absconded (an unfortunate model for the narrator's own retreat at story's end).

The narrator does, however, possess two primary means of communion: reading Aspern's work, and organizing, legitimizing, and perpetuating Aspern's "truth," whether bibliographical or biographical. In either case, the narrator projects himself, "lives into," a fantasy of encountering the author in the text, a fantasy extended to places Aspern merely visited—as though they posted signs reading "Jeffrey Aspern slept here." His fantasy compels the narrator to infiltrate hearts and hearths alike, in a perverse metaphysics of presence whereby former lovers are presumed to "channel" the indwelling spirit of the now dead poet.

This is a sorry sort of *vzhivanie*. As a votary trying to vault himself into his deity's innermost precincts, the narrator succumbs to what Max Weber called "the spell cast by persons," an always available and defective mode of aesthetic transference.[31] His various attempts to conjure up Aspern in his absence constitute a kind of live-entering by proxy, a cult of the intercessor which parallels the narrator's hagiographic romance with the text: "The sacred relics [the papers] . . . after all were under my hand—they had not escaped me yet; and they made my life continuous, in a fashion, with the illustrious life they had touched at the other end" (38).

The narrator affirms his standing in an elitist clerisy most extravagantly in his vision of Aspern as a benevolent guardian angel: "I had invoked him and he had come; he hovered over me half the time; it was as if his bright ghost had returned to earth to tell me that he had regarded the affair as his own no less than mine and that we should see it fraternally, cheerfully to a conclusion" (37).

I would argue here that the narrator's fantasy of authorial inhabitation in the text does not simply betray an egregious tendency toward intentional fallacy; it coincides with his delusion that authors are "housed" in the persons they affect, that one can hear their voices reverberate, and look them in the face by looking into a pair of eyes which theirs had reflected. Just as the narrator lives out that fantasy by lodging with the Bordereaus, parasite to host, so he inveigles Juliana to perform the same connective function for him that he imagines she served for Jeffrey Aspern. And by inhabiting Tita's affections in order to plunder her legacy, he completes the circuit.

"We stare at people in fiction as we would never do in life," writes a contemporary critic.[32] But such staring nevertheless indicates a certain form of acknowledgment, as Cavell reminds us—rejection, for instance, or passive witnessing. Tita cannot resist the narrator's importunate gazing, his solicitations to her to come out of the dark. Nor can Aspern—whether in *bio* or *graphy*—contest the obsessive scrutiny he has no choice but to endure. But in Juliana, the narrator encounters a face, in Levinasian terms, which will not dissimulate its forms, will not disclose itself; it remains defiantly "impenetrable."[33] At the doorstep to her person and her house, Juliana ensures that outsideness will not be carelessly breached; she, as it were, puts the narrator "in his place."

In Juliana's case, the story's various metaphors of lodging or inhabitation become conspicuously economic. The narrator's propensity for transgressing personal boundaries and infiltrating other consciousnesses founders when an ostensibly social relation becomes nakedly monetary and commodified. He registers his frustration early in the story, having just met Juliana: "it had begun to act on my nerves that with these women so associated with Aspern the pecuniary question should constantly come back" (32). His interpretive excess, the tyranny of semiosis he imposes—"There was no end to the questions it was possible to ask about them and no end to the answers it was not possible to frame" (48)—is persistently flattened by Juliana's relentless conversion of terms into economic values. (Indeed, "terms," for Juliana, represents the linguistic and economic counterpart to the narrator's "confidence.")[34]

Conversation between the narrator and Juliana takes the form of a transaction, a bargain struck. When Juliana receives the narrator into her apartment, the terms of "intimacy" and "inhabitation" shift to accommodate the link between receiving guests and receiving payment. As the narrator construes it (with characteristic self-importance), "I had descended on her one day and taught her to calculate" (68). In any case, the transaction becomes an occasion for forced entry and entry denied, and traces the link between home and inhabitation, parasite and host.

Presumably, the narrator's mercantile role, if conveniently fudged by him, never entirely eludes Juliana: "You talk as if you were a tailor" (70). Indeed, as far as securing Aspern's papers goes—his only aim in "inhabiting" the Bordereaus—he never amounts to anything more than a boarder in Juliana's sibylline eyes, an alien guest (as the etymology of "guest" nicely ambiguates) to be kept at bay. As he perhaps never fully understands, he joins the company of the Bordereaus as another of his story's victims; the severe narrative ethics of the story dictates that having feigned his own narrative and elicited others' in bad faith, the narrator becomes his story's topic, not its master.

The economic/semiotic circuit in *The Aspern Papers* comes to revolve finally around a concrete object: a cameo-sized portrait of Aspern. Not only does this portrait objectify aesthetic, monetary, and ethical value, but it also magnetically attracts to it the various filings, as it were, of theme and figure I have specified so far. Most obviously, it stands for the economic basis for the narrator's presence at the Villa. The narrator pays exorbitantly for his lodgings, the money being a compensatory legacy for Tita. Juliana precisely answers the narrator's personal and social extortion of Tita with a blatantly commercial one of her own.

Second, the portrait stands for the money which Aspern's papers can realize. As a "publishing scoundrel" (89), the narrator wishes to secure the commodity value of the papers, however nobly he strikes the aesthetic pose. The portrait represents this commodification materially. It is always potentially for sale, and at the end of the story it indeed changes hands, finding its way into the narrator's own. That may signify his continued "possession" by Aspern's spirit, but more important it conveys the nonliquidity of the narrator's social currency; like the portrait, the narrator's sympathies have no real exchange value: they never really leave home, in an Odyssean movement of return from the "same back to the same."

Third, the portrait offers to the narrator the most potent *sign* which his overactive semiotic machinery can work upon. Does the portrait signify the papers and their accident of ownership and possession? That is, does whoever owns the portrait own the papers, or will the portrait merely have to substitute for the papers as sign for referent. Is Juliana's disclosure of it a potential deal, a test, or a trick? (For Tita, certainly, the portrait ultimately signifies the failure of the narrator's confidence, of his attempt to pass from mere inmate to intimate.)

Fourth and last, it represents materially the attempted transposition of aesthetic and intersubjective values. It represents the division between them as finally secured—again, economically, in the form of a bargain. And it represents the difference in respective value—how the price of art and the price of personal integrity stand in regard to each other, like the narrator and Tita at story's end.

The narrator of *The Aspern Papers*, like his counterpart in "The Real Thing," hunts for value (a quality Marx ascribed to capitalist and miser alike). The latter traffics in image capital, bent on turning an artistic as well as a financial profit on liquid commodities of plastic character; Marx would call him a miser who has come to his senses, because he circulates his exchange-values (regardless of the personhood they debase) in order to realize whatever return he can.[35] The narrator of *The Aspern Papers*, in contrast, is a capitalist gone mad. He converts even social relations into hoarded artistic capital. In this respect, however, the story neatly juxtaposes one kind of hoarding with another—Juliana's semiotic thrift, her refusal to let private meanings circulate publicly (as her dying accusation—"you publishing scoundrel"—makes abundantly clear).

In *The Aspern Papers*, aesthetic duty operates economically, as a struggle for value; social duty operates similarly, as a matter of house management, and so also a struggle for value. However, the narrator's extravagance within the one clarifies his parsimony in the other. As he lives into art and Aspern, he acts as host and parasite both, never at home, never *en soi*, always extra-vagant (as Thoreau would say) from his own borders. But in his effect on others, in crossing over their separate thresholds, he merely gives the impression of leaving himself in order to face and make present the other, make him or her *other*. To the degree that he remains always at home, he stays paradoxically always an exile. To the degree that he infiltrates the homes of others, he brings with him the very spirit of the unhomely—"the uncanny."

Does the "unreliability" which motivates such behavior finally explain the story's real ethical burden? For, as narrator in addition to plotter, he inspires nothing but distrust. "The one who has the word 'I' at his or her disposal," writes Cavell in his essay on *Lear*, "has the quickest device for concealing himself." The narrator's perceptions may just as easily be misperceptions, his construals, misconstruals, and thereby he forfeits the measure of believability which readers might accord him. Even at the end, the narrator incriminates himself: he writes to Tita that he has sold the portrait, sending her a larger sum than he expected to get for it, but he lies: he keeps the portrait for himself.

In *The Rhetoric of Fiction*, Wayne Booth points to James's revision of the text's final sentence: from "When I look at it my chagrin at the loss of the letters becomes almost intolerable" to "When I look at it, I can scarcely bear my loss—I mean of the precious papers." Booth reads the revised sentence as a sign of the narrator's self-awareness.[36] But if the real nature of his loss does in fact suggest itself to him, it still remains inconsistent with the narrator's tone in the rest of the story, which is, after all, a restrospective account.

Booth emphasizes just this dissonance in narrative voice as the great defect of *The Aspern Papers*. Three voices alternate, he argues—the narrator's self-betrayals, his evocations of the past, and a blend of the two; each competes for the readers' attention and, more important, their trust, their confidence. "We are confined," Booth says, "to the drama of [the narrator's] scheming" (359), forced as a result to hear the voice ring false even in his moments of plangent reverie. (One obvious way to specify the reader's role in *The Aspern Papers'* economy of representation, then, would emphasize the way in which the narrator coaxes and inhabits our reading of him at the same time as he insinuates himself into the lives of his fellow characters.) By referring to these moments as "straightforward . . . which, taken out of context, might be indistinguishable from James's own voice" (361), Booth hits upon the important connection with James's theory of memory which I mentioned above.

If the narrator effectively insinuates himself into Aspern's past, James has already provided a model for such license in his image of the "long arm grasp[ing] an object at the other end of our table."[37] Rather than being undermined by an inconsistency of voice, at the level of representational ethics *The Aspern Papers* carefully aligns memory and defective modes of live-entering as essentially similar mechanisms. In "Author and Hero in Aesthetic Activity" Bakhtin contrasts two forms of memory: memory of one's own life, a retrieval of its content, and memory of another's life, "the golden key to the aesthetic consummation of a person": "Memory is an approach to the other from the standpoint of his axiological consummatedness. In a certain sense, memory is hopeless; but on the other hand, only memory knows how to value . . . an already finished life, a life that is totally present-on-hand" (*AA*, 107).

Similarly, in his early work Levinas casts the structure of ethics as the structure of time. The approach of the Other is always oncoming and unforeseeable, and thus the very image of futurity. But it summons the past as well, inscribing within the subject the trace of an immemorial past, a condition of being always already responsible.[38]

The narrator can bestow no such temporal plenitude in the face of alterity, neither the aesthetic justification described by Bakhtin nor Levinas' exorbitant responsibility. His pathological relation to Aspern's past deforms both his ethical duty to the Bordereaus' present and his own self-identity: except for the possible ambiguity in the story's last sentence, his mercenary impulses remain intact. If he bestows the shape of "an event, a plot, a storyline," in Bakhtin's words, on Aspern or the Bordereaus, he does so not for the sake of valuational and consummating form, but for property. Indeed, the next to last words in "The Real

Thing" could as easily belong to this narrator: "I'm content to pay the price—for the memory."

Thus the story adds to the hoarding of artistic capital and the hoarding of meaning, the hoarding of time. And thus the narrator stands revealed as a self adrift in a world which ministers to persons. As Amelie Rorty puts it, "The continuity of the self is established by memory . . . it is difficult to think of bundles of properties without an owner, especially when the older idea of the person as an agent and decision-maker is still implicit."[39] Being content to pay the price for the memory not only shows the narrator's neurotic subservience to Aspern's biography but, more important, exposes the defective narrative-ethical sense which allows him to exploit the Bordereaus' seeming "plotlessness."

As I argued for "The Real Thing," *The Aspern Papers* makes its own demands outside the narrator's ken. Yet if, as before, we posit a straight line from *implied* author through narrator to "authorial audience,"[40] we sidestep the questions raised by James's own stance, which he records in his preface. For his acquistive view of ransacking the past does not differ much from the narrator's own. In the context of this story, James's figure for the artist—a dog burying and digging up its bone of value—calls to mind instead a miser at his hoard.

I am claiming that at those moments in the text when Booth suspects the presence of James's own voice overlaid on top of the narrator's, he does not err. The first-person narrators in this story and "The Real Thing" speak doggedly, as it were, with voices resembling their master's. But what Booth must consequently impute to James's lapse in artistic sense—the delicate balance of morality and form—I ascribe to the text's autonomous level of representational ethics instead, a level which again speaks over its author's head.

Arguments about textual autonomy in James's work are not new. Hillis Miller, for instance, correctly locates an operative level of such autonomy in both James's fiction—*What Maisie Knew*—and his criticism—the preface to *The Golden Bowl*.[41] But he errs far more seriously, I think, than Booth in confining it to linguistic autonomy—a law of unreadability whose "productive" but necessitarian force the text exemplifies. Rather, a text such as *The Aspern Papers* or "The Real Thing" shows how narrative can trip up attempts by author as well as narrator to appropriate or redirect its ethical force.

And indeed being "tripped up" by ethics is my whole point here. Thus the following image from James's preface to *The Golden Bowl*: "Into his very footprints the responsive, the imaginative steps of the docile reader that I consentingly become for him all comfortably sink; his vision superimposed on my own image in cut paper is applied to a sharp shadow on a wall, matches, at every point, without excess or deficiency" (*AN*, 336).

But, as Miller notes, James admits to an alternative experience when he re-reads his earlier work, a mis-stepping at absolute variance with this falling lanugorously back into the past: "It was, all sensibly, as if the clear matter being still there, even as a shining expanse of snow spread over a plain, my exploring tread, for application to it, had quite unlearned the old pace and found itself naturally falling into another, which might sometimes indeed more or less agree with the original tracks, but might most often, or very nearly, break the surface in other places" (*AN*, 336).

Along with Miller, I too see the necessity of "something both hidden and revealed" in James's image, a play of snow and footprints.[42] But instead of seeing it as deconstructive *différance*, the "law which gives itself without giving itself," I interpret that play as the force of narrative ethics. In interrupting the equable surface with "breaks in other places" *The Aspern Papers* imparts for me its final and perhaps most crucial lesson about borders and border-crossing. Or to domesticate James's image and bring it indoors, once again, we could say, a basement presence of ethical unrest has made itself felt in one of James's houses of fiction.

In the final such house in this chapter, the novella *In the Cage*, the many breaks in surface, the temptation of easy alignments, the difference between reading footprints or signs, on the one hand, and reading persons, on the other—all these features give form, shape, and dimension to narrative ethics as a governing property of the text, as its "shining expanse." The story's title may indeed convey its protagonist's plight, x-raying my image of residence with one of inter(n)ment instead; a cage, after all, is a house reduced to bare bones. But I suggest that we read it alternatively: as betokening a scene of judgment, a public tribunal, if you will, which holds the author, his third-person narrator, and readers all to account.

In the Cage

Let me begin, however, with another social code which often oversees the reach of law or justice. If the protagonists of "The Real Thing" and *The Aspern Papers* are hemmed in by a closed system of representation, those "in the cage" are truncated as well—reduced to the bare currency of alphabetically linked senders, receivers, and decoders whose sign-capital represents their sole medium of exchange and social relation.[43] In such a symbolic economy, persons and spaces alike are defined by insides and outsides, frames and cages, inclusions and exclusions. The governing structure for all such divisions, of course, is class.

But "class" here encompasses more than considerations of simple social disparity, since the text reveals a certain class hierarchy of narrative level as well, where elitist author and bourgeois narrator collude at the expense of social-climbing characters. *In the Cage* thus raises the ante substantially on the ethics of representation encountered thus far by frankly drawing us inside its put-upon protagonist; that is something neither "The Real Thing" nor *The Aspern Papers* tries to do.

The story's third-person narrator shares much in common with the polite observers of James's longer fiction. In the preface to *The Golden Bowl*, James explains the advantage of an interposed narrating consciousness this way: "The somebody is often, among my shorter tales I recognise, but an unnamed, unintroduced and (save by right of intrinsic wit) unwarranted participant, the impersonal author's concrete deputy or delegate, a convenient substitute or apologist for the creative power otherwise so veiled and disembodied" (*AN*, 327).

What happens when such a deputy becomes a jailer instead, displacing onto *character* the veils and disembodiment of authorial privilege, when narratorial superego (to replace Marx with Freud) colludes with authorial id at lonely ego's expense—a sort of "fiction and its discontents"?[44] In that lonely ego—the story's telegrapher-protagonist—James exploits a "light vessel of consciousness" (in age midway between, say, Maisie in *What Maisie Knew* and Isabel Archer in *The Portrait of a Lady*, but in social standing, inferior to both) who remains unique, I believe, in his oeuvre. In choosing her from a "lower class," James does something which he does not do to his "heroes" elsewhere; he diminishes and cheapens her at the outset—irrespective of her "moral worth"—and therein complicates the text's "moral reference."

And yet to call her by the Bakhtinian name "hero" actually misprizes the telegrapher's problematic status in the story, since, as I will show, she is part author too. Indeed, that audacity is precisely the target of the text's *ressentiment*, for I will track a singular competition between the story's two dominant consciousnesses, the narrating and the narrated one. Although the former ensures the latter's oblivion of sorts by never telling us her name—an important gap in a text obsessed with absence—that very anonymity may prove her real worth after all, a possibly opaque depth of "contextual privacy" left unplumbed by the text.[45] (Other characters' proper names float detached as empty signifiers, or else stick greasily to their owners, like "Mudge," the name of the protagonist's fiancé.) Unlike the Monarchs, royalty in name only, the unnamed telegrapher gets to lord over her customers in a small-scale "muffled majesty" of her own devising. A purposeful allegory of Jamesian impersonality? Or the footprints of a more muffled majesty within the text? That is what the next few pages will explore.

Outside Looking In

In its first few pages, the Euclidianism of *In the Cage* goes so far as to distinguish station not just between classes but within class. We see the telegraph operator and her domain—a general store's telegraph cage—juxtaposed with a friend, Mrs. Jordan, and hers—floral arrangements for wealthy patrons' houses. In the conversation these two share, Mrs. Jordan flaunts the freedom expressed by her arrangements as a token of the liberty her occupation allows her; she penetrates the airy social regions above her, "because a door more than half open to the higher life couldn't be called anything but a thin partition."[46] Conversely, "what [the telegrapher] could handle freely, she said to herself, was combinations of men and women" (178). The narrator thus establishes as a point of contrast the degree of intimacy each woman shares with her social "betters," the extent to which each is granted recognition.

For each of these women's imaginative self-projections, there is an inside to be penetrated and an outside where one resides. Mrs. Jordan's spatial horizons restrict her to acts of peeping and furtive penetration; making "free of the greatest houses" entails the merely physical stepping inside of spaces which normally exclude her; she experiences a temporary and purely decorative intimacy. Still, if only temporarily, she does "step inside" the homes of the upper class, prompting her to feel that she has "lived into" their lives, her "imagination quite [doing] away with the thickness" of social partition. "Our girl," as the narrator calls the telegrapher, responds pointedly, "Then you *do* see them?" (180), articulating the distinction between a real insider's connection, on the one hand, and mere stolen perimeter glances, on the other.

The telegrapher insinuates for us here her own more authentic brand of live-entering, which consists of converting the accidental details of her elliptical contact with the rich into narrative and story. "Combinations of men and women" provide the skeletal information which she transforms into plotted fiction, "filled with a torrent of color, accompanied with wondrous world-music" (186). Thus does she irrealize what is for her the thinly realized real, with actual people yielding her a pretext for the creation of literary character. But notwithstanding such authorial hegemony, her house of fiction must still answer to the more privileged intrusions of others; in the telegraph cage which defines her social and occupational space, it is her customers' outsides which frame the limits of her interior demesne.[47]

For each woman, as readers discover, the spatial opposition of outside/inside only seems dialectical; ultimately, outside remains outside and inside, inside, the women ending their respective adventures of allegory almost exactly in the places where they began. Mrs. Jordan may "do" the upper classes, and the telegraph girl may "have" them, but in each case, that stylized account represents the revenge of the faceless—the merely functional—on those who have faces. Each fictionalizes, then, in a manner dictated by her occupation. (Mrs. Jordan's brand of fictionalizing more closely approximates lying than creative invention, however, since she stretches the truth about her subservient relation to the rich in order to exaggerate her intimacy with them. But in the story, fabrication comes naturally to both women.)

Still, only the telegraph girl experiences the "boundless freedom" of the artist—qualified, to be sure, by the dimensions of her cage. But then this same spatial confinement yields a great imaginative advantage. The narrator nonironically describes the view from inside the cage as "prodigious": "her eyes for types amounted to genius . . . a triumphant vicious feeling of mastery and ease, a sense of carrying [people's] guilty secrets in her pocket" (188). And in the end, she alone possesses what Bakhtin calls the surplus of vision to remedy the deficits which the characters she "authors" actually incur. On the one hand, she projects into this authored world an author-spectator, a "fictional ego who attends the events as a kind of non-voting member."[48] But on the other, she also actually inserts herself into that world as an author-participant, an impersonation, really, of someone on the level with her characters who can interfere in and have an effect on their lives. Thus, to recall James's formulation, she acts quite literally as an "unnamed, unintroduced, and unwarranted participant." If her job keeps her for the most part veiled and disembodied, her creative divination allows her to act as her own "convenient substitute."

Inside Looking In

Fictional and class borders overlap in this story in a way which recalls *The Aspern Papers;* here too, the conditions of live-entering appear wholly aesthetic, but reap practical consequences. Only in their early stages do the girl's projections remain self-contained; later, her semiotic peepings have real, if ultimately limited, effect as a fantasy of fulfillment through reading cedes to the fantasy of authorial power—to make, control, and even impose meaning on others' lives.

Thus, besides being a fairly obvious image for text or writing, the "cage" in which the girl works symbolizes for me a Gyges-like technology of seeing without being seen, or as the text puts it, of knowing "a great many persons without their recognizing the acquaintance" (174). Unlike Gyges' ring, however, the cage secures a degree of power only by being conspicuously linked to the service of others. The narrator describes it as relegated to that part of the store most susceptible to being invaded by an aggregate of commercial odors; if this position enables the telegrapher to identify those odors "without consenting to know their names" (175), it also allows her clientele to insinuate themselves through the cage's bars without consenting to know hers.

The cage thus confuses boundaries of inside and outside; through its bars indiscriminately pass the odors of the surrounding merchandise, the elbows of co-workers, and the coded bits of private lives which the telegrapher scans and communicates without "really" penetrating: "Her observer's nose brushed by a bouquet, yet she could never really pluck a daisy" (184). At the same time, however, the telegrapher alone occupies the cage's interior space, a sort of interpretive holy of holies for her priestly function.

Erving Goffman speaks of a category of persons whom others treat in social encounters as if they were not present, whereas in fact they may be indispensable for "sustaining the social performance." He terms these "non-persons," not only because of the menial tasks that they discharge but also because they function as instrumentalities, extensions of the steering wheel, broom, or telegraph that they manipulate.[49] Discursively speaking, the girl's function bears comparison with Roman Jakobson's communications model: channel—addresser—code—

message—context—addressee. Essentially an extension of the "channel" or medium, a telegrapher becomes the anonymous vehicle for sending the messages she encodes.

But when this story's telegrapher decides to follow, actively decode, and reconstruct messages rather than simply transmit them, she transforms a pragmatic model of communication into a model of authorship. She begins to exploit, by mediating them, all the different levels of "gaps" her position affords her: the gap between words in any individual message, the gap between messages, the gap between the presences and absences of her customers, the gap between social classes, and, finally, the gap between incident and plot.

"Her imaginative life was the life in which she spent most of her time" (178), the narrator tells us. Since the characters who people her fictional world come to her already impersonated (they mask themselves behind aliases), she feels free to mythologize them, turning them from "characters" into "figures," referring to Lady Bradeen, for example, as "Juno." Thus elevated, her characters come to possess, to occupy her—"their presence continued and abode with her" (182)—much as the spirit of Jeffrey Aspern hovers over *The Aspern Papers'* narrator.

Writing for the Plot

This is the stuff of authorship because by assembling decontextualized moments in others' lives, moments of "bristling truth and high reality" (185), the telegrapher can fill them out on the model of a *mythos* she is all too familiar with: the typical plot of a ha'penny romantic novel. Like an ultimate "reader for the plot," she overcodes proairetic incident with hermeneutic speculation, mediates *histoire* and *discours*, detects without fear of detection. "She read into the immensity of [her customers'] intercourse stories and meanings without end" (188). Like an accomplished practitioner of the *Poetics*, she plays peripeties off possible anagnorises, pitting moments of *kairos*—"the flashes, the quick revivals, absolute accidents all" (182)—against *chronos*, the measured flow of temporal sequence.[50]

Unfortunately, as ethical relation, "recognition" remains something largely withheld from her, a source of persistent ambivalence: "It was at once one of her most cherished complaints and secret supports that people didn't understand her" (177). The kind of recognitions she herself dispenses on the outside may partially explain this paradox. In

Mrs. Jordan she "recognized an equal," and only finally does she decide to recognize Mr. Mudge, her fiancé; in their mundanity and easy decodability, such outside associations thus gloss her complaints with a "secret support" she presumably takes for granted.

Her own fictionalizing seems to follow upon the immediate and sensuous effect her customers have upon her. After a long description of a story built upon a few details the telegrapher has gleaned from one customer's cryptic messages to another, the narrator remarks, "all this, every inch of it, came in the waft [Lady Bradeen] blew and left" (181). Similarly, after this addressee's first appearance, "She felt her pencil dabbing as if with a quick caress the marks of [Captain's Everard's] own, and put life into every stroke" (183); as in *Lord Jim*, a kind of pathetic fallacy governs her desire to bring these characters to life by plotting their actions through mimetic invention.

Since Everard's reality eventually pales beside the novelistic adventures she creates for him (indeed, later in the story Everard even appeals to her for plot assistance, as a character might solicit an author), her "tracing" accomplishes more than a passive following of story lines. In a sense, she becomes an amateur detective "creating" plot from story, as though story served only to realize plot.

She "misses" the real answers, the narrator explains, but "presses the romance closer by reason of the very quality of imagination it demanded and consumed" (201). She fills in the gaps of narrative—"appointments and allusions, all swimming in a sea of allusions still, tangled in a complexity of questions" (184)—in the same way as her job requires her to count the spaces between words in a given message. But despite the vicarious interest which the very limits of her caged space generate, amidst this "world of whiffs and glimpses, a panorama fed with facts and figures," being an author has an end outside itself: "the possibility of her having for [Everard] a personal identity that might in a particular way appeal" (185). "It's not that the muffled majesty of authorship doesn't here *ostensibly* reign; but I catch myself again shaking it off and disavowing the presence of it while I get down into the arena and do my best to live and breathe and converse with the persons engaged in the struggle that provides for the others in the circling tiers the entertainment of the great game" (*AN*, 328).

Obviously it is James who speaks here, but his sentiments double, I think, for the girl's own. The narrator, however, captures this pathos of romantic *vzhivanie* when he calls it "the hazard of personal sympathy," since the girl can author everything but her own inclusion within the plot. After she had novelized a "golden shower" out of the minute droplets of lives removed from hers, "what still remained fresh was the immense disparity, the difference, and contrast from class to class of every instant, every moment" (186).

Money, Language, Thought

As in "The Real Thing" and *The Aspern Papers*, a merciless economics explains such disparity. A thousand tulips at a shilling for Mrs. Jordan over and against a thousand words at a penny in the telegraphy cage somewhat mitigates the equality between the women, but the difference is negligible compared with that which keeps them both solidly outside the worlds they peer into or brush against. Thus, superficially, the girl can muster resentment at the follies she witnesses, telling Mudge contemptuously, "what I like is to loathe them. You wouldn't believe what passes before my eyes" (201). But she says this more for his benefit than for hers, since in fact curiosity, not loathing, keeps her from looking for other employment. The narrator also observes the conflicted quality of her fascination with her clientele, mixed as it is with superiority and disgust, the *ressentiment* of the nonperson. "What twisted the knife in her vitals was the way the profligate rich scattered about them, in elegant chatter over their extravagant pleasures and sins, an amount of money that would have held the stricken household of her childhood, her poor pinched mother and tormented father and lost brother and starved sister, together for a lifetime" (187)

Mudge parasitically enjoys the girl's proximity to circulating capital, preferring to be, if only by proxy, "where the money was flying and not simply and meagerly nesting" (201). To this extent the girl's associations in the cage and her association with Mudge outside it run along what she calls parallel lines (or, more precisely, concentric circles). Just as she traces over the signs in a semiotic circuit which translates mundane facts into ethereal meanings, so Mudge likes to keep himself close to an economic circuit, "where everything was knit together in a richness of pattern that it was good to follow with one's fingertips" (202).

Not a member of the "supersensible fry," as James refers to his novels' more affluent characters, but an instance of middle-class small fry in a *nouvelle*, Mudge knows that the telegraph girl plays an obscure but important role in the market economy: "What did the [telegraph] sounder, nimbly worked, do but keep the ball going" (203). Indeed, he cannot understand why else the girl would derive pleasure from her station, the only distinctly right thing being "to be prosperous at any price" (202).

The telegraph girl, by contrast, generates a nonmonetary yield from her clientele, a kind of aesthetic usury, something Mudge finds vaguely disturbing. His business ethics allow only for interest derived from the upper class's transfer of commodities into capital, not for interest *in* their affairs or that to be made from their unwitting transfer of narrative details into plot. Where Mudge understands only the return on one's investment, for example, staying close enough to the excitement on the Bournemouth pier to enjoy it without having to pay an admission fee, the girl conceives of expenditure and remuneration in an entirely different way: "she got back her money by seeing many things, the things of the past year, fall together and connect themselves, undergo the happy relegation that transforms melancholy and misery, passion and effort, into experience and knowledge" (230).

Fiction's currency circulates here in a manner similar to that remarked on by Hillis Miller in his description of Trollope's mimesis I cited in the previous section. But authorized coinage, a currency's "true" value, matters less in this instance than simply maintaining its circulation. Indeed, the girl finds commerce interesting only when she keeps it with herself in her capacity as an author-izor, so to speak, of coinage. "Oh, how she tried to divest this of all sound of the hardness of bargaining. That ought to have been easy enough, for what was she arranging to get?" (220). Even when she finds she must divulge her secret pleasure to Mudge, she bears no real expense; she had already learned the thrift in "merely spending enough words to keep him imperturbably and continuously going" (230).

Telling the truth to Mudge, she now realizes, does nothing to mitigate her authorial power, because she decides to do so as an author—for herself alone—thereby sustaining the private import of her aesthetic projections, even in the act of making them public. "This truth filled out for her there the whole experience she was about to relinquish, suffused and coloured it as a picture that she should keep and that, describe it as she might, no one but herself would ever really see" (232).

And yet, as I will show, the text may have the last word on what and even whether she really sees.

Inside Out

The gap between economic and social classes, a deficit the girl can never personally make up, is offset by the surfeit of fictional meaning with which she can liberally endow her customers' correspondence. The balance, however, ceases when economy, semiosis, and authorship converge: she confesses to Mudge to a "relation" of sorts with Captain Everard on the outside, a transgression of ostensibly inviolate boundaries.

At first, that relation oscillates between the presences and absences dictated by her job. If Everard departs after giving the girl a message to send, he can always be counted on to return for an answer, or to send another message. The girl exploits this advantage by calling Everard's attention to the telegrapher, as it were, behind the telegraphy; she pushes the "inside" of the cage out. The merest banter about the weather convinces the girl that whatever she and Everard might say conceals a deeper communion, "the fullness of their silence" (236), as the narrator puts it. For once a customer speaks to rather than through the telegrapher; but the sending of signs only continues: "Everything, so far as they chose to consider it so, might mean almost anything. The want of margin in the cage, when he peeped through the bars, wholly ceased to be appreciable. It was a drawback only in superficial commerce. With Captain Everard she had simply the margin of the universe" (205).

Eventually, the girl contrives to meet Everard outside the cage, and for a moment divisions of inner and outer cease to dictate the conditions of intersubjectivity. The girl's plotting of recognitions suddenly yields to the compelling need for recognition. The play of signification gives way to the drama of Signification, in Levinas' sense, the exposure of self to other in which Face and Discourse replace sign and clandestinity as the media of encounter. "Redressing the equivocal by . . . coming to the assistance of the sign given forth" (*TI*, 91) opens up an interior world formerly sheathed in apparition and coded meanings; the romance of fabulation, "the harmless pleasure of knowing," as the girl confesses, suddenly entails unexpected responsibilities. Having successfully transformed telegraphy into authorship and reversed inside and outside, the girl finds herself obliged by a narrative ethics—she must extend her perceptual surplus to a character and, like some gender- and class-crossed Henry Higgins, bring her Eliza-Everard to life.

But isn't ethics principally Everard's affair, one might object, not hers? After all, to the degree that he exploits her services, he bears some responsibility for her status as nonperson in the first place; the girl has always been a means to him, in the most mechanical of senses. But precisely because Everard is a somewhat fictional entity even without the girl's creative imagination, a creature of two dimensions, he cannot bear the weight of any palpable ethical significance; he is a "Captain" in the same way Conrad's Jim is a "Lord." Despite the girl's romantic magnifications—"your selfishness, your immorality, your crimes" (226)—the story unequivocally assigns him triviality. The telegrapher's apt condemnation of his entire "set"—"the horrors . . . they show me with as good a conscience as if I had no more feeling than a letter box" (226)—must include him within its rebuke as well.

Her indignation, however, does not conceal the fact of her own indiscretions, her own culpability. While in the cage, for instance, she has occasion to rectify one of Lady Bradeen's messages. "There was a word wrong, but [Lady Bradeen] had lost the right one and much depended on her finding it again" (213). Just previously, the girl had reveled in "the high company she keeps," scanning diligently the features before her for clues, "filling out some of the gaps, supplying the missing answers" (211).

"The anarchy of the spectacle" Levinas calls such speechless mystification. Only finally does the girl make her presence known, not through real speech but by supplying the missing word, for the first time inserting herself materially into the correspondence. Lady Bradeen's consequent bewilderment—"How did you know?"—betokens a triumph of sorts, given voice by the girl herself: "How little she knows, how little she knows . . . How much I know, how much I know" (211).

In the same exchange with Everard quoted above in which the girl tells him that the "horrors" amuse her, disabusing him of any apprehension, she admits that his crimes please her as well: "I like them, as I tell you—I revel in them" (226); her earlier confession to Mudge proves entirely genuine. But although the story does, like "The Real Thing" and *The Aspern Papers*, implicitly gesture toward a moral high ground and leave no one uncensured, once again an autonomous "un-

derground" level of narrative ethics exerts a greater and more telling
pressure.

See Here!

As "the fine risk of approach" (*OTB*, 94), language disenchants, according to Levinas. It proposes the world through speech as the common
property of ethical subjects. As Saying, as a coming near the other
person, its performativity can "unsay" the dead letter of the Said, the
very domain of telegraphy. More important, language as expression
creates the conditions for acknowledging the persons involved *as* distinctly other; through discourse one "breaks through [her] own plastic
essence, like someone who opens a window on which [her] figure is
outlined."[51] The telegraph cage forms such a window and outline, yet
the girl repeats outside of it the same conditions which prevail within.
Even on a presumably more equal footing, she continues to deal with
Everard in cipher, a concatenation of gaps and traces; thus does her
"relation" with Everard pursue its "pursuit of signs": "for when she was
most conscious of the objection of her vanity and the pitifulness of her
little flutters and manoeuvres, then the consolation and the redemption
were most sure to glow before her in some just discernible sign" (210;
my emphasis).

The anarchy of the spectacle underwrites their social commerce too.
After they meet and recognize each other from opposite sides of the
street—significantly, across a gap—they walk together "in the absence
of anything vulgarly articulate," their connection "beautiful behind and
below the mere awkward surface." Everard's continued silence after she
admits she hasn't eaten, allows her to imbue even the *absence* of expression with enchantment: "She had known he wouldn't say, 'Then sup
with *me*,' but the proof of it made her feel as if she feasted" (219).

Even after the apparent fulfillment of her ongoing fantasy, she sustains the aura of fictionality; when she adds to the blankness of their
discourse a stock romantic formula—"I'd do anything for you. I'd do
anything for you"—the narrator observes, "Didn't the place, the association, and circumstances perfectly make it sound what it wasn't? and
wasn't that exactly the beauty?" (221). "By the mere action of his
silence, everything they had definitely not named, the whole presence
round which they had been circling, became part of the reference,
settled in solidly between them. It was as if then for a minute they sat

and saw it all in each other's eyes, saw so much that there was no need of a pretext for sounding it at last" (227).

But the cage's "sounder" only *seems* no longer in effect. Everard contributes to the illusion of tacit knowledge with wooden replies; when the girl confesses the "harmless pleasure of knowing," repeating, "I know. I know. I know," Everard assents, "Yes; that's what has been between us." As with Mudge, telling means conserving, prolonging the enchantment. In the form of phatic but revealing interjections like "I say!" or "See here!" defective language extends the equivocal play of vision and secrecy. "'See here—see here!'—the sound of these two words had been with her perpetually; but it was in her ears today without mercy, with a loudness that grew and grew. What was it they then expressed? What was it he had wanted her to see? She seemed, whatever it was, perfectly to see it now—to see that if she should just chuck the whole thing, should have a great and beautiful courage, he would somehow make everything up to her" (238).

Michael Levenson notes that in James's later work, two formal devices—metaphor and typification—work to deny the individual a margin of uninterpreted space; like good detectives, they tap the phone lines of contextual privacy, and co-opt quiddity with figure or abstraction. A countervailing option, however, can and does carve out such a space, according to Levenson, a privilege belonging solely to the indexicals.[52] These are the facts of language which register momentary points of view, like Strether's "Then there we are" at the end of *The Ambassadors;* three of the four words in this quotation function deictically, positioning their speaker relative to other vectors of time, space, and person.

"See here!" performs no such service, for character or for reader; it doesn't validate subjective perception so much as convey the irony of distorted vision masked by the vocabulary of designation, of reference. "See here!" is a world away from "Here am I," the totality, if you will, to its infinity. The force of its imperative implodes rather than explodes; its locating one-dimensionalizes space instead of curving it. Each of the indexicals in the latter statement performs, moves, goes forth, like the biblical Abraham, toward an elsewhere; the "here" directs itself implicitly to a yonder, and the "I" offers itself—accusatively, as Levinas says—to an other.

But "See here!" does not possess such ethical orientation; like the interiority which is this text's governing spatial locus, it points down and in, not up and out (and as far as the girl is concerned, it promises more than it delivers, whatever it is she imagines she now "sees"). Which is why it is of a piece with its banal partner "I say!" since far from being a substitute for genuine expression, Saying is ethical sincerity itself, "a way of giving everything, of not keeping anything for oneself," as Levinas puts it. Everard, on the contrary, remains clandestine to the last.

Telegraphy and Its Discontents

Everard and the girl transport this newfound politics (or phatics) of the ineffable back with them to the cage, which now presents occasions, the girl believes, for meta-telegraphy: "From the first flash of his re-appearance she had read into it its real essence. . . . She continued to recognize in his forbearance the fruit of her dumb supplication" (238). Characteristically, she overreads his absences by assuming she is their cause. In a final scene of farewell, romantic fiction and tongue-tied portentousness à la Jim prevail: "Goodbye." . . . And the once more, for the sweetest faintest flower of all: "Only I say—see here!" (245).

In fact, however, the indexical carries more weight than either of them realizes, because only in her capacity as telegrapher, *here*, in the cage, does seeing make a difference, does the girl finally have any genuine effect. When Everard and Lady Bradeen's correspondence reaches a crisis, Everard returns to the cage after what seemed a permanent absence in order to retrieve a certain message. Confronted directly with all the evidence she had willfully repressed, the girl then realizes "above all . . . how much she had missed in the gaps and blanks and absent answers—how much she had to dispense with: it was now black darkness save for this little wild red flare" (247). Like any character already immersed in a rival plot, Everard doffs chivalric pretense for the venality of a cad.

But if the girl deceives herself as to her value inside the fiction, she has only to recollect that she is its "author" and can exert authorial control. Thus she acts the functionary in response to Everard's purely instrumental need. With full knowledge of its sound in her mouth, the girl officiously tells him, "'I see—I see.' She managed just the accent they had at Paddington when they stared like dead fish" (250). And, indeed, she merely and clearly "sees here."

Without having to search for the message, she produces it from memory, writing a number on the back of Everard's card. His errand accomplished, the clue successfully found to be unincriminating—"If [the message]'s wrong it's all right"—Everard turns on his heels and leaves her world forever. In a neat piece of arithmetic, just as the telegrapher augments herself by supplying a word for Lady Bradeen, so she is subtracted by repeating the identical action with Everard.

How does she weather this defeat? By transferring the muffled majesty of authorship into a character's majestic heroism: "Now it was a great surface, and the surface was somehow Captain Everard's wonderful face. Deep down in his eyes was a picture, a scene—a great place like a chamber of justice, where, before a watching crowd, a poor girl, exposed but heroic, swore with a quavering voice to a document, proved an *alibi*, supplied a link. In this picture she bravely took her place" (250).

Authoring in fiction, to paraphrase Cavell once again, shows what authoring in actuality is and what are its stakes. The girl craves the satisfaction of being recognized, but recognized for her importance within a spectacle she has manipulated. As an author, she simply indulges in theatricalization, which, Everard's own play-acting notwithstanding, converts the other person into a character. When, by contrast, someone breaks through the masks imposed by others, writes Bakhtin, "he introduces, as a participant with a definite role, an element of a particular *story* into my dream, whereas what is really needed is an author who does not himself participate in the event" (*AA*, 31). With no access to such redemptive live-entering, the telegrapher permits herself the luxury of behaving like a ha'penny Walter Mitty instead.

In the Cage ends with a set piece involving the girl and Mrs. Jordan. Each forces the other to recant an inappropriate form of *vzhivanie*. Mrs. Jordan undoes the false impression she has given of being on some equal, intimate footing with Lord Rye, by way of her involvement with Lord Rye's "loved friend," Mr. Drake. (In point of fact, Mr. Drake attends Lord Rye as his butler.) Likewise, the girl is made to confront the gap between her plotting of romantic fiction, and the real, rather tawdry and illicit circumstances of her characters' "correspondence."

Telegraphy of any sort suddenly seems quite useless, its "sounder" quieted by another, deeper sort: "Her interlocutress had, in the cage, *sounded* depths, but there was a suggestion here somehow of an abyss quite measureless" (263). Mrs. Jordan, about to become that odd contradiction, a live-in outsider, and the girl, caged once more, "could now only look at each other across a social gulf" (261). Inside and outside reassert their normative status, the gap between them reinstated. Moreover, the author/reader abdicates her majesty, having learned from Mrs. Jordan the meager role her imaginings had played all along. Having all along desired original response, in Robert Frost's phrase again, the girl has merely projected her own copy-speech back to herself. Her wan reply to Mrs. Jordan, "I see. I see," simply recycles one more time the hollow trace of an exercise of faulty vision. Yet my purposeful mention of the word "trace" introduces an implication of the story I have so far left unexplored.

Traces

A signifier of cumulative significance in *In the Cage*, "trace" suggests three related but distinct connotations. First, it signifies the girl's authorial plotting, the mimetic detective work in which she traces the lives of her characters, as she traces the alphabetic characters of Everard's message. Second, it hints at the alternation of presence and absence, the trace of tone in the other, that is, how the girl could be "with the absent [Everard] through her ladyship, and with her ladyship through the absent" (211). Third and finally, it betokens both the signs the girl interprets as evidence for the plots she constructs, and the signs she awaits from Captain Everard, the trace which would be "the consolation and redemption sure to glow before her in some just discernible sign" (213).

In Levinas' work, however, the word resonates in a single but powerful sense. In his essay "The Trace of the Other," Levinas compares with several different kinds of writing the "signifyingness" of the Other which engraves itself without signs or encounter, in a perpetual escape from my horizon. When paying a check, he says, one leaves a manifest trace of the payment, "inscribed in the very order of the world."[53] Ethical relation, however, involves a kind of overprinting from below which interrupts that order. The trace left does not conform to an interpretable system of signs which a graphologist might decipher. "There is a difference," Kierkegaard once wrote, "between writing on a blank sheet of paper, and bringing to light by the application of a caustic fluid a text which is hidden under another text."[54]

Thus, in the second example, a letter leaves traces of its writer ineffably, without leading to disclosure through analysis of the writing or the style. Levinas compares this indelibility which cannot be "traced" to a surface cleared of the tracks or prints which might identify one's presence; the act of wiping away, and not fragmentary evidence of the signs themselves, signifies that a passage has occurred. Unlike James's "clear expanse of snow spread over a plain," where footprints old and new "break the surface," the trace, as Levinas says, "disturbs surfaces in an irreparable way."[55] That is how narrative ethics works as well, for this and the other two texts by James in this chapter—by overprinting from below.

To conclude, I want to return to a point I made earlier about the narrator-"deputy" and the telegraph girl's competition as fictionalizers. *In the Cage* begins in free indirect speech, or narrated monologue. Occasionally it employs quoted monologue—"what [the girl] could handle freely, she said to herself, was combinations of men and women" (178). Usually, however, it renders the girl's consciousness through the narrative mode Dorrit Cohn calls psycho-narration, the focalized reporting of another's thoughts.[56] But presiding over such important distinctions in narrative voice is a pronounced and permanent division in social class and aesthetic sensibility, opening wide the gulf between "authorship," on the one hand, and real authority, on the other.

On a fairly obvious level, the story prohibits translation into figural, first-person narration; the girl simply could not tell her own story, as is not the case for more polished and linguistically sophisticated narrators like those of "The Real Thing" or *The Aspern Papers*. For reasons both aesthetic and moral, James found figural narration of this type unsatisfying for his purposes over a long stretch of fiction; in the preface to *The Ambassadors* he refers to first-person narration as "the darkest abyss of romance," the kind of abyss laid bare, for instance, in a text like *The Sacred Fount*.[57]

In his longer third-person fictions, by contrast, James runs a remarkable inquiry into the opaqueness and lucidity of subjective consciousness—its "quality of bewilderment"—alongside a more implicit inquiry into the propriety of third-person narration. Often, like the "parallel lines" of the telegraph girl's double life, these two inquiries cross and merge. In *What Maisie Knew*, for example, psycho-narration guides Maisie's expanding consciousness, gradually ceding it greater authority by minimizing narratorial analysis or aside. Similarly, in *The Portrait of a Lady* (the meditative vigil chapter being perhaps the most impressive example) the temporal flexibility—the give of tense which narrated monologue permits—becomes nearly inextricable from the interpenetration of narrator and protagonist.

In the Cage works differently.[58] It juxtaposes authorial privilege with the special circumstances of a protagonist given special literary powers of vision. But the relationship seems almost causal—as though the girl's telegraphy of gaps and traces sets off and provokes the narrator's nearly seamless telepathy into her thoughts, as though he "gets back at her" for daring to poach on his premises. But this *ressentiment* backfires. The effect of the juxtaposition, I am arguing here, is to force representational aspects of narrative form into readers' awareness as ethical problems. If a lowly telegrapher can so presume, what then do we make of the presumptions of a more sophisticated message sender like the story's narrator, or its author? As if by accident, gaps and traces in a minimalist paradigm of communication open sightlines to possibly analogous features in James's fictional project as a whole, in all its towering verisimilitude. "Moral reference" and "boundless freedom," in other words, may not be as cozily and unproblematically aligned as James suggests.

The "frank and brave *nouvelle*," as James terms this story's genre, can foreground features of narrative ethics which the longer fiction, in its multiple centers of consciousness or lavish exploration of subjective perception, can frequently conceal. Hence the interesting dearth of typical Jamesian "talk" in *In the Cage*, so much a staple of the late fiction or of stories like "The Beast in the Jungle." Instead of the almost contentless dialogue of social finesse which we find there, discourse in "The Real Thing," *The Aspern Papers*, and *In the Cage* falls to a level, again, of gaps and traces.

In both these respects—narratorial perspective and dialogue—gaps and traces serve ultimately to underscore what I have described as perhaps the founding condition of intersubjective relation: the ethical separateness of persons. From behind and below the textual surface such gaps and traces indicate, with Levinasian surreptiousness, an always possible divergence between an author's "moral" intention and a text's ethical structure. They permit what Levinas calls the "upsurge" of alterity in ethical encounter, the putting-into-question of a self's "boundless freedom," and the investing of it as critique.

When James observes in his preface to *The Ambassadors*, "There is the story of one's hero, and then, thanks to the intimate connexion of things, the story of one's story itself" (*AN*, 313), he means his own search for value and form, which "can least be likened to the chase with horn and hound." The texts in this chapter, as I have endeavored to show, intimate a third possibility: the *story's* story of itself. In that story, where representations of the discrete and interior lives of persons are concerned, art's horn and hound may yield only bone. And thus does art "let go of the prey for the shadow."[59]

5

Creating the Uncreated Features of His Face: Monstration in Crane, Melville, and Wright

One thing is necessary, of course, but only one: that men have a countenance at all, that they see each other. . . . The power to dissolve all that is rigid already inheres in the glance. Once an eye has glanced at us, it will glance at us as long as we live.

Franz Rosenzweig, *The Star of Redumption*

The face, it is inviolable; these eyes absolutely without protection, the most naked part of the human body, offer, nevertheless, an absolute resistance to possession, an absolute resistance in which the temptation of murder is inscribed: the temptation of an absolute negation. The Other is the sole being that one can be tempted to kill. This temptation of murder and this impossibility of murder constitute the very vision of the face. . . . The being that expresses itself, that faces me, says no to me by his very expression. . . . Violence can aim only at a face.

Emmanuel Levinas, *Totality and Infinity*

Be that as it may, how it was that upon the rocking waters of the ocean the human face began to reveal itself; the sea appeared paved with innumerable faces, upturned to the heavens; faces, imploring, wrathful, despairing; faces that surged upwards by the thousands, by myriads, by generations.

Thomas de Quincey, *Confessions*

Everything about history that, from the very beginning, has been untimely, sorrowful, unsuccessful, is expressed in a face—or rather a death's head.

Walter Benjamin, *The Origin of German Tragic Drama*

As the barber foamed the lather on the cheeks of the engineer he seemed to be thinking heavily. Then suddenly he burst out, "How would you like to be with no face?"

Stephen Crane, *The Monster*

MY READINGS OF texts in the previous two chapters trace features of narrative ethics in a fairly text-centered fashion. By advancing what thus may appear to be simply one more formalism which lacks the explicit pressures of "culture" or "history," I must seem in some quarters merely to have installed "ethics" in the place of some other free-standing and reified category. I hope the claims I put forward in Chapter 2 persuade otherwise, but the risk of "ideological confusion" may perhaps remain.

Indeed, in going so far as to argue for an "autonomous ethical principle" which cuts across, or at least inscribes itself within, authorial intention, as I do in the previous chapter, I suppose I veer perilously close to the style of acontextual close reading for which ideological critics so often fault deconstruction.

To make the comparison more difficult to dismiss, the play of resistance—of solicitation and repudiation—which I ascribe to a text's ethical self-understanding does, I admit, begin to look not unlike *differance*—a kind of clandestine norm for reading. The easy explanation: since Levinas (from whom I draw in this regard) does not stand entirely outside the trends of poststructuralist thought in France, an affinity with both its philosophical concerns and interpretive style probably cannot help surfacing in readings which attempt to correlate Levinasian concepts with a theory of literary interpretation.

The explanation which begs the question: like deconstruction, narrative ethics assumes that literary texts are perfectly capable of un-saying themselves, that is, being interrupted from within. What is linguistic rupture for deconstruction, however, is *prima facie* ethical upsurge for narrative ethics. And *prima facie*, or face, is this chapter's special concern.

Still, it may reasonably be objected, where does all of this leave politics? Making intermittent common cause with deconstruction would seem to make me especially vulnerable on this score, because it creates an *impasse* for the political. As Simon Critchley frames it, "If politics is the moment of the decision—of judgement, of justice, of action, of antagonism, of beginning, of commitment, of conflict, of crisis—then how does one take a decision in an undecidable terrain?" (*ED*, 188).[1]

Needless to say, "undecidability" plays no major part in this study. But neither so far has politics. Or so it seems. For if I consistently employ verbs like "perform," "enact," "respond," and "answer for," am I not raising political questions, am I not speaking as much in a political register as an ethical one? What exactly are the political implications of narrative ethics, anyway?

Superficially, at least, Levinas doesn't seem to help much here. He has been accused of subordinating political and cultural considerations to a transcendental ethics whose attention to the particular thus appears quite selective.[2] For, this argument goes, is not "the neighbor" precisely an ethnically specific, culturally defined other, for whom allegiance or at least ethical concern must ineluctably tap into universal principles of law or reason? And yet for Levinas, materially based conceptions of human action seem to becloud the purity, the originary shock of alterity by appealing to the very realm of system and institution which Levinasian ethics vigorously contests.

Thus Levinas will say, "Morality is what governs the world of political 'interestedness,' the social interchanges between citizens in a society. Ethics, as the extreme exposure and sensitivity of one subjectivity to another—[disinterestedness which precedes our interest in being]—becomes morality and hardens its skin as soon as we move into the political world of the impersonal 'third'—the world of government, institutions, tribunals, prisons, schools, committees, and so on."[3]

To objections which set at issue hard realities of "appropriation," or "skin" in the context of racism and ethnic persecution, Levinas would oppose his own insistence on ethics as first philosophy, as the armature which undergirds "the moral-political" order which is embodied in that culminating list above. The political world of the impersonal "third," "the other of the other," thus seems to have at best an epiphenomenal relation to ethics, to the irreducible and primordial event of face-to-face encounter.

But the question of politics stands over literary as well as social "interchange." How, therefore, can such putatively essentialist and ahistoricist thought as that of Levinas (or of Cavell and the early Bakhtin, for that matter) open literary texts to the question of politics, to contexts larger than the synchronic frameworks of "acknowledgment," "answerability," or "the face"?

For one thing, while Levinas does not emphasize politics as such, there are significant implications for political philosophy in his work, for "community based on the recognition of difference, of the difference of the Other to the same . . . difference affirmed through Yes-saying to the stranger."[4] Both of Levinas' major works, *Totality and Infinity* and *Otherwise Than Being*, begin by situating themselves in relation to history and politics—to the permanent changes wrought by war in this century.

His sally against politics' complicity with totalitarianism (conspicuously placed in the first paragraph of *Totality and Infinity*)—"The art of foreseeing war and winning it by every means—politics—is enjoined as the very exercise of reason" (*TI*, 21)—implies that any humane politics must be grounded in and mediated by ethical critique, if it is to avoid this panoptic hubris. The only just politics begins as an ethics.

Moreover, "situating the self in public space" (to borrow Seyla Benhabib's phrase) is an integral dimension of Levinas' philosophy. All of the central Levinasian modalities—proximity, expression, facing—key into that dimension as constitutive features of "justice." With the entry of "the third party," the radical asymmetry which justifies the relation of self and other is itself justified—in a double sense—through an equality on the largest scale: The other's "equality within his essential poverty consists in referring to the *third party*, thus present at the encounter, whom in the midst of the destitution the Other already serves . . . The *thou* is posited in front of a *we*. To be *we* is not to 'jostle' one another or get around a common task. The presence of the face, the infinity of the other, is a . . . presence of the third party (that is, the whole of humanity which looks at us)" (*TI*, 213). Human community is thus a symmetry built around an asymmetry; "fraternity" is a healing which still crucially depends on the wounding, the trauma, of one to another.

This composite image of community in fact offers me a much more direct answer to the question I posed above, since all the texts I read in this chapter—Stephen Crane's *The Monster*, Herman Melville's *Benito Cereno*, and Richard Wright's *Native Son*—crucially depend on such a dynamic of salve and wound, of Other and the others. Each proposes the "question of politics" as fundamentally linked to questions of ethical difference and recognition.

All incorporate the narrative structures and events which I have elaborated so far, but amplify their meaningfulness politically. Recognition, for example, and Levinas' concept of the face become pressure points on the scale of communities and cultures, not just of persons. Rather than restricting *face* to a descriptive image for individual alterity, these works of fiction assign it intercultural and interethnic force—otherwise than and beyond—the force of intersubjectivity.

Before I proceed to the answer to my question, however, I shall take a short but instructive detour. As it has several times already in this book, work by J. Hillis Miller on ethics and literature contrasts significantly with my own, and in doing so serves to clarify the boundaries of this study and the aims which guide it. Miller's book *Hawthorne and History: Defacing It* develops four themes which bear on my discussion in this chapter: (1) allegory as a common boundary between realism and romance; (2) the exact role accorded "history" in the interpretation of a literary text; (3) the ethical demands on interpretation which a text reads out; and (4) the literary representation of *face*—the difference between having and not having one, conferring it and taking it away, its revelation and/or concealment.

For a proof-text, Miller selects Hawthorne's "The Minister's Black Veil," a story whose themes and images perhaps stand behind many texts of ethnic-American fiction where face, the physical and psychosocial expression of identity, either figures or suffers disfigurement.[5] He places it in the middle of a rhetorical argument which proceeds, as he says, "from Theory to Example to Reading to History" (*HH*, 106). Each of these putatively stable referents, like the minister's black veil or like Bartleby (to whom Miller several times alludes), proves, rather, to be refractory to our interpretive will. (For economy's sake, I proceed directly to his argument's *dénouement*.)

Among other things, Hawthorne's story tells a twofold (as the Veil itself is "twice-fold") parable of History: a historical event becomes both "the inadvertent re-enactment of earlier events" and "the irruption of a sign or system of signs into the historical continuum" (*HH*, 111–112). The story shows the performative as opposed to representable nature of history, enacting that lesson uncannily; all literary language, we discover, ushers in the uncanny by necessarily escaping the hegemony of both History and Theory (presumably its twin guarantors).

Miller concludes by explaining how, therefore, even his own theoretical pretensions must bow before the story's central image—a veiled face which invites unmasking, but only to evince another mask.

> Just as surely as the citizens of Milford projected a face behind the black veil of the Reverend Hooper and assumed that the missing face was an index of personality behind the veiling mask of the face, so have I projected faces, selves, and voices on these white pages, filigreed in black. I cannot read the story without doing this, even though the point of the story is to put into question the prosopopoeia on which its functioning as a narrative depends . . . the stubborn presupposition that behind every mask is a face, and behind every face, as behind every sign or configuration of signs, there is somewhere a personality, a self, a subject, a transcendental ego. (*HH*, 123–124)

As the tropological undoing of normative assumptions—both critical and intersubjective—about readability, the story's conceit ultimately inscribes itself, as Miller would say, in a general discrepancy within and among historical occurrences. "History" is a name we give to events which have already effaced their meanings or, rather, which have become defaced through our imputation of meaning *to* them. "In personifying the absent, the inanimate, or the dead, each repetition of those events imposes or projects a face on the veil, or creates a face that acts a veil" (*HH*, 124).

That Miller finds prosopopoeia to be inescapable while all the time critiquing its phenomenalist effects proves the story's—or any text's—resistance to theory. But such an insight, as I have argued before, merely closes the door on argument, leaving the rest of us, like so many K's, stymied "before the law" of tropological disarticulation. In Miller's view, Reading and History make sense only in terms of both their performative and necessarily incalculable effects, and thus does literary figure—the donnée of a veiled face—"read" Theory, Example, Reading, and History alike.

But like its sister concepts, history (or our experience of it), I am afraid, cannot so easily reduce to the disarticulations of a rhetorical trope.[6] Rather, with Levinas and Claude Lanzmann, I would argue that beings have an identity before the accomplishment of history, before the fullness of time. To invoke them through "the projection of a face" simply provides the material coefficient to the ethical summons which Levinas sees as residing primordially *in* a face. It is ethics, in this sense, which irrupts into and cuts across constructed historical time. This "'beyond' of history draws beings out of the jurisdiction of history and the future; it arouses them in and calls them forth to their full responsibility . . . All the causes are ready to be heard" (*TI*, 23).

By "showing forth," the face itself, we could say, conduces to a form of monstration. Or rather, it is or does monstration. Miller momentarily hints at one especially significant linguistic and phenomenalist consequence of this fact, but he does not tie monstration to the face per se (an interesting lacuna, given the context of his discussion)—"*Monster:* the word means 'showing forth,' the demonstration of something hideously unlawful or unique, for example a monstrous birth" (*HH*, 102).

In Stephen Crane's novella *The Monster*, Henry Johnson, a black man, is transformed into a "monster" when a fire burns away his face. Crane's text ties defacement directly to two very different kinds of exterior monstrosity: physical disfigurement, on the one hand, and the inhumanity shown by a town's men and women toward one no longer "recognizable," on the other. Hawthorne's town of Milford and Crane's town of Whilomville differ to the degree that in one the townspeople project a face upon a veil which hides a face, and in the other the townspeople project a veil upon a face which has disappeared.

Milford folk, like their Reverend, disguise their respective individual monstrosities; Whilomville folk share in a collective monstrousness by refusing to face an individual calamity. Crane's text does invoke Hawthorne's rather explicitly—at one point in the story Henry is swathed in "a heavy crepe veil." But by actually destroying a face, *The Monster* reveals a "power of blackness" wholly foreign to the sensibility of both "The Minister's Black Veil" and Miller's reading of it.

Miller, of course, does not choose his proof-text idly, Hawthorne's story being perhaps the tale of tales to demonstrate the self-canceling properties of prosopopoeia—as it were, from behind the veil. (The appeal of the story for Miller's textual approach is telling: a human face remains conspicuously hidden under "text"—a double-folded piece of black crepe. As a standing affront to interpretive desire, Hawthorne's man with a veiled face could just as easily be a man in an iron mask: doubly imprisoned, he remains forever unknowable—just like a text's "inner meaning." Put another way, like Bartleby, the text "prefers not to" when asked to signify.)

Appropriately or not, the most fruitful moment of Miller's analysis for me is to be found off its beaten track—in a brief excursus on the ideological meaning of "masking" as Puritan sexual repression or gender reversal. Anticipating an objection, Miller explains that the gendered ideology reflected in wearing the veil "causes the social structure of repression and policing, and not the other way around" (*HH*, 88). This is an extraordinarily valuable concept for my own readings in this chapter.

In the texts I have selected, social structures of repression and policing follow not from seeking a face behind a veil but rather from the social act of projecting a veil upon a face. In each text, the possession of a black face already provides the culture of definition with a pre-text—humanity reduced to physicality—for defacing or misrecognizing it; being culturally "marked," in other words, legitimates a more violent marking of the face through actual disfigurement.

As Frantz Fanon once wrote, "there are times when the black man is locked into *his body*," or as Ralph Ellison put it, "on the moral level I propose that we view the whole of American life as a drama acted out upon the body of a Negro giant."[7] And in light of Miller's analysis of prosopopoeic agency in Hawthorne, face in these texts works, I wish to argue, precisely as pre-text, as a phenomenal fact prior to an image of writing or figuration.

Moreover, each text could be said to treat monstration in a double sense: on the one hand, the showing forth of a face and, on the other, the engendering of a monster. The point at which these vectors cross is the point of a cruelly infinite cultural semiosis: we call something monstrous because we can overload it with always new signs and meanings, such endless interpretability being merely the sign of *our* desire to keep "the monster" always at a distance, to keep it monstrous. Hence my recourse to Levinas, and the political ramifications which follow from the ethical obligation to see, not through a glass darkly, but face to face.

Thus in all three of this chapter's texts, Levinas' concept of ethical transcendence—the scene of recognition which forms around the acknowledgment or repudiation of a face—can be asked to play a pivotal and similarly dual role. It can signify either a material focus within a textual field of representation or a metonym for the body politic within a field of social representation—the face of social (in)justice.

It is in the latter case, I hope to show, that Levinas' privileged realm of the intersubjective defers to politics, where a single face of a representative Other looks out at, commands, or becomes the object of, a crowd of gazers; the Other shows the way to the others.[8]

One can choose between two envisioned outcomes for intercultural "recognition," it seems to me. The first is frankly utopian. It regards as seeing through a glass darkly the view that "being" is contingent on "race"; it looks forward to the recognition of a "true" self lying just beneath the skin—the cultural meaning of "seeing face to face." The second, more Sartrian option has been ably described by Frantz Fanon: "He who is reluctant to recognize me opposes me. In a savage struggle I am willing to accept convulsions of death, invincible dissolution, but also the possibility of the impossible."[9] Only from the permanent material fact of being "sealed," as Fanon puts it, in whiteness or in blackness arises the possibility of ethical encounter grounded in productive difference.

We can never see "face to face" if that means a faceless universalism which neutralizes contingent features of appearance, because faces are always marked, sized, colored.[10] This is quite different from Miller's point about the chimera of transparency, since it points to the demand for only a more strenuous exertion to make out, accurately, the features of another's face. (It also shows, I believe, how his idiosyncratic analysis of prosopopoeia—the "ideologically confused" inference of personality and self behind a human face—fails crucially to account for phenomenological realities of being and race which, in the texts that follow, the marring of a face paradoxically brings to light.)

Of these two possible outcomes, it is the second, in its severity, its emphasis on incommensurability, and its adumbration of violence and trauma, which stands closer to the spirit of Levinasian ethics. It also stands closer to the spirit of the three pieces of fiction I treat in this chapter.

To introduce each one briefly:

1. Stephen Crane's *The Monster*, a text which lies midway between realism and allegory, suggests that the surface and the interior of a person may for all intents and purposes be treated as equivalent when selfhood has already been determined to be a racial and therefore an aberrant or "monstrous" category. I include a brief comparison with Charles Chesnutt's short story "The Web of Circumstance."

2. Herman Melville's *Benito Cereno*, analogously, shows how metaphor and symbol impede seeing the racially different other. Despite the text's revolutionary ethos, its black characters never escape the doubly hollowing effect of representational "monstration."

3. Richard Wright's *Native Son*, finally and most problematically, complicates its own naturalistic urgency by drawing from the same imagistic well as that tracked by Melville's and Crane's texts (a precursor for it, I speculate, can be traced in the "Kabnis" section of Jean Toomer's *Cane*); in this respect, Wright's novel reaps an inadvertent legacy of horror: call it, if you will, "the son of *The Monster*."

As indices of history, all three texts demand something more than a disjunctive theory of historical event and historical relation. Indeed, the immediate and grotesque historical context underlying each—the deadly serious minstrelsy that was American slavery for *Benito Cereno*, the "second slavery" of postbellum Jim Crow legislation for *The Monster*, and the liberal democratic failure to come to terms with both these monstrosities for *Native Son*—simply defies a romantic sense of "history" as a synonym for "uncanny." As Geoffrey Hartman has observed, "To recall the past is a political act: a 'recherche' that involves us with images of peculiar power, images that may constrain us to identify with them."[11] That constraint demands a sense of the uncanny truer to the German, that *unheimlich* capacity to alienate and estrange, and drive us forth from home. I return to this point at the end of each of the following readings.

The Monster
Mask and Face

In an essay on Stephen Crane, Ralph Ellison refers to what he calls "the noncommittal mask of his prose."[12] But among realist authors, Crane remains distinctive precisely for the stylisms which belie that mask: a mannered obtrusiveness, for example, side by side with a naturalist account of events unmediated by any narrative presence. I find Ellison's word choice particularly interesting for two reasons: its echo of another Ellison phrase—"the black mask of humanity"—an emblem for white authors' failure to render black experience without distortion; and its usefulness for calling attention to the textual veil which lies over Henry Johnson's exposed facelessness in the short work entitled *The Monster*. Both implications will surface again in the analysis to follow. (As to the second, needless to say, I use the word "veil" with some caution: in Crane's story, any face to be covered has literally disappeared, and poses therefore an intrinsic barrier to projections about the person behind it.)

Literalizing beyond the notion of property the original subtitle of *Uncle Tom's Cabin*, "a man who was a thing"[13] (a theory of "dual realities" which found its ultimate legal sanction after Reconstruction, in Plessy v. Ferguson), Crane does to his character in the most extreme sense what the Reverend Mr. Hooper in "The Minister's Black Veil" freely chooses to do—with no violence—to himself: he deflects signification "by removing one of its essential elements, the face, though leaving the rest, the voice, gesture, form, figure, and name" (*HH*, 74). To this degree, as Ellison's phrase implies, *The Monster* does feature its own level of purely textual disfigurement and mantled writing. This is the aspect of the novella analyzed at length by Michael Fried in *Realism, Writing, and Disfiguration*.

The core of Fried's argument involves the interesting theory that Crane's unconscious fixation on "the scene of writing" derives from his "seeing through" writing's communicative dimension to the material facts which make up its production—letters, paper, printed lines—the purely physical aspects of inscription. In other words, the literary objects of representation together with their "real" content cede to the activity of representation itself. This anxiety in turn is reflected (or, better, rendered) in Crane's penchant for upturned and disfigured faces—faces that are textually dead. Literary figuration, in effect, usurps human figure.[14]

In light of this theory, Ellison's phrase "the noncommittal mask of [Crane's] prose" acquires a more sinister and complex meaning, since the mask of textuality actually serves to expose (while concealing) the specifically literary disfigurement of human faces. Fried's reading works deconstructively to the degree that it sees *The Monster* as leaving readers suspended between a metaphorics of inscription, on the one hand, and a "'manifestly' social subject," on the other.[15]

For me, however, interest in the text derives less from the "theme" of that social subject—moral guilt and responsibility—than from representational effects better explored, I believe, in terms of narrative ethics. *The Monster*'s most important feature for me becomes the cultural meaning which it assigns to recognition. Social structures of representation, the story says, require a complicitousness from which even the act of reading cannot exempt itself. A politics of reading, in other words, is a far more overdetermined feature of this text than any metaphorics of writing.

To anticipate myself slightly, I wish to argue that since "representation" in *The Monster* pivots from material facts of language to material forces of culture and society, the question of face cannot be subsumed under an ethically neutral theory of writing (Fried) or of rhetoric (Miller). Nor can it be fully grasped in the terms of a conventionalist social allegory about responsibility, that is, saving or losing face.[16] Rather than being content with analyzing a polarity between these approaches, I would claim that the one quite literally conveys the other. In Lee Clark Mitchell's words, "As always in Crane, ethics is revealed to be fully complicit with discourse, and the triumph of the story therefore lies in enacting on its rhetorical surface the dilemma of race it represents."[17]

We see this develop in the various ways through which both Whilomville and the text systematically deny Henry Johnson recognition or response, through racist constraints on his identity and expressive power which are intact before the story even begins. (In this, Whilomville merely operates with the full constitutional sanction of Jim Crow, which, in Charles Chesnutt's words, "branded and tagged and set apart" such as Henry Johnson "like an unclean thing.") Text and town construct a culturally sanctioned and counter-moral barrier to prosopopoeia; there is no common human self correlated with Henry's black face. Henry Johnson lives under a veil far more ontologically devastating in its effects than the Reverend Hooper's, as the children's taunt which habitually dogs Henry before his accident makes clear: "Nigger, nigger never die / Black face and shiny eye" (145).[18]

(This couplet uncannily returns in a similar anecdote related by the literally self-effacing narrator of James Weldon Johnson's *The Autobiography of an Ex-Coloured Man*. In this text, however, there is no "black face" to correlate with the narrator's race, since he *passes*.[19] To spin a fanciful intertextual link, it is almost as though Johnson decided to write a cautionary tale about the "mask of whiteness" in order to show the effects of a more benign, but still self-canceling ontological devastation.)

What the text calls an "odious couplet" in fact undermines the townspeople's opinion of Henry's fate after he is dragged out of the fire: "As for the negro Henry Johnson, he could not live. His body was frightfully seared, but more than that, he now had no face" (144). The couplet moreover predicts his real fate; his bandaged appearance later on "allowed only one thing to appear—an eye" (145). (One must presume that Henry's color does not disappear along with his face, but that he is still recognizably black, if no longer recognizably himself).

The Ex-Colored Man

In this respect, the story gives the lie to the first and more optimistic of the two outcomes for intercultural recognition which I described above. Henry's subjectivity is never granted recognition by white culture. His blackness survives both the disfigurement of person and the extinguishing of self. If the children's couplet simply prognosticates, the one chanted by one of the town's adults—"He has no face in the front of his head / In the place where his face ought to grow" (156)—serves as an inadvertent piece of cultural critique, since it describes not only Henry's physical predicament but his social fate as well.

The text, of course, participates in this racism, neutralizing Levinasian monstration by merging it with the specifically cultural monstering which transforms, in Frantz Fanon's phrase, a "phobogenic object" into minstrel-show parody: "Henry's face showed like a reflector *as he bowed and bowed, bending almost from his head to his ankles*" (129). In this same section, one of the men in the barbershop, commenting on Henry's courting apparel, says, "Why he always dresses like that when he wants to make *a front*" (129). (Obviously, "frontage" in this text is a far less genteel, but in a way more material entity than it is in James's "The Real Thing"; Crane's "real thing"—a no more genteel nor less material matter of social standing—is, of course, racism.)

This question of inner identity versus front, self versus face, and one form of monstration versus another is the story's chief preoccupation, and not solely in respect to Henry, though the narrator focuses upon him first as he strolls to the Farraguts: "It was not altogether a matter of the lavender trousers, nor yet the straw hat with its bright silk band. The change was somewhere far in the interior of Henry. But there was no cake-walk hyperbole in it. He was simply a quiet, well-bred gentleman of position, wealth, and other necessary achievements out for an evening stroll, and he had never washed a wagon in his life" (127).

Behind the seeming irony the passage suggests not a divergence of surface and depth but a continuity between them, since both remain entirely circumscribed within the narrator's perspectival horizon. Displacing that perspective onto the town, the narrator says, "In fact, the people without resembled the inhabitants of a great aquarium that here had a square pane in it. Presently into this frame swam the graceful form of Henry Johnson" (128).

Is Henry's true self the stableboy and infantile companion to Trescott's son ("In regard to almost everything in life they seemed to have minds precisely alike"; 124)? Or is it rather the servant "set free" to don outlandish livery and court Bella Farragut in her home on Watermelon Alley? It doesn't much matter since in both cases, Whilomville—storybook America—sheathes his black skin in the white mask of projective identity. But so, as a matter of course, does the text.

Henry Johnson never entirely becomes an "ex-colored man" (a different order of monstrosity altogether, as I note above). But worse, before the fire burns his selfhood away, Johnson's blackness ensures for him, the town, and the narrator that his manhood will forever be in doubt, a fate precisely captured in Orlando Patterson's phrase "social death" (from the title of his book *Slavery and Social Death*). To be an "ex-man," in other words, one has to be accorded the attributes of "a man" to begin with.

To Jimmie Trescott Henry says revealingly, "I ain't gwi' have you round yere spilin' yer pants, an' have Mis' Trescott light on me pressen'ly" (126). But the entire story "lights on" him from first to last as something less or other than a man, whether faced or faceless, since color, not the features of his face, ultimately defines manhood in the logic of racism. In the words of a more articulate Johnson, "And this is the dwarfing, warping, distorting influence which operates upon each and every coloured man in the United States. He is forced to take his outlook on all things, not from the view-point of a citizen, or a man, or even a human being, but from the view point of a coloured-man" (*Ex-Coloured Man*, 21). Echoing W. E. B. Du Bois by counterposing a black man's self—the part of his identity "disclosed only in the freemasonry of his own race"—with his "role"—the blackface he is forced to wear—Johnson goes on to speak of the "dual personality" which results: "I have often watched with amazement even ignorant coloured men under cover of broad grins and minstrel antics maintain this dualism in the presence of white men" (22).

In *The Monster*, however, the narrator certifies that Henry maintains this "cover" even on Watermelon Alley, the all-black part of town, where he inspires "kowtow on all sides, and a smiling show of teeth that was like an illumination" (129). The text, in effect, exhausts Henry's personhood through a relentless racial optics. As Patricia Williams observes, "The words of race are like windows into the most private vulnerable parts of the self; the world looks in and the world will know."[20]

Indeed, an empty blank like so many of Crane's characters, Henry amounts simply to the sum of the features attributed to him—whether by the racist prosopopoeia which "grants" him a distorted face in the first place, or by the inhumane prosopopoeia which cancels and strips it from him after his accident. In the story's centerpiece scene of moral deliberation, Judge Hagenthorpe tells Dr. Trescott: "He will be your creation, you understand. He is purely your creation. Nature has evidently given him up. He is dead. You are restoring him to life. You are making him, and he will be a monster, and with no mind" (147).

The suggestion of *Frankenstein*, I think, is deliberate, as is the repeated identification of Trescott with Henry in the tale. More important, however, by "sponsoring" Henry's monstrousness, by "creating" him, Trescott merely transfers to himself a role already exercised by the townspeople in treating Henry as a menial black; if nature has given Henry Johnson up after the fire, white culture had already made of him "a completely artificial man," consigned to wear either blackface or noface.[21]

Just as Conrad's *Lord Jim* maims its hero, Crane's text actively sabotages its monster, disfiguring him before, during, and after he loses his face (the narrator's description of the accident itself is rococo in the extreme). In that respect, the exclamation Reifsnyder the barber repeats to his customers several times, "supposing you don' got a face!" neither aims ultimately at an authorial audience nor functions any more ambiguously than the famous closing question another fictive barber asks—"Comb it wet or dry?"—in Ring Lardner's "Haircut." By the same token, Hagenthorpe's pronouncement quoted above remains circumscribed within the text's own ideological boundaries; it need not, in other words, be taken as applying to Whilomville in general as opposed to just Dr. Trescott. The text, in short, speaks in concert with its narrator.

Crowds and Power

In a fundamental sense, then, the monstrosity in *The Monster* derives from the peculiar representational consequences of a black man's losing his face. The question one wants to ask of this story is, why must "the monster" be black? Or, again, would white facelessness be any less monstrous than black facelessness? "Justice," says Levinas, "does not link up beings already akin" (*TI*, 63). By contrast, it remains the peculiar and damning feature of American society that color creates two entirely different sets of beings, each of which, defined by the existence of the other, becomes "already akin" as a group. American justice, we could say, shows two faces (a constitutional fact in the wake of the Supreme Court's 1896 decision in *Plessy*).

A willingness not to look past a certain point flies in the face of an injunction to look *at*—not *past*—a demand which the face-to-face relation legislates as primordial justice. What Levinas thus calls "nonadequation"—a link between beings "absolutely foreign" to each other—can only be neutralized from without (since the face itself issues an incontrovertible moral summons)—by being encompassed in the panoramic perspective of another: "This inequality does not appear to the third party who would count us. It precisely signifies the absence of a third party capable of taking in me and the other. . . . The inequality *is* in the impossibility of the exterior point of view, which alone could abolish it" (*TI*, 251).

But the third party is also necessarily present in the face of the other because the whole of humanity, as it were, "presides" over my encounter with another and "looks at us." Alternatively then, the face-to-face relation sanctions all other distributive, civic, and fraternal relationships: "Like a shunt, every social relation leads back to the presentation of the other to the same without the intermediary of any image or sign, solely by the expression of the face" (*TI*, 213).[22] This creates a fairly obvious problem for political philosophy, since Levinas posits a metaphysical condition in force before a social contract, an "original condition" more originary than the one which founds the community or the state.

It also creates a problem for interpreting *The Monster*. Structurally speaking, the narrator assumes the role of the third party throughout. Here we see a crucial ethical difference between retrospective figural narration like Marlow's in *Lord Jim* and the entirely complicit third-person narration of *The Monster*, which seems to revel, as I say, in Henry's defacement. But turned around, so to speak, the narrator's encompassing gaze enables us to apply Levinasian pressure to its representational strategy; it "faces off" characters against one another rather than discreetly, "self-effacingly" describing them.

But perhaps more important, Crane's novella poses as one of its central phenomenological facts the Hydra-headed (and -faced) third party—the crowd or mob. Indeed, perhaps nothing more graphically contests the prophetic or religious force Levinas ascribes to intersubjective relation—the Face says, "You shall not kill"—than that stark symbol of racial violence, a lynched body with a black face.

Beyond comparisons of blacks to monkeys and watermelon, for the ultimate empirical referent of this text's racist terminology, one need look no further than the horrific image made famous by Billie Holiday—"a bitter crop: strange fruit hanging from a poplar tree." (The 1890's, of course, saw the high watermark not only of the erosion of black rights won during Reconstruction but of a mania for lynching which stretched across the South.)

That is why juxtaposed crowd scenes play such a crucial role in *The Monster*. Except for a single scene in which Henry accompanies Dr. Trescott to the Williams', he always appears to groups of others (a fact that seems to have gone unremarked in the critical literature). The successive tempests Henry creates at Theresa Page's birthday party, the Farraguts' home, Trescott's barn, and Alek Williams' home all crucially involve, in Thomas de Quincey's wonderful phrase, a "sea of faces." Similarly, at Reifsnyder's barber shop, in the description of a Saturday evening in town in section 4, and in the sections dealing with the fire, crowds gather and lend themselves to scene painting.

One discerns a movement here from anonymous crowd scenes in which Henry is negatively present (through foreshadowing or, as in section 10, through premature "deaths") to specifically domestic crowd scenes, which he actively disturbs. But once again, Henry's situation merely exposes prior deformities in the social structure which represses him. If Henry's identity cannot escape defacement, neither can social relations transcend crowd logic or glaring opposition: Hagenthorpe and Trescott, Hagenthorpe and Williams, Trescott and Jimmie, Martha Goodwin and Carrie Dungen, Trescott and Winter, Trescott and his wife all "face each other down."

Ethics and the Face

When Levinas equates the face with discourse, expression before theme or sign, he says the words it first "speaks" in the purity of signification do not convey an appeal, as in Rousseau's "love me" or "help me" from *The Essay on the Origin of Language*, but rather a command: "You shall not kill." "Power, by essence murderous of the other, becomes, faced with the other and 'against all good sense,' the *impossibility of murder*, the consideration of the other, or justice" (*TI*, 47). The face resists without resisting or, rather, the face does not resist: it speaks. Violence succeeds precisely by avoiding the face, by angling away from the "no" which is inscribed on it.[23]

We find this prophetic formula unexpectedly but pointedly worked out in Charles Chesnutt's ironic short story about black stature outside the law and within it, "The Web of Circumstance." I turn to it here because of the contrast it offers not only to the standing presence of crowds and the always foregrounded perspective of a "third-party narrator" in *The Monster*, but also to the latter's inability to grant its black protagonist a bona fide interior.

In Chesnutt's story, a blacksmith, Ben Davis, is convicted of a theft he has not committed and, after attempting to escape from jail, is sent to prison for five years. The stolen object in question is a white man's whip, the very image of white mastery and injustice. To compound the irony, what convinces the judge and jury of Ben's guilt is that after admiring the whip he was heard advocating economic self-sufficiency for blacks. This is a fatal double bind neatly summed up by a reply to Ben's common sense philosophy from a white man early in the story: "You're talkin' sense, Ben. . . . Yo'r people will never be respected till they've got property."[24]

When he is released and returns home, Ben discovers that during his imprisonment the real thief, his apprentice, had taken up with his wife (now dead, along with their children), and had sold his property. After concocting a plan for revenge against the original owner of the whip—the mistaken but understandable focal point for all his rage— Ben falls asleep in some shrubbery on the white man's property.

Dreaming of bygone domestic happiness as well as of the degradation of prison life, he awakes to find the Colonel's daughter standing over him, innocently offering to place flowers upon his face. The sight undercuts his desire for revenge, and he prepares to leave, whereupon the Colonel arrives, and seeing a "desperate-looking negro, clad in filthy rags" (322) running toward his daughter (whom he must pass in order to escape), shoots Ben dead.

Two interrelated features in this text call for comment against the background of what I have said so far about Crane's story: an insistent imagery of faces and a thematics of monstration.

The narrator lavishes attention on faces at three important junctures in the story. Tom, the real thief, attends Davis' trial throughout, and when the verdict is delivered, the narrator comments, "*The eyes* of the prisoner were glued to the jury box, and he looked more and more like a hunted animal" (304); and goes on to make plain Tom's expression of satisfaction: "If the face is the mirror of the soul, then this man's soul, taken off its guard in this moment of excitement, was full of lust and envy and all evil passions" (304). Prosopopoeic linkage of surface and depth here proves to be unequivocal and wholly just.

Another description of a face occurs when Davis is sentenced to jail; the narrator employs a similar dynamic of exposure and observation: "Several people were looking at Ben's face. There was one flash of despair, and then nothing but a stony blank, behind which he masked his real feelings, whatever they were" (313). In this case, however, one could say a "black mask" that registers inhumanity in others descends upon a black man's face.

If Tom answers to a conventional correspondence theory about physiognomy and moral worth, Ben demonstrates a "nonnormative," racial tactic of self-silencing and disguise. To adapt Levinas here, "Man can repress his saying, and this ability to keep silent, to withhold oneself, is the ability to be political."[25] Such responses as Ben's represent standing political moments in slave narratives and works of black American fiction.

The third and crucial instance involves Ben's transfiguration upon waking.

And as he slept, he dreamed of his childhood; of an old black mammy taking care of him in the daytime, and of *a younger face, with soft eyes, which bent over him sometimes at night.* . . . "Poo' man! Poo' man sick, an' sleepy. Dolly b'ing some flowers to cover poo' man up." A sweet little child, as beautiful as a cherub escaped from Paradise, was standing over him. . . . It was so strange, so unwonted a thing, that he lay there with half-closed eyes while the child brought leaves and flowers and laid them on his face . . . and arranged them with little caressing taps." (320–321)

As the girl ventures farther away to collect more flowers, "Ben Davis watched her through eyes over which had come an unfamiliar softness." Houston Baker has used the trope of the "black hole" to describe those imagistic moments when characters in African-American fiction descend underground (as in Wright's "The Man Who Lived Underground" and Ellison's *Invisible Man*) or enter a state of dormancy (as in *Beloved* and *The Autobiography of an Ex-Coloured Man*). Akin to the symbolic descent into the South in much black fiction, the black hole represents a domain not merely of holeness but of wholeness, "an achieved relationality of black community in which desire recollects experience."[26]

Sleep, as in Proust or Bunyan, would seem to perform a function very similar to this, but Chesnutt's story resists that thematics by introducing the important feature of reciprocal witnessing—a sleeping face observed by another face which is itself the first object to be noticed upon waking. Ben's condition, in this scene especially but throughout the story, remains one of exposure and vulnerability.

Although the text masks Ben's face once again—this time by flowers—the response of the child represents pure beneficence and care, an ethical response to a summons which is an appeal for cover. That the girl is white, is the Colonel's daughter, and is described in sugary and sentimental tones invites an ironic reading of the story's dénouement—fairy tale wrenched back into the depredations of racist ideology.

(Indeed, this interpretation would neatly complement another salient feature of the text. The encounter with the girl and her flowers, with fairly obvious self-consciousness, hearkens back, as I argued for Crane's text, to scenes in Shelley's *Frankenstein* where the monster encounters young girls, though here the allusion gathers its signifyin(g) force in the context of the tradition of black folk heros—outsize and outlaw figures like Stagolee: the Frankenstein monster as "bad nigger").

Monstration is a dual phenomenon in "The Web of Circumstance," however: the showing forth of a face and the metamorphosis (ultimately canceled) into a monster. They coincide when the ethical relation of two faces encountering each other intercepts Davis' near-monstrous transformation:

After five years of unrequited toil, and unspeakable hardship in con-
vict camps—five years of slaving by the side of human brutes, and of
nightly herding with them in vermin-haunted huts—Ben Davis had
become like them. (317)

It is true the thought occurred to Ben, vaguely, that through harm to
her he might inflict the greatest punishment upon her father; but the
idea came like a dark shape that faded away as soon as it came within
the nimbus that surrounded the child's face. (321)

"Assumptions of nonidentity read off the dark page of a black man's
face," according to Michael Warner, describe Whilomville's hermeneutic toward Henry Johnson.[27] A presumption of need and human
relatedness, conversely, becomes the quite accidental sign of ethical
responsibility in "The Web of Circumstance." It, too, is read off the
dark page of a black man's face. In Chesnutt's story, justice (a pre- or
nonlegal entity) does link beings not already akin, and the imperative
"You shall not kill" blends into the annunciatory "Here am I," both
signified in a down-turning face answering the one which looks up into
it. (Levinas typically refers to differences of "height" in ethical relation.)

Running parallel to its ironic critique of blacks' ensnared status
"before the law," "The Web of Circumstance" constructs a representational web of human relations in which ethical claims can, notwithstanding, be seen to follow from the irreducible dimension of the
face to face. The fact that the plot ultimately thwarts such claims does
not so much cancel their efficacy as draw attention to the double-faced
condition of justice for black Americans.

Unlike Shelley's *Frankenstein*, in which Viktor's child is murdered
because he shares his father's revulsion at a monster, "The Web of
Circumstance" shows a white child attending to, caressing, and thus
undoing the monstrousness taking shape in the face before her, uncreating the resultant "creation" of social inhumanity. The irony I
spoke of above comes to seem less definitive if one sees Chesnutt as
being at least hopeful about a respite from prejudice in childhood, if
not in the institutions and polity overseen by adults; there *is* a difference between "Poo' man! Poo' man! sick and sleepy" and "Nigger,
nigger never die." To this extent, at least, Chesnutt's story stages an
optimistic version of *creating the uncreated features of his face* against the
truly monstrous minstrelsy of social and legal inequity. (It should thus

also be seen in conjunction with Chesnutt's late story "The Doll," another bitterly ironic tale of justified black rage arrested by an ambivalent token of childhood.)

The Avoidance of Face

The Monster, by contrast, offers not even this qualified benison, and in its own perhaps inadvertent way serves as a far more savage critique of African-American social death, a web of cultural will, not mere "circumstance." Jimmie Trescott, once possessed of "a full sense of [Henry's] sublimity" (125) and now the legatee of his self-sacrifice, repudiates Johnson as "the monster" along with the rest of his townsfolk. Not alone in Henry's presence, but cheered on by the derisory exclamations of a children's "mob," Jimmie, significantly, dares only to touch Henry "delicately on the shoulder" (170); he neither looks at his veiled face directly nor ventures to remove the veil. The narrator describes Henry's response and its arresting effect:

> The monster on the box had turned its black crepe countenance toward the sky, and was waving its arms in time to a religious chant. "Look at him now," cried a little boy. They turned, and were transfixed by the solemnity and mystery of the indefinable gestures. The wail of the melody was mournful and slow. They drew back. It seemed to spellbind them with the power of a funeral. They were so absorbed that they did not hear the doctor's buggy drive up to the stable. Trescott got out, tied his horse, and approached the group. Jimmie saw him first, and at his look of dismay the others wheeled. (173)

The last sentence in this passage incorporates a motif repeated time and again in the text: accusatory faces linked to faces rebuked. In addition to the various instances of upturned faces which mime the original conditions of Henry's disfigurement, Whilomville faces contest one another in tense and unequal opposition throughout the text's many scenes of dialogue and encounter; the fact that such scenes are comprehended "panoramically" by the third party of the narrator merely compounds their static and neutralized intersubjectivity.

Just as "the monster" refers with equal accuracy to both Henry and the town of Whilomville, so Henry's defacement repeats on a material plane not only his cultural status as a thinglike person, but also the entire ethical aberrancy of the society which limits his acknowledgment. And whereas Chesnutt's story ends by contrasting a similarly

anamorphic picture of social morality with a sole encounter of benevolent facing and acknowledgment, Crane's begins, in a scene between
Jimmie and Dr. Trescott, with a short "lesson" in effacement and
avoidance which prefigures the rest of the story.

In his essay on *Lear*, Stanley Cavell suggests two possible explanations for a son's fear of recognition by his father: his own shame and
his shame over his father's impotence. The first, which Cavell calls the
wish to avoid being recognized or, rather, the wish to be "recognized
without being seen, without having to bear eyes upon oneself" (*MWM*,
280), describes Jimmie's ignominy at the end of section 1: "During the
delivery of the judgment the child had not faced his father, and afterward he went away, with his head lowered, shuffling his feet" (124).

It also describes the variations on this initial encounter which the
story compulsively repeats, the passage I quoted above being one such
instance and the conversation between Trescott and Judge Hagenthorpe in section 11 being a more damning scene of judgment because
it involves the reproval of a judge: "The judge abased himself completely before [Trescott's] words. He lowered his eyes. He picked at
his cucumbers." [146] Henry causes a similar reaction: "The bandages
on the negro's head allowed only one thing to appear—an eye which
unwinkingly stared at the judge. The latter spoke to Trescott on the
condition of the patient. Afterward he evidently had something further
to say, but he seemed to be kept from it by the scrutiny of the unwink-
ing eye, at which he furtively glanced from time to time" (145–146).

Indeed, no one in Whilomville save Trescott can bear either to
recognize or to suffer recognition from Henry Johnson; hence the
relation of reciprocal monstrousness in the story. Lear's appeal to
Gloucester, "If thou wilt weep my fortunes, take my eyes" (as Cavell
reads it), signifies a desire to be a Gyges in reverse, free from having
to witness the gazes of others. Henry's cyclopic obstinacy implies a
different sort of bargain: if you could bring yourself to condole with
my calamity, you must use *my* eye, the eye from a black man's face, to
see it, since your eyes do not register black experience, since you are
quite "color-blind."

But, shockingly, so indeed are the other black characters, as depicted
by the narrator. Crane subjects the other black man in the story, Alek
Williams, to the same racist condescension and ridicule as Henry.
Similarly, Henry is received alternately with terror and comic antics by
Bella Farragut, his former fiancée, and her mother. When Henry calls

on Bella Farragut a second time, "she shielded her eyes with her arms and tried to crawl past it, but the genial monster blocked the way" (164).[28]

Sheer terror at bodily disfigurement? Horror in the face of black defacement? The narrator leaves no doubt that the story's blacks serve rather for comic relief. Crane's use of last names or categorical locutions (as for instance "the monster" or "the thing"), as Michael Warner notes,[29] signals his withdrawal in his fiction of sympathy from the characters he describes; I am arguing, however, that the text insists that neither Henry Johnson nor the other blacks in the story merit such sympathy to begin with.

Although the narrator himself introduces the distinction between "front" and "deep interior" in regard to Henry, clearly the latter means nothing because its value gets displaced onto the former. (One sees here the limitations of Fried's rhetorical argument about deep and surface "writing" structures in the context of narrative level and agency.) In *The Monster*, blacks possess no interior phenomenological reality, only the exterior, phenomenal fact of blackness, or its empirical equivalent, facelessness.

(Likewise, whereas one of the two unadulterated "moral" actions in the story—Trescott's saving of Henry—receives implicitly compassionate treatment from the narrator, the other—Henry's saving of Trescott's son—is undercut with racist "theorizing": having "given up almost all idea of escaping from the burning house, and with it the desire, [he] was submitting, submitting because of his fathers, bending his mind in almost perfect slavery to the conflagration"; 137.)

Levinas subtitled his first long work *An Essay on Exteriority* to contest the traditional philosophical theory of the subject as rooted in the interior self. Instead, he argued, subjective freedom becomes comprehensible only as it is justified through exterior relation. The face of the other, while it signifies only relative to itself beckons me out of *myself* at the same time: it calls my subjectivity into question and makes it transitive.

We could say that Levinas, in common with the logic of Crane's story, relies on a concept of interchangeable surface and depth. Unlike *The Monster*, however, which uses such a concept to suspend the force of ethics, Levinas uses it to institute ethical authority instead. Indeed, with some justification, I would argue that the erasure of Henry's face paradoxically dramatizes his status as the Levinasian figure par excellence: man as he is infinitely other, man—because he is faceless—as face, and not as "man."[30] Indeed, for Levinas, the other is never man, but "the stranger, the widow, the orphan," the phrase from Isaiah which, in the context of Crane's text, logically entails both "the faceless" and "the colored."

Henry Johnson, as I said earlier, makes Levinas' concept of the face concrete in a profoundly political sense. As a black man in a racist society, he is already infinitely other—a condition, from white people's perspective, of negation, not ethical surplus. But as a faceless black man, he stands primordially denuded, "naked, without covering, clothing, or mask."[31] With his single eye looking out of a face thus "divested of form" (20), he represents the monstrousness of monstration, the unbearability of pure auto-signification: "The face has turned to me, and this is the very essence of its nudity" (*TI*, 75). (The word for face in Hebrew, incidentally, *panim*, incorporates the root meaning "to turn," which underlies both *panim* in its connotation of "outside" and *pnim*, meaning "inside.")

Does this then explain Henry's monstrosity, the double fact of the cultural murder which his society subjects him to and the textual murder which the story itself commits?[32] I would demur, since that would credit both Henry and the text with more ethical authority than each seems actually to possess. Henry does not serve as a figure of heroic resistance to the force of ideology; and *The Monster* does not pose an unambiguous ethical solution.

By implication, readers do not bear a hermeneutic burden of "saving the person in the text" like that which I located in my reading of Anderson's "Loneliness." Cranian ethics functions like Conradian ethics to the degree that readers assume not the caretaking role of Trescott, but the specular role of a "fourth party" comprehending both the narrator's perspective and the face-to-face relations of the novella's characters.

Ethics, I argue, does not reside somewhere in the text as an exemplary lesson to be decoded. Judge Hagenthorpe's weak lament "it is hard for a man to know what to do" (148) possesses exactly the same nugatory rhetorical force as Reifsnyder's "supposing you don' got a face!" and both echo the deflationary effect of the narrator's commentary on Henry's disfigurement: "amid flames and low explosions drops like red-hot jewels pattered softly down at leisurely intervals" (139). These sentences only seem to carry the story's "message."

Nor does ethics reside in the individual acts of rescue in the story, both more aptly designated by Hagenthorpe's phrase "blunders of virtue." Nor, finally, does ethics reside in the form of a conceptual category for understanding human behavior, as befits a naturalist like Crane. "Right and wrong" answers to the same disfiguring process as the removal of an individual human surface; like a face, morality possesses merely surface value in the story, and like Henry's face, it is sterilized.

In terms of narrative ethics, however, Crane's text does performative if not epistemological work, up to and including its own self-incrimination. It runs a set of changes on the single motif of monstration as the monstrousness of defective facing, hence the story's structure (like that of *Lord Jim*) of mimetically similar, juxtaposed scenes undercutting any larger and totalizing narrative logic.

The dissonance represented by a faceless black man repeats itself on all levels of the text—imagistic, rhetorical, thematic, narrative, and, last, ideological. Either, in visual terms, faces stare out at one another in futile recapitulation of the story's central fact: The Judge and Trescott "remained for a time gazing at each other, their faces illuminated with memories of a certain deed" (30). Or, in discursive terms, language ultimately terminates in the hollowed-out but at the same time purified expression of Henry Johnson's mournful wail.

Skepticism and Face

I argue, finally, that *The Monster* can be read as a kind of stripped-down and inverted analogue to Levinas' concept of ethics, its photo-negative, if you will. (In this respect, Crane's story works much like *Winesburg, Ohio.*) As Lyotard, Derrida, and Levinas himself have observed, the Levinasian project continually risks the logical difficulty of relying on constative discourse to describe a fully performative, or prophetic, "ethical reason."

The way the other appears to me as a face, summoning and commanding me; the "going beyond" of alterity and the "going beyond" of subjective responsibility; the invocation that is ethical discourse; the investiture and justification of autonomous freedom—all these ethical concepts should be construed as, rather, ethical events, categories of action, not knowledge. "Duties become greater in the measure that they are accomplished," says Levinas. "We know this relation only in the measure that we effect it" (*TI*, 76).

Levinas' work could be said to build into itself the undoing of its own rationalist scaffolding; it invites readers, therefore, to "perform it." I call *The Monster* a negative form of Levinasian ethics because it does not really believe in the conditions of alterity it puts forth. It shares Levinas' anti-epistemological bias. It includes itself in the representational and ideological violence it exposes. It places interiority and not just the surfaces of selfhood under erasure (precisely because it knows only the exterior fronts of persons). It undermines conventional theories of value and agency. And yet it remains completely skeptical.

Thus when Levinas speaks of "the manifestation of a face over and beyond form," he does not describe Henry Johnson's "meaning" in the story, although such a description may seem entirely apt: "Form—incessantly betraying its own manifestation, congealing into a plastic form, for it is adequate to the same—alienates the exteriority of the other. The face is a living presence; it is expression. The face speaks. The manifestation of the face is already discourse. He who manifests himself comes, according to Plato's expression, to his own assistance. He at each moment undoes the form he presents" (*TI*, 66).

Let me, then, recast this into political terms. Henry has no face. His expression, such as it is, remains unintelligible, perhaps not intrinsically, but at least to others. According to Levinas, "Discourse is rupture and commencement, breaking of rhythm which enraptures and transports the interlocutors—prose" (*TI*, 203), something the text emphatically denies Henry. Similarly, in "undoing the form he represents," he cannot come to his own assistance because, confined to the representational space which racism assigns him—"black" or "thing" but not "man"—he effectively lacks both form and figure even before losing his face. In "manifesting himself" he appears only as others have defined him, not as he experiences himself to be. Or more accurately in Henry's case, he seems to experience himself (at least before the disfigurement) as others have described him. In Levinas' sense, therefore, he cannot manifest himself.

Frantz Fanon writes in *Black Skin, White Masks*, "One day the White master, without conflict, recognized the Negro slave. But the former slave wants to make himself recognized" (217). Levinas' sense of recognition eschews Hegelian mediation because it believes neither in struggle nor in synthesis. Clearly, however, Henry Johnson's existential situation prohibits those very things which the passage above legitimates for him as an ethical subject. Fundamentally, as monster, he cannot be an ethical subject, he cannot be *kath'auto:* he can only be black . . . or faceless.

Lee Clark Mitchell's remains the only recent commentary on the story to deal complexly and at length with its racial content. It, too, invokes the trope of prosopopoeia but only in order to underscore "an oscillation at [the story's] heart" (181) between projecting a face and stripping it away. To counter strictly visual analyses like Fried's, or those like de Man's (and Miller's) which insist on the muting of reality which language as trope produces, Mitchell sees prosopopoeia rather as implying ultimately voice and the power to speak. As he observes, "the moral issues of *The Monster* as well as its brutal account of race do not become apparent until we escape the tyranny of the eye" (177).

"Henry's face showed like a reflector" (*The Monster*, 129). As one form of monstration, a face not only shows but tells, and for Levinas, as the sign of ethical responsibility, face equates with speech, discourse, expression, not vision.[33] As the "more monstrous" form of monstration depicted by the novella, Henry Johnson himself represents Levinasian face in its purest, yet paradoxically most horrific form: speech in the absence of visual recognizability. But as Mitchell notes, Henry is even more monstrous because he still has a voice after his face has been burned away. Although when Henry isn't wailing, he speaks what seem like human sentences, "his words cannot mean what they seem to say because they should never have been spoken at all; men without faces should lack mouths and voices" (185). Mitchell, however, sees Henry's continued ability to speak as an expressive triumph.

> He challenges the silence that is disfiguration's expected consequence with a "wail" that might be construed as representing a form of purified speech . . . Little as his personal tragedy can be diminished or gainsaid, he has achieved nonetheless a curious power that speaks to the condition by which meaning is formed. . . . The only one to escape [the story's counter-ethical logic] is Henry, and he has moved beyond our words (if also necessarily with our words) into a realm we cannot hear because we cannot face. (192)

I admire this reading but ultimately I do not agree with it. It transforms Henry into the sort of radicalized Levinasian hero to which I alluded earlier—pure face and expression because impossibly faceless, yet still able to speak. Henry, I would argue however, does not escape, and this fact gives the novella its peculiar ethico-political force. He enacts all the features Levinas lists in the passage above, but together they produce only a negative "traumatism of astonishment," not its positive counterpart, which is the "idea of infinity" produced by the other in me, a desire for that which both exceeds and contests.

And "what exceeds and contests" the story implicitly expresses in terms of racial otherness. Rather than monstrously freeing Henry to speak, the text forces him to become Levinas' "political man" by default: his voice may wield a "curious power" but it remains entirely contained, muffled, by the narrator's. The face speaks, ethically speaking, but it does not signify. Indeed, as an example of mystified expression, Hooper's withdrawal in "The Minister's Black Veil," I would say, appears a more potent political gesture by comparison. Thus a different sense of "the political," I believe, must come into play here.

Skin and Bones

Cultures construct difference according to all sorts of imagined bodily facts which, by means of a paralogism, may have nothing to do with real physicality; hence, as Sander Gilman shows, the "blackness" traditionally ascribed to "the Jew."[34] Racism, like antisemitism, may be a constitutive and endemic feature of human relations, but as the different legacies of American and colonialist history demonstrate, it also proves to be context-dependent. (Admittedly, this is also the difficulty of using Fanon as a gloss on black-American texts.)

In Crane's *The Monster*, a man's sacrifice and personal tragedy burden a town with an ethical responsibility which it has no will to assume. By literalizing the town's already intact representational structures, Henry's facelessness—his now absolute difference from others—and his ethical need paradoxically make him a monstrous exemplification, a limit case, we could say, for Levinas' ethical philosophy. But the story's representational logic in fact reduces to the idea that because of color, Henry Johnson is already enframed in a negatively political and therefore, I want to say, extra-ethical fate.

Even without the addition of "the third party," Henry's necessarily political horizon moots metaphysical concepts of ethical primacy; no one can face him, not even readers. Color, not face, becomes the nontranscendable metaphysical and phenomenological category in the text. Crane's story says that as the image and standing fact of intercultural difference, a black man has no face to begin with; he thus cannot initiate or enter into ethical relation, and the physical extinguishing of his face thus makes his entirely but reductively political being even more apparent.

If, as Fanon writes, "with the Negro, the cycle of the biological begins,"[35] then in "the Negro's" case, the story says, we must equate biology with the political, and not with the ethical. This, of course, represents part of the text's racism, as it dissolves self-standing ethical valuation into attached surface value on the model of a black man's identity dissolving with his face. Along with Henry, one cannot escape the story's conclusion that blacks in a text by a white author like Stephen Crane remain extra-ethical because paradoxically they possess only political representability—"representability" without, however, the advantage of political representation tied necessarily to ethical action. Like Fanon's Caribbeans, these blacks have been "seen," but have "not attained the truth of this recognition as an independent self-consciousness" (*Black Skin, White Masks*, 219). Or as Ralph Ellison puts it in *Invisible Man*, "Responsibility rests upon recognition, and recognition is a form of agreement."[36]

The story's self-canceling representational ethics, one must say, indicate as clearly as anything the essentially counter-moral nature of slavery and its various second-order institutionalized racisms because of the politico-economic nature of their terms; they reduce metaphysical categories to the level of property and object—a "man who is a thing." Obviously, then, Henry Johnson's accidental capacity for monstration—of face and of facelessness—substitutes for a prior and essential monstrosity—skin, or color—something that can only become truly invisible with the wholesale disfigurement of a self to its skeleton.[37] In this connection I note again that Levinas' later work represents subjectivity in even more profound and complex physiological terms than those he uses in *Totality and Infinity*—as exposure, as sensibility, as *skin*. Politicizing Levinas, I will say that "blacks"—humanity as skin—present the unambiguous and paradigmatic "Other" in American history and culture.

Racism need not aim at murder, but can aim at profit and containment. In that way it ensures that its victims remain objects. But as *The Monster* shows, racism also aims at suffering. "To inflict suffering," says Levinas, "is not to reduce the Other to the rank of object, but on the contrary it maintains him superbly in his subjectivity." It requires his "lucidity and witness," for as hated object, the Other can "never become object enough" (*TI*, 239).

Henry, I maintain, never does leave the confines of the text because, though stripped of face and publicly recognized identity, he still has yet to become *object enough for it* (that is, the text)—hence its fascinated need to stage repeated facings which are only successive defacings. Paradoxically, however, all of Whilomville together with the narrator necessarily undergoes the same deformation; the townspeople deface their own subjectivity to the extent that they extinguish difference—an act "only possible," as Levinas radically maintains, *"starting from me"* (*TI*, 40). We see Crane's characteristic flatness and abstraction of character particularly suiting this text, then. *The Monster* says that in marring the surface of its black populace, American culture hollows out itself.

Over New Year's day in 1991, a gang of white men cornered two black girls in a Bronx neighborhood and painted their faces and clothes white. A century after the writing of Crane's novella, the everyday disenfranchisement which black Americans routinely undergo was brutally literalized in a violent act of making people "lose face." Such things do not merely "irrupt" into history or "inadvertently re-enact" earlier historical events, as Hillis Miller claims. They demonstrate an enduring representational logic which literary texts like Crane's *The Monster* make available but do not transcend.

Transcending history, as Levinas says, requires that the invisible must manifest itself if history is to lose its right to the last word; its judgment, which is set forth in the visible, remains "necessarily unjust for the subjectivity, inevitably cruel" (*TI*, 176). Henry Johnson, a faceless black man in a work of fiction, and two unnamed black girls, live and painted white, offer us two kinds of invisibility that, in *our* acts of uncovering and exposing them, may indeed attain the status of "the visible"; this is how they "lead back to evidence."

But these figures' greater function, it seems to me, lies perhaps on what Ralph Ellison calls "the lower frequencies," in their capacity to submit to judgment the judgment of history itself, to speak, instruct, and dictate with the power wielded only by those who have been placed "under shadow." Such figures become "negatively aestheticized"; one order of representation (images of "blackness" or of "the negro," like the Sambo doll in *Invisible Man*) cancels the possibility of another: social weight and political authority.

Freed not from the tyranny of violence, but only from the tyranny of "the shadow"—the term Levinas himself uses to describe the dehumanizing capacity of representation—Henry Johnson and the two young girls, if they do escape at all, leave the void of "faceless faces, soundless voices, lying outside history" under our presiding gaze. And only through such release do we renounce home a little, and wander forth ourselves.

Benito Cereno
Shadows and Light

My reading of Crane ends with a quotation from Ellison's *Invisible Man*, a work which itself ends on an explicit albeit ambivalent note of "social responsibility," of release from the shadows and a return to history. But the novel *begins* otherwise, with its own quotation, drawn from the final recognition scene in Melville's *Benito Cereno*: "You are saved," cried Captain Delano, more and more astonished and pained; "you are saved: what has cast such a shadow upon you?" Benito Cereno's answer, "The negro," does not appear in Ellison's epigraph; but its negative presence, we could say, "shadows" the rest of the novel.

Ellison's text meditates at length on the peculiar and catastrophic equivalence drawn by Western cultures between racial identity and a naturalized theory of color perception. Call this the ideology of chromatics: "black" means the absence of light, the negative to its positive. Fanon-like, the novel stages as its first scene an act of revolutionary violence that ends just short of murder—a mugging by an invisible man which aborts with the mugger's realization that he casts no shadow.

How does one cast an effective shadow? Indeed, need one cast a shadow at all? For doesn't the dialectic of shadow and substance parallel the defining terms of a racist account of human relation? Must "creating the uncreated features of a face" involve ontological categories of shadow and light? *Invisible Man* asks these and similar questions.

Melville's story, antithetically, written from the narratorial and cognitive perspective of white men, assumes at the outset that cultural and individual perception proceed according to the play of shadows; shadows may not fully illuminate either light or act, but they remain inseparable from them both, "troubled gray vapors among which they [are] mixed" (217).[38]

We may take this as a general description of Melville's work, wherein typically inverted or suspended antinomies find a kind of literalization in the black, white, and in-between gray of *Benito Cereno*. But *Benito Cereno*'s color scheme clearly possesses special significance. Thus while Ralph Ellison may stand self-consciously within a long-standing tradition of American allegorists, something basic separates his concept of the allegorical role color plays in the phenomenology of race from Herman Melville's.

Am I saying simply that black authors and white authors differentially represent black characters?[39] (The fact that *Benito Cereno* has been read as either a pro-abolitionist or a racist text, with convinced batteries of critics lined up on either side, shows how loose are the moorings on which allegory as a representational strategy depends generally.) Valid or not, perhaps the distinction is better framed in terms of readership. Insofar as we can make such determinations, Melville and Ellison (to take the present examples) aimed at very different audiences.

Thus one might compare Melville's Hegelian epigraph for "The Bell-Tower"—"Like negroes, these powers own man sullenly; mindful of their higher master; while serving, plot revenge"—with Ellison's Melvillian one in *Invisible Man*. The first is a not very subtle hint to a white audience that the "labored" story in fact allegorizes the national ruin which is part and parcel of institutionalized slavery; and yet it speaks about, but does not address, black Americans. Ellison's epigraph, which raises perhaps a profounder point about the more insidious institution of allegory, speaks, on the contrary, to a mixed audience (which is still, rhetorically speaking, separate yet unequal).[40]

Shadowy Creatures, Your Creatures

But the text of *Benito Cereno* itself plays with such ratios of perception and reception. As Philip Fisher has persuasively argued, within its governing structure of either/or relationships, we find an instrumental logic which levies social difference, classifying members as opposed to strangers, insiders as opposed to those without.[41] Sartre has described how such a split works on the level of audience reception, but from a pole diametrically opposite to Melville's. In the introduction to Frantz Fanon's *The Wretched of the Earth*, he writes:

Europeans, you must open this book and enter into it. After a few steps in the darkness, you will see strangers gathered around a fire; come close, and listen, for they are talking of the destiny they will mete out to your trading centers and to the hired soldiers who defend them. They will see you, perhaps, but they will go on talking among themselves, *without even lowering their voices.* This indifference strikes home: their fathers, *shadowy creatures, your creatures,* were but dead souls; you it was who allowed them glimpses of light, to you only did they dare speak, and you did not bother to reply to such zombies. Their sons ignore you; a fire warns them and sheds light around them, and you have not lit it. Now, at a respectful distance, it is you who will feel furtive, nightbound, and perished with cold. Turn and turn about; *in these shadows from whence a new dawn will break, it is you who are the zombies.*   (13; my emphasis)

I cite this passage for two obvious reasons. Instead of the deliberately ambiguous picture of a suppressed slave revolt which we find in *Benito Cereno, The Wretched of the Earth*—as described on its original dust-jacket—serves as "a veritable handbook for successful revolutionary practice." If Melville's allegory leaves open the question of whether its shadow falls on readers unsure as to its intent, Fanon's book on the contrary aims deliberately at a readership it has very carefully selected.

In contrast to the prevailing conditions in the sea-bound world of *Benito Cereno,* stranded between Europe and America, in Fanon's "third world" no one whispers, nor do "master and man . . . act out in word and deed . . . some juggling play" (*Benito Cereno,* 267). A straight, clear, and transparent line runs from revolutionary intent through achievement to interpretability, since, as Fanon puts it, "the attempt at mystification, in the long run, becomes impossible" (*Black Skin, White Masks,* 95).

(This, conversely, is Fanon's amazingly trenchant description in *The Wretched of the Earth* of the colonial world, especially telling in light of Melville's story: "In this becalmed zone the sea has a smooth surface, the palm tree stirs gently in the breeze, the waves lap against the pebbles, and raw materials are ceaselessly transported, justifying the presence of the settler: and all the while the native, bent double, more dead than alive, exists interminably in an unchanging dream" [51]. The political ambiguity of *Benito Cereno* derives in part from its having substituted one dream or shadow-play for another—revolt and liberation as theater, not fact.)

Readers of Melville's text cannot occupy the kind of sure and certain perch which Fanon assigns to demystification; it is no simple thing to pierce this text's gray vapors, to unmask its masquerade. If Fanon's text need not lower its voice to accommodate the presence of a certain quotient of its readers, Melville's goes on whispering in front of both its readers and its "singularly undistrustful" Captain. And thus its political and ethical questions, I will argue, center ultimately on how auriculate are its readers (any decision we make about Melville's racial sympathies notwithstanding). Unlike *The Monster*, however, which collects its representational tensions around the image of an unreadable face, *Benito Cereno* holds out its own reflexivity as the puzzle that cannot quite be made clear.

Captain Delano, we know, sees and actively ponders everything; he simply fails to interpret his perceptions outside a bland and stereotyped frame of reference. But through him and through the thinly submerged narratorial perspective which enframes him, readers see the same things. What has been described as a "mystery story" actually diverges in an important respect from that formulaic structure.

In conventional detective fiction, two apparently conflicting orders of *vraisemblance* intersect: the reader's fallible misreading of signs and the supervening adjustments of the detective. Melville's story works somewhat in reverse. It underscores the ambiguous nature of its signs both internally (by having them read off by a fallible detective) and externally (by cluing readers to the double nature of the ongoing tableau by means of Delano's very waverings between trust and mistrust).

Yet this seemingly solid vantage point becomes instead a vanishing point within the text's frame of an entirely different system of *vraisemblance*—the legal deposition. As in *Lord Jim*, rigid empiricism not only fails in its own way to capture the "meaning" of the event, but also runs afoul of the same gap in knowing which the narrator exposes in Captain Delano: "So that the tribunal, in its final decision, rested its capital sentences upon statements which, had they lacked confirmation, it would have deemed it but duty to reject" (289).

The riddle-structure of Melville's story, its "tautology," in Eric Sundquist's apt phrase, is more than simply an epistemological or textual property. Indeed, my whole aim here is to put pressure on the hermetic or involuted direction of the text's own representational energies by insisting, as I did with *The Monster*, on their political and ethical effects, their role in ideological mimesis.

And here again, I'm interested in showing how political ramifications grow out of ethical narrative structures—tableaux of perception and cultural difference, of showing and telling, of face and discourse. Like two other "mariner texts" with which it shares certain elements, *Othello* and *Lord Jim*, *Benito Cereno* fuses the intersubjective and the intercultural by focusing on the image of face and stymied expression. Like Crane's story, Melville's makes and unmakes a black monster.

Eric Sundquist's contextualization of *Benito Cereno* against the background of antebellum fears and hopes of black revolution remains definitive. I defer to his excellent analysis of the novella's allegorical intent and of its precise historical anatomy of slavery and revolution— the peculiarly suspended state which both afflicts democratic principles and animates African-American resistance in antebellum America.[42] As Sundquist rightly observes, the story's knot of tautology presides equally over the self-canceling institution of slavery and an America which has yet to disentangle or simply cut it. Suspension and simultaneity establish the text's own revolutionary credentials by becalming the entire societal ship of state and calling it radically into question.

Yet there is a way in which the would-be insurrectionists of the *San Dominick*—the oakum pickers, hatchet cleaners, Atufal in chains, and Babo the subversive genius—remain insidiously subjunctive, fictional creations on every level. Not independent figures of resistance, but rather Old and New World property, the stuff alike of Aranda's legal ownership, Delano's clouded perceptions, the deposition's reconstitution of order, and Melville's abdication of authorial intent. Shifted from historical moment to the transverse plane of representational ethics, the insurrectionists fall crucially short of "creating themselves" (Fanon's phrase), let alone creating the uncreated features of a self-defining African-American face.

In Babo, the still point of suspension across whose "black body" the two white captains clasp dilatory hands, "casting earnest glances . . . too overcome to speak," one sees not only a genuine "hive of subtlety," but also a monster that escapes the immediate political confines of the text. In him, one sees, if you will, the ethical-representational transformation of "tautology" into a fascination with teratology instead.

For once again the ethical problematics of monstration, of facial exposure and readability, coincide with the individual and cultural sleep of reason which breeds monsters. That coincidence comes to the ghastliest of heads in the final paragraph's shocking image of Babo decapitated, at once staring and stared at: "Some months after, dragged to the gibbet at the tail of a mule, the black met his voiceless end. The body was burned to ashes; but for many days the head, that hive of subtlety, fixed on a pole in the Plaza, met, unabashed, the gaze of whites" (307).

Significantly, the incident of the exhibited head does not appear in the historical account on which Melville based his story.[43] In the rest of this analysis I want to trace the peculiar representational logic which seems to require its presence. Here Melville's culpability in a "racially motivated" violation is less important to me than the cultural availability of such an image and its powerfully counter-ethical significance: a literally dis-figured black face positioned to return the gazes of others. That "dis-articulation" is itself the end result of the commodity fetishism of person into artifact, a process which the economy of literature, as I have argued, can exploit as well as thematize, but which the institution of chattel slavery of necessity demands.

The Panoptics of Not Seeing

Above, I explained how Crane's text, by collapsing the difference between depth and surface, exposes the sociological mechanism by which ethical value and the problematic of identity—cultural "face"—are conveniently stripped away; a body of people, if you will, is selected for defacement. Henry Johnson, a legacy of Reconstruction, deconstructs before our eyes a pasteboard mask of facelessness which has replaced another mask of antic and infantile expression.

In *Benito Cereno*, Babo is also assigned two masks: the theatrical imposture he enacts aboard ship and the muteness which follows his capture. The text makes both of these explicit, referring to the first, after Delano receives his "flash of illumination," as a "mask torn away" (284), and to the second as follows: "His aspect seemed to say, since I cannot do deeds, I will not speak words" (307). (Earlier, at the first ritualized staging of another slave's recalcitrance/chastisement, the text has Babo "murmur," "How like a mute, Atfual moves" [236]. Atufal remains silent throughout this interrogation.)

We have met this aspect before in Ben Davis' elected silence during conviction in "The Web of Circumstance." And we will meet it again in *Native Son*.[44] But imagistically, Babo's aspect joins with Henry Johnson's to form, for practical purposes, the two most common culturally licensed masks for black representability: a voiceless face or a faceless voice. In both cases, the natural link between what Levinas calls manifestation and expression is cruelly severed.

Melville signals that disjunction early on by means of Delano's vision of black men as a "throng of dark cowls"—monks presumably vowed to silence, as well as mantled from the world. Similarly, upon climbing aboard the *San Dominick* to hear "as with one voice . . . a common tale of suffering" (221), Delano again introduces the split: "While Captain Delano was thus made the mark of all eager tongues, his one eager glance took in all faces, with every other object about him" (221). And once more, "that first comprehensive glance . . . rested but an instant upon them, as impatient of the hubbub of voices" (222). Between Delano and the narrator, the reader must track a constantly obversative relation between sight and speech, perfectly symbolized by the "ritual of whispering"—communication seen but not heard.[45]

Delano's vision is telescopic, as I noted above, something the narratorial perspective obliquely mocks in the extravagant simile it uses to describe the sun (Delano's guiding star): "wimpled by the same low, creeping clouds, [it] showed not unlike a Lima intriguante's one sinister eye peering across the Plaza from the Indian loop-hole of her dusk *saya-y-manta*" (218). Delano's sensibility being anything but sinister of course, the novella's first few pages monitor his ever encroaching, ever more totalizing progress into what the text calls "sudden disclosure": "Both house and ship—the one by its walls and blinds, the other by its high bulwarks like ramparts—hoard from view their interiors till the last moment. . . . The ship seems unreal; these strange costumes, gestures, and faces, but a shadowy tableau just emerged from the deep which directly must receive back what it gave" (222).

Although the legal deposition in effect lifts the veil from the shadowy tableau Delano is made to witness; although nature resolves the non-differentiated state of the story's beginning (Delano notes with frustration that the ship "showed no colors") into clearly demarcated blues, blacks, and whites under a "bright sun" at story's end; and although marine enchantment gives way to the hard terrestrial facts of reinstituted social order and inequality, one still feels that a shadowy tableau remains intact for the text's failed revolutionary blacks, leaving them, as the narrator of William Cowper's poem "The Castaway" says of himself, quite "whelmed."

It is within Amasa Delano's comprehensive glance (and with the help of a complicit narrative voice) that such a shadowy tableau—"the very expression and play of every human feature" (245)—takes shape; the transpositions of servitude and mastery exist only for Delano's eager perceptual consumption. Thus when the narrator speaks of Don Benito as "shut up in oaken walls" and "chained to one dull round," the "hypochondriac abbot" to his cowled throng, the "full ironic meaning" (in Henry James's phrase) perhaps escapes Delano.

Yet the transposition of slave and Cavalier in effect becomes both product and property of Delano's legitimating vision. He sees them; therefore, they exist. Hence when the narrator ironically speaks of "the noisy confusion of the *San Dominick*'s suffering host" as "repeatedly challenging [Delano's] eye" (227), not only does this locution repeat the cleavage between sound and sight, but it also meaningfully unsays itself, since the would-be rebel blacks never really challenge Delano's eye at all. As with the name, so with the man: a "masa."

In the preceding chapter, I spoke of the ethical culpability which witnessing entails, the share watchers have in the production or creation of images. Accordingly, within Delano's mild and balmy ken, we find Babo's dark and villainous "aspect" engendered, as Melville's text in turn, I would insist, preserves, sustains, and extends it outward; one order of monstration—the politicized (in this case meaning "unconscious") perspective of third-personal gaze—breeds another.

Again, whether Delano sees "correctly" is the sort of epistemological question which the text itself suspends. The point is, rather, that the line of sight from *Bachelor's Delight* (Delano's ship) to the *San Dominick* functions exactly like that habitually directed by the town of Whilomville toward Henry Johnson. It legitimates the image-repertoire through which it frames the objects it views. Like Dr. Trescott, it both shepherds and cloaks its monsters.

But Delano's point of view, crucially, incorporates the viewpoints of others, above all, the anti-Levinasian face-to-face exchanges of Babo and Don Benito. The latter's own looks oscillate between the downcast and the "half-lunatic." His fainting and refusal to eye Babo at the tribunal suggest a self-blinding which exactly matches Babo's self-silencing—consider, for instance, the scene in which Don Benito covers his face with both hands, having been urged by Captain Delano to look at one more incomprehensible occurrence (247).

We understand Don Benito's aversion *in exact relation* to Babo's habitual perspective, since Babo's eyes and face remain consistently glued to the Spaniard's. This is a commonplace in the stable of black portraiture for white authors—the black man as inverse double, as "shadow figure."[46] But (in Levinasian argot) as Babo's literal "attendance" at his master's "manifestation" might suggest—"unwilling to leave him unsupported, the black man with one arm still encircled his master, at the same time keeping his eye fixed on his face" (229)— Babo's concentrated devotion possesses almost all the features which Levinas assigns to his paradigm for ethical relation: face locked onto face, eyes "threaded on a double string," solicitude, asymmetry, height, even and most ironical of all, mastery, since, as Levinas says, "The Face, from its height, teaches Mastery" (*TI*, 91).

And yet the face-to-face encounters which we witness in *Benito Cereno* are absolutely counter-moral, the stuff of deception not revelation. Accordingly what Sundquist identifies as a "contagion of silence" in the story establishes a discursive correlative to the misrecognizing facial link among characters, and as such performs the parallel negation to Levinas' concept of discourse as expressive communion.

The Freemasonry of Face

Far from being a power-relation, the face to face in its ethical mode dispels or neutralizes power; it appears always as "a positive value." The face is not an object-cognition, says Levinas. Looking in this case means expression rather than perception. The orientation of the face indicates its dissimulating character: to turn the face frontward, as I said above, constitutes the very gesture of truthfulness.

Of course, Babo and Don Benito's collusive freemasonry in *Benito Cereno* belies all these meanings, as watchfulness translates into surveillance, vulnerability into the leverage of power, honest communion into consummate deception, and, finally, ethical mastery into the servile repetition of the word "master" (simultaneously subverting and preserving the status quo). And all of this transpires within and for the benefit of Captain Delano, whose own limpid insinuations of positive value fail to register the cyclical ambivalence acted out before his "inexperienced eyes" (230). Perhaps then, he's not "a masa," after all. The following sequence of perspectives in the text shows the entire triangulated pattern:

Captain Delano again glanced at Don Benito, but the latter's eyes were averted.

[Babo's] disengaged face, meantime, with humble curiosity, turned openly up into his master's downcast one.

[Delano] paused. The sound of the hatchet-polishing fell on his ears. He cast another swift side look at the two. (242–243)

But perhaps the three most conspicuous facial images in the text after Babo's decapitated head (each in its own way prefiguring it) remain defaced ones: the *San Dominick*'s stern-piece, "a dark satyr in a mask, holding his foot on the prostrate neck of a writhing figure, likewise masked" (220); the narrator's image for the similitude of innocence and guilt, which, "through casual association with mental pain, stamping any visible impress, use one seal—a hacked one" (249); and the lathered face of Don Benito "sculpted" by Babo's razor.

The text invites a symbolic reading of such images. For example, the stern-figure "pre-figures" Delano's tableau-vivant in the whaleboat when he crushes Babo's neck while holding the fainting Don Benito— an emblem of victorious but oblivious America *passant* over a felled Europe-cum-Africa. But this is to accept overtly Melvillean symbolism at, as it were, face value; when Delano remarks of the key around Atufal's neck, "padlock and key—significant symbols, truly" (238), the text casually gives the game away (as it does again when it reuses this imagery in reference to the deposition).[47]

Another way to interpret the image of masked faces, then (whether such was Melville's intent or not), falls in line with Levinas' definition of allegory: that is, the very temptation to bestow masks on faces—to allegorize them—in the first place. *Benito Cereno* says that when this intersubjective violation becomes intercultural, the price is registered by the image of a severed black head. If violence "can only aim at a face," then racial violence proves it with a vengeance—through decapitation.

Take the second image, of the hacked seal. Eric Sundquist notes of this metaphor, as well as others in the text, that the narrative voice makes it seem as though it originates from Delano, "existing on the page as in his imagination," while partially withdrawing it at the same time, "leaving the shadow of suggested meaning between the mind that embodies and the mind that creates" (113).

Later, he says that this also describes the mechanism of metaphor itself, which suspends two significations, "separating and joining them by the 'shadow' of meaning that falls between." I would qualify the epistemological emphasis here by simply suggesting that within an available vocabulary of cultural imaging, such metaphorization necessarily leaves the object of definition, in this case "the Negro," in eternal penumbra. This is in effect how cultures create monsters—by creating the uncreated features of their faces.

The third image, Benito's lathered face, works combinatively. In the shaving scene, a ritual of masking/unmasking ends in a ritual of disfigurement. Sundquist sees it as the preeminent moment of tautological suspension in the text, "the metaphoric at the absolute verge of becoming literal," the levels of story and discourse both "carrying out 'plots' and expressing in mimic action their mutual authority through a suspended and agonizing ritual."[48]

Among its several orders of reversal, the scene transposes the customary face-to-face relation of Babo and the Spaniard; this time, Don Benito looks up, fixated, into Babo's face, the two having exchanged merely one mode of ominous fascination for another. In Melville as in Levinas, to look up is not the same as to look down. Again, Levinasian themes of exposure, suppressed power, and what the text calls "manipulated" subjectivity become negatively illumined, the ethico-political shadow to a counter-ethical tableau.

For obviously, here and elsewhere in the story, socially legislated positions of dominance and deference do not *visibly* shift; instead, they express themselves in shadow through the "innocent lunacy or wicked imposture" of theatricalized relation. (Again, the metaphorization of ordinary shipboard reality, and by implication, of American society, merely etches in sharper relief the already metaphorical role a certain segment of the population is forced to play.)

An important aspect of the shaving scene not often noted, however, is the preponderance of "colors." In this most crucial of symbolic scenes in the story, the "graying" of normally dualistic conditions is temporarily set aside, not only for the blacks, blues, yellows, reds, and whites of the Spanish flag, but for the markedly counterposed hues of white shaving soap, black skin, and red blood. The lather is "intensified in its hue by the contrasting sootiness of the negro's body" (266), and the blood shows itself in "spots which stained the creamy lather under the throat," at the sight of which "immediately the black barber drew back his steel" (267).

The gray in *Benito Cereno* belongs to Delano's muddled perception, and in that respect does correspond to the shadow of equivocating metaphor upon which Sundquist hangs the text. But according to the story's (and its culture's) rigorous chromatic logic, shadow, as Don Benito makes perfectly clear, means "Negro," and not the suspended space between black and white. The shaving scene dramatizes the fact that mock role reversals and epistemological doubt both pivot around the fixed points of color.

Frantz Fanon calls this the Manichean nature of the colonial or racist society, the only stable level of reciprocal exclusivity in *Benito Cereno*'s world of black, white, and gray. (Hence, perhaps, the telling coincidence of Fanon's elaboration in *The Wretched of the Earth* on the colonial world's motionless Manicheism as "a world of statues" (51) and Melville's description of Babo as a "Nubian sculptor finishing off a white statue-head" (269).

"The Spaniard behind—his creature before: to rush from darkness to light was the involuntary choice" (280). Just so, Fanon speaks not of reversals but of full substitutions, one man's place taken up by another: "To wreck the colonial world is henceforth a mental picture of action which is very clear, very easy to understand. . . . To break up the colonial world does not mean that after the frontiers have been abolished lines of communication will be set up between the two zones. The destruction of the colonial world is no more and no less than the abolition of one zone, its burial in the depths of the earth or its expulsion from the country" (*The Wretched of the Earth*, 41).

This is not the world of the *San Dominick*, where mirrorings define the frontiers of mystified communication. This is why, shortly after the shaving scene, Babo must receive the blood stain correlative to Don Benito's; in what Delano insipidly calls "a love-quarrel," the Spaniard strikes the Negro. Babo and Don Benito remain blood brothers in a negative and self-canceling sense.

Shadows Cast

To be "Negro" in this story is to be ontologically marooned, "sealed in blackness," to use Fanon's phrase. When *Benito Cereno* does not refer to its two captains by name, it calls them the Spaniard and the American respectively. By contrast, Babo is never identified by the narrator as the African but is called "the creature," "the monster," "the black," and, most frequently, "the Negro."

The legal deposition obsessively ties identity to the fact of blackness in its studied repetition of the phrase "the Negro Babo." Hence whether Don Benito's explanation of the shadow over him connotes merely "blackness" per se, as some commentators have insisted, or Babo specifically, makes little or no difference. Babo and blackness alike possess no interior life of their own in Melville's text, but only the surface reality of projective representation, of ad hoc differentiation: of color.

But the name "Babo" clearly attaches to both face and demonization; like Crane's story half a century later, Melville's relies on a deeply ingrained racist image-repertoire which interrelates images of blackness, face, and monsters. I find it intriguing that one possible etymology finds the source of "Babo" in the Hausa word for "no."[49] Levinas, one recalls, defines the face as that which says no by its very expression, and Fanon's entire work is devoted to revolutionary Nay-saying. The more common etymology links Babo to "baboon," a term of racial opprobrium which projects animal monstrosity onto a black face. To my ears, however, the name "Babo" lies ambiguously and uneasily suspended between *abo*lition on one side and *barba*rism on the other.

I have found it useful to appeal to Levinas' own image-repertoire to show how all three images of face, blackness, and monsters coalesce around a disfigurement in recognition, a scarring of human acknowledgment. (In addition to the many levels of "uncompleted" thought and action which Sundquist identifies in the text, Stanley Cavell's idea of the hindered completability of acknowledgment can also be said to shadow it throughout.) Similarly, the centrality of generic formulas for anagnorisis in *Benito Cereno* at some level merely serves to mask the text's mostly unconscious staging of failed or violently repudiated ethical recognition.

As with my reading of *The Monster*, I would argue that *Benito Cereno* generates a representational ethics/politics that it cannot fully control. I say "ethics" because the dehumanization of an entire people is expressed in terms of the narrative and authorial murder done to a human face—the very sign of ethical relation, of the most exposed and most individualized attribute of personhood, which says, "You will not do murder." I say "politics" precisely because of the representative value accorded a single human face: a black face functions to signify black people.

For, indeed, Babo's face or head metonymizes his (non)humanity. The text ends with this description: "As for the black—whose brain, not body, had schemed and led the revolt, with the plot—his slight frame, inadequate to that which it held had at once yielded to the superior muscular strength of his captor" (307). Again, even if Melville intends his text as an attack on slavery and slaveholders (as Sundquist argues), *Benito Cereno* nevertheless both contains and passes on one more textually legitimated image of a black face violated through monstration—held out, as it were, for disfigurement. Even as Melville may profoundly incriminate his contemporary audience's own Delano-like obtuseness, its fatuous reliance on natural law as a framework for "capturing" blackness and black Americans, the text sustains its own blind spot: its own defect in the mechanics of face to face.

In Shakespeare's *Othello*, Iago expertly forges a counter ethical link between culturally enforced (mis)recognition and the engendering of monsters when he says, "Hell and night must bring this monstrous birth to the world's light" (1.3.409). Although Iago refers here to the plot he hopes to hatch, his mention of Othello's name immediately before in conjunction with animal imagery artfully collocates all these things: a plot, a black man, and monstrousness.

When transferred to the horizon of Melville's text, however, this idea of plot is perhaps better expressed through the word which Melville reserves for describing the fate of Billy Budd—"marplot." As in *Othello*, in *Benito Cereno* narrative manipulation of a black man both cancels the revolutionary threat he poses, and lays bare the emplottedness of African fates in the New World, the shadow which stands over "the Negro" and "blackness," making them plotted elements in an enduring racist narrative.

Despite itself, then, Melville's text establishes another link in an enduring American significatory chain which makes and unmakes blackness by "uncreating" the features of a face. A link all the stronger, I would argue, for the silence it bequeaths to Babo at story's end, which is no less a capitulation to the culture which defines him than to the power to contest that culture (as Sundquist argues) by holding itself in reserve. The story's logic of tautology, finally, must hold in check even the representational freedom which it cannot help denying to its black characters.

The *Unheimlich* Maneuver

As I did in the preceding section, I conclude this reading by opening it up to history and to its "beyond." One of the severest lessons of *Benito*

Cereno—the reason for me that it betokens a representational ethics—is the very mobility of the images it circulates, the reversals, transpositions, and reattachments of meaning within the text. But by "mobility" I mean something beyond a textually contained series of displacements which mirrors back for us a historical conundrum—the "dread," as Melville put it, of tautology. Babo's severed head and defiled face pass out of the story and into "history," that is, into the collective hands of a culture's capacity for, and failure of, imagination—its large-scale ethics of representation.

This leakage, I have argued, ultimately outpaces *Benito Cereno*'s subversive intent, forcing its revolutionary energies into reiterative as well as genuinely interventive directions; what goes around, in other words, just keeps going around. The "shadowy tableau" of the story's black characters remains a perpetual estrangement, an intact code of "strange costumes, gestures, and faces."

Such is one side effect of "tautology" as a lens for critique: the graying of certain unequal blacks and whites which are perhaps all the clearer for being kept separate. Indeed, I'd like to construe the "shadow" of *Benito Cereno* with which I began my reading as an image, finally, for the text itself, a still occluded interval between the "white lies" of successive historical daylights.[50] One of *Benito Cereno*'s two logics (or ethics) of monstration, in other words—the de-facing of a black man—can't help undercutting the other—the "showing forth" of an America tormented by and through slavery.

Like *The Monster*, Melville's text casts a long shadow. It falls onto other texts, as witness the following sentence from William's Faulkner's *Light in August* (the manic reworking of *Benito Cereno*'s tautological syntax): "But after that I seemed to see them for the first time not as people, but as a thing, a shadow in which I lived, we lived, all white people, all other people." That shadow falls onto a whole culture and polity as well as onto individual persons. And it falls onto history itself, where merely fictive shadows become lived ones. As I noted in the last chapter for some of Henry James's fiction, and as I am suggesting here for *Benito Cereno*, *unfree* values—even when they are the object of representation and critique—can still circulate back into the world again with a vengeance.

Consider, for instance, the tautology, the knot, that is Michael Jackson—perhaps the most famous black man in history. If, as he sings, "It don't matter if you're black *or* white," why has he remade or unmade his own blackness? (While respecting his announcement on television that he suffers from a skin disease, I pose the obvious question: Why light make-up, then, and not dark? why white, not black?)[51]

How to understand this self-chosen effacing of a black face? Would it be so far-fetched to consider in this light Jackson's preoccupation, ironic or not, with the physical remains of the Elephant Man, the nineteenth century's most famous "monster"? One explanation for the phenomenon of Michael Jackson, then, involves tautology at its most uncanny: revolutionary power at the point of suspense, projected back on or against the self; the mechanism—call it the *unheimlich* maneuver—by which an image-repertoire of race hatred, in a final, bizarre transposition, finds a home inside the very interior life which such an image-repertoire intrinsically denies.

The alien become improbably native? *Alien* (the movie) as a type for self-bred monsters? An insidious pop cultural inflection of "domestic violence"? Such questions pry us away from home one last time, as I turn to face this chapter's final instance of monstration and perhaps its most compelling, thickly realized native son: Bigger Thomas, not only ensnared "in a tangle of black shadows,"[52] but marred as well by the white shadows in which many blacks are made to live.

Native Son

How *was* Bigger born? (I signify here on the title of Wright's prefatory essay, "How Bigger Was Born," which he provided for the second edition of *Native Son*.) And how does such a question fit within a framework of narrative ethics? After all, the novel was written and received in the spirit of naturalist fiction or the protest novel, genres more political than ethical. Yet *Native Son* raises central questions, both hidden and overt, about the role it asks its readers to play. And though I have said as much for *The Monster* and *Benito Cereno*, to speak about Wright's novel primarily in terms of its "effect" (an illusory term, to be sure) means confronting what Bakhtin calls its answerability in the world.

But again, even here, I am less interested in interrogating the intentionality of a text than in speculating on the passage through it of an image-repertoire both larger than and anterior to the novel's own. Hence I will first consider certain intertextual parallels between *Native*

Son and other texts, and then look briefly at some examples of the novel's critical reception.

UnderWrighting

Like *The Monster* and *Benito Cereno*, Wright's text couples images from what I have established in the preceding sections as two orders of monstration which together "aim at" a black face. But unlike Crane's and Melville's stories, which contain images very similar to those in Wright's text, this novel was written by and not simply about a black man; no white man, observes one critic, could have written *Native Son*, since its most extraordinary quality is its very "niggerness."[53]

Obviously, of course, the question of intentions cannot fail to arise, since presumably one best construes the role played by a text's representational ethics by having already stabilized the author's rhetorical thrust—ironic, parabolic, realistic, and so on. And yet, to be sure, a text's blindnesses can be as instructive as its insights. Take, for example, the following examples of uncanny intertext. Wright describes Bigger's capture by the police in the following way: "Round him surged a sea of noise. He opened his eyes a little and saw an array of faces, white and looming. 'Kill that black ape!' Two men stretched his arms out, as though about to crucify him; they placed a foot on each of his wrists, making them sink deep down in the snow. His eyes closed, slowly, and he was swallowed in darkness" (699).

In *Benito Cereno*, Melville describes Delano as having "ground the prostrate Negro" with his feet, binding his hands, while Babo "made no resistance." Afterward, as I noted above, Babo refuses to speak. Likewise, in detention, Bigger Thomas "steadfastly refused to speak" (700). Beyond Wright's image of "an array of faces," what makes an interesting but perhaps unspectacular parallel compelling for me is Bigger's willful lapse into unconsciousness upon arrest—the text says "he chose not to struggle anymore" (701)—and his even more telling fainting fit at his inquest, the result of the accumulated pressure of staring white faces; when he wakes, as in Stephen Crane, "a white face loomed above him."

Here Wright has, as it were, fully merged Babo and Don Benito or, more precisely, merged their respective strategies in the face of the implacable—silence on the one hand and loss of consciousness on the other. Like Babo, Bigger silences himself; like Don Benito, he covers his face with his hands during his inquest. Fainting, as Philip Fisher observes, constitutes "the opposite act to solving the riddle" in *Benito Cereno*—Don Benito opts out of the web of circumstance for which he bears partial responsibility.[54] Likewise in *Native Son*, fainting offers the one alternative to white America's construction of plot and counterplot, as Bigger turns away "from the long train of disastrous consequences" (701) that is the marplot narrated by the text.

I do not argue here for a case of conscious borrowing, let alone a knowing resolution of Melvillean tautology. But if we take Bigger's fainting as analogous in a way to Don Benito's, I find it fascinating that Wright does what Melville does not: he merges power and powerlessness, white and black, defiant staring down and being stared at—a both/and instead of an either/or. Though I defer a full treatment of the question to later in my analysis, this would be one way of answering how Bigger was born. That is, in addition to the extensive factors and variables Wright lists in his Jamesian preface to *Native Son* to account for Bigger's birth, Bigger's character incorporates what I would call accidental properties, drawn from the same cultural vocabulary which underwrites *The Monster* and *Benito Cereno*.

Here is a second candidate for such underWrighting. The "Kabnis" section of Jean Toomer's *Cane*, a work rarely mentioned in relation to *Native Son*, begins in a manner remarkably evocative of the first pages of Wright's novel. The parallel becomes even closer if one looks at the first draft for *Native Son*, which omits the alarm clock and describes at greater length Bigger's transition from sleep to wakefulness. But Ralph Kabnis attempts the transition in the other direction; unlike Bigger, he reads in bed, trying to fall asleep. Toomer describes his immediate surroundings with the kind of insistent imagery of black-against-whiteness which pervades *Native Son*: "whitewashed hearth and chimney, black with sooty saw-teeth," "rosin yellow" walls, "black cracks" between, "the warm whiteness" of his bed, and the song lyrics he hears, "White-man's land. / Niggers, sing."[55]

Directly, Kabnis dreams:

> Near me. Now. Whoever you are, my warm glowing sweetheart, do not think that the face that rests beside you is the real Kabnis. Ralph Kabnis is a dream. And dreams are faces with large eyes and weak chins and broad brows that get smashed by the fists of square faces. The body of the world is bull-necked. A dream is a soft face that fits

uncertainly upon it . . . God, if I could develop that in words. Give what I know a bull-neck and a heaving body, all would go well with me, wouldn't it sweetheart? If I could feel that I came to the South to face it. If I, the dream (not what is weak and afraid in me), could become the face of the South. (81)[56]

Not only, as in Wright's text, does a rat jolt the sleeper into consciousness, but the overdetermined rage which characterizes him becomes compressed up front in the text into a symbolic act of murder. In displaced and misogynist frustration, Kabnis hurls his shoe at a chicken, then seizes and decapitates it, saying, "Got you now, you she-bitch." "Kabnis whirls the chicken by its neck and throws its head away. Picks up the hopping body, warm, sticky, and hides it in a clump of bushes. He wipes blood from his hands onto the coarse scant grass" (82). Bessie's fate at the hands of Bigger in *Native Son* does not loom far off.

We can see the title of Toomer's novel fanning out in two not unrelated directions—"roots": *Cane*; and fugitive rootlessness: *Cain*. The title *Native Son* is similarly double-voiced. But it is the crossing of two motifs within these texts—the presence of faces and the often monstrous violence which is aimed at them or which they desire—I would claim, that constitutes the parallel which draws them together so uncannily.

All three sections of *Native Son* alternate directed and averted glances—the same perceptual rhythm which is theatricalized in *The Monster* and *Benito Cereno* and "resolved" into the respective images of Henry's horrifying one-eyed face and of Babo's still staring and stared-at head. White faces in *Native Son* arc in a Melvillean circle from the grotesque—the face of a policeman is described, like Captain Ahab's "pasteboard masks," as "stuck like a piece of white pasteboard above the top of the hole" (692)—to the redemptive—Bigger "saw Jan as though someone had performed an operation on his eyes, or as though someone had snatched a deforming mask from Jan's face" (715).

Throughout the novel, Bigger remains both painfully conscious of white faces looking at him (making him, as the narrator puts it, "feel his black skin") and mostly unconscious of his own looking out into a world rigorously circumscribed by whiteness—snow on the ground, white skywriting, white high society on a movie screen. In Dan McCall's superb formulation, racial misery here equals indecent exposure; an unerring transfer of distorted recognition-energies compels Bigger in the direction of heads: crushing, severing, and being haunted by them.[57]

In much the same way, Kabnis modulates with unaccountable logic from invoking faces to envisioning them smashed, from personifying himself as a face to stifling consciousness in the form of tearing from its neck the head of a chicken. That act itself seems the sympathetic displacement of a more complex cultural ambivalence, expressed in a song which comes to Kabnis at night; a black mother sings of lulling and then killing a white baby.[58]

Estranged from community, both Kabnis and Bigger Thomas resort to the alienated violence which aims at faces and heads, the sites of consciousness and recognition. But they differ to the degree that consciousness makes Kabnis impotent, while Bigger's internal blockage seems preconscious; the narrator must convey his thoughts to us. If Bigger always "goes for the head," as Roger Rosenblatt puts it, he does so because he is venting the unconscious *ressentiment* bred of a prior cultural decapitation.[59] But both Bigger and Kabnis in effect try to remove their own faces by "blotting out" (the locution which the narrator habitually uses) and "smashing" (Kabnis' phrase) the faces of others.

Monsters inhabit both texts. The prosecuting attorney in *Native Son* calls Bigger an "infernal monster." Toomer, likewise, describes Ralph Kabnis as breeding a monster within himself: "Th form thats burned int my soul is some twisted awful thing that crept in from a dream, a goddamn nightmare, an wont stay still unless I feed it" (110). Hence the most problematic connection of all which I want to draw between these two texts. Kabnis (and Jean Toomer) divulge a personal ambivalence, a racial self-hatred which draws deep from the culturally inscribed well of bigoted representationality. Wright did not seem to suffer from such ambivalence, and yet *Native Son* draws, I argue, from the same well.

Here again, conscious authorial impulses are less important to me than the charged and compressed valences of "monstration" which thrust themselves into both authors' work. But black authors? My point is precisely the intrinsically ambi-valent power of a cultural vocabulary of "race" to cross the color line, so to speak, of the text. The chain which links blackness to face to monstrosity is a legacy which all Americans inherit, willingly or not, as hard to disinherit as that piece of chain which Invisible Man carries with him throughout the novel, and cannot seem to get rid of.

In Chapter 4, I spoke of Levinasian and Bakhtinian themes of recognition and answerability as impinging on literature in the form of an autonomous ethical image-repertoire which invests even texts of an overtly "moral" cast with an internally differentiating power. I have used the term "representational ethics" to describe this nonrhetorical agency, a mechanism which, in *The Monster*, *Benito Cereno*, and here in *Native Son*, grafts political meanings onto originally intersubjective images and tropes; neutral faces thus become either black or white, the "simple" act of looking becomes marked as white (objectifying) or black (objectified).

The difficulty which this interpretive scheme introduces (even for the James stories) lies in the fact that the images do not then read out as transparently "ethical." On the contrary, they negatively confirm an ethical principle by conspicuously violating it: the face, instead of being the ethical summons which says "no" to appropriation, hatred, or violence, becomes the target for all these things; difference, instead of being the ground of humility or respect, serves as the excuse for a reifed subjectivity and its "drama" of power. (Hence the logic of an agonistic and privative model for recognition like Fanon's, from the perspective of which "metaphysical" theories such as Levinas' necessarily appear exorbitant and impossibly utopian.)

Two Types of Signifying

Contemporary studies of African-American literature assume as basic not merely a stable cultural inheritance but a dynamic system of tertiary revision. This applies, of course, inter- as well as intraculturally, for black-American fiction defines itself as much within or against a tradition of "American" literature as of "African-American" literature. To paraphrase Henry Louis Gates, Jr., the African-American reader reads and critiques white as well as black texts as an act of rhetorical self-definition, "allowing . . . the black person to move freely between two discursive universes."[60] Thus for Gates, in addition to a text like Paul Lawrence Dunbar's *Sport of the Gods*, *Native Son* signifies on fiction by Norris and Dreiser (and, as its preface states, on stories by James, Hawthorne, and Poe)[61] just as Ellison's *Invisible Man* signifies on it.

Here I am saying something slightly different. Wright's novel does not "signify" on texts by Melville and Toomer in Gates's sense of the term. (Though I do not elaborate the connection, *The Monster* also, I think, stands behind—or rather at the "head" of—Wright's novel.) Rather, standing impediments to individual and racial Signification (with Levinas' capital "S") circulate through all these texts in ways which the texts themselves do not entirely control. (Usually, when critics speak of a deficiency in authorial control in respect to *Native Son*, they mean its overemotionalism; it should be clear that I intend the sense of "control" quite differently: narrative ethics will make its presence known, authorial intention—even when "moralistic"—notwithstanding.)[62]

We can think of this pulse within the text as a "call and response" in addition to the call and response of cultural poetics or of folklore, a signifying structure, to use Gates's term, of ethical (and counter-ethical) relation. Thus *Native Son* exploits, sometimes quite paradoxically, a common stock of images which it simultaneously critiques and endorses, and this is the ethical burden which it leaves to readers. As in Melville's case, the varied critical reception of Wright's novel partly follows, I believe, from a logic dictated by the ambivalent structure of the text itself.

To take another example, the third section of *Native Son*, "Fate," which consists of a long didactic summing-up by Bigger's lawyer (and for that reason has been critically decried as nonorganic or digressive), serves a function exactly parallel to Don Benito's deposition in *Benito Cereno*. Each legal action re-contains, even co-opts, the energies let loose by the narrative which precedes it; each employs a language which converts its protagonist's experience, fitting it to procrustean "theories." Each, in its own way (and for different motives), unsays what the text has said immediately before it.

Does this mean then that Wright consciously or unconsciously imitated Melville? Or that Wright blundered in resisting the negative capability which would have left his novel self-sufficient and unencumbered from within? In fact, it need mean neither of these things, but instead a kind of discursive collision or cross-fertilization, a cementing together of different discourses, different ideological energies.

In this case, whatever Wright's intentions for it, a legal or sociological "account of fact" attempts not merely to defuse the potency of Bigger's revolutionary actions, but also to re-contain, to "sociologize," the now politicized representational energies which show how racism, objectification, stereotyping, and other forms of cultural violence actually take place. Moreover, one can see the "Fate" section of the novel as redirecting strictly narrational energies, as both Buckley's prosecutorial designs and Max's crucial denial of acknowledgment at the novel's end together squelch or overpower Bigger's "liberating" acts of confession. Max, for instance, literally walks out on Bigger: "Max's eyes were full of terror. Several times his body moved nervously, as though he were about to go to Bigger; but he stood still. . . . Max groped for his hat like a blind man; he found it and jammed it on his head. He felt for the door, keeping his face averted" (849). The Wedding Guest goes about his business; pity and fear do not enable but rather cripple acknowledgment; one protects oneself from the other by covering the head, and looking away.

Valerie Smith reads this scene (and the novel as a whole) as an opportunity for Bigger to transcend the emplottedness which has deformed his life by taking over and actually telling his own story;[63] Max is effectively discharged as "narrator for the defense." Thus at one point the narrator tells us, "The impulsion to try to tell was as deep as had been the urge to kill" (733). But the "cold breath of peace" (781) that comes from confession (which Smith interprets as the fruits of authorial control) is described by the text itself almost immediately afterward as merely a "short respite of rest." And crucially, the narrator points out that Bigger understands only the tone not the meaning of Max's speech during the trial; so his own storytelling skills remain in doubt.

Even if his own words loose the narrative fetters which bind him, Bigger's story has already been told: Max "captures" Bigger through symbolism no less confining than the narrator's: "A man's life is at stake. And not only is this man a criminal, but he is a black criminal. . . . The complex forces of society have isolated here for us a symbol, a test symbol. The prejudices of men have stained this symbol, like a germ stained for examination under the microscope" (804).

A broadside against "our whole sick social organism," this amounts really to one more instrumentalization of black personhood—humanity's "black mask," the black man as metaphor, Bigger Thomas as a "mode of life." In Ralph Ellison's words, "Gradually [the Negro] was recognized as the human factor placed outside the democratic master plan, a human 'natural' resource who, so that white men could become more human, was elected to undergo a process of institutionalized dehumanization."[64]

In fact, I would argue, Bigger's narrative almost never belongs to him alone, since it is continually "thematized" and assimilated to somebody else's narrative control. Beyond the equally short respite of free indirect style allowed him in an otherwise insistent framework of psycho-narration, Bigger possesses almost no independent life of his own within the text; what he has is angry recoil or glued-on motive.[65] As he himself puts it, "what I killed for, I *am*." Even here, however, the unconscious "colonization" of his own words by the courtroom rhetoric of his lawyer undercuts Bigger's self-fashioning: "When a man kills, it's for something. . . . I didn't know I was really alive in this world until I felt things hard enough to kill for 'em. . . . It's the truth, Mr. Max" (849).

In concert with what I have called the underWrighting of the novel in which he appears, Bigger stands out as an almost entirely overwritten character, and thus shares the common fate of a character, like Pip in *Great Expectations*, who cannot get outside of plot. Thus the levels of narration in the novel actively conspire with a cultural repertoire of images linking face to monstrousness in order to leave Bigger to "Fate," the section of the novel which escorts him from police station to court to prison.[66] Now in a racial context, an author sentences his character to the "fate of imprisonment," which Levinas talks about in relation to Poe (a fate doubly ironic in this case given Wright's acknowledgment of Poe in the final sentence of "How Bigger Was Born").

This Thing's Bigger Than You

I return now to the issue of readership with which I began, important enough for Wright that he initiated an extra-textual dialogue with his readers through his prefatory essay to the novel. Wright's profiles of the several Biggers he has known reflected in the composite Bigger of *Native Son* betray a continuity with, a shadow-life to, Wright's own personal history. Like him, those figures began by feeling "estranged from the religion and folk culture of his race" (859).

That outsiderness is the one feature of Wright's life and fiction which critics of disparate stripes uniformly begin with when they discuss his work—the "deep sense of exclusion" (863) which generates "the Bigger Thomas reaction," the modus vivendi for his rebellion. "More than anything else," Wright says, "I was fascinated by the similarity of the emotional tensions of Bigger in America and Bigger in Nazi Germany and Bigger in old Russia. All Bigger Thomases, white and black, felt tense, afraid, nervous, hysterical and restless" (865). (The strange analogies to National Socialism and Stalinism which Wright draws, I must say, are even harder to justify now than at the time of publication, 1940.)

Now although immediately afterward Wright speaks of Bigger as a "symbol of American life," he obscures the symbolism by multiplying Bigger once again, this time as either a "white" or a "black" Bigger. I continue to find these equivalences mystifying because as the name suggests, to be a "black Bigger" just *means* to be Bigger, since to be a "Russian," "Nazi," or "white" Bigger connotes at most the *ressentiment* of diminishment; only "Bigger Thomas" incorporates the nonshareable condition, the native son's patrimony, of "niggerness."

Wright expresses a hunter's fascination with Bigger: "Bigger won over all . . . claims . . . because I felt that I was hunting on the trail of more exciting and thrilling game." "What Bigger meant had claimed me because I felt with all of my being that he was more important than what any person, white or black, would say or try to make of him, more important than any political analysis designed to explain or deny him, more important, even, than my own sense of fear, shame, and diffidence" (869).

It is hard for me not to hear the ironic oversound here of Boris Max's dilemma in defending Bigger (omitted in the 1940 edition)—"How can I make my voice heard with effect above the hungry yelping of hounds on the hunt" (805). Wright's incongruous image of a big-game hunt startles even in context, and he then compounds it by confessing to an allure which supersedes any external claim on Bigger's "Biggerness." (As Charles Johnson says of the novel, it achieves in the end a dimension "bordering on racial mythology—the hunt for the killer-slave.")[67]

Thus Bigger would seem to have a life independent of the text after all, at least until Wright conspires with it to track him down. And though this is not Wright's intent, I find it difficult not to think of that larger-than-textual-life as Bigger's provenance in a by-now-familiar image-repertoire which precedes him. As his lawyer aptly puts it, "This thing's *bigger* than you son" (745).

In one sense, that means, as Wright himself was aware, giving back to a white readership its own distorted image of blackness, its own grotesque projection of "the Negro." When Bigger "goes for the head," he is trying to fight his way out of racist encephalopathy—out of the white imagination which has birthed and still houses him. Wright's own expressed desire to purge himself of Bigger in the preface attests to the complex levels of cultural exorcism this entails. But in another sense, as both James Baldwin and Ellison differently complained, Wright cannot help indelibly writing Bigger directly back into that imagination because he makes him a "creature" of telltale face, of recognition expressed as cynegesis—hunting and tracking.

Reading Wright

In his essay "Literary Theory and the Black Tradition," Henry Louis Gates, Jr., quotes a question posed by Sartre—"To whom does Richard Wright address himself?"—in order to redirect it as a question for criticism or theory.[68] The question is, no doubt, irresistible, and I will follow Gates's lead in signifying on it momentarily. But first I want to stay within the original dimensions of Sartre's question, to contemplate the phenomenon of split readership, a double audience of black and white readers, in order to underscore the uncanny, "bigger than" effect Wright's novel can have, which I see as an index of the text's own more complex politics of representation. I turn briefly to a two-toned pair of responses which Wright's "double simultaneous postulation" (as Sartre termed it) provoked from readers roughly contemporaneous with both novelist and philosopher.[69]

Consider James Baldwin first. Baldwin begins his much anthologized essay "Many Thousands Gone" with an implicit nod toward *Benito Cereno:* "The Negro in America, gloomily referred to as that shadow which lies athwart our national life, is far more than that. He is a series of shadows, self-created, intertwining, which now we helplessly battle. One may say that the Negro in America does not really exist except in the darkness of our minds."[70]

For my purposes, Baldwin's analysis catches fire when he speaks of "the Negro face," which, if it cannot be made white, is blanked and made invisible, or else reified by being invested with white guilt. As though he were Levinas writing on racial inequality, Baldwin says, "Wherever the Negro face appears a tension is created, the tension of silence filled with things unutterable" (28). One remembers that in Levinas, the face above all signifies expression, the language of pure difference, but Baldwin notes profoundly that black faces, especially in literature, produce only two typical effects: silence or dread.

Moreover, when he speaks specifically of *Native Son*, Baldwin calls Bigger a "monster created by the American republic" (32), and observes that "this is an arresting and potentially rich idea and we would be discussing a very different novel if Wright's execution had been more perceptive and if he had not attempted to redeem a symbolical monster in social terms" (32). The redemption of a monster in social terms is, of course, the mission undertaken by Dr. Trescott in Crane's *The Monster;* and that text shows the motives for such redemption to be merely conventional, its results disastrous. A culture cannot exorcise its symbolic demons symbolically. This, as I see it, forms also the hard fact illustrated by Melville's *Benito Cereno.*

Baldwin says, in carefully chosen words, "The 'nigger,' black, benighted, brutal, consumed with hatred as we are consumed with guilt, cannot be *blotted* out" (37). He is absolutely correct, I think, when he concludes that Max's defense of Bigger implicitly admits that black experience is as "debased and impoverished" as the culturally available set of defaced and defacing images portrays it to be.

Bigger murders faces because he finds himself suffocated by a black mask molded by white *in*humanity. But that grotesque fulfillment of the white imagination's worst fears serves only to postpone indefinitely a less exotic, phenomenologically "genuine" encounter with the alterity (for whites) of black culture. In effect, Bigger merely recreates the already created features of his face. The only creativity allowed him by the text's narrator is the creativity of violence (Bigger's murder of Mary is termed an "act of creation"). For Fanon's optimistic image of self-creation, we must substitute Baldwin's image of "Bigger living in the skull."

Yes, Bigger imagines himself differently after he kills, and he does after a fashion begin to "plot" his own story. Surely, however, that plot is a borrowed one, the marplot of internalized race hatred. At least this is how I understand the logic of Wright's decision to have Bigger commit the more heinous act of motiveless black-on-black murder (on the heels of rape): "And yet, out of it all, over and above all that happened, impalpable but real, there remained to him a queer sense of power. *He* had done this. *He* had brought all this about. . . . He was living, truly and deeply, no matter what other might think, looking at him with their blind eyes" (669).

But all these thoughts take place behind and beneath an entirely pasteboard black mask. In ironic counterpoint, one may hear again echoes of Faulkner's *Light in August* in Joe Christmas' realization "But I have never got outside that circle I have never broken out of the ring of what I have already done and cannot ever undo," as he watches the ineradicable "black tide creeping up his legs, moving from his feet upwards as death moves."

In diametrical contrast to Baldwin, Irving Howe lauds *Native Son*'s belligerence by thrusting it directly in the face of its two-tone readership. In "Black Boys and Native Sons," he writes, "A blow at the white man, the novel forced him to recognize himself as an oppressor[; a] blow at the black man, the novel forced him to recognize the cost of his submission."[71]

Bigger is thus understood relative to other resourceful characters in Wright's fiction—Mann in "Down by the Riverside," Silas in "Long Black Song" from *Uncle Tom's Children*, the protagonists of "The Man Who Was Almost a Man" and "The Man Who Lived Underground" from *Eight Men*, Cross Damon of *The Outsider*, and Fishbelly Tucker of *The Long Dream*. Or we can assign him folkloric status—as an avatar of Nat Turner and Stagolee, an existential hero or Fanonian revolutionist, the monster as *Volksmensch*.

Howe argues for the incontrovertible authenticity of Bigger as a figure of sociological truth while at the same time admitting his origins in "white fantasy and white contempt" (111): "Naturalism pushed to an extreme turns here into something other than itself, a kind of expressionist outburst, no longer a replica of the familiar social world but a self-contained realm of grotesque emblems" (114). I find this passage central, obviously, because of its notions about social replication and an image-repertoire of "grotesque emblems." One could, without much difficulty, describe both *The Monster* and *Benito Cereno* in the identical terms; yet those texts stand generically apart from Wright's naturalism. (Indeed, I think the question of tagging *Native Son* a "naturalist" text is at best problematic, since Wright himself oscillates in his preface between, on the one hand, espousing Zolaesque theories of environment and experimental method and, on the other, remarking on the "expressionist outburst" with which Bigger periodically entered his consciousness.)

Howe later calls preposterous the idea that Wright, "for all his emotional involvement with Bigger, could not see beyond the limitations of the character he had created" (108). But why is that so implausible? Could we not, contrariwise, envision here a subtle order of invisibility which courses textually underground, a "swift and imperceptible flowing" (Ralph Ellison's phrase) of literary and cultural history? The realm in which Bigger lives, breathes, and has his being, in other words, is not self-contained, but protean, mobile, liquid. What Howe underestimates is just that "bigger than" effect which I alluded to above. (Negatively reassessing *Native Son* as "crude," as Howe later does in "At Ease with the Apocalypse," qualifies his already myopic view of the text in exactly the wrong direction.)

But Baldwin makes a similar error himself, I think, since Bigger's monstering simply *cannot* purify or otherwise redeem that other level of monstration—the "Negro face"—within the text. Monsters do not easily bear an allegorical or socially symbolic stamp; to defy meaning is the nature and function of the monstrous in the first place. (One suspects that Ellison made Invisible Man a mock-picaresque instead of a "monster" partly for just this reason, as a generation later Toni Morrison in *Beloved* swathed the infanticidal character of Sethe in lyrical gauze.)

It may well be, as Baldwin argues, that recognizing, sublimating, and creatively exploiting the Bigger Thomas that lives in every black skull is in fact a liberating act, one which "lends to Negro life its high element of the ironic." Still, it would seem that after, or rather because of, Richard Wright bogeymen cannot unambiguously do duty for the disenfranchised or dispossessed within the black imagination.[72]

Given the blind spots which one can thus detect in such passionate and disparate readings of Wright as Baldwin's and Howe's, perhaps the question of Wright's "addressivity" is better pursued within another context: neither readership, nor authorship, but instead the novel's own base level of image and trope.

Base, Race, and Face

Bigger Thomas, his lawyer tells us, lives behind a veil, an image the narrator also exploits when he speaks of the "curtain" or "wall" which separates Bigger's world (and consciousness) from "ours." As I argued in answer to Hillis Miller's thesis at the beginning of this chapter, living "behind the veil" represents an ontological dilemma for black Americans which cannot be rightly appreciated through, as it were, the veil of "ideological confusion." Indeed, texts like *Native Son, The Monster,* and *Benito Cereno* all illustrate the tragic conflation of reference with phenomenalism which underlies the logic of racism; in this sense the representational self-consciousness of these texts introduces order, not disorder, into the workings of ideology as it shapes cultural perception. In this way also they demonstrate the integral link between intersubjective and intercultural horizons of encounter and recognition.

Among the various categories of difference which can be read out of (and which connect) these three texts, the one which is hard to ignore is the racial identity of the author. Does one not after all reckon with Crane's, Melville's, and Wright's texts on blackness, as I have said, as texts written by a white man or a black man? But how black (or white) is figuration? Henry Louis Gates asks this very question in another of his essays, "Criticism in the Jungle," whose implications supersede those involving author and readers.[73] Gates ponders this question in order to argue that the best black literary criticism will escape an intellectual *bovarysme collectif* if it follows the lead of African-American texts themselves, whose idiom figures forth a double-voiced or two-toned set of utterances.

But while he thus meticulously deconstructs doctrines of essentialism, be they projective like white racism or reactive like "Negritude," Gates still draws a continuous mimetic line from history to literature to theory. It is a line which, perhaps not ironically, ends up running at cross purposes with the very deconstructive premise Hillis Miller defends in *Hawthorne and History*. Whereas Miller uses text to disarticulate all other categories, Gates as I interpret him, implies that behind even textual veils hide real and potentially damaged faces.

And in terms of figuration, the dominant and most reusable sign of external difference remains the face. I want therefore to inflect Gates's question I quoted above by marking figuration not as "black" or "white" but as ethico-political, as the claim of difference on persons, cultures, and texts. Of the many instances of face imagery in Wright's face-obsessed book, a sequence of three stands out in particular, and it is these with which this chapter's analysis of representational ethics shall conclude. The first occurs when Bigger reconnoiters with Bessie just after Mary's murder:

> The streets were empty and silent, stretching before him white and
> clean under the vanishing glow of a long string of street lamps. . . .
> As he walked beside her he felt that there were two Bessies: one a
> body that he had just had and wanted badly again; the other was in

Bessie's face; it asked questions; it bargained and sold the other Bessie to advantage. He wished he could clench his fist and swing his arm and blot out, kill, sweep away the Bessie on Bessie's face and leave the other helpless and yielding before him. He would then gather her up and put her in his chest, his stomach, some deep place inside him, always keeping her there even when he slept, ate, talked. (575)

The second describes the fulfillment of Bigger's desire:

Her breath guided him in the darkness; he stopped where he thought her head must be. . . . Quickly, to make certain where he must strike, he switched on the light, fearing as he did so that it might awaken her; then switched it off again, retaining as an image before his eyes her black face in deep sleep. . . . Soon he seemed to be striking a wet wad of cotton, of some damp substance whose only life was the jarring of the brick's impact. . . . Then a dreadful thought rendered him incapable of action. Suppose, when he turned on the flashlight, he would see her lying there staring at him with those round large black eyes, her bloody mouth open in awe and wonder and pain and accusation. . . . But he had to look. He lifted the flashlight to where he thought the head must be and pressed the button. . . . There! Blood and lips and hair and face turned to one side and blood running slowly. (666–667)

Finally, when the coroner wheels Bessie's body into the courtroom as evidence, the narrator describes Bigger's reaction when the sheet is removed:

The sight, bloody and black, made Bigger flinch involuntarily and lift his hands to his eyes and at the same instant he saw blinding flashes of the silver bulbs flicking through the air. His eyes looked with painful effort to the back of the room, for he felt that if he saw Bessie again he would rise from his chair and sweep his arm in an attempt to blot out this room and the people in it. Every nerve of his body helped him to stare without seeing and to sit amid the noise without hearing. (755)

The play of light and darkness, alternately illuminating and obscuring lurid scenes of recognition in all three passages is unmistakable. Arcing in a sequence, together these moments in the text describe a circle within which a black face becomes subject to repeated defacings, the joint product of character and author. The implausible introduction as evidence of Bessie's corpse into a public courtroom merely compounds the fascination that Wright seems to take in defacement (with which we should compare Crane's). The narrator's voicing of Bigger's indignation in this same scene does not appreciably diminish the authorial culpability here (all the more striking considering that we are witnessing a scene of judgment in a court of law).

If there is a "self-contained realm of grotesque emblems" to be found within the novel, it is the circle traced by these images which together form the novel's hollow core. Coupled with Bigger's implicit bestiality, the presence of these emblems of defacement suggests that "monstra-tion" as a cultural strategy of black representability does not "stay put," but rather influences the figurative imaginations of black and white writers alike. Signifying on Gates, I would say that in the case of *Native Son* figuration may aim at color, but at the same time it exercises a kind of color blindness in aiming at the human face.

The sheer political potency of such emblems may bear on race, but it originates in terrain beyond race, I believe, and beyond authorial control. It resides, rather, in an underlying ethics symbolized by the "no" to violence uttered by a face. "Race and superstructure" models, according to Gates, err in their essentialist approach to text; a frankly transcendentalist intent, however, explains the "base and race" model of politics as ethics as I have developed it here; and it is not just for euphony's sake that what links the novel's representational base and its politics of race is the ethical import of the human face.

In the 1988 presidential campaign, a television commercial added one more portrait of monstrosity to the American image-repertoire of black faces. Willie Horton, a prisoner let out on furlough who there-upon committed another crime, was exposed to us as one of those Biggers whom Wright describes in his essay, the life models from whom he drew. Inadvertent historical reenactment? I would say, no. Rather, it was the logic which Emerson termed "compensation" or, in the phrase of another Ralph Waldo (Ellison), the return to history of those invisible men who have "plunged outside it,"[74] forced out, like Bigger, "before they born."

The Republicans are commonly credited with circulating a mug shot of Willie Horton himself, when in fact their commercial showed only a revolving door through which passed anonymous, faceless, essentially invisible men. As if in dialectical compensation, however, a freeze-frame of Horton's face did make itself known as it migrated, like a traveling exhibit, from one news program to another.[75] We needed a face, evidently; and the gap was dutifully filled with a "monstrous" image face obligingly provided for fascinated and denuding eyes.[76] Like the one-eyed non-face of Henry Johnson, the decapitated yet still staring face of Babo, or the mutilated face of Bessie upon which Bigger displaces the indecent exposure of black visibility, Willie Horton's face looked out at us otherwise than and beyond our polite cultural frame of reference, implacable in its anti-anagnorisis.

Images such as these, I have argued, supply an always available cultural resource; they circulate with an uncanny power of their own. Indeed, in Willie Horton's case, the news media did the Republicans' work for them through what we can only call supplementary monstration: they gave their monster a face. The violence which aims at a face requires our staring, as it does the culpable eyes of Whilomville, of Amasa Delano, of prosecution and defense in Bigger Thomas' trial.

An upsurge into democratic space, performing a function they have not themselves chosen, all these "imploring, wrathful, despairing" faces—Babo's, Henry Johnson's, Bessie's—look out, and in so doing summon forth "the third party." In that way, they defy our easy specularity, beckoning us to leave home, and denying history the last word. Only in that way do we make the invisible visible, and only in that way does ethics, with political rectitude, "lead back to evidence."

6

Telling Others:
Secrecy and Recognition
in Dickens, Barnes, and Ishiguro

Writing is the trespass of oneself upon the other and of the other upon me.

Maurice Merleau-Ponty, *The Prose of The World*

I have discovered that all the unhappiness of men arises from one single fact, that they cannot stay quietly in their own chamber.

Blaise Pascal, *Pensées*

Are you unable to give me your sympathy—you who read this? Are you unable to imagine this double consciousness at work within me, flowing on like two parallel streams which never mingle their waters and blend into a common hue?

George Eliot, *The Lifted Veil*

A s the title and epigraphs for this chapter suggest, literary texts play host to various kinds of homelessness, even and perhaps especially that most *heimlich* of discursive forms, first-person narrative, where "home" fits into the quiet chamber of the narrating "I." Since in this chapter I will concern myself with the oversound of voices which make that first person multiple (the *unheimlich within* the *heimlich*, as it were), it is appropriate that two voices from my introductory chapter return together here, to speak again. First, Stanley Cavell: "a first-person account is, after all, a confession; and the one who has something to confess has something to conceal. And the one who has the word 'I' at his or her disposal has the quickest device for concealing himself."[1] Second, Philip Roth: "With autobiography, there's always another text, a counter-text, if you will, to the one presented."[2] Consider the following nonfictional instance.

On the second page of his autobiography, when John Stuart Mill refers to himself as the "eldest son of James Mill, the author of the *History of British India*," he suggests nothing so much as an isomorphism of son and book, the fraternal if not identical twins of their father's middle age. Mill's *Autobiography* pens the story of a mind educated according to preestablished principles and opinions, and in doing so parrots a writing already performed for him by its author's father. Mill's "penning" (to "cop" from Cavell's essay on Poe) can thus signify either release or incarceration. Mill's is the task of auto*de*biography—mastering a simultaneously overwritten and "underwritten" life by rewriting it oneself.

Of course, such mastery eludes Mill, at least within the literary confines of the *Autobiography*. Further, in handing the text over to his wife for revision its author seems to have multiplied the complexities of authorship, the diversity of voice, which the project of self-writing inflicts on him. Much of the pathos of Mill's *Autobiography*, I believe, derives from its vulnerability to other kinds of writing or textual "support." These take two shapes—deliberate: references to his father's writings or to a set of literary and political works which he needs to help explain his feelings; and inadvertent: "collisions," as it were, with certain works of fiction which the *Autobiography* wants to call to mind (most conspicuously in Mill's day, Dickens' *Hard Times*).[3]

As an instance of the first weakness, consider that in Mill's prefatory list of the three reasons for writing "a memorial of so uneventful a life as mine,"[4] self-acknowledgment—the modest praise of a plastic and adventuresome mind—comes second, safely contained between a testimonial to his father's educational method, on the one side, and obeisance to the moral stature of others, most notably his wife, on the other. One can of course attribute this stance to nineteenth-century standards of propriety and autobiographical decorum, traits which, however, typically and often knowingly served their authors as convenient fictions.[5] I prefer to think of it instead as a sign of self-alienation, of an inability to be separate, *chez soi* (Bakhtin's, Cavell's, and Levinas' precondition for a genuine readiness for another). *On est parlé*—one is spoken, as Sartre writes of Flaubert, or, to paraphrase Sartre in turn, *writing . . .* is other people.

But it is at the second of these two textual crossroads that this final chapter will situate itself; for it is Dickens, not J. S. Mill, who will occupy my attention here—and not *Hard Times* (as one might perhaps expect) but *Bleak House*. That novel goes Mill's *Autobiography* one better by distributing its split in narrative consciousness between two distinct narrators. Yet between them, Esther Summerson and the omniscient narrative voice share the identical problematic of secrecy, the same hedge around recognition, which Mill's *Autobiography* illumines in, as it were, half light.

And since I am multiplying voices here, let me articulate the hinge between Mill and Dickens (or nonfiction and fiction) by way of a third voice and genre—the literary critic D. A. Miller: "Writing the self, then, would be consistently ruled by the paradoxical proposition that the self is most itself at the moment when its defining inwardness is most secret, most withheld from writing—with the equally paradoxical consequence that autobiography is most successful only where *it has been abandoned for the Novel*."[6] Add to this paradox the one I have already alluded to, that the crowning literary expression of the sovereign self—autobiography—betrays deeply embedded intersubjective claims and is at some level "half someone else's," and the ethical problematic for reading becomes once more acute.

To return to the example of Mill for a moment, the *Autobiography*'s self writes under the duress of what has to be seen as an overwrought and overwritten intersubjectivity. In staking his claim to vocal autonomy, Mill inadvertently exposes what Bakhtin claims is the irresistibly heteroglot nature of language, or as George Steiner memorably puts it, "the disparity between the uniqueness, the novelty of his emotions and the word coinage of words."[7] For the author of the *Autobiography*, language functions less as a prison house than a haunted house— through Mill's ghostwritten narrative, we, as it were, "hear voices." (The title of Mill's text, by the way, conspicuously lacks a possessive pronoun—not *My Autobiography*, just *Autobiography*.)

In the declension of J. S. Mill's identity and narrative autonomy, we might say, dative and accusative cases precede the nominative. Or as Mill puts it himself, "I never thought of saying to myself, I am, or I can do, so and so. I neither estimated myself highly nor lowly: I did not estimate myself at all" (21). We discover this text's pathos as well as its irony then in the tenuousness of its *auto* and the exogamous complexities of its *graphy*: Mill can only tell himself through the wadding of others.

In one of his early, "first-person plural" essays, Montaigne remarks, "We are never in ourselves, but always beyond," an attestation not simply of narrative "desire," but of internal differentiation: when I confess, I implicitly acknowledge the presence of an other or others who interpellate me from within.[8] In this respect, not only does self-writing work performatively, but it has perlocutionary effect.

The specifically ethical claim which a text like Mill's makes on us lies then in the intricate "life-support" apparatus which undergirds it, the tubes, wires, and cables of a medicinal codependency which enables and enfeebles its author at one and the same time. (Indeed, sometimes the text becomes painful enough that we are tempted to switch the machine off.)

And it is this intersubjective fact of connectivity that I want to focus on here, the magic and sometimes indelible effect one person can have discursively upon another. Such texts as Mill's ask from readers a certain hermeneutic generosity, a tactfulness, an ethical surplus of recognition; they require our seeing them against a background which they themselves remain unaware of. If we are all authors, as Bakhtin has said, who must cite ourselves, since we cannot be ourselves, Mill's "throwing" his own voice appears especially torturous, because for him self-citation so often means other-citation. The task of reading defines itself precisely as mediating the task of autobiography which a text like Mill's exemplifies. Another way to say this is that certain texts possess "open secrets" which entreat careful revelation, not easy disclosure.

And thus in this final chapter I return to the tie between narrational and hermeneutic ethics which I traced in my initial readings of Coleridge and Anderson. "Telling Others," my title, should consequently be understood as fanning out in several directions at once: narration to others, narration about others, and narrating persons, as it were, "in the indicative"—simultaneously speaking and bespoken.

All of these trace vectors or, better, rhythms of secrecy, a systole and diastole not simply of facts, of information consciously or unconsciously withheld, but of self and voice. Beckoning gestures oscillate with acts of self-mantling. This does not correspond to Cavell's claim about concealment lurking just under the surface of confession, but rather suggests the inverse relation: clandestinity which solicits, indeed, summons interpretation, a dynamic Levinas calls "rubbing the text."

And yet, doesn't literary criticism, in its capacity as a hermeneutic of suspicion, make all texts open secrets, and necessarily rub them the wrong (or from this perspective, right) way? Doesn't it provide an arena where the dialectic I have just described shifts from rhythmic revelation and concealment alongside a text to a transactive tug of war across it, in short, between a text's secrets and their would-be demystifiers? Those are questions which Mill's text inadvertently and *Bleak House* quite deliberately thematize and transact in an ethics of secrecy and recognition.

Indeed, I find strong legitimation for such an approach to these texts precisely in the tendency for "ethics" to be peeled away by critics like so much transparent skin, the better to savor the psychoanalytic and textual "meat" it protects. But "ethics," to take the opposite tack, constitutes not expendable transparency but rather the central "open secret" which demands a reckoning in Mill's *Autobiography* and *Bleak House* alike.

As Bakhtin has said of the novel, it "always includes in itself the activity of coming to know another's word, a coming to knowledge whose process [it] represent[s]" (*DI*, 353). The same activity which Mill unconsciously and incompletely attempts in his *Autobiography* is the one uniformly practiced by Esther Summerson, Inspector Bucket, Mr. Tulkinghorn, and all the other lay detectives and lay narrators within the confines of *Bleak House*.

Accordingly, instead of seeing the plot of Dickens' novel as determining all other narrative features, I treat its proliferation as in some way a response to the interplay of voices; the *telling* or the *hoarding* of secrets serves as the glue which binds person to person, and only consequently, person to plot.[9] In effect, by thus binding themselves through the communication of secrets and narrative invention, the novel's characters justify and explain their connectivity in light of the Court of Chancery's random manipulation of lives (it is not by chance that the name of such an institution contains the word "chance").

Plot, I will argue, forms answers to the pressures of narration and human nearness, rather than the other way around, the same motivating pressures, I have claimed, which painfully underwrite Mill's *Autobiography*. (This argument need not, I caution, be seen as against the grain of the formal compositional structure within which Dickens actually worked—the serialized form of the multiplot novel with its characteristic tempo of peaks and lulls.)

In the second part of this chapter—compounding a leap between genres with a vault over centuries—I continue my analysis with two examples drawn from contemporary fiction: *Flaubert's Parrot* by Julian Barnes and Kazuo Ishiguro's *The Remains of the Day*. I do so not because Dickens is a prescient postmodernist, but because the ethical problem of narration in *Bleak House*—when cleared of its Dickensian clutter—can be seen as a topic in its own right for much recent prose fiction. In this way do nineteenth-century texts like Dickens' (and Mill's, for that matter) point us toward literature of a much later date, as indeed, texts like Barnes's and Ishiguro's can be said to look back in return.

Sometimes explicitly, sometimes not, all the texts I have looked at in the previous chapters highlight the same problematic of secrecy and recognition which I discuss, as it were, openly here. In the buried lives and "secret treasons of the world" unearthed in *Lord Jim*, *Winesburg, Ohio*, and *In the Cage*; in the differing modes of deception exposed in "The Real Thing," *The Aspern Papers*, and *Benito Cereno*; in the fascinated crime and horror structures of *The Monster* and *Native Son*—in all these, secrecy and recognition map another set of coordinates, another boundary for narrative ethics.

The readings which follow, then, like those which preceded, respond to the texts' own internal drive toward *sollicitation*—a French word which Levinas uses for the energy and labor which serious interpretation always demands. *Sollicitation*, in this sense, means not benign entreaty, but something harder, more percussive—something like the directed rhetoric Dickens employs when he describes Jo's death, or the forcing of secrets which propels Inspector Bucket, Tulkinghorn, Lady Dedlock, the Snagsbys, Esther, and others through the novel. *Bleak House* "moves on" all its characters, from story to story, from secret to secret, as profoundly as do the forces which goad the perpetually forward movements of Jo, the text's "rejected witness"[10] and ultimate mobile signifier for its interlocutionary web of "open secrets."

Sollicitation is the overt burden of Barnes's and Ishiguro's novels as well, each, in different but still quite consonant ways, the legatees of Mill's *Autobiography*, the ones it has been "abandoned for"; each could be said in a way to have added to the *Autobiography* its own personal pronoun. Each, also, inhabits its own bleak and haunted house which alternately exposes and protects secrets—houses let, so to speak, by the acts of reading and interpretation. For both text and reader, it is secrecy which dictates the terms of recognition, which guards "not merely isolated secrets about the self but access to the underlying experience *of* secrecy."[11]

Bleak House

Dickens wrote two great confessional narratives, *David Copperfield* and *Great Expectations.*[12] In them, through the intelligent manipulation of story, the narrative "I" progressively differentiates himself from a set of constraining influences—from his other self (the enounced or past self), from his doubles (Orlick for Pip and Steerforth for David) and those who impinge most closely on his consciousness, and, finally, from certain images of him in the reader's imagination which he defends against. In this respect, Dickens merely follows a standard Bildungsroman pattern, a fact which *Bleak House* signals very early on in the (no doubt ironically) titled first chapter of Esther Summerson's narrative, "A Progress."[13]

While only in a limited sense "the hero" of the novel, Esther does control more than half of its narrational space (34 of 67). She thus represents the only other confessional identity outside of David and Pip in Dickens' fiction. *Bleak House*, of course, is a hybrid, unique in

Dickens' oeuvre; its first- and third-person narrators divy up between them the eight hundred or so pages of reportage and anagnorisis, the latter sometimes discovered as the reader discovers them, sometimes hedged and prepared for in advance.

If *Great Expectations* can be thought of as a novel about emplottedness or fiction-making and *David Copperfield* as about the growth of consciousness, the "aesthetics of education," then *Bleak House*, I will suggest, is about secrecy. The word is obsessively repeated in the text, as its overarching topic: the hoarding or dispensing of secrets through narrative.

Accordingly, narration—telling or Saying—assumes fundamental importance in the novel, a matter of both guise and style—hence names or nicknames like "Conversation Kenge" or "Bucket" (the very image of collected life stories). As a policing of stories, *Bleak House* displays a counter-text to the sort of unmonitored prodigality of story we see, for example, in *Winesburg, Ohio*. At any rate, the double narrative in *Bleak House* stands out sufficiently in Dickens' work that any reading of the novel needs to come to terms with it.[14]

Telling as Confessing

Through its two narrators, the novel defines storytelling as a process through which one either keeps or divulges secrets. It is fair to ask, then, whether the need to fashion, pass on, and otherwise direct the flow of narrative may at some level, conscious or not, depend on a kind of confessional guilt. If that premise is true, as I believe it is, it would go a long way toward explaining why the novel's most effective narrator is a member of the Detective Police.

In *The Novel and the Police* D. A. Miller has argued cogently that the novel requires the presence of Inspector Bucket because it needs to resolve legal undecidability by means of a detective "story." As I explain later in my analysis, I see Bucket rather as the narratorial "solution" for the "story" which is acted out by the twin narrators on the level of discourse; the homeless boy Jo's plaintive query, "Is there *three* of them, then?" (directed at the text's seeming fondness for veiled ladies), is something we can wonder about its narrators as well.

But why a detective as narrator, rather than the more customary relation—a narrator as detective? Consider the odd link between confession and stolen objects which we find in Rousseau and Augustine:

there the ethics of storytelling and the ethics of secrecy so thoroughly
intertwine that it becomes quite impossible after a certain point to
tell which motivates or underlies which. Similarly for *Bleak House:*
not only does Bucket narrate; he "hears" and extracts confessions as
well.

Confession's purpose is to rectify (if possible) unethical action
through ethical language. As de Man says, "To confess is to overcome
guilt and shame in the name of truth [through] an epistemological use
of language in which ethical values of good and evil are superseded by
values of truth and falsehood."[15] Thus since Esther commits no crime,
she technically has nothing to "confess."

But where Bucket reveals secrets for reasons which are epistemological and hermeneutic, "professional," in a word, other characters in the
novel divulge their secrets for more performative reasons, since in its
broadest sense confession functions intersubjectively not just veridi-
cally; it is a narrative-ethical, as well as a sense-making, act.

For confession, in one of its dictionary meanings, also connotes
acknowledgment—perhaps not in the strict Cavellian sense, but still
implying an avowal of limits before others; confession, as in the confession of a secret, produces a reckoning of both facts and persons.
Even as benign and banal an act of disclosure as Esther's first step into
the world of secrecy—confiding to her doll—shows this interplay
clearly:

> And so she used to sit propped up in a great arm-chair, with her
> beautiful complexion and rosy lips, staring at me—or not so much at
> me as at nothing—while I stitched away, and told her every one of
> my secrets. . . . I had always rather a noticing way—not a quick way,
> O no!—a silent way of noticing what passed before me, and thinking
> I should like to understand it better. . . . Imperfect as my under-
> standing of sorrow was, I knew that I had brought no joy, at any time,
> to anybody's heart, and that I was to no one upon Earth what Dolly
> was to me. (19)

Esther plays an ambivalent Penelope here, stitching fabric and un-
stitching her inner life, giving material form to *Bleak House*'s overcod-
ing of both the proairetic and the hermeneutic by the semic of fact and
story, in other words, by the need, simply, to tell another. One can
even, I think, take the doll here as a figure for the reader or narratee,

the status of whose staring and responsiveness—whose collaborative role in the novel—Dickens problematizes at the outset.

Compare a very similar moment in another text about secrecy, Henry James's *What Maisie Knew*, where Maisie confides in her doll, Lisette:

> Everything had something behind it: life was like a long, long corridor with rows of closed doors. She had learned that at these doors it was wise not to knock—this seemed to produce from within such sounds of derision. Little by little, however, she understood more, for it befell that she was enlightened by Lisette's questions, which reproduced the effect of her own upon those for whom she sat in the very darkness of Lisette.[16]

Where Maisie imagines her doll as "enlightening" her with transactive questions, Esther regards her doll as simply a silent interlocutor who passively shares her own desolated state.[17] Maisie instrumentalizes Lisette mimetically, "changing places" in order to facilitate her steady progress toward coming "to know" (as she will soon gain perspective by shuttling between her parents' homes). Esther, on the contrary, lives pathetically into, and identifies with, Dolly to the extent of abandoning her as she was herself abandoned (Esther covers the doll in a shawl and leaves her in the garden).

I think we more willingly trust the Jamesian narrator as a barometer of Maisie's state than we do Esther's confessional monologue as a measure of her own. Why? Recall my argument about *In the Cage*. Esther's habitual self-depreciation and withdrawal into inner, unspoken depths should give us pause, I think, and make us wonder about her investment in keeping her secrets secret. Maisie simply "plays" adult; by contrast, Esther in her reticence at times seems to be the reverse: an adult "playing" child.

The retrospectivity of Esther's narrative makes the conscious withholding, of course, even more troubling. Her coyness is of a different order entirely from, say, David Copperfield's discreet promise of narrative autonomy at the beginning of his story, where he resolves to "bring [his life's] secrets to life." Do we then lean toward *Bleak House*'s anonymous narrator over Esther for similar reasons? I think that we do, and the reason for our preference depends fundamentally on the different treatment of "authoritative" discourse and "inner persuasive" discourse which we find in *Bleak House.*

Of the many seeming oppositions in the novel, I think it is safe to say that only the difference between distinct narrative voices remains for the most part uncollapsed. As many critics have noted, the novel's symbolism and language tend ultimately to confuse any easy opposition in the text, between, say, system and chaos, or Chancery, fog, and Krook's spontaneous combustion, on one side, and the Jarndyces' eventual domestic security, on the other.

Given the sudden termination without resolution of the lawsuit, Bucket's error in judgment and consequent failure to catch up to Lady Dedlock in time, Richard Carstone's death, and Miss Flite's portentous loosing of her birds, very little real "progress" takes place in the novel, besides that conveyed through the artifices of plot. Any closure in the novel, as D. A. Miller puts it, "even as it [i]s achieved, misse[s] the essence of what it aspired to grasp" (97). Or in the text's own words, "And thus, through years and years, and lives and lives, everything goes on, constantly beginning over and over again, and nothing ever ends" (89).

Miller provides perhaps the most intelligent reading of this self-canceling tendency in the novel, turning, for instance, at the end of his analysis to consider how even the Jarndyce family remains suspended in a state of paradox: "In the same degree that [Esther's insecurity] propagates the worry and anxiety needed to maintain the family, it keeps alive the ever-present danger of its fall" (104). Miller does not discuss the two narrators, but it seems logical to treat their role in the novel as also a matter of discipline and restraint. Except that in this case, the discipline is double-voiced, and the question of ideological allegiance centers on the ethics of secrecy as a function of, or check on, narrative ties that bind.

Clearly, "enmeshment" defines the novel at its most basic levels of character, story, and discourse. The sources for such enmeshment need not, however, be located in invisible sites of power, but can be situated in a given ethical collectivity which the sending and receiving of stories makes evident, a cross referencing which Miller's otherwise brilliant reading forces him to disallow. It would be a mistake to neutralize the force of ethics in *Bleak House* by assimilating it to Dickens's reformist or moralist intentions (whether they are then endorsed or demystified), since that would obscure a central dimension in which such enmeshment actually plays out: that involving tellers and listeners.

Telling/Being Told

The two questions to resolve about the novel's double narrative are: why does Dickens use it? and what is the best way to distinguish the narrators? The answer to the first can be found encoded in this chapter's title: the pressure of others on any narrating "I." The second question requires a short detour by way of Bakhtin.

In line with his concept of language as a ceaseless oscillation between centripetal and centrifugal forces, Bakhtin distinguishes between twin ideological potencies, the *authoritative* and *inner-persuasive:* the first is the voice of dogma and social control—"education by cram" (22) as J. S. Mill puts it—and the second is predicated on self-assertion—"retelling in one's own words."[18] Authoritative discourse is closed, finite, quoted; internally persuasive discourse is open, experimental, assimilated.

Given the critical consensus on *Bleak House* and the tendency to subtend the two narrators, one might expect simply a neat division of these two terms along narratorial lines: authoritative—third-person narrator; inner-persuasive—Esther. Where, for instance, one critic sees Esther as a "thin verbal mask," in effect, merely a dodge for the rhetoricality which underlies all of Dickens' narrators, another sees her as "a transparency," a necessary mimetic foil for the other narrator's elaborate verbal opaqueness.[19] I see the eponymous and anonymous voices in *Bleak House*, rather, as performing two kinds of similarly inner-persuasive narration, each invested in its own way in negotiating and opposing the voices of authority.

"Novelistic double-voicedness cannot be unfolded into logical contradictions or into purely dramatic contrasts," says Bakhtin (*DI*, 356). Although he speaks here of utterances' internal dialogism, the double-voiced structure of *Bleak House*'s narration falls under the same restriction, I think; the contrast between its narrators belies their essentially similar function.

We can see the affinity between the two narrators, for example, precisely in that area most often used to distinguish them, verb tense. "The internally persuasive word is either a contemporary word, born in a zone of contact with unresolved contemporaneity, *or else it is a word that has been reclaimed for contemporaneity*" (*DI*, 346; my emphasis). Functionally identical pressures of "contemporaneity," I believe, impinge both on the third-person narrator's present tense and on Esther's retrospective narration.[20]

Thus I will say that each narrator opposes an internally persuasive word of his or her own—as irony, as emotion, as declarative statement—to the ambient surround of authoritative discourse. Moreover, each, as reporter or commentator, serves to *channel* all the other small-scale internally persuasive discourses—Guppy's, Tulkinghorn's, Vholes's, Mr. Chadband's, and so on—and their multiple conflicts over "others' words." As for the voices of authority, Bakhtin insists they remain completely external to a person. Thus it is that the language of Institution in this novel, "the bills, cross-bills, answers, rejoinders, affidavits, issues, references to masters', masters' reports" (26)—the entire mass of Chancery's sentences—belongs preeminently to the authoritative world.

As much as any novel by Dickens, *Bleak House* teems with reprocessed languages. It plays with the boundaries of various speech styles, not only "hybrid constructions" (the combination within a single utterance of two speech styles) but discrete discursive signatures, "islands of scattered direct and purely authorial speech, washed by heteroglot waves from all sides" (*DI*, 307).[21] The ocean which generates such waves is far from tranquil or limpid; at the same time as it extends ever outward, it englobes and concentrates its speakers, assimilating them through a complex network of substitutions—metaphors, nicknames, documents—and appropriating them through what J. Hillis Miller calls "the instinctive habit of interpretation."[22]

Yet in my view the text disciplines and constrains this double-edged multiplicity by filtering it through an instinctive habit of narration—the double-voiced narratorial structure and the consequent relationship we construct between its twin narrators. We shift from one to the other throughout; the intimacy of "Esther's Narrative" will periodically draw us from the third-person narrator's telescopic purview, and we are constantly measuring the objective narrator's control and qualified omniscience against the insipidity of Esther's prose, with *its* incessant qualifications.

Of course, the novel is too self-consciously heteroglot to impute to the narrators themselves authorship of the language world which they jointly depict. They simply narrate and report, actions sufficiently culpable in their ethical consequences not to warrant the added complexity of fictionalization per se. Furthermore, the model of narrative transmission which the twin narrators thus place before us is precisely what is imitated by the actions of the novel's characters; hence we need to see the secrets hoarded and dispensed within the story relative to the two major narrational tracks which pass them on and control their flow.

Tellings, Lookings

Above, I described Esther's manner of confiding secrets as a child as paradoxically closed rather than open. We see a similar dynamic operating in the following example, where Esther recounts her response to an offer from Jarndyce: "What the destitute subject of such an offer tried to say, I need not repeat. What she did say, I could more easily tell, if it were worth the telling. What she felt, and will feel to her dying hour, I could never relate" (23).

Writing the self requires that it be withheld from writing. And thus does confession become concealment and "autobiography" shade into the fictive. When it comes time for the third-person narrator to withhold his first secret, he, too, speaks of childhood and family. But unlike Esther (who is, as we know, writing after the fact), he purports merely to disclose others' secrets for them, while not necessarily able to see through them. In chapter 2, he introduces Lady Dedlock as follows:

> On Sundays, the little church in the park is mouldy; the oaken pulpit breaks out into a cold sweat; there is a general smell and taste as of the ancient Dedlocks in their graves. My Lady Dedlock (who is childless), looking out in the early twilight from her boudoir at a keeper's lodge, and seeing the light of a fire upon latticed panes, and smoke rising from the chimney, and a child, chased by a woman, running out into the rain to meet the shining figure of a wrapped-man coming through the gate, has been put quite out of temper. My Lady Dedlock says she has been quite "bored to death." (11)

Beneath the veneer of irony, and the more baroque overlay which follows this passage, a secret has been obliquely (and inadvertently) signaled, but it has also been kept.

The juxtaposition of this kind of narrative secretiveness with Tulkinghorn's entrance shortly thereafter is important. The text describes

Tulkinghorn as having "as many cast-iron boxes with [the Dedlock] name outside, as if the present baronet were the coin of the conjurer's trick, and were constantly being juggled through the whole set" (13). Tulkinghorn is *Bleak House*'s aspirant to the throne of authorship and commanding omniscience, what the text calls "the acquisition of secrets" (451). He receives salutations with "gravity, and buries them along with the rest of his knowledge" (14); he is an "oyster of the old school, whom nobody can open" (119), who "carries family secrets in every limb of his body, and every crease of his dress" (147).

Tulkinghorn, then, "hoards" others' secrets (he speaks of them as a kind of "property" [581]), whereas Esther preserves them and her third-person counterpart respects their right to be kept hidden until they need to be revealed; Tulkinghorn uses recognition as a threat, as a means of proairetic extortion, while the text's narrators bow to its hermeneutic autonomy. It is important, however, to see that these positions differ according to degree, not kind. Indeed, Dickens' point seems to be not the disreputability of secrecy, its resemblance to lying or deception, but rather its proper use or abuse. Narratives and narration, like other forms of social conversation, depend as much on the need to keep certain matters concealed as the desire to see them exposed. Call this the tactfulness of text.

Bleak House, then, sets before its readers a continuum along which its narrators and characters retain and divulge their secrets, some for good, some for ill. (The one narratorial mode the novel tends to eschew, however, is free indirect style. Because of the novel's obsession with secrecy, the internal contrast between narrators, and the array of character-narrators on either side of them, the "publicizing" function of free indirect style becomes structurally, if not thematically, out of place.)

The coercive subterfuge of Tulkinghorn (or the French maid Hortense's malignant deceit) simply warps the ordinary bars against transparency which regulate human interaction. As Esther says of two of the novel's characters (more ambiguously than she knows), "I think the best side of such people is almost hidden from us" (101)—a sentiment quite at odds with her unequivocal description of Mrs. Pardiggle as "an inexorable moral Policeman," a figure of indiscriminate invasiveness.

Still, even Esther's staring at others' grief does not stand so completely outside the "rapaciously benevolent" (93) world of Mrs. Pardiggle that its transmission to us as narrative report should not give us pause: Esther inadvertently violates, by exposing it to us, the very "side" of people she acknowledges to be hidden. (Perhaps, as reluctant muck-raker, she is obliged to do so, but it remains ethically inconsistent.) Jarndyce's bed-trick at the novel's end similarly bears a family resemblance to the more insidious substitutions of Hortense, Guppy, and Mrs. Jellyby. All these activities confirm the significance of contagion in the text as a model for the metonymic chain which links persons and their various open secrets.

As with telling, a continuum of "looking" arcs through the text. Again, Tulkinghorn legislates. His scrutiny and incessant eyeing of Lady Dedlock initiates a pattern of one-sided specularity, some of it harmless, like Jarndyce's covert spying on Esther in chapter 3—"for he caught my glance, appearing to read her thoughts" (60)—much of it baleful, like Mrs. Snagsby's surveillance of her husband or Hortense's habitual espionage, "a watchful way of looking out of the corners of her eyes without turning her head" (143). Guppy's eyes follow Esther perpetually until he is preempted by her disfigurement. Krook does not take his eyes off Jarndyce, observing him "with the slyness of an old white fox . . . lowering his grey eyebrows until they appeared to be shut, and seem[ing] to scan every lineament of his face" (181). The following sequence is representative: "Mr. Weevle casts an eye about him. Mr Guppy's eye follows Mr. Weevle's eye. Mr. Weevle's eye comes back without any new intelligence in it. Mr. Guppy's eye comes back and meets Mr. Smallweed's eye" (492).

At the poles of this spectrum, the text situates Tulkinghorn's "expressionless mask" and Jo's pathetic "O my eye!" (as though forced looking actually hurt). If Tulkinghorn "shows nothing but his shell," Jo "knows nothink," coerced into observation, several times con-scripted as witness and pointer, compelled either to look or to tell. ("Jo's Will" is the most ironically titled chapter in the novel—he is the ultimate "victim of circumstance.")

Scrutiny, narration, and pursuit in the novel align as correlative activities, each reducing to the common action which the text calls "following."[23] Hence, as I will discuss shortly, the central importance of Tulkinghorn and Bucket (along with their pointing fingers) as two kinds of exemplary "follerers." Hence, as well, the text's obsessive figuration of faces, mirrors, and veils, the most famous being Esther's *dévoilement* of her disfigured face as she draws back the muslin curtain of a mirror. Here the necessity of telling is coupled with the difficulty of looking.[24] "Face," in other words, becomes discursive exposure.

Such a moment as this affirms Terence Cave's claim that "recognition scenes in literary works are by their nature 'problem' moments rather than satisfaction or completion."[25] From a certain point of view, the scene represents a pure instance of "autobiography as defacement," the literalization of a trope. De Man calls autobiography both a "specular" and a "privative" structure, and thus it is wholly appropriate that we find Esther looking at an altered self which has undergone a kind of death. As Jo says of another disguised woman in the text, "It is her and it an't her."

In calling autobiography "defacement," de Man is chiefly concerned with the narrative act of retrospection, since it involves summoning a figure who has in fact passed away (which is how de Man understands the trope of prosopopeia). Again, quite appropriately, it is in this scene before a mirror that Esther's self-canceling act of confession finds its peak moment: when Esther looks at herself, in de Man's words, she enacts "the restoration of mortality by autobiography—the prosopopoeia of voice and the name—[which] deprives and disfigures to the precise extent that it restores."[26]

De Man's view, however, remains anti-narrative to the extent that it obscures the particular relation between looking (or showing) and telling which I want to bring out. Esther recaptures a scene of recognition, but she does not share with readers what in fact she sees; her revelation is kept concealed, one more in Esther's string of open secrets, her own "flaming necklace"—the nightmare of metonymy which she recounts: ". . . strung together somewhere in great blank space, there was a flaming necklace, or ring, or starry circle of some kind, of which *I* was one of the beads!" (432). In turn, Esther's blend of seeing and speaking occupies merely one slot in *Bleak House*'s catalogue of specular and narrative kinds, each separated from the others by degrees.

It is important to note that *Bleak House* does not project a single model of secrecy, a theme from which it then derives a set of variations. Rather (to continue the musical metaphor) secrecy functions like a ground bass upon which the text plays multiple figurations. The two narrators, for example, make their disclosures in superficially similar yet different ways. When Esther expresses confidences, she will tell us that she has withheld information from another: "I put my arms around [my guardian's] neck and kissed him; and he said was this the mistress of Bleak House; and I said yes; and it made no difference presently, and we all went out together, and I said nothing to my precious pet about it" (540).

The subterfuge with Ada, "her precious pet," is placed subtly in relief by the set of coordinated clauses which hide the obversative relation of the final clause—"and I said nothing." And an open secret is placed before us in the same manner as well: "and it made no difference presently," suggesting that it will some other time. (Significantly, this passage closes a scene in which Jarndyce communicates to Esther not by mouth but by letter, about which "he did not say a word," but merely waits for Esther's reply.)

Alternatively, Esther withholds information directly from readers: "What more the letter told me, needs not be repeated here. It has its own times and places in the story" (453). Or again, "I don't know what it was. Or at least if I do, now, I thought I did not then. Or at least—but it don't matter." (365).[27] And perhaps most famously, "I have forgotten to mention—at least I have not mentioned—that Mr. Woodcourt was the same dark young surgeon whom we met at Mr. Badger's. . . . that Mr. Jarndyce invited him to dinner that day. Or, that he came. Or, that when they were all gone, and I said to Ada, 'now my darling, let us have a little talk about Richard!' Ada laughed and said—But, I don't think it matters what my darling said. She was always merry" (182).

This passage reverses the syntactic peculiarity of the one above. An obversative clause interrupts and preempts a string of sequentially entailed statements. (Esther eventually confesses this secret at the end of chapter 35, but she repeats the habit many times therafter, notably by keeping hidden to readers the fact of Ada's marriage in chapter 50.) Thus, even on the sentence level, Dickens brilliantly encodes the concatenating structure of secrecy *as* narrative. And thus does *Bleak House* end on Esther's unfinished sentence.

When the third-person narrator discloses secrets, he, too, employs a dual method. On the one hand, he will seem to discover revelations along with his readership, as in his description of Krook's death: "What is it? Hold up the light. Here is a small burnt patch of flooring; here is the tinder from a little bundle of burnt paper, but no light as usual, seeming to be steeped in something; and here is—is it the cinder of a small charred and broken leg of wood sprinkled with whites ashes, or is it coal? O horror, he IS here! and this from which we run away, striking out the light and overturning one another into the street, is all that represents him" (403).

On the other hand, he imparts secrets to us but keeps them concealed from characters.

> From the ceiling, foreshortened Allegory, in the person of one impossible Roman upside down, points with the arm of Samson obtrusively from the window. Why should Mr. Tulkinghorn, for such no-reason, look out of window? Is the hand not always pointing there? So he does not look out of window.
>
> And if he did, what would it be to see a woman going by . . . even though she were going secretly? They are all secret . . .
>
> But they are not all like the woman who now leaves him and his house behind, between whose plain dress and her refined manner, there is something exceedingly inconsistent. (200)

We can, of course, ascribe the difference between the two narrators' modes of secrecy to the simple contrast in structure indicated by their different temporal frames or to Dickens' authorial purposes in orchestrating the plot. But I see it equally as a function of the two narrators' respective holds on inner-persuasive discourse. The anonymous narrator's identity is never in jeopardy while he narrates. Esther, by contrast, cannot fully or successfully confess. As in the case of Mill's *Autobiography*, self-writing can be fraught with background, a shadow-text which third-person narration can accordingly escape.

Consequently, the more that individual characters within the story become implicated in secrets which they must at some point confess, the more mobile or driven they become. Lady Dedlock, Mr. Snagsby, George Rouncewell, Phil Squod, and, preeminently, Jo all fall to this side of the novel's narratorial continuum. Conversely, the more characters find it efficacious to hinder or divert the flow of confession, the more stationary and immured in the storage of confidences they become. Grandfather and Bart Smallweed, Vholes, Krook, and, ultimately, Tulkinghorn all exhibit this tendency.[28]

Telling as Policing

> It is not a free appropriation and assimilation of the word itself that authoritative discourse seeks to elicit from us; rather, it demands our unconditional allegiance. Therefore,

> authoritative discourse permits no play with the context
> framing it, no play with its borders. . . . A playing with
> distances, with fusion and dissolution, with approach and
> retreat, is not here possible.
>
> Bakhtin, *DI*

A playing with distances, with fusion and dissolution, with approach and retreat, is the routine affair of Inspector Bucket. With his pointing finger, however—in its real utility and consequence—he points up the distance he has traveled from the rigid *habitus* of authoritative discourse as law. For the ethos of law is the spirit of the nonnarratable: of stasis, blockage, and calcified social intercourse, presided over by Tulkinghorn and the unmoving, foreshortened figure of Allegory in his office.

Lest a notion of authority and "outer-persuasion" be equated with the narrative entity known as "third-person," the text seems to demand the figure of Bucket; as his very name implies the gathering up and unifying of random differences within a single container, so indeed he correlates the novel's narratorial differences within a single hybrid mode of discourse. (The text does, however, make him known to us as "this *third person*" [275], and for me that establishes his ideological rather than narratorial credentials; Bucket personifies what Levinas calls the political world of the impersonal "third," in its purely instrumental and technological capacity. To the extent that he is the state's spy, he is, as it were, a "secret" agent.)

To say that Bucket resolves the novel's narratorial tension implies not that he is a "better" narrator in the sense of being morally superior, but only that he is a more effective and self-sufficient one. He is not a flawless detective, as evidenced by his failure to overtake Lady Dedlock; and the ambiguity over exactly which sphere—public or private—he serves as instrument is not unimportant.

Yet it is because he is so performative, so *engagé*, in his narrational task that he nicely offsets both Esther's inconsistent confessionality and the objective narrator's seeming objectivity. Ideologically, he serves the authoritative interests he has sworn to uphold. Structurally, however, he serves to unify the inner-persuasive energies of the text's two narratorial tracks—on the one hand, by securing not indulging in confession; on the other hand, by bridging the gap between extradiegetic narrator and story by inserting himself into the story which had narrated him from without.

But "story" in *Bleak House* is not exclusively a medium for detection, and it's important to see Bucket as just one (albeit the most masterful) of the novel's many accidental tourists of narrative. The novel's characters tell more than publicly available detective stories: they narrate their own secret and idiosyncratic ones, too. When the wards of Jarndyce first meet Miss Flite, she relates in compressed form her life story, the details of which she intermittently fills in as the novel progresses: "I was a ward myself. I was not mad at that time. . . . I had youth and hope. I believe, beauty. It matters very little now. None of the three served, or saved me" (34). When she has a minute alone with Esther, Caddy Jellyby leaps at the chance to discharge the same autobiographical task.

Mrs. Badger treats Jarndyce and company to an extensive "Biographical Sketch" of the life and deaths of her first two husbands, Swosser and Dingo, and similarly, Mr. Turveydrop provides Esther with his own personal history of deportment, as does Phil Squod in reciting their past adventures to Mr. George. More pathetic are the autobiographies which Charley Coavins, Gridley, and Liz volunteer. A set of narratives is shared between parents and children: Jarndyce imparts to Esther what he knows of her childhood; Lady Dedlock does the same—by letter; George Rouncewell relates his buried past to his mother, asking her to keep it concealed from his brother until such time as he can reveal it himself. Jarndyce provides happy closure in front of the new Bleak House by confessing to Esther that he has told Mrs. Woodcourt "all our story—ours—yours and mine" (752).[29]

Bucket's specularity surpasses all the other modes of "eyeing" which dot the text; he is after all Inspector Bucket, oscillating between seeing, seen, and, like Gyges, seeing unseen. Snagsby describes him as "appearing to possess an unlimited number of eyes" (281). Does he not then merely share Tulkinghorn's "purview," that of narratorial panopticon? The "omniscient" narrative voice articulates the difference between them, however: "Contrast enough between Mr. Tulkinghorn shut up in his dark carriage, and Mr. Bucket shut up in *his*. Between the immeasurable track of space beyond the little wound that has thrown the one into the fixed sleep which jolts so heavily over the stones of the streets, and the narrow track of blood which keeps the other in the watchful state expressed in every hair of his head!" (628). The chapter in which this passage appears is entitled "The Track," an ideal image for Bucket as both detective and narrator, "steering" character and reader alike "over the crossings and up the turnings" (599).

Bucket is the exemplary narrator, first- and third-person in one; "time and place cannot bind Mr. Bucket" (680). He is the exemplary reader: "the velocity and certainty of his imagination . . . is little short of miraculous" (670). Not only does he seem to know other's thoughts, but he voices them on their behalf, with particular emphasis on the word "you," as when he tells Gridley, "You want excitement, you know to keep *you* up; that's what *you* want" (314). Or when he tells Sir Leicester, "*You* know life, you know, sir. . . . *you* don't want to be told, that, from information I have received, I have gone to work" (632). Indeed, when he tells Snagsby, "I don't mind telling *you*" (276), he perfectly encapsulates the force of his narratorial prerogative: "I say what I must say, and no more" (678).

(He employs this method even with objects: "His great hand comes upon a handkerchief. 'Hum! Let's have a look at *you*,' says Mr. Bucket, putting down the light. 'What should *you* be kept for? What's *your* motive? Are you her Ladyship's property, or somebody else's. You've got a mark upon you, somewheres or another, I suppose?' He finds it as he speaks, 'Esther Summerson.' 'Oh!' says Mr. Bucket, pausing, with his finger at his ear. 'Come, I'll take you'" [671].)

The subtlety of that prerogative can be seen in the way Bucket folds his own short autobiographical story into a question and answer session with the Dedlock's footman in order to find something out. We see its full extent, however, in "Springing A Mine" (chapter 54), where Bucket not only arrests the detective story, but arrests somebody *through* story. Synthesizing the person and time frames of the novel's two "official" narrators, he dispenses plot and apprehends person through what can only be called "narration by incarceration."

Bucket's complex performance begins retrospectively and ends in the narrative present by unifying *discours* and *récit*, an arc neither of the novel's primary narrators is capable of tracing himself or herself. A symphonic, not polyphonic, narrator, he discloses secret after secret, and arranges set scenes of anagnorisis as he pieces together the story which he has been hired to "tell." Even his pauses confirm his power as they create narrative suspense, effectively "arresting" the motley group of amateur detectives who have competed with him: Grandfather Smallweed, Chadband, and Mrs. Snagsby. As he tells Smallweed, for

instance, "I am damned if I am a going to have my case spoilt, or
interfered with, or anticipated by so much as half a second of time, by
any human being in creation . . . Do you see this hand, and do you
think that *I* don't know the right time to stretch it out, and put it on
the arm that fired that shot?" (643). Not only, I would venture, does
Bucket implicitly include any presumptuous readers in his admonish-
ment, but for the only time in the text, he highlights the "I," not the
"You."

Bucket's story reaches its climax when he implicates Mademoiselle
Hortense directly to her face, as well as in the presence of Sir Leicester;
Bucket thus discloses his information at one and the same time to
accused, witness, and the greater audience of witnesses who read along.
In line with the astonishing fact that Dickens has effectively given over
the reins of narration to Bucket at this point (the chapter consists
almost entirely of direct speech), most of the accompanying commentary from the third-person narrator shows Bucket's bodily closing-
in on his focal suspect as the analogy to the act of narration. For
example,

> Mr. Bucket, breaking off, has made a noiseless descent upon Made-
> moiselle, and laid his heavy hand upon her shoulder.
> "What is the matter with you now?" she asks him.
> "Don't you think any more," returns Mr. Bucket, with admonitory
> finger, "of throwing yourself out of window. That's about what's the
> matter with me. Come! Just take my arm. You needn't get up; I'll sit
> down by you. Now take my arm, will you? I'm a married man, you
> know; you're acquainted with my wife. Just take my arm."   (650)

And again: "Now my dear, put your arm a little further through
mine, and hold it steady, and I shan't hurt you!" (652). The text aptly
describes the effect on Hortense of this convergence of capture by hand
and by mouth: "the very atmosphere she breathes seemed to narrow
and contract around her, as if a close net were being drawn nearer and
yet nearer around her breathless figure" (651): "It is impossible to
describe how Mr. Bucket gets her out, but he accomplishes that feat in
a manner peculiar to himself; enfolding and pervading her like a cloud,
and hovering away with her as if he were a homely Jupiter, and she the
object of his affections" (651).

This is narrative seduction at its wiliest; the anonymous narrator
goes so far as to concede Bucket's mastery by confessing his own

descriptive inability—"it is impossible to describe." I agree with D. A. Miller's observation that Hortense's verbal qualifications at the end of this scene locate the flaw in Bucket's expertise: "However skillfully prosecuted, the work of detection appears capable only of attaining a shell from which the vital principle has departed" (96). "An oyster of the old school," perhaps only Tulkinghorn manages to keep pearl and shell together, but he is murdered, and his "repository of noble confidences" is eventually pried open. But in his capacity as narrator, I argue, Bucket remains unimpeached.

His purpose, then, would seem to be the literal foregrounding of narration in a novel intensely invested in the ethics of telling and listening. Bucket, as it were, gathers up the disparate energies of inner-persuasive discourse and forges a performative tale which disenchants the world of clandestine secrets and neutralizes the dangerous lure of subterfuge.

He quite overtly shows both the negative consequences of keeping harmful secrets and the process by which they are most effectively dismantled. Of course, he is a policeman, and the job before him is the solution of a criminal case. Still, by so clearly drawing attention to the procedural aspects of telling and knitting together story, he calls attention to the burden assumed by ordinary narrative discourse in transporting people's inner worlds into public space.

And yet, the novel must return to the ordinary to gain such a perspective, to restore narratorial balance, which means that Bucket's function, like Tulkinghorn's before him, must be exhausted within the text. Only finished sentences belong to him (despite the flaw he makes in detection); in the final analysis, thematization and the closure of the Said are his metier. But the novel, however, retains an investment in the unfinished, in the aperture of Saying as pure unvocalized signification.

Telling as Not Telling

In *Bleak House*, the act of "following" possesses the triple meaning of observation, narration, and pursuit; to follow is to eye is to shadow is to tell. All three of *Bleak House*'s primary narrators—first-person, third-person, and Bucket—finally converge in all three of these dimensions in the aptly titled chapter "Pursuit." As is typical of the entire text, secrets pass from and through the three in concentric wise.[30]

In the course of the several chapters' long pursuit of Lady Dedlock, all three of these narrators permit a gap to surface in their narratives while they severally "follow" death. First, most simply, Bucket, whom ostensibly "nothing escapes" (681), exposes such a gap performatively by following the wrong woman; second, in announcing "Look what I am bringing you, who watch there! Who will tell [Sir Leicester]?" (702), the anonymous narrator augurs Lady Dedlock's demise by registering a little death of his own. The content of the narrator's question (it absolves him of having to impart the secret), its form (as prosopopoeia), and the object which it endows with voice (the day—as phantom, "cold, colourless, and vague")—all suggest that this narrator, too, has been prevented from fully "following" what he tracks. (De Man writes that "by making the death speak, the symmetrical structure of prosopopoeia implies, by the same token, that the living are struck dumb, frozen in their own death" [*RT*, 78].)

Last, Esther withholds her feelings from us at the very moment in which she reveals the novel's climactic anagnorisis. "I proceed to other passages of my narrative," (714) she says, twice. By omitting to narrate her reaction to the events that have just "happened to" her, she fails to "follow" as well. Readers must follow for themselves here, as they must once more when they arrive at Esther's (and the novel's) final, uncompleted utterance. But here Esther makes only more discursively obvious the various gaps of self which yawn within her ongoing act of confessional narrative. And in doing so, she imitates (or is imitated by) the novel's own split structure.

In multiplying the set of gaps which fissure a single narrative task into several narrators, the text of *Bleak House* exposes on its narrative surface the cleft between private and public worlds, between one's own and someone else's, which creates the conditions of secrecy, and which Bucket, as I say, cannot entirely resolve. It seems that as we reach the end of the novel we discover that not all its secrets will be ours. In the person of Esther, at least, the last voice we hear, the text remains precariously poised over the abyss of confession, which it, like Bucket, cannot fully master.

In its final chapters *Bleak House* leaves narration in biblical rather than Homeric guise; its first- and third-personal voices opt, however, not for an Abrahamic "Here am I" but for the clandestinity of one more open secret. When Eric Auerbach speaks of the novel in *Mimesis*, he emphasizes its progressive canvassing of both exterior reality (realism) and interior sensation (modernism), leaving nothing unexamined or undisclosed. In the novel, he argues, Western realism completes its long turn away from elected silence to *apokalypsis.*

Ironically, however, it is the biblical model which Auerbach associates with exactly those suspenseful dislocations of narrative form routinely exploited by prose fiction (though Auerbach himself makes the connection to epic, not novelistic, discourse). I have extended Auerbach's suggestion in my reading of *Bleak House* by foregrounding, as it were, this biblical notion of narrative background, of a penumbra around character and discourse which preserves the value of intersubjective claims over hermeneutic desires.

And thus it is fitting that *Bleak House* keep its own council on the ethics of secrecy, preferring an open question to the resolution of full disclosure; to recall Sissela Bok, "Secrecy guards, therefore, not merely isolated secrets about the self but access to the underlying experience *of* secrecy."[31] Along with its own habit of narration, as I have called it, the novel anticipates readers' own typically profligate habit of interpretation.

And thus along with its other matters for the police, the act of reading is placed "under arrest" at the novel's very end. We may be able to predict how Esther should have completed her final sentence, but we do not in fact see or hear it. If *Bleak House* "has an exposed sound" (64), that sound is finally not the whoosh of exposure, but the clap of book covers signaling that some of a text's secrets have remained hidden.

Remainders

In spirit, at least, the two texts I discuss briefly in this final section, *Flaubert's Parrot* and *The Remains of the Day*, look back to both Dickens and Mill. What Mill conveys accidentally, and Dickens through thematic counterpoint, however, Ishiguro and Barnes address explicitly: writing *through* others in order to write the self. Moreover, the gaps of self and intersubjective space which come to light, conspicuously afflict these texts more palpably, if not more profoundly, than either of the Victorian ones, since each narrator himself "comes to knowledge" in the process of narrating his story. Each, in a way, is his own Hortense, delaying capture as long as possible, but each is also his own Bucket, exposing a set of secrets in the presence of witnesses—the readers who look on and listen.

Ishiguro's novel—the more Mill-like of the two—purports to be the week-long diary of a butler for a country estate in 1950's England, at the height of Harold Macmillan's Conservative ministry before its downfall in the wake of the Profumo scandal. The narrator painfully documents just how ill-suited he and a no longer tenable code of service and "dignity" have become in a world of tarnished honor. Against that background of cultural decline, the butler, Stevens, narrates his own small story; as the history of unwavering "professionalism" and the costly subordination of self to role, it merits that famous description with which a similar narrative of societal *malheur* begins: John Dowell's *incipit* to *The Good Soldier* as "the saddest story."

Flaubert's Parrot is the more obviously postmodern and "playful" text. An inside narrative, it secretes the autobiographical confession of its narrator, an English physician, within an artful disquisition on the life and work of Flaubert. The narrator's own story is carefully encrypted in chapters such as "The Flaubert Bestiary," an inventory of the various animal references found in Flaubert's letters and fiction, or "Examination Paper," which is, indeed, a mock exam on the vexed relation between art and life (the text's main preoccupation).

Gradually, one understands such anti-novelistic technique to be the postmodern corollary to the theory about novel and autobiography which I cited earlier in this chapter: that the former must lay bare its artifice in order to prepare the ground for the latter.

Looking Away

"I'm saying that you trust the mystifier more if you know that he's deliberately choosing not to be lucid," says the narrator of Barnes's novel. "You trust Picasso all the way because he could draw like Ingres. But what helps? What do we need to know? Not everything. Everything confuses. Directness also confuses. The full-face portrait staring back at you hypnotises. Flaubert is usually looking away in his portraits and photographs. He's looking away so that you can't catch his eye: he's also looking away because what he can see over your shoulder is more interesting than your shoulder."[32]

"You can't define yourself directly" (95), he says elsewhere, because one always must struggle with the form of autobiography, ensuring that it does not force one to miscalculate the delicate business of revelation—showing either too much of "the full face" or an "unwished impersonality." Thus the narrator speaks of himself by way of Picasso and Ingres, by way of Flaubert, by way of analogy. This principle of indirection, which the narrator calls "looking away," forms the armature on which both narratives in these texts will rest.

Moreover, it informs each text as a narrational as well as a perceptual technique. "Looking away" offers us a final metaphor for describing the kinetic relation between revelation and concealment at the vexed heart of autobiographical fiction. In cases such as Mill's, Esther's, Geoffrey Braithwaite's, and Stevens', the act of telling implies, indeed enacts, its own negation, its own commitment to the "underlying experience of secrecy"; telling the self to others, in other words, just means "to look away." And as "looking away," the readerly coefficient here involves a kind of sympathy, as sympathy itself involves what Roberto Unger has called a "recognition of comic incongruity."[33]

To think about what's involved here, we might appeal by analogy to the ordinary operations of sense perception (a comparison already sanctioned in my readings of Dickens and Mill), specifically the phenomenon known as "figural transformation," which takes place when one surface kinetically "occludes" another. In James J. Gibson's words, "It specifies the existence of an edge in the world, and the depth at the edge, but it does even more. It also specifies the existence of one surface behind another, that is, the continued existence of a hidden surface."[34]

Each of the narrators of *Flaubert's Parrot* and *The Remains of the Day*—Geoffrey Braithwaite, M.D., and Stevens, a butler (he never imparts his first name)—betrays the existence of such hidden surfaces. This is their burden of comic incongruity that asks to be recognized—"wiping-out" and "shearing-across" a texture of occluded feeling and event through conspicuous narrative overlay. In Barnes's novel, metaphor supplies the optical trick; in Ishiguro's, a kind of after-image prevails instead.

When Braithwaite says, "'Life! Life! To have erections!' I was reading that Flaubertian exclamation the other day. It made me feel like a stone statue with a patched upper thigh" (12), he actually discloses the edges of multiple imbricated worlds, different orders of "mapping": the mapping onto the real world of a statement with an aesthetic frame around it (despite the paradoxical fact that it "speaks" about "life"); the mapping onto one's physical self of "artifactuality" (again, in contrast to the content of Flaubert's observation); the mapping onto one's own world of another's; the mapping onto the present of the distant past; the mapping onto direct speech of the indirection of metaphor.

Metaphor forms the obvious rhetorical analogue to the lamination of different surfaces in the material world. Accordingly, the title *Flaubert's Parrot*, itself a polyvalent metaphor for authorial voice, suggests that the task of autobiography is part metaphor: writing the self as an act of occlusion.

By contrast, the title of Ishiguro's novel—befitting its more prosaic and anything-but-Flaubertian narrator—signifies not crafted metaphor but something more "natural," a linguistic stutter, an accident of language: "the remains of the day" can mean either diurnal ruin ("the butt-ends of my days," in J. Alfred Prufrock's pithy phrase) or, less ominously, merely what is left of the day before nightfall. For Stevens, unlike Braithwaite, the occlusion of narrative surfaces does not come about through an integument of metaphor, of art sheathing life. It is produced instead by the appearance of a world which emerges from behind the one he discreetly and courteously escorts us through; we see that world, mostly unbeknownst to him, through a sort of discursive double exposure.

Like Barnes's system of metaphor, however, Ishiguro's model of after-imaging also incorporates several levels. Thus Stevens' narrative folds together the story of global and cultural events; the story of the passive collaboration of his employer, Lord Darlington, with the Germans in the war years occludes a local horizon of domestic duties and chores. The story of Stevens' professional service as butler occludes an inner life of feeling and human connection. The story of narration itself occludes a set of details it prefers not to tell (Stevens' gradual sense of accumulated personal loss and traduced professional loyalty). And finally at the level of simple sense impression, the story of the narrator's field of vision occludes that which it necessarily excludes—this is the story, in other words, of "looking away."

On this last level of what I call the novel's structure of accidental interruption, we find a motif of averted or otherwise obscured glances. The following passage is representative; Miss Kenton—a co-employee who has since moved on—has entered Stevens' personal chamber, and has importunately requested to see the book he is reading:

She reached forward and began gently to release the volume from my grasp. I judged it best to look away while she did so, but with my person positioned so closely, this could only be achieved by my twisting my head away at a somewhat unusual angle. Miss Kenton continued very gently to prise the book away, practically one finger at a time. The process seemed to take a very long time—throughout which I managed to maintain my posture—until I finally heard her say: "Good Gracious, Mr. Stevens, it isn't anything so scandalous at all. Simply a sentimental love story."[35]

Just as Miss Kenton interrupts Stevens by accident, so she accidentally disturbs a professional veneer to disclose a world of tender feeling hiding just beneath. So also does she mime, on the level of story, Stevens' own accidental self-revelation on the level of discourse, which surfaces only as a consequence of the narrative act. Accordingly, the novel asks us to ponder whether beneath its matter-of-fact surface also hide the lineaments of "a sentimental love story." Just as ghosts haunt the great house in which Stevens has worked, and as they flit about Mill's *Autobiography*, so ghosts of a sort inhabit the story which Stevens meticulously relates.

Leaving Home

Like taking a leap or falling in love, Stevens' autobiographical narrative is a kinetic act—hence the novel's conceit of an atypical journey away from home marked by entries in a diary.[36] For Stevens and his tale, the epigraph from Pascal which stands at the beginning of this chapter has especial import. In Stevens' case, however, unhappiness waits merely to be discovered in the course of leaving the security of his private chamber, an unhappiness which has always lurked there, unacknowledged.

In the same way, Barnes's Braithwaite, an aficionado of Flaubert, begins a story of encrypted secrets away from home: in front of a statue of Flaubert in Rouen. His journey, being ostensibly a desire "to chase the writer" (12) (or rather the writer's voice), directly enables the act of finding his own; it is as if, to recall Merleau-Ponty, he must trespass upon the home of another in order to occupy his own more fully, and provide us with access to it in the bargain.

Metaphor, obviously, besides "looking away," also serves as a means of "leaving home." Through its metaphorical intricacy, *Flaubert's Parrot* says that writing the self requires the pathos of leaving home through language, should one seek to open to others "the secret chamber of the heart" (127). It depends on a condition of intentionally thrown or parroted voice quite distinct from the unconsciously inhabited quality which voice assumes in *The Remains of the Day* (though the lesson of trespass each text communicates is identical).

If Stevens' narrative works through the implications of accident as interruption and interruption as accident, Braithwaite's rehearses an interruption of another sort, a governing structure of delay and willful juxtaposition. In carefully closing in on a self which "emerges from behind," *Flaubert's Parrot* "specifies appearance but not the materialization of a ghost."[37] Ishiguro's novel also specifies "appearance," but adds to this unifying function, which Coleridge called "esemplastic," something of the ectoplasmic as well.

Throwing Voice

We could say provisionally that Ishiguro's is to Mill's text as Barnes's is to *Bleak House*. The first exposes purely accidental features of confession, at variance with itself as it strives to remain discreet, while Barnes's text discreetly sediments a set of private revelations artfully coded through a mask of Flaubertian allusion and detail; if Stevens is an "autobiographer," then Braithwaite is a "personificator."[38]

It is wholly appropriate then that *Flaubert's Parrot* "thinks of itself" as a novel (albeit a novel in the tradition of *Bleak House*, given its passion for the heteroglot), and *The Remains of the Day*, by contrast, inclines toward fictive autobiography. The difference between the two texts bears out again D. A. Miller's thesis that writing the secret self inevitably modulates from autobiography to the novel in proportion to the increasing pressure to encrypt one's secrets. As Braithwaite himself frames this idea, "If the sweetest moment in life is a visit to a brothel which doesn't come off, perhaps the sweetest moment in writing is the arrival of that idea for a book which never has to be written, which is never sullied with a definite shape, which never needs to be exposed to a less loving gaze than that of its author" (116).

And yet, obviously, this is wishful thinking; the best, easiest, and most "unsullied" confession is that which remains safely virtual; written secrets, however carefully hedged, are always open secrets.[39] The analogy between the book unwritten and the life untold, let alone the life unlived, breaks down fairly quickly, however. The most reliable form of pleasure, as Braithwaite approvingly says in glossing Flaubert, may be the pleasure of anticipation. But Braithwaite's narrative, by contrast, dilates only in order to perfect the finished form which autobiography must eventually assume at its end. And what that form depends on is the hard, perhaps not ultimately pleasurable labor of truth.

Autobiography is not really abandoned for the novel in this case so much as temporarily ventured away from; or, to think of it another way, autobiography is "thrown" from within the novel, as a ventriloquist's voice is projected through a dummy to play its trick. Personification and autobiography remain closely allied, and Ishiguro's and Barnes's texts converge upon a median point even though they may seem to differ on either side of it.

Thus each of these novels progresses toward an eventual anagnorisis, Barnes's with careful deliberateness, Ishiguro's under the pressure of accreted accidents. In each, the counter-text functions solely to offset, to illuminate the secrets which its narrator slowly decrypts. In *The Remains of the Day*, that counter-text comprises both the life that did not happen and the past that is structurally identical to it, seen and understood only in retrospect, when it no longer matters. As Braithwaite says obliquely of himself—but it is just as true for Stevens—"It is not just the life that we know. It is not just the life that has been successfully hidden. It is not just the lies about the life, some of which cannot now be disbelieved. It is also the life that was not led" (121).

In *Flaubert's Parrot*, books, Flaubert, and art form a counter-text of virtuality which mediates the life which could not but be lived. Thus Braithwaite will ask repeatedly, "How do we seize the past? How do we seize the foreign past?" Or, as Stevens puts it in *The Remains of the Day*, with all the poignancy of incipient realization, and without irony's safety-net, "Naturally, when one looks back to such [turning points] today, they may indeed take on the appearance of being crucial, precious moments in one's life; but of course, at the time, this was not the impression one had. Rather, it was as though one had available a never-ending number of days, months, years. . . . There was surely nothing to indicate at the time such evidently small incidents would render whole dreams irredeemable" (179).

Here, in the first of only three such moments in the text, Stevens' voice conspicuously changes register, as a world of secrets newly discovered wells up from beneath its occluded surface.[40] Yet for all its pertinacious metaphorical hedging, Braithwaite's voice, too, escapes him on occasion and throws itself, so to speak, by accident. In the course of an ongoing diatribe against critics for being defective readers, and having launched into a familiar opposition between what Stevens calls the "vagaries" of social relationship, on the one hand, and the erotics of reading, where "domesticity need never intrude," on the other, Braithwaite remarks, "Look, writers aren't *perfect*, I want to cry, any more than husbands and wives are perfect. . . . I never thought my wife was perfect. I loved her, but I never deceived myself. I remember . . . But I'll keep that for another time" (76).

Braithwaite seems to undo this moment of *vraisemblance* (and others like it) when he observes in a subsequent chapter, "When a contemporary narrator hesitates . . . does a reader in fact conclude that reality is being more authentically rendered?" (89). I emphasize, however, that Braithwaite's own image for contemporary fictional technique—cubism—aptly describes the structure of his own narrative: a postmodern ironic veneer which "shears across" an underlying realist sensibility. As he himself asks, "Does irony preclude sympathy?" (155)[41]

Rubbing Text

The reflexive or concentric irony of postmodern fiction hypnotizes on its own account. But what prevents *Flaubert's Parrot* from being merely, however ingeniously, mechanical is the ethical weight it places on narration; the disguised pathos in its voice determines the quality of readers' belief. Ironic fiction demands belief of a certain kind, because a successful irony enjoins a peculiar readerly alliance: just as an ironist bids, teases, flirts with readers (lest they forget the purely libidinal allure of the text), so readers in consequence are flattered, gratified, and seduced by the ironist's assumption that they will appreciate his ironies. A mutual sizing up, irony is textual athletics; when well played on both sides, the game rewards both sides as winners. But that explains how readers believe, not why.

We trust Picasso all the way not simply because he could draw like Ingres, for that is respect, a polite relation, but because "we know our man," which is familiarity, an ethical relation, the one Levinas calls Sensibility. The form irony takes will excite us, but it is its timbre which domesticates. *Flaubert's Parrot* manipulates the postmodern—readerly erotics and the pleasure of the text—in order to abandon it for real-ism—the ethics of secrecy and the failure of married love.

Thus, to return to the question of secrecy, Braithwaite's running complaint against critics amounts essentially to a fence built around hermeneutic propriety; he advocates a chastened as well as loving demeanor for both texts and persons. Of the panel which opens the "secret chamber of the heart," Braithwaite says, "Sometimes you find [it], but it doesn't open; sometimes it opens, and your gaze meets nothing but a mouse skeleton. But at least you've looked. That's the real distinction between people: not between those who have secrets and those who don't, but between those who want to know everything and those who don't. This search is a sign of love, I maintain" (127).

The desire to "know everything" can be tyrannous, as I noted for Tulkinghorn, inside the text or outside it, as in the case of the herme-neutics of suspicion applied to a work like Mill's *Autobiography*. But here, I think, Braithwaite means something closer to Levinas' concept of "rubbing the text": *sollicitation* as a labor of love.[42] Both Barnes's and Ishiguro's novels, as fictive autobiographies about autobiography, train readers in an ethics of secrecy as vigorously moral as any exercised by Victorians such as Dickens or Mill.

Toward the end of his narrative, Stevens juxtaposes two scenes in which the desire not to know everything is put in the dock. In the first, after informing Stevens of her intention to marry, Miss Kenton asks, "'Are you not in the least interested in what took place tonight between my acquaintance and I, Mr. Stevens?" (218). In the second, Mr. Car-dinal, a critic of Lord Darlington's political improprieties, asks, "Aren't you struck by even the remote possibility that I am correct? Are you not, at least, *curious* about what I am saying?" (225). In both cases, Stevens "looks away," interrupted either by "matters of global sig-nificance taking place upstairs" or by the pressing requirements of "the gentlemen" across the hall. In the latter instance, Cardinal pointedly remarks, "How could you not have *seen* it?" (223; my emphasis).

Performing Self

Whereas the parrot metaphor in Barnes's novel rebukes the imperti-nent desire for a reliable frisson with the past or the text or another person, Ishiguro's novel rebukes the opposite tendency to submerge a sharable private world wholly within public role and professional tact.

To recall the observation by David Brudney I quoted in Chapter 2, "maintaining surface can be a way either to avoid or to acknowledge intimacy." Or, as Hans-Georg Gadamer defines tact in *Truth and Method*, "to pass over something does not mean to avert the gaze from something, but to watch it in such a way that rather than knock against it, one slips by it."[43]

For the novels at hand, then, where *Flaubert's Parrot*, as Novel, meticulously tends a surface in order to disclose the open secret which resides beneath, *The Remains of the Day*, as Autobiography, obediently attends a surface with tactful subservience, in order to maintain the pretense that surface is all there really is.

Of course, Ishiguro's text is a novel, and thus at its outermost level qualifies the conceit of dignified ignorance, as the narrator gives way to occlusion by the author—the novel's feat of "cultural impersonation."[44] But Stevens would hardly agree with the following sentiment about impersonation, expressed by the narrator of Philip Roth's *The Counterlife* (a perfect alternate title for Ishiguro's book, incidentally): "What people envy in the novelist aren't the things that the novelists think are so enviable but the performing selves that the author indulges, the slipping irresponsibly in and out of his skin, the reveling not in 'I' but in escaping 'I,' . . . the gift for theatrical self-transformation."[45]

Within the text Stevens neither slips in and out of his skin nor impersonates others. While he is obliged to conceal his identity now and again (people still associate Darlington Hall with fascist sympathies) he understands his raison d'être to be the seamless inhabitation of the private individual by the entity known as "Stevens." Hence, in one of the rare metaphors he assays, Stevens—a son of Abraham, not Noah—likens the shedding of one's role to "removing one's clothing in public" (210). "A butler of any quality must be seen to *inhabit* his role, utterly and fully; he cannot be seen casting it aside one moment simply to don it again the next as though it were nothing more than a pantomime costume. There is one situation and one situation only in which a butler who cares about his dignity may feel free to unburden himself of his role; that is to say, when he is entirely alone" (169).

Stevens makes this claim more than once in the novel; the question of correctly defining "dignity" remains a constant preoccupation. And to be sure, the public does not fully occlude the private self, which is

Stevens' minor tragedy. But whether he is ever "entirely alone" in the novel, I think, is the more important question, since his diary entries clearly address an imagined audience. And as I said above, propriety demands that he inhabit his role even in a purely discursive context, writing being merely another, albeit atypical, function which a butler must dignifiably perform; like Mill, he thereby calls his readership to concomitant vigilance.

Barnes's narrator demands the same circumspection but construes the meaning of "performance" quite differently. Also something of an accidental writer, as English and rooted in his professional identity as is Stevens, Braithwaite nevertheless sees performance not as service but rather as skillful and deliberate impersonation, closer to the sense of "performing self."[46]

And yet Braithwaite's use of Flaubert as secret sharer does *not* conduce to a slipping irresponsibly in and out of his skin. As what we might in fact call a personificating J. S. Mill, Braithwaite defines fiction's connection to autobiography in quite another way (appropriately enough, through the example of Mauriac):[47]

> [Mauriac] writes his *Memoires*, but they aren't his memoires . . . Instead, Mauriac tells us about the books he's read, the painters he's liked, the plays he's seen. He finds himself by looking in the works of others. . . . Reading his "memoirs" is like meeting a man on a train who says, "Don't look at me, that's misleading. If you want to know what I'm like, wait until we're in a tunnel, and then study my reflection in a window." You wait, and look, and catch a face against a shifting background of sooty walls, cables and sudden brickwork. The transparent shape flickers and jumps, always a few feet away. You become accustomed to its existence, you move with its movements; and though you know its presence is conditional, you feel it to be permanent. Then there is a wail from ahead, a roar, and a burst of light, the face is gone forever. (96)

By this point in the novel, readers have been sufficiently trained in the text's pattern of superimposed surfaces to grasp the implications here of "looking away": to speak about the difficulty of seizing the past or of ever really knowing someone or of transcending loss is precisely to enact the refractory truth of self-revelation.

And thus Braithwaite's narrative keeps the ground situation ever present exactly by means of such diversionary parallelism; within the nested metaphors of the passage above, for example, one discovers a deeply embedded reference to his wife—"the face is gone forever." It is actually her infidelity and death which form the core of the "pure story" the text slowly and carefully unfolds. Similarly, the railway image joins several more in the narrative which link Braithwaite's story to Flaubert's: "Has anyone made a comparative study of the spread of railways and the spread of adultery?" (109).

However, Braithwaite does not intend the stereographic effect of multiple frames to produce a *vertige* of endlessly reflexive mirrorings: Flaubert, the authorial alter ego; Flaubert's mistress, Louise Colet; Ellen, Braithwaite's dead wife; Braithwaite himself. (The narrator's Francophile tastes incline toward Flaubert, not Robbe-Grillet.) Rather, as in *Bleak House*, storytelling presses "narrative seduction" into the service of making readers confront the sheer enmeshment of lives and stories which autobiography—as narrative ethics—complexly "nets."

Signs and tokens such as these constitute what Braithwaite himself calls "submerged parallels" and "references," and it is through them that we discover the stratifications of his story:

> Three stories contend within me. One about Flaubert, one about Ellen, one about myself. My own is the simplest of the three—it hardly amounts to more than a convincing proof of my existence— and yet I find it the hardest to begin. My wife's is more complicated, and more urgent; yet I resist that too. Keeping the best for last, as I was saying earlier? I don't think so; rather the opposite, if anything. But by the time I tell you her story, I want you to be prepared: that's to say, I want you to have had enough of books. . . . Books are not life, however much we might prefer it if they were. Ellen's is a true story; perhaps it is even the reason why I am telling you Flaubert's story instead. (86)

In the chapter entitled "The Flaubert Apocrypha," having inventoried and "pacified" the necessary set of details, Braithwaite concludes, "writing can begin" (125). That is, the narrator of contemporary fiction knows he must first disenchant in order to tell his secrets, engage in a "demythologizing to induce depathologizing," as Philip Roth puts it.

But Roth's own fictional ego, Nathan Zuckerman, poses a counter-argument. Despite the elaborate precautions one takes, autobiography still manipulates, as any confession must; it mythologizes and re-pathologizes all over again. Hence the importance of Braithwaite's profession and the analogies (or disanalogies) between writing and medicine which the text constructs. "You produce desolation," wrote George Sand to Flaubert, "and I produce consolation." Braithwaite asks his readers, "Do you want art to be a healer? Send for the *Ambulance George Sand*. Do you want art to tell the truth? Send for the *Ambulance Flaubert*" (136).

The narrator's seemingly morbid fascination with the many deaths of Flaubert's friends and with Flaubert's metaphors of decay and disease clarifies itself when we discover that not only did his wife try to commit suicide, but Braithwaite himself terminated her life-support: "The patient. Ellen. So you could say . . . that I killed her. You could just. I switched her off. I stopped her living. Yes." But immediately after, the narrator supplies the rationale, the necessity behind all his fictiveness and literary manipulation: "Ellen. My wife: someone I feel I understand less well than a foreign writer dead for a hundred years. Is this an aberration, or is it normal? Books say: She did this because. Life says: she did this. . . . Books make sense of life. The only problem is that the lives they make sense of are other people's lives, never your own" (168).

Literature may not be a pharmacopoeia, but autobiography, at least, can dispense medicinal effects, be they purgative for the writer or prophylactic for the reader. (Hence the clinical cast we find in Coleridge's *Rime of the Ancient Mariner*, Conrad's *Lord Jim*, and Anderson's *Winesburg, Ohio*, or the contagion-structure and the scenes of nursing in *Bleak House*, or the deathbed twinning of Mariner-patient and Wedding Guest–healer in Turgenev's famous story "The Country Doctor," or the temptation to "switch off" the hermeneutic life-support to Mill's *Autobiography*—all these texts link narrative in some way or another with therapy.)

It is the interruptive structure in both *Flaubert's Parrot* and *The Remains of the Day* which most overtly activates this question of attention, of care, of ministering to oneself or to others. When Braithwaite confesses that he "switched off" his wife, he simultaneously looks "away" from narrative obfuscation and toward hermeneutic clarity, as he looks away from his wife and toward us; death paradoxically heals narrative rupture and pivots the story toward recognition and readerly compassion. When, in Ishiguro's novel, Stevens actually comes to confess in the course of his story, when, to use the vocabulary of moral philosophy, "agent-regret" suddenly breaks in upon—interrupts—the placid, deliberative surface of a rational "life-plan,"[48] he also can be said to have hit upon the palliative uses of narrative.[49]

Interruptions

Above, I contrasted the two novels in terms of either the accidental or the willful quality of interruption each demonstrates. The distinction is not ironclad, since Braithwaite does falter on occasion, and Stevens, it can be argued, consciously modulates at several places from disturbing recollections to those which are more anodyne. Generally, however, the distinction holds, the difference between two kinds of memory, like Proustian *memoire volontaire* and *involontaire*: where Braithwaite distributes the segments of his narrative in the way which best suits his carefully plotted juxtapositions, Stevens dis-covers his own secrets in the act of narrating them.

In *Flaubert's Parrot*, a logic of displacement guides the sequence of chapters, securely containing the mobile effect of the submerged parallels and references which lie within. For instance, the chapters entitled "Snap!" and "Emma Bovary's Eyes" serve as rebukes of a sort to readers; the first mocks their insufficient understanding of Flaubertian irony, the second, their lapses of discretion and sympathy toward writers. Both chapters buttress "Cross-Channel," the second most crucial chapter in the novel after "Pure Story," since it is the one which quite literally suspends Braithwaite between Britain and France on a ferry. As he addresses an imagined interlocutor, the uncomfortable proximity between them (read: between him and us) threatens, for the only time in the narrative, to disturb the assured ironist's calculated poise.

Thus in "Snap" an offhand remark about writers feeding "mistakes" to reviewers—"I see the novelist at the stern rail of a cross-channel ferry, throwing bits of gristle to the hovering gulls" (79)—wraps a protective film around the narrator's uncharacteristic rhetorical lapse and consequent need to "look away" in "Cross-Channel": "You'd guessed that, at least—that I'm English. I . . . I . . . Look at the seagull up there. I hadn't noticed him before. Slipstreaming away, waiting for the bits of gristle from the sandwiches" (89).

The next two chapters, "The Train-Spotter's Guide to Flaubert" and "The Flaubert Apocrypha," perform the same function; they create more diversionary security against the fast-encroaching plot, a movement begun in earnest (though still hedged) in the chapters entitled "The Case Against" and "Louise Colet's Version." One more chapter of entirely nonnarrative play, "Braithwaite's Dictionary of Accepted Ideas," is needed before the narrating of "Pure Story" can finally take place.

By contrast, the sequence of chapters in *The Remains of the Day* is purely formal, following the order of diary entries for a six-day trip, all but one recorded in the afternoon or evening—in the remains of the day. The set of transitions and interruptions within these entries between private and public matters (the two are never far apart and are always in some sense co-implicated) answers to a different logic than Braithwaite's—either the wish "not to know" or the simple randomness which controls Stevens' encounters with people along the way. When Stevens meets such people, he is invariably provoked to speak obliquely about himself, since they tend to mistake him for gentry rather than realizing he is "help." Often, the occasion for these encounters is a real accident: either he loses his way or he has trouble operating the car.[50]

As with Braithwaite, three stories contend within this narrator, three distinct and layered narrative pulses, one could say, which control the flow of his story. At the most temporally immediate level is the narrative of the journey itself; it consists of the random details of place, the relation of incidental happenstances, and the intermittent activity of writing itself. It can occasionally be reflexive, as the following sentence shows: "But for the tranquility of the present setting, it is possible I would not have thought a great deal further about my behaviour during my [earlier] encounter with the batman" (121). It seems to possess at times a discreetly nuanced symbolic quality. For the most part, however, it performs the yeoman's work of simple narrative transport.

Between its formal divisions, however, a background flux of reverie and association commands Stevens' attention, typically signaled by markers such as "Incidentally, now that I come to think further about it . . ." or "It is probably apt at this point to say a few words concerning . . ." The chance nature of these transitions determines the string of anecdotes and remembrances which make up Stevens' "accidental" autobiography. For example, as he sits composing one of his entries, he looks out the window and notices a sign for the town of Mursden, where, he recalls, the firm of Giffen and Co. made the finest silver polish available during the war.

Thence he drifts into a small discursion on the bygone standards of

silver polishing in the great houses, which reminds him of Lord Halifax's favorable comment one evening about the delightful appearance
of the silver at Darlington Hall; it was the same evening, Stevens
realizes, on which Halifax met with Ribbentrop in 1939. This further
prompts him to remark on Lord Darlington's flirtation with Oswold
Mosley and the British Union of Fascists, his reputation as an an-
tisemite, and how one's employer's morals do not exist independently
of his servant's standing.

The silver-polishing theme pivots his thoughts one final time to the
question of "polishing errors" he himself has recently made under the
indifferent eyes of his new employer. In this way he circles back from
the global to the domestic, and permits himself to imagine the possibility that Miss Kenton may return to Darlington Hall after a long
absence and a possibly failed marriage to assist him in his duties, this
particular sequence of recollections thus ending in the present on an
unmistakable note of fantasized wish fulfillment. The silver having
done its associational work, Stevens closes his diary entry with thoughts
of Miss Kenton, his last sentence registering perhaps the most meaningful kinetic occlusion in the entire sequence: "Still, I must say, I did
spend some long minutes turning those passages over in my mind as I
lay there in the darkness, listening to the sounds from below of the
landlord and his wife cleaning up for the night" (141). "The landlord
and his wife" in some suppressed sense "refers" to himself and Miss
Kenton, but he does not indicate to us that he recognizes such a
connection. Thus does Stevens glide through his memories, alternately
looking and looking away.

Against or rather within this measured amble appears a third
rhythm—not of time, however, but of appearance: the coded text of
dignity, service, and concentrated attention which invites us to look
beyond to its after-image, the ghostly counter-text of words and feeling
left unexpressed, of averted glances, of the desire not to know. Whether
conscious or not, the logic of eclipse—the perceptual rhythm between
what appears and what remains in shadow—is controlled entirely by
narrative ellipse—Stevens' interruptive resistances. We thus become
privy to dramatic and even tragic moments, defined by the structure of
looking away, as we saw in *Flaubert's Parrot*, which modulates in and
out of them. The saddest of these is perhaps the death of Stevens'
father, Stevens' narrating of which mimetically reproduces the competing claims on his attention at the time.

For the duration of his speaking to us, however, Stevens sees most of his more flagrant self-deceptions deflate and collapse, and we witness the scales fall as he does (though he merely shows us, and avoids telling us). Many times he qualifies earlier observations with the locution "I may well have been mistaken about this." From "I have, I should make clear, reread Miss Kenton's recent letter several times, and there is no possibility I am merely imagining the presence of these hints on her part" (10) to "I am inclined to believe I may well have read more into certain of her lines than was perhaps wise" (180), from "A 'great' butler can only be one who can say that he has applied his talents to serving a great gentleman—and through the latter, to serving humanity" (117) to "You see, I *trusted*. All those years I served him, I trusted that I was doing something worthwhile" (243), we see the full contour of Stevens' story-long anagnorisis.

And yet Stevens' narrative confession does not accomplish full recognition so much as permit him merely restricted and partial glimpses. That is in the nature of his permanently occluded manner of negotiating the world. Sometimes, he need not comment, and we respect his taste, his "dignity." He recalls, for example, a moment in which he was publicly shamed—paraded before one of his employer's guests and examined on his knowledge of world events so that he would demonstrate the smallness of the common man's perspective—but he records this occasion and an equally painful scene of shaming at the hands of Miss Kenton discreetly, without rancor or self-pity.

Alternately, however, he can be overly liberal with self-congratulatory pride for "having been given a part to play, however small, on the world's stage" (188), and can sustain such saving blindness even to the end. But, benighted or not, a thought such as this occurs to him only as a consequence of having embarked on narrative, of having "left home": "As I say, I have never in all these years thought of the matter in quite this way; but then it is perhaps in the nature of coming away on a trip such as this that one is prompted towards such surprising new perspectives on topics one imagined had long ago been thought through thoroughly" (117).

The Art of Good Waiting

The Remains of the Day, with its delicate recognition plot, affirms along with the texts of Barnes, Dickens, and Mill that "recognition" remains a problem, a "scandal" as Terence Cave puts it in his book, *Recognitions*, and not a guarantor of either satisfaction or resolution. This applies, of course, to readers' responses as well as to the texts.

Stevens' more painful belated realizations are quickly covered up and suppressed; he looks away. Attentive readers, however, witness both what he prefers not to see and what he does see. And if Stevens' narrative has succeeded, whatever his intentions for it, it has instructed them a little in the art Stevens calls "good waiting": "that balance between attentiveness and the illusion of absence" (72) This is the art not of occlusion but of double vision: keeping two surfaces co-present. It is the tactful capacity for recognition, for seeing "comic incongruity." It is something which Stevens, along with John Stuart Mill, can only unknowingly solicit, but which Braithwaite, along with Dickens (and Flaubert), can more pleasurably enjoy and exploit. Braithwaite knows what his story means, which is why he so carefully prepares us for it; Stevens, unaccustomed to irony—or as he calls it, "bantering"—knows both more and less that he tells. Each narrator, however, presumes on our sympathy, our tact.

We withdraw from Braithwaite's narrative with perhaps a different sense of the way such tact works than we take away from Stevens', but we have received a brief glimpse, a palimpsest really, of Picasso drawing like Ingres. Our recognition of that fact, like our recognition of Stevens' momentary vacation from the haven of self, is our way of leavening sympathy with the necessary irony that separates art from life. It is how we track the pathos and the comic incongruity of open secrets, of Autobiography and Novel as they shade into each other.

Texts of secrecy and recognition, of interruption both willful and accidental, *Flaubert's Parrot* and *The Remains of the Day* solicit from readers the same ethical surplus which Enoch Robinson asks, which the Mariner asks of the Wedding Guest, which Jim asks of Marlow, which the Monarchs ask of their painter and the telegrapher of her auditors "outside the cage," which Henry Johnson asks through the nudity of face, which Jo asks from the many tellers and "follerers" who take up his story. This is one way of explaining why both Barnes's and Ishiguro's novels contain the sign of remainder in their titles, the parrot which cannot be tracked down, and the day which is still left to en-joy—the evening, as Stevens' bench-companion tells him, being "the best part of the day" (244). In each, something is left over, inaccessible, unexposed.

The desire to know everything, as Braithwaite says, is a sign of love. It is also a sign of reading. And a sign of excess. And so, reading sometimes demands the contrary sign of looking away, of stopping short, of realizing that texts, like persons, cannot entirely be known, that they must keep some of their secrets. It is, finally, the sign of interruption which identifies the reader's share in the act of telling the self to others, the dialectic of revelation and concealment, of leaving home and looking away, of knowing and acknowledging, that is narrative ethics. "Besides stopping in order to understand, there is another kind of interruption, more mysterious and more important. It introduces waiting, which measures the distance between two speakers, and not the reducible distance but the irreducible."[51]

—

Conclusion

The tale is not the narration of an event, but the event itself, the approach to that event, the place where the event is made to happen—an event which is yet to come and through whose power of attraction the tale can hope to come into being too.

Maurice Blanchot, *The Sirens' Song*

He spake with somewhat of a solemn tone,
But when he ended there was in his face
Such easy cheerfulness, a look so mild,
That for a little time it stole away
All recollection, and that simple tale
Passed from my mind like a forgotten sound.
A while on trivial things we held discourse,
To me soon tasteless. In my own despite
I thought of that poor woman as of one
Whom I had known and loved. He had rehearsed
her homely tale with such familiar power,
With such an active countenace, an eye
So busy, that the things of which he spake
Seemed present, and, attention now relaxed,
There was a heartfelt chillness in my veins.
I rose, and turning from that breezy shade
Went out into the open air, and stood
To drink the comfort of the warmer sun.
Long time I had not stayed ere, looking round
Upon that tranquil ruin, I returned
And begged of the old man that for my sake
He would resume his story.

William Wordsworth, *The Ruined Cottage*

ALTHOUGH HE MAY seem to do so, the speaker in *The Ruined Cottage* does not "look away." Nor, though he admits a chill upon his heart, does he find himself glaciated by story as does the Wedding Guest in Coleridge's *Rime of the Ancient Mariner.* He rises, not to "shake off" the effects of what he has just heard, but to pause, "To drink the comfort of the warmer sun," before the narrative resumes. He "waits," in Maurice Blanchot's sense, and marks in time and space the interruption which measures the distance between himself and Margaret, "that poor woman"; although the storyteller's story in a sense reclaims her and makes her "present," enabling the speaker to imagine he has "known and loved" her, she remains irrevocably absent to him.

In the expanded version of this poem included in the first book of *The Excursion,* three separate acts of rising mimetically reproduce one another at each of the story's three diegetic levels: Margaret rises from her seat to tell her tale to the storyteller; he rises from a bench outside her house, some months later before she picks up where she had left off; and the poem's speaker rises from the same bench, years after that, just before begging the storyteller, "for my sake," to resume his story.

In Turgenev's short story "The Country Doctor" a similar mimetic relay takes place. The narrator, sick in bed, reaches out and takes the hand of the doctor who has just spontaneously related a "rather re-markable incident": the story of a patient on her deathbed who, before she expires, reaches out to him, and offers her love; at each diegetic level, overwhelmed by narrative—of which he is either recipient or narrator—the doctor momentarily turns away.

In each of these texts, embedded narratives give birth to those which nest them. Nevertheless, each remains self-contained, bearing out Walter Benjamin's contention that a story "preserves and concentrates its strength" while retaining its "germinative" power.[1] Two other premises of Benjamin's famous essay "The Storyteller" apply to these texts as well. Each text features a "self-forgetful listener" (91), obliged by the "chaste compactness" of the story he hears to retell it, to imitate its content in some palpable way. And each tells the story of a death, "the sanction of everything that the storyteller can tell" (94).

But, certainly, while death can be called the common topic of Wordsworth's and Turgenev's texts, as well as those of Coleridge, Conrad, Wright, and many of the others in the previous six chapters, each, I have tried to show, fundamentally concerns the process—the motivation, the act, and the consequences—of storytelling itself. The layering of story*tellings* whose absence Benjamin laments in the novel's world of solitary individuals, need not, I have argued, disappear with the form and practice of oral narrative. Indeed, the genius of prose fictional form is to incorporate within itself the promise of transmission and hermeneutic responsibility which traditional storytelling legislates externally. *Contra* theories of its authoritarianism, its power leverage, the novel, above all, transacts inner-persuasion across the dimensions of text.

Like the storytellers in *Bleak House*, texts of narrative ethics range across a spectrum. In Wordsworth's and Turgenev's texts, for instance, the act of turning away on the level of story is counterbalanced on the level of discourse by an implicit "turning toward" or addressivity of utterance, as Bakhtin calls it, "a link in the chain of speech communion" which forges intersubjective alliance.[2] However, as the mimetic transfers within *Bleak House*, *Winesburg, Ohio*, the James stories, and across the three texts discussed in Chapter 5 indicate, addressivity can mean a wholly negative inscription of the other, narrationally as well as representationally. It need not preserve the other "under the sign of the neutral," as Blanchot puts it, but may appropriate and defile him or her under the same sign instead.

As I have remarked before, narrative ethics is often a matter of force, a concept which cuts two ways. If the force of story in *The Ruined Cottage* makes the narrator feel as though he has known and loved Margaret, the force of representation, of repudiating and defacing others, in *The Monster* and *Benito Cereno* implicitly confirms Henry Johnson's and Babo's representational power, the way in which they impinge on an unhappy (culture's) consciousness. And "the experience of secrecy," as shown in the last chapter, involves both bliss and bale, the need to keep knowledge from others as well as to retain authority over it oneself.

As we know from Coleridge, the sheer experience of narrating or witnessing stories can transform persons in ways they often cannot control. Indeed, the mere representation of an other, the translation of human "background" into fictional form, is fraught with ethical tensions. Even dumb, unanswering physicality calls its perceivers and fabricators to account. Consider the following example from Bruno Schultz, an analogue to Levinas' notion that representation can immure the human form into a kind of "still life" clothed in "old garments":

> Figures in a waxwork museum . . . even fair-ground paradoxes of dummies must not be treated lightly. Matter never makes jokes; it is always full of the tragically serious. Who dares to think that you can play with matter, that you can shape it for a joke, that the joke will not be built in, will not eat into it like fate, like destiny? Can you imagine the pain, the dull imprisoned suffering hewn into the matter of that dummy, which does not know why it must remain in the forcibly imposed form which is no more than a parody? Do you understand the power of form, of expression, of pretense, the arbitrary tyranny imposed on a helpless block, and ruling it like its own, tyrannical, despotic soul? You give a head of canvas and oakum an expression of anger and leave it with it, with the convulsion, the tension enclosed once and for all, with a blind fury for which there is no outlet. The crowd laughs at the parody. Weep, ladies, over your own fate, when you see the misery of imprisoned matter, of tortured matter which does not know what it is, nor where the gesture may lead that has been imposed on it for ever.[3]

It is but a step from here to the Monarchs' fate in "The Real Thing," and but a few more to Babo's and Henry Johnson's in *Benito Cereno* and *The Monster*. Is the despotism of form, of expression, of pretense any less grievous for heads of paper and type than for those of canvas and oakum? Evidently, the fate which is character has something to teach about the fate which is sentience, about the hands which shape and the face which gestures. What Cavell calls acknowledgment, Bakhtin answerability, and Levinas ethics is just this recognition of our part in that shaping, in that gesturing.

But as we know from Wordsworth, form and the communication of form also bring about the grace of moments, even amid ruin and the irremediable. *Lord Jim* teaches us that, and so in its own strange way does *Winesburg, Ohio*. The "neurological novels" of A. R. Luria intervene in the lives of their impaired subjects, too late, it is true, to effect remedy or cure, but meaningfully enough to make broken lives whole again through story.[4] One of the lessons of A. B. Yehoshua's *Mr. Mani*, to take another example, is that selves and cultural histories can each be knit together through the power of narrative and plangent representation.

As I have endeavored to show through all my readings, narrative ethics is not merely a property of texts. The kind of narrative "repair" I just alluded to continues in the "morrow of the book," where the "presiding" hands of readers open, close, and intervene in the worlds of Stevens and Braithwaite, of Bigger Thomas and Enoch Robinson.

A theory of narrative ethics entails the perhaps peculiar notion that characters' fates take place in the presence of readers, that Stevens' waiting in *The Remains of the Day*, as Sartre says of Raskolnikov, becomes in some way readers' own. I say peculiar, because this idea may seem to imply a "borrowing" of consciousness from book to reader which my ongoing argument about intersubjective boundaries explicitly discounts. What it means, rather, is that readers' "waiting" is quite different from Raskolnikov's or from Stevens', for that matter.

It is the waiting of interruption, a bearing witness at an irreducible distance, rather than the hope for, or belief in, merger; we cannot approach a character, as Stanley Cavell says, "not because it is not done, but because nothing would count as doing it" (*MWM*, 324). More is true of such an entity, continues Cavell, "than we take in at a glance, or in a generation of glances. And more that we are responsible for knowing. Call him our creation, but then say that creation is an exhausting business" (335). Call that exhaustion the catharsis of narrative ethics, the labor of resistance and response, the "fate" that is rubbing the text. Narratives that bind and narratives that release, "the stories that help and the stories that hurt": in each case, texts tax readers with ethical duties which increase in proportion to the measure with which they are taken up. The ethics of reading is to think the infinite, the transcendent, the Stranger.

If, finally, "the storyteller," as Benjamin says, "is the man who could let the wick of his life be consumed completely by the gentle flame of his story" (108–109), then readers, in coming ever closer to the story, alternately warm themselves before it and draw off a measure of its air.

The latter consequence carries with it the severer ethical burden, since the voice of the text may always have the last word, a word through which it in Saying and we in Acknowledging each die just a little. "'You are a storyteller,' a friend said to me one day. How can I be when words and images always cut in and want to be heard with their own aura, when the story is built out of counter-stories, and when silence lies in wait for the world?"[5]

Notes

1. Narrative as Ethics

1. See Stanley Cavell, *In Quest of the Ordinary: Lines of Skepticism and Romanticism* (Chicago: University of Chicago Press, 1988).

2. This "logic" of skepticism, structurally analogous to religious faith in its persistent haunting of the claims of reason, becomes a prominent theme in Emmanuel Levinas' later work, and offers an extremely interesting point of contact with Cavell's project. See the relevant passages in Levinas, *OTB*; Jan de Greef, "Skepticism and Reason," in *Face to Face with Levinas*, ed. Richard Cohen (Albany: State University of New York Press, 1986), 159–180; and Robert Bernasconi, "Skepticism in the Face of Philosophy," in *Re-Reading Levinas*, ed. Robert Bernasconi and Simon Critchley (Bloomington: Indiana University Press, 1991), 149–161.

3. As another important essay, "Aesthetic Problems in Modern Philosophy" indicates, Cavell knows well that the problem of paraphrase to some degree persists because of an arbitrary division between aesthetic language and other kinds of discourse. *MWM*, 73–96.

4. Maurice Blanchot, "Interruptions," in *The Sin of the Book: Edmond Jabès*, ed. Eric Gould (Lincoln: University of Nebraska Press, 1985), 43–54.

5. Chaucer's *The Canon's Yeoman's Prologue and Tale*, for instance, remains a definitive text about being bound and released through narrative. Wordsworth's *The Ruined Cottage* (which I discuss briefly in the concluding chapter) and many dramatic monologues—by Browning, Meredith, E. A. Robinson, Robert Lowell, and Richard Howard, for instance—also demonstrate the force of narrative ethics at work in poetry.

6. *NDR*, 15.

7. For Genette's explanation, see *Narrative Discourse: An Essay in Method*, trans. J. E. Lewin (Ithaca: Cornell University Press, 1980), and *NDR*; see also Didier Coste, *Narrative as Communication* (Minneapolis: University of Minnesota Press, 1987), and Shlomith Rimmon-Kenan, *Narrative Fiction: Contemporary Poetics* (London: Routledge, 1984).

8. William Scheick's *Fictional Structure and Ethics: The Turn-of-the-Century*

English Novel (Athens: University of Georgia Press, 1990) is representative. Other recent approaches which have raised the "ethics" banner are *CWK, ED, ER,* Tobin Siebers, *The Ethics of Criticism* (Ithaca: Cornell University Press, 1988), and vol. 79 of *Yale French Studies, Literature and the Ethical Question* (1991). See also Zygmunt Bauman, *Postmodern Ethics* (Oxford: Blackwell, 1993).

9. See, for example, Ian Watt's classic *The Rise of the Novel* (Berkeley: University of California Press, 1957) or, more recently, Nancy Armstrong, *Desire and Domestic Fiction* (New York: Oxford University Press, 1989).

10. Tobin Siebers' *Morals and Stories* (New York: Columbia University Press, 1992) is representative.

11. Northrop Frye, *The Anatomy of Criticism: Four Essays* (Princeton: Princeton University Press, 1957), 63. (Frye's subsequent description of it as "the sense of the real presence of culture in the community" is not far removed from what is now called "cultural literacy.")

12. See Hans Robert Jauss, *Towards an Aesthetic of Reception* (Minneapolis: University of Minnesota Press, 1986), Frank Lentricchia, *After the New Criticism* (Chicago: University of Chicago Press, 1980), and Tzvetan Todorov, *The Fantastic: A Structural Approach to a Literary Genre* (Ithaca: Cornell University Press, 1975).

13. See, for example, *The Question of the Other,* ed. A. B. Dallery and C. E. Scott (Albany: State University of New York Press, 1989), *The Nature and Context of Minority Discourse,* ed. Abdul JanMohamed and David Lloyd (New York: Oxford University Press, 1990), Tzvetan Todorov, *On Human Diversity: Nationalism, Racism, and Exoticism in French Thought,* trans. Catherine Porter (Cambridge: Harvard University Press, 1993), and Julia Kristeva, *Strangers to Ourselves,* trans. Leon Roudiez (New York: Columbia University Press, 1991). In his introduction to Michael Theunissen's *The Other: Studies in the Social Ontology of Husserl, Heidegger, Sartre, and Buber* (Cambridge: MIT Press, 1984), Fred Dallmayr points out that these trends are not purely speculative. As he says, "the post-Cartesian turn to 'otherness' is nourished by the broader mutations and dislocations of our age: dislocations manifest in the confrontations between Western and revitalized non-western cultures on a global scale, and also in the clash between social classes and experiential lifeworlds" (x).

14. Fabio Ciaramelli, "Levinas' Ethical Discourse: Between Individuality and Universality," in *Re-Reading Levinas,* 83–105.

15. *Face to Face with Levinas,* 23.

16. The distinction belongs to Seyla Benhabib, as developed in *Situating the Self: Gender, Politics, and Communicative Ethics* (New York: Routledge, 1992).

17. See Paul Taylor, *The Moral Judgment: Readings in Contemporary Meta-Ethics* (Englewood Cliffs, N.J.: Prentice Hall, 1963), for a selection of positivist models which restrict the sense of ethics to the projection of human values upon a neutral world. By contrast, a pragmatic and fluid definition of ethics

guides the projects of Martha Nussbaum, such as *LK*, and of Hans-Georg Gadamer, such as *Truth and Method*, trans. D. G. Marshall and J. Weinsheimer (New York: Continuum Press, 1993). See also the collection of essays on the continental tradition of discourse ethics, *The Communicative Ethics Controversy*, ed. Seyla Benhabib and Fred Dallmayr (Cambridge: MIT Press, 1990).

18. The title of this section is taken from one of the chapters in Julian Barnes's *Flaubert's Parrot*, one of the most penetrating of forays into the vagaries of narrative self-revelation, a text I discuss extensively in Chapter 6.

19. I paraphrase Nathanael West's *A Cool Million* here.

20. Sherwood Anderson, *Winesburg, Ohio* (New York: Penguin, 1978), 176. Further references are to this edition.

21. I borrow this phrase from Ian Hacking's article by the same name in *Reconstructing Individualism*, ed. Thomas Heller (Palo Alto: Stanford University Press, 1986), 222–236.

22. Compare some of Hawthorne's stories, "Wakefield" or "The Artist of the Beautiful," for instance, or Melville's *Bartleby the Scrivener* for nineteenth-century American precursors of this sort of self-reflexivity (what Baudelaire, in possible homage, perfected on an even smaller scale in his *petit poèmes en prose*).

23. Edmond Jabès, "Book of the Dead: An Interview with Edmond Jabès," in *The Sin of the Book: Edmond Jabès*, 17.

24. Emmanuel Levinas, "Reality and Its Shadow," in *Collected Philosophical Papers*, ed. Alphonso Lingis (Dordrecht: Martinus Nijhoff, 1981), 6–7.

25. It should be evident that such a notion of "performance" differs significantly from a pluralist model of readerly production such as Wolfgang Iser's. (The relevant texts are *The Act of Reading: A Theory of Aesthetic Response* [Baltimore: Johns Hopkins University Press, 1978] and *The Implied Reader: Patterns of Communication in Prose Fiction from Bunyan to Beckett* [Baltimore: Johns Hopkins University Press, 1975].) If we construe Iser's textual approach as a kind of "ethics," then it is the ethics of liberal pluralism: text and reader generously link arms as each other's confederates. In Iser's "schemata" and "indeterminacies" and "structurations," there is no sense of cost, price, resistance, or rebuke: the act of reading draws no blood. In short, texts, for Iser, are *merely* open books; but for me "merely" opening a book automatically confers an ethical burden. (See the related critique of George Poulet's "phenomenological" approach in Chapter 2.)

26. "Kant believes that the work of art first exists as fact and that it is then seen. Whereas, it exists only if one looks at it and if it is first pure appeal, pure exigence to exist. It is not an instrument whose existence is manifest and whose end is undetermined. It presents itself as a task to be discharged; from the very beginning it places itself on the level of the categorical imperative." Jean-Paul Sartre, *"What Is Literature?" and Other Essays* (Cambridge: Harvard University Press, 1988), 34.

27. J. Hillis Miller, "*Lord Jim:* Repetition as Subversion of Organic Form," in *Fiction and Repetition: Seven English Novels* (Cambridge: Harvard University Press, 1982), 40.

28. Michel Foucault, *Les mots et les choses: une archéologie des sciences humaine* (Paris: Gallimard, 1966), 22.

29. The term rabbinical tradition uses to describe the sacredness of Torah is *m'tamei ha yadaim* ("to make the hands impure"), emphasizing the text's physical (but implicitly hermeneutic) power of contagion. I defend the analogy between scriptural and literary answerability in "Jew/Greek Is Greek/Jew: Hebrew Means Crossover" in *Reconfiguring Jewish Identity: Literary and Cultural Essays in an Autobiographical Mode*, ed. Shelly Fisher-Fishkin and Jeffrey Rubin-Dorsky (Minneapolis: University of Minnesota Press, 1995).

30. See Theodor Adorno, "Punctuation Marks," in *Notes to Literature*, trans. Sherry Weber Nicholsen (New York: Columbia University Press, 1993), 91–97.

31. This textual dilemma can also be decribed in strictly linguistic terms. In his *Problems in General Linguistics*, trans. M. E. Meek (Coral Gables: University of Miami Press, 1966), Emile Benveniste shows how grammatical person depends on a splitting between enunciation and enounced. Only the proper name can assure consistent referentiality in written texts, because "I" hides both a second person (I talk to myself) and a third (I am he who writes); the gaps among these are merely masked by lexicalized usage. (See also Phillipe Lejeune, *On Autobiography*, trans. Kathleen Leary [Minneapolis: University of Minnesota Press, 1989]). Enoch's splitting between enunciation and utterance expresses the tragedy of a life story, each of whose attempts at total expression depletes and fissures it a little more. From this perspective, Anderson's story shows how discourse so completely disarticulates itself from within that any question of real identity factors out. But my reading suggests that since the text is aware of this fact, it shows further that this grammatical predicament merely stands for a personal or interpersonal one. Hence, it "catches" voice in language and leaves it "falling" through successive distantiations into readers' actual but nonrecuperative hands. (In *Winesburg, Ohio* generally, hands function as a metonym for thwarted communication.)

32. See *RT*, and my treatment of it in the next chapter.

33. See Adrian Peperzak's formulation, which I have paraphrased here, from his essay "Presentation," in *Re-Reading Levinas*, 51–66.

34. In an early essay, "Author and Hero in Aesthetic Activity" (in *AA*), Mikhail Bakhtin coins the term *vzhivanie*, or "live-entering," to denote acts of empathy or imaginative projection. See Chapter 3 for a full exposition of this concept.

35. On the difference between orders of witnessing in reading fiction versus theatrical performance, see Cavell's essay on *King Lear*, "The Avoidance of Love: A Reading of *King Lear*" in *MWM*, 267–353, as well as my discussion of it in Chapter 2. Cavell's insights work for a theory of fiction, I think, exactly

because "the company we keep" while reading remains textual. Theater offers a respite in community that reading provides only *inside* the book.

36. The dispersal of a potentially collective audience in *The Rime of the Ancient Mariner* ("And he stoppeth one of three") and the selecting of a single interlocutor in *Winesburg, Ohio* or *Lord Jim* represent unmistakable signals to me that the ethical stakes in such texts will ride on individual isolation within and before a work. There are, however, forces which mitigate the face-to-text dynamic which I emphasize here, for instance, Levinas' concept of *le tiers*, or the "third party." In looking at me through the face of the other, the third party relaxes the dialogic severity of the ethical relation by situating both self and other within a public, and therefore political, realm. I treat this subject at greater length in Chapter 5.

37. See, for example, Julia Kristeva: "Ethics used to be a coercive, customary manner of ensuring the cohesiveness of a particular group through the repetition of a code—a more or less accepted apologue. Now, however, the issue of ethics crops up wherever a code (mores, social contract) must be shattered in order to give way to the free play of negativity, need, desire, pleasure, jouissance, before being put together again, although temporarily and with full knowledge of what is involved." "The Ethics of Linguistics," in *Desire in Language: A Semiotic Approach to Literature and Art* (New York: Columbia University Press, 1980), 23. Perhaps not ironically, however, the hard postmodern position can be equally coercive; Jean-François Lyotard's model of phrasal enchainment, for example—prescriptive and normative assertions legislate descriptions—would neutralize any theoretical claims I might want to make here.

38. Bakhtin, "Author and Hero in Aesthetic Activity," in *AA*, 111.

39. Compare Hannah Arendt's analysis of the hero in *The Human Condition* (Chicago: University of Chicago Press, 1958), 186. Seyla Benhabib brilliantly situates Arendt's project—a sociopolitical parallel to Bakhtin's and Levinas'—in the contemporary debate over universalist models of ethical and political theory. As she writes, "Speech and action have a revelatory quality: they reveal the wholeness of the doer . . . Only if somebody else is able to understand the meaning of our words as well as the whatness of our deeds can the identity of the self be said to be revealed. Action and speech, therefore, are essentially interaction. They take place between humans" (*Situating the Self*, 127). Charles Taylor and Paul Ricoeur have each defined moral personhood as the capacity to be addressed and to respond; its distribution into first, second, and third persons creates both narrative and ethical relations. Finding oneself "addressed" by ethical demands, in effect, establishes one's place in regard to others as well as to one's own life; it locates, in a word, one's "address." See Charles Taylor, *Sources of the Self: The Making of the Modern Identity* (Cambridge: Harvard University Press, 1990), and Paul Ricoeur, *From Text to Action*, trans. Kathleen Blamey and J. B. Thompson (Evanston: Northwestern University Press, 1991), and *Oneself as Another*, trans. Kathleen Blamey (Chicago:

University of Chicago Press, 1992), and also *The Narrative Path: The Later Works of Paul Ricoeur*, ed. T. P. Kemp and David Rasmussen (Cambridge: MIT Press, 1989).

40. Barbara Hardy, *Tellers and Listeners* (London: Athlone, 1975), 4.

41. D. A. Miller's formulation, from *The Novel and the Police* (Berkeley: University of California Press, 1988), 84.

42. See, for example, Peter J. Rabinowitz, *Before Reading: Narrative Conventions and the Politics of Interpretation* (Ithaca: Cornell University Press, 1987).

43. I paraphrase Ralph Ellison's *Invisible Man* here. Strangely, in their frequent allusions to Roland Barthes's *S/Z*, theorists of narrative have tended to neglect perhaps its most useful contribution to method: the *multiple* nature of narrative coding, for instance, proairetic (the code of actions), hermeneutic (the code of truth and disclosure), semic (the code of thematic context), symbolic. To these I have added an "ethical" code, which need not, however, eclipse specifically historical or political components of a given text. Thus Stephen Crane's *The Monster*, which I treat in Chapter 5, requires—outside whatever Crane's own intentions for it happened to be—that its allegory of defacement be read in strictly political terms: as representing the further disempowerment of black Americans after Reconstruction. But failures of recognition which dictate the degree to which one is seen or shunned are both specific and general, a matter of personal as well as cultural guilt.

44. The remark is Jacques Derrida's. See Critchley's *ED* for a reading of Derrida which emphasizes his commitment to both critical responsiveness/responsibility and performativity. Critchley's rapprochement between Derrida and Levinas here is entirely apposite. Still, if deconstructive reading, in Critchley's words, "must move *à travers* the text" (26), then my reading of deconstruction through the lens of narrative ethics demands a similar "athwartness" by calling into question the dictates of a presiding, rigorous, and immodest specularity. Stanley Cavell conducts a parallel critique in "Counter-Philosophy and the Pawn of Voice," in *A Pitch of Philosophy: Autobiographical Exercises* (Cambridge: Harvard University Press, 1994), where he takes issue with what he sees as Derrida's jaundiced and untragic notion of human "voice."

45. As Cohen writes, "Knowing must always decide beforehand what will count as knowledge. . . . For knowledge to be knowledge it must turn upon itself, retrieve its project, deliberate, probe, and prove." In contrast, "The movement that sustains knowledge while remaining outside of knowledge is the ethical situation. . . . This is not because ethics makes some truths better and others worse, but because it disrupts the entire project of knowing with a higher call, a more severe 'condition': responsibility." *Face to Face with Levinas*, 3–8.

46. See Charles Altieri's *Act and Quality: A Theory of Literary Meaning and Humanistic Understanding* (Amherst: University of Massachusetts Press, 1981) and *Canons and Consequences: Reflections on the Force of Imaginative Ideals* (Evanston: Northwestern University Press, 1991); Luis Costa Lima, "Social Repre-

sentation and Mimesis," *New Literary History*, 16 (Spring 1985), 447–466; Paul Ricoeur, "Mimesis and Representation," *Annals of Scholarship*, 2, no. 3 (1981), 15–32; Christopher Prendergast, *The Order of Mimesis: Balzac, Stendhal, Nerval, and Flaubert* (Cambridge: Cambridge University Press, 1987); and Alfred Schutz, *The Structures of the Lifeworld* (Evanston: Northwestern University Press, 1984).

47. Consider Habermas' communicative ethics model. Just as speech remains a faulty model of presence for Derrida, so for Habermas recourse to the individual subject cannot justify a philosophy of language. However, even this intersubjective model of communication needs to rest on something deeper than discursive accord. Yet in his devotion to consensus, his determination to nail shut the case against subject-centered reason, Habermas, in a strange way, forces himself to reify intersubjectivity; by placing so much weight on group praxis, he undervalues just those concrete and contingent acts of responsible authorship that place the ethical self in the balance. See Jürgen Habermas, "Discourse Ethics: Notes on a Program of Philosophical Justification" in *Moral Consciousness and Communicative Action* (Cambridge: MIT Press, 1990), 43–117, as well as "The Generalized and the Concrete Other" in Benhabib's *Situating the Self*, 148–177.

48. The distinction is developed by David Perkins in *Is Literary History Possible?* (Baltimore: Johns Hopkins University Press, 1992), where he adroitly defends both the impossibility and the necessity of doing literary history.

49. See Wolfgang Iser's *Act of Reading* for the argument from literary theory and Anthony Giddens' *The Consequences of Modernity* (Palo Alto: Stanford University Press, 1990) for the argument from sociology.

50. See Vincent Pecora, *Self and Form in Modern Narrative* (Baltimore: Johns Hopkins University Press, 1989), 7.

51. See Miller, *The Novel and the Police*, and Richard Eldridge, *On Moral Personhood: Philosophy, Literature, Criticism, and Self-Understanding* (Chicago: University of Chicago Press, 1989).

2. Toward a Narrative Ethics

1. Blanchot, "Interruptions," in *The Sin of the Book: Edmond Jabès*, 44.

2. The affinity between Levinas and Derrida has already received a great deal of attention. In addition to Critchley's *ED*, see *Re-Reading Levinas;* Robert Bernasconi, "The Trace of Levinas in Derrida," in *Derrida and Différance*, ed. David Wood and Robert Bernasconi (Evanston: Northwestern University Press, 1988), 13–29, and "Levinas and Derrida: The Question of the Closure of Metaphysics," in *Face to Face with Levinas*, 181–202; and Susan Handleman, "Jacques Derrida and the Heretic Hermeneutic," in *Displacement, Derrida, and After*, ed. Mark Krupnik (Bloomington: Indiana University Press, 1983), 98–129.

3. I find unacceptable, for instance, Shoshana Felman's argument that de

Man's silence functioned as a mode of bearing witness (unsaid or unsaying testimony, one might call it). One has only to measure it against the *yizkor* (memorial) prayer to his murdered family with which Levinas introduces *OTB*. That Levinas chose to leave this epigraph untranslated—it's easy to assume, for instance, that it simply parallels the other (translated) epigraph which precedes it—creates a "possibility of not reading" which calls into question the "impossibility of reading" that Felman defends on de Man's behalf. (Her conscripting of Primo Levi throughout the essay in order to articulate de Man's mutedness strikes me as even more disturbing.) See Felman, "After the Apocalypse: Paul de Man and the Fall to Silence," in *Testimony: Crises of Witnessing in Literature, Psychoanlysis, and History*, ed. Shoshana Felman and Dori Laub (New York: Routledge, 1992), 120–164, and the entire memorial issue *The Lesson of Paul de Man, Yale French Studies*, 69 (1983), especially Minae Mizumura's essay, "Renunciation," 81–97.

4. De Man's puritanism stems from his early Heideggerian prejudice against an empirical self "fallen" into facticity that only "a transcendent type of self that speaks in a work" can redeem (*BI*, 50). Matthew Roberts traces de Man's debt to Heidegger in "Poetics, Hermeneutics, Dialogics: Bakhtin and de Man," in *RB*, 115–134, from which I draw in my subsequent discussion of Bakhtin.

5. Paul de Man, *Allegories of Reading: Figural Language in Rousseau, Nietzsche, Rilke, and Proust* (New Haven: Yale University Press, 1979), 206.

6. Christopher Norris treats this question extensively in *Paul de Man, Deconstruction, and the Critique of Aesthetic Ideology* (New York: Routledge, 1988). See especially the chapter "De Man and the Critique of Romantic Ideology" and the relevant essays by de Man, "Sign and Symbol in Hegel's Aesthetics," *Critical Inquiry*, 8 (1982), 761–775, and "Phenomenality and Materiality in Kant," in *Hermeneutics: Questions and Prospects*, ed. Gary Shapiro and Alan Sica (Amherst: University of Massachusetts Press, 1984), 121–144. See also Rodolphe Gasché, "In-Difference to Philosophy: De Man on Kant, Hegel, and Nietzsche," in *Reading de Man Reading*, ed. Wlad Godzich and Lindsay Waters (Minneapolis: University of Minnesota Press, 1990), 259–294, and Dieter Henrich, "Beauty and Freedom: Schiller's Struggle with Kant's Aesthetics," in *Essays in Kant's Aesthetics*, ed. Ted Cohen and Paul Guyer (Chicago: University of Chicago Press, 1982), 237–257 for a different perspective on Kant's legacy to the history of aesthetics.

7. De Man, *Allegories of Reading*, 206.

8. "Pointing" in language, of course, is called deixis, and deixis (Roman Jakobson's "shifters" and Emile Benveniste's discursive *énonciation*) provides the crux on which de Man turns language against both itself and the self. Cavell's statement implies that forcing the issue epistemologically this way, if it clarifies anything, reveals the limitations of epistemological reasoning, the dead-end (to catch de Man *tu quoque*) of rhetorical criticism.

9. De Man, in *Allegory and Representation*, ed. Stephen J. Greenblatt (Baltimore: Johns Hopkins University Press, 1981), viii.

10. Compare the identical example in Bakhtin, and his very similar analysis in "Author and Hero in Aesthetic Activity" (*AA*, 79).

11. Stanley Cavell, *Disowning Knowledge* (Cambridge: Cambridge University Press, 1987). On Cavell's terms, see "Knowing and Acknowledging" and "The Avoidance of Love" in *MWM*. See also the articles by Gerald Bruns and James Conant in *Critical Inquiry*, 16, no. 3 (Spring 1990), 612–632, and 17, no. 3 (Winter 1991), 600–630, for an important clarification of Cavell's terms.

12. Critchley lights on the pedagogical impulse at work in this "narrowly textual" sense of ethics which is associated with J. Hillis Miller's *ER*. "The problem, on a Levinasian view, is not so much, 'Is there an ethical structure or law of reading?' as 'How does the ethical relation to the Other enter into the textual economy of betrayal?'" (*ED*, 48).

13. Sartre, *"What Is Literature?" and Other Essays*, 31.

14. This is meant to call up George Poulet's "Criticism and the Experience of Interiority," in *Reader-Response Criticism: From Formalism to Poststructuralism*, ed. Jane Tompkins (Baltimore: Johns Hopkins University Press, 1981), 41–49, which in its devotion to readerly entitlement is the perfect foil for Sartrean "accountability."

15. The question of such status is systematically covered in Thomas G. Pavel's *Fictional Worlds* (Cambridge: Harvard University Press, 1986) and Robert McCormick's *Fictions, Philosophies, and the Problem of Poetics* (Ithaca: Cornell University Press, 1988).

16. *BI*, 18.

17. Emmanuel Levinas, *L'au-delà du verset* (Paris: Minuit, 1977), 136.

18. Bakhtin, "Towards a Philosophy of the Act," quoted in *RB*, 112.

19. On Bakhtin's neo-Kantianism, see Michael Holquist, *Dialogism: Bakhtin and His World* (London: Methuen, 1990), and see the introduction to *AA* for a very good treatment of this direction in Bakhtin's thought. See also Gary Saul Morson, *Mikhail Bakhtin: Creation of a Prosaics* (Palo Alto: Stanford University Press, 1990).

20. On de Man's language, see Neil Hertz's essay, "Lurid Figures," in *Reading de Man Reading* 82–104.

21. Bakhtin's Soviet counterpart, the psychologist Lev Vygotsky, argues very similarly from the perspective of developmental psychology; the self is always a dialogue, a disputed border between consciousnesses. See *Thought and Language* (Cambridge: MIT Press, 1983).

22. A very cogent discussion of Bakhtin's reshaping of Kantian architectonics toward the intersubjective (dubbed in a very Levinasian phrase "the rule of Altruity") can be found in Wlad Godzich, "Correcting Kant: Bakhtin and Intercultural Interactions," *boundary 2*, 18, no. 1 (1991), 5–17.

23. Matthew Roberts quotes this statement in his essay in *RB*, 122. Heidegger, however, makes an important distinction between assertive and hermeneutic uses of language in his early work, and his analysis of truth as disclosure situates interpretation in terms of a mediating rather than a grasping function;

aletheia is a mode by which things of themselves come to presence. Levinas, in contrast, sees "disclosure" as a mode of totalizing vision which "links up beings already akin"; it both interferes in and resists ethical engagement (*TI*, 73, 195).

24. Walter Benjamin *Schriften*, ed. Theodor Adorno (Frankfurt on the Main: Suhrkamp, 1955), 1:146.

25. Paul Valéry's analogy for conversation, cited by Blanchot, "Interruptions," in *The Sin of the Book: Edmond Jabès*.

26. See Roberts' valuable analysis in *RB*.

27. Whereas de Man's essay on Walter Benjamin deforms by assimilating, his essay on Bakhtin merely repudiates. De Man is not at his best when "wresting truth" from such writers. In a nutshell, de Man cobbles together three sentences from different places in a two-hundred-page essay to deconstruct Bakhtin's entire project; he merely asserts the contradictory relationship between dialogism and hermeneutics without proving it; and in neutralizing Bakhtin's discourse on the grounds of an epistemological error not in fact Bakhtin's, he himself incurs the very charge of "dialectical imperialism" which he wishes to ascribe to Bakhtin. Indeed, one wants to call de Man's nondialogical imperialism here more than mere bad faith, since it has distinctly political implications. It is at moments like this, when the political reality of the critics he reads is factored out—the exile which resulted in deprivation for Bakhtin, the exile which led to death for Benjamin—that the "biographical argument" for de Man's critical perversities becomes very "difficult to resist."

28. Emmanuel Levinas, "Phenomenon and Enigma," in *Collected Philosophical Papers*, 61–74.

29. See Jacques Derrida, *Limited Inc, ABC*, ed. Gerald Graff (Evanston: Northwestern University Press, 1988).

30. Siebers, *The Ethics of Criticism*, 30, 39.

31. For treatments of that bridge, see Altieri's *Canons and Consequences;* Onora O'Neil, *Constructions of Reason: Explorations of Kant's Practical Philosophy* (Cambridge: Cambridge University Press, 1989); Hannah Arendt, *Lectures on Kant's Political Philosophy* (Chicago: University of Chicago Press, 1982); and Wlad Godzich, "Correcting Kant." Finally, see Richard Wollheim's essay "The Plausibility of Literature as Moral Philosophy," *New Literary History* 15, no. 1 (1983), 185–192, for a non-Kantian framework of idealizing textual encounter across different levels of reading.

32. From Wlad Godzich's introduction to *SS*, xiii. See, among other narratological models and methodologies, Vladimir Propp's *Morphology of the Folktale*, 2nd. rev. ed. (Austin: University of Texas Press, 1968), Claude Brémond's *Logique du récit* (Paris: Seuil, 1973), Tzvetan Todorov's *Poetics of Prose* (Oxford; Blackwell, 1977), Algirdas Greimas' *Du sens* (Paris: Seuil, 1971) and "Elements of a Narrative Grammar," *Diacritics*, 7 (1977), and F. K. Stanzel, *A Theory of Narrative*, trans. Charlotte Goedsche (Cambridge: Cambridge University

Press, 1984). Shlomith Rimmon-Kenan, *Narrative Fiction*, and Didier Coste, *Narrative as Communication*, offer the best summaries of this material.

33. On monist and dualist positions regarding form and content, see Geoffrey Leech and M. H. Short, *Style in Fiction* (London: Longman, 1981). See also the recent collection of essays which recuperates thematics, *The Return of Thematic Criticism*, ed. Werner Sollors (Cambridge: Harvard University Press, 1993).

34. See Ricoeur, *From Text to Action* and "Mimesis and Representation." Ricoeur bases semiotic intelligibility on a prior rationality, something like Aristotelian phronesis, "a transcendental, not psychological function" ("Mimesis and Representation," 24–25). Ricoeur applies Kant's notion of schematism to the literary imagination to explain how textual action is remade in terms of the transformative readability of human action; readers transfigure plot and character, and liberate them, as it were, from the prison of the text. See also in this vein Maurice Natanson, "The Schematism of Kantian Agency," in *New Literary History*, 15 (1983), 135–162.)

35. See, for example, Martha Nussbaum's catalogue of stylistic decisions about topic—voice, point of view, *consistency*, *generality*, and *precision*—in the introduction to *LK.*

36. See Seymour Chatman's *Story and Discourse: Narrative Structure in Fiction and Film* (Ithaca: Cornell University Press, 1980) and Jonathan Culler's *The Pursuit of Signs: Semiotics, Literature, Deconstruction* (Ithaca: Cornell University Press, 1981) for an interesting discussion of this duality.

37. Levinas, "Reality and Its Shadow," 13. Thus Genette will separate narrative discourse from its objects, like character, the latter being a second-order and therefore less analytically dependable category. See *NDR*, 136. Genette one-dimensionalizes narrative discourse at the same time that he subordinates problems of representation. Accordingly, he appeals to Aristotle's assertion that character functions as a bearer of the plot's action, that *mythos* legislates ethos; but this reads the *Poetics* reductively and implies a static relation between agents and the actions which they presumably serve. In contrast, in Chapters 5 and 6, I borrow Aristotle's trope of anagnorisis (recognition) and use it as a constitutive narrative element resonating far beyond the constraints of emplotment.

38. See, for example, Dorrit Cohn, *Transparent Minds: Modes for Presenting Consciousness in Fiction* (Princeton: Princeton University Press, 1978).

39. See Christopher Prendergast's important *The Order of Mimesis.*

40. From within belles-lettres, Levinas' very Jewish dubiety about representation—as invention, as mystification, as idolatry—is given its strongest statement by Cynthia Ozick. As she writes in her introduction to *Bloodshed and Three Novellas* (New York: Knopf, 1976), "the story-making faculty itself can be a corridor to the corruptions and abominations of idol worship, of the adoration of the magical event" (11). See also in this context the pertinent

explication of Walter Benjamin's theory of allegory by Doris Sommer in "Allegory and Dialectics: A Match Made in Romance," *boundary 2*, 18, no. 1 (1991), 60–82. Sommer emphasizes the mutual "scarring" that takes place between allegory's two levels of signification, wonderfully captured by Benjamin's own aperçu "Allegories are, in the realm of thoughts, what ruin are in the realm of things."

41. Rimmon-Kenan, *Narrative Fiction*, 30.

42. See John Perry, ed., *Personal Identity* (Berkeley: University of California Press, 1973); Amelie O. Rorty, ed., *The Identity of Persons* (Berkeley: University of California Press, 1976); Paul Ricoeur, *Oneself as Another*; Charles Taylor, "The Concept of a Person," in his *Language and Human Agency* (Cambridge: Cambridge University Press, 1985); and Richard Wollheim, *The Thread Of Life* (Cambridge: Harvard University Press, 1986).

43. See Prendergast, *The Order of Mimesis*.

44. These phrases are the titles of two contemporary guides to "reading otherwise": *Resisting Novels: Ideology and Fiction* (New York: Methuen, 1987) by Lennard Davis and *Room for Maneuver: Reading (the) Oppositional (in) Narrative* (Chicago: University of Chicago Press, 1991) by Ross Chambers.

45. Stephen Halliwell, for instance, describes Aristotelian mimesis as a means of signification, not just simple imitation. Aesthetic response does not remain vicarious or extrinsic to a work but, like Bakhtin's "participatory consciousness," involves being subjected to form, as one contemplates it. Halliwell's unpublished essays to which I refer are "Aristotelian Mimesis and Theories of Artistic Representation," and "Pleasure, Emotion, and Understanding." See also Gerald Else, *Aristotle's "Poetics": The Argument* (Cambridge: Harvard University Press, 1957), and Kathy Elden, *Poetic and Legal Fiction in the Aristotelian Tradition* (Princeton: Princeton University Press, 1986), both of which compare the *Ethics* and the *Poetics*; see also Göran Sörbum, *Mimesis and Art* (Uppsala: Scandinavian University Books, 1975), and Martha Nussbaum, *The Fragility of Goodness* (Cambridge: Cambridge University Press, 1986).

46. See Slavoj Žižek, *The Sublime Object of Ideology* (London: Verso, 1992), for an important analysis of Lacanian categories with reference to the ideological-political field.

47. Prendergast, *The Order of Mimesis*, 212.

48. See, for example, Fredric Jameson, *The Political Unconscious: Narrative as a Socially Symbolic Act* (Ithaca: Cornell University Press, 1981); Peter Brooks, *Reading for the Plot: Design and Intention in Narrative* (New York: Vintage, 1985); Marie Maclean, *Narrative as Performance: The Baudelairean Experiment* (London: Routledge, 1988); and Ross Chambers, *SS* and *Room for Maneuver*.

49. In *L'école du spectateur: Lire le théâtre II* (Paris: Seuil, 1981), Anne Ubersfeld refers to this act more ominously as "the rape of the spectator." Other studies parallel Chambers' work here as well. In *Reading for the Plot*, for

example, Peter Brooks adapts Freud to develop a theory of textual dynamics fueled by desire. René Girard's theory of mimetic desire in *Deceit, Desire, and the Novel: Self and Other in Literary Structure*, trans. Yvonne Freccero (Baltimore: Johns Hopkins University Press, 1986), also shows how narrative "relationship" can affect representation. Levinas' sense of desire (the metaphysical drive to the other) contrasts dramatically with all of these (see *TI*).

50. Chambers uses the term "situational self-reflexivity" to describe both narrative fiction's awareness of its literariness and its conditions for "readability," the range of discursive and cultural meanings which it maps. Narrative acts distribute frames or roles to the participants, a "textual mirroring," as Chambers calls it, which takes two forms: "narrational embeddings" (dramatizations of narrative communication within the story, as in *Lord Jim*) and "figural embeddings" (tropes of communication like the hands in *Winesburg, Ohio* or of aesthesis, as in James's "The Real Thing" and *The Portrait of a Lady*). Obviously, I see formal categories such as these as involving a distinctly ethical uptake which exceeds the requirements of a strictly textual "metaphorization" (*SS*, 35).

51. See Stanley Cavell, *Pursuits of Happiness: The Hollywood Comedy of Remarriage* (Cambridge: Harvard University Press, 1986), and also Richard Eldridge's discussion of marriage and contracts in *On Moral Personhood*.

52. Such infiltration by formalism detracts from the otherwise instructive study by Marie Maclean, *Narrative as Performance*, which analyzes the performative aspect of narrative in a number of directions besides self-reflexivity. For other work in this area, see Bernard Duyfhuizen's *Narratives of Transmission* (Rutherford: Fairleigh Dickinson University Press, 1992), Susan Lanser's *The Narrative Act* (Princeton: Princeton University Press, 1981), William Labov's *Language in the Inner City: Studies in Black English Vernacular* (Philadelphia: University of Pennsylvania Press, 1972), and Mary Louise Pratt's *Towards a Speech-Act Theory of Literary Discourse* (Bloomington: Indiana University Press, 1982).

53. Nussbaum, *LK*, Booth, *CWK*, Siebers, *The Ethics of Criticism*, Taylor, *Sources of the Self*, and Habermas, "Excursus on Leveling the Genre Distinction between Literature and Philosophy," in *The Philosophical Discourse of Modernity: Twelve Lectures*, trans. F. G. Lawrence (Cambridge: MIT Press, 1990), 185–210.

54. For this pragmatic critique of ethical theory's utility, see especially Bernard Williams, *Ethics and the Limits of Philosophy* (Cambridge: Harvard University Press, 1985). Actually, a postmodernist critique would be less salient here than Williams' because of its focus on knowledge as disinterested reflection, something none of the accounts I have listed either advocates or defends.

55. By signaling the economic here, I wish merely to draw out certain levels in the process of exchange and mediation which may remain obscured in even Nussbaum's attentive analysis. See Edward J. Ahearn's *Marx and Modern Fic-*

tion (New Haven: Yale University Press, 1989) and Carolyn Porter's *Seeing and Being: The Plight of the Participant Observer in Emerson, James, and Faulkner* (Middletown: Wesleyan University Press, 1981) on the intersection of wealth and refined judgment in James.

56. I paraphrase Charles Taylor's phrase from *Sources of the Self.*

57. See D. A. Miller's *Narrative and Its Discontents: Problems of Closure in the Traditional Novel* (Berkeley: University of California Press, 1985) for the concept of narratable versus nonnarratable experience.

58. Booth rightly attributes sentimental force to our experience of narrative literature, but his trope of friendship, in my view, despite an extensive table of "ratios," serves him less precisely than he may wish. Two clarifying frames for Booth's idea, I think, can be found in Aristotle's chapters on friendship in *Nichomachean Ethics* and *Eudemian Ethics* (which, curiously, Booth does not invoke) and in Jacques Derrida's "The Politics of Friendship," *Journal of Philosophy*, 35, no. 11 (1988) 632–644. But even Derrida's (implicitly Levinasian) choice of friendship, as Thomas McCarthy argues in the same issue, may represent a less than ideal context in which to think about social polity and law, let alone narrative ethics. Levinas himself might approvingly cite Nietzsche's *Zarathustra:* "I am not teaching you the friend but rather the neighbor."

59. Leo Tolstoy, *"What Is Art?" and Essays on Art*, trans. Aylmer Maude (London: Oxford University Press, 1955), 121–123.

60. The two exemplification models which best state their case can be found in Nelson Goodman's *Ways of Worldmaking* (Indianapolis: Hackett, 1978) and Max Scheler's *Formalism in Ethics or Non-Formal Ethics of Value: A New Attempt towards the Foundation of an Ethical Personalism*, trans. M. S. Frings and R. S. Funk (Evanston: Northwestern University Press, 1973). Both are insightfully critiqued in Edith Wyschogrod's *Saints and Postmodernism: Revisioning Moral Philosophy* (Chicago: University of Chicago Press, 1990).

61. When asked to describe the role of the audience for his film *Shoah*, Claude Lanzmann replied, "To accompany the dead. To resurrect them. And to make them die a second time, but to die with them." Quoted in Jay Cantor, *On Giving Birth to One's Own Mother: Essays on Art and Society* (New York: Knopf, 1991), 162.

62. Richard Brudney, "Knowledge and Silence: *The Golden Bowl* and Moral Philosophy," *Critical Inquiry*, 16, no. 2 (Winter, 1990), 419. Further page references are given in the text.

63. To Charles Altieri, for instance, literature offers us an "expressive grammar" for trying on "ethical identities," the foundation for which is the power of example: "Texts become representative . . . by their capacity to make what they exemplify seem shareable in clarifying or negotiating certain situations" *Canons and Consequences*, 15). In other words, examples build a moral constituency from the ground up instead of, as in Kant, from the top down. But the model, like Altieri's description of it, remains simply too abstract.

3. We Die in a Last Word

1. Joseph Conrad, *Lord Jim* (New York: Penguin, 1957), 20:161. All chapter and page references are to this edition.

2. In *The Romantic Sublime: Studies in the Structure and Psychology of Transcendence* (Baltimore: Johns Hopkins University Press, 1986), Thomas Weiskel uses the phrase to describe certain Romantic conceptualizations of the sublime. In another chapter contrasting Burke and Kant, he underscores Burke's interesting suggestion of "criminality" in aesthetic watching; when people witness the sublime, they experience feelings of relief similar to those of a successfully escaped fugitive. But on the latter score in Conrad's novel, Jim remarks, "Isn't it awful a man should be driven to do a thing like that—and be responsible?" (10:94). Burke's analogy hints subliminally at the role which ethical responsibility thus plays in ostensibly pure aesthetic experience.

3. Sherwood Anderson, *The Teller's Tales: Short Stories* (Schenectady: Union College Press, 1983), 20.

4. Edmund Husserl, *Ideas* (New York: Macmillan, 1962), 92.

5. On the complexity of Conradian impressionism, see Michael Levenson's *Modernism and the Fate of Individuality: Character and Novelistic Form from Conrad to Woolf* (Cambridge: Cambridge University Press, 1991).

6. See "The Avoidance of Love," in *MWM*, 298. As I have said previously, Cavell makes his criterion the simultaneity of occurrence and description which theater depends upon for its effect. True, first-person narration and third-person narration each carry real epistemological flaws, but they can be mediated, or at least revealed, through the interstices—the interruptive pauses—of face-to-face conversation.

7. Bakhtin's concept of *vnenakhodimost'* ("outsideness" or "extralocality") echoes both Levinas' and Cavell's insistence that morality begins with the separateness of persons. Indeed, the boundedness of human relation governs acts of live-entering, and continues in aesthetically generous articulation of the spaces in between. See *AA*, 95.

8. Compare in this vein Tzvetan Todorov's correlation of "themes of vision" with "themes of the self," and "themes of the other" with "themes of discourse" in *The Fantastic*.

9. See Miller, *"Lord Jim."*

10. Compare what Marlow says of Gentleman Brown, a photo negative of the French Captain in the way he perversely adapts "abstract disinterest" to occasions for manipulative self-interest: "Notice that even in this awful outbreak there is a superiority as of a man who carries right—the abstract thing—within the envelope of common desires" (44:304). Conrad persistently stages mirrorings and correspondences of this kind, to cast doubt on reflectionism per se, I think, and its tendency toward "optical forgery."

11. On "knowable cultures" and their significance for the British novel, see Raymond Williams, *Culture and Society* (Oxford: Oxford University Press,

1984) and *The Country and the City* (New York: Oxford University Press, 1973). For interesting studies of the link between story and cultural identity, see Homi K. Bhabha, *Nation and Narration* (New York: Routledge, 1991); Julia Kristeva, *Nations without Nationalisms* (New York: Columbia University Press, 1992); and Marc Shell, *Children of the Earth: Literature, Politics, and Nationhood* (New York: Oxford University Press, 1992).

12. See Ian Watt's concept of "thematic apposition" in *Conrad in the Nineteenth Century* (London: Chatto and Windus, 1980).

13. Anatole Broyard, "About Books: Does Your Analyst Read Henry James?" *New York Times Book Review*, April 16, 1989, 14.

14. Bakhtin's remark, as quoted in Holquist, *Dialogism*, 79.

15. Mikhail Bakhtin, *Problems of Dostoevsky's Poetics*, trans. Caryl Emerson (Minneapolis: University of Minnesota Press, 1984), 242.

16. See Aaron Fogel, *Coercion to Speak: Conrad's Poetics of Dialogue* (Cambridge: Harvard University Press, 1985).

17. See Janet Malcolm, "Reflections: Journalism, Part II," *The New Yorker*, March 20, 1989, 76.

18. See, however, Philip Rieff, *Freud: The Mind of the Moralist* (Chicago: University of Chicago Press, 1979); Roy Schafer, "Narration in the Psychoanalytic Dialogue," in *On Narrative*, ed. W. J. T. Mitchell (Chicago: University of Chicago Press, 1981), and *Retelling a Life: Narration and Dialogue in Psychoanalysis* (New York: Basic Books, 1992); and Paul Ricoeur, *Freud and Philosophy: An Essay on Interpretation*, trans. Denis Savage (New Haven: Yale University Press, 1978), for arguments for the ethical purposiveness of therapy as performance.

19. Brooks, *Reading for the Plot*, 262.

20. Conrad continually recycled plots and characters. *Lord Jim* cannibalizes elements from *Alymer's Folly* and *An Outcast of the Islands*, just as "Youth," *Heart of Darkness*, and later *Chance* reuse the Marlow figure. And as he did several times in his career, Conrad paused during the composition of a longer work of fiction—*Lord Jim*—to write a shorter, having begun *Heart of Darkness* in mid 1899.

21. See Terence Cave, *Recognitions: A Study in Poetics* (Cambridge: Cambridge University Press, 1988).

22. These are two of the six textual codes Roland Barthes specifies in *S/Z* (New York: Hill and Wang, 1974). The proairetic in any story constitutes its level of sequenced actions; the hermeneutic, in contrast, consists of those secrets whose unfolding makes a plot a "plot."

23. See Roland Barthes, *The Pleasure of the Text* (New York: Hill and Wang, 1975), and Jacques Lacan, "On a Question Preliminary to Any Possible Treatment of Psychosis," in *Ecrits*, trans. Alan Sheridan (New York: Norton, 1977).

24. In his biography of Conrad, *Joseph Conrad: A Chronicle* (New Brunswick: Rutgers University Press, 1983), Zdzislaw Najder quotes from the journals of Conrad's wife: "he lives mixed up in the scenes and holds converse with the

characters" (357). *Lord Jim* invites a similar "confusion," a living into characters' textual and personal fates. Marlow thus can be said to draw energies of transference from both co-character and author, living into the one, standing in for the other.

25. In *Reading People, Reading Plots: Character, Progression, and the Interpretation of Narrative* (Chicago: University of Chicago Press, 1989), James Phelan divides character into three components: the mimetic (the cluster of recognizably human attributes), the synthetic (marks of artifice and fictivity), and the thematic (signs of certain commonly employed cultural codes). Bakhtin's own distinction between personality (unfinished and at some level sacrosanct) and character (constructed and mediated) as "person components" offers a parallel framework.

26. George Eliot, *Middlemarch* (New York: Penguin 1978), 87:890. Further references are to this edition.

27. Until this point in Genesis, the Lord speaks "unto" man without naming him individually. The name/answerability formula occurs again in stories involving each of the Patriarchs, in Exodus 3:5 when G-d speaks to Moses from the midst of the burning bush, and in Isaiah 6:9. As *me voici*, Levinas develops the trope as an expression of subjectivity held hostage to the other, the French syntax capturing the "accusative" structure of responsibility exactly. A. B. Yehoshua's *Mr. Mani* (1989) makes the "binding" trope integral to its unique treatment of addressivity and temporality across five demi-dialogues.

28. Fogel, *Coercion to Speak*, 226.

29. Edmond Jabès, *The Book of Dialogue*, trans. R. Waldrop (Middletown: Wesleyan University Press, 1983), 14.

30. Walter Benjamin, *Illuminations* (New York: Schocken, 1969), 71.

31. Only sporadically does language produce a free-floating, incantatory magic in *Winesburg, Ohio*. It renames a person by fiat in "Tandy." It self-hypnotizes, as in "An Awakening," when George, no longer bound by rules of syntax, pours out a string of words like so many musical notes. It sweeps all before it in a tidal wave of verbiage in "A Man of Ideas." And by a kind of parthenogenesis it reproduces itself during ongoing speech in "The Thinker": "Into his mind came a desire to tell something he had been determined not to tell" (139).

32. John Ruskin, *Works* (New York: Longmans, Green, 1903), 13:72.

33. In *Winesburg, Ohio*, I see "grotesque" and "uncanny" as essentially synonymous categories, though strictly speaking one refers to an aesthetic category and the other to a literary theme. See Todorov's *The Fantastic* for a discussion of their distinguishing features in the context of genre.

34. See Gershom Scholem, *On the Kabbalah and Its Symbolism*, trans. Ralph Mannheim (New York: Schocken, 1974).

35. Toni Morrison, *Beloved* (New York: Dutton, 1988), 53.

36. Indeed, de Man goes as far as to affirm, scandalously, "it is this errancy of language, this illusion of a life that is only an afterlife, that Benjamin calls

history. As such, history is not human, because it pertains strictly to the order of language. . . . For now we see that the nonmessianic, nonsacred, that is the *political* aspect of history is the result of the *poetical* structure of language, so that the political and poetical here are substituted, in opposition to the notion of the sacred" (*RT*, 92–93).

4. Lessons of (for) the Master

1. Maurice Natanson, "The Schematism of Kantian Moral Agency," 21.

2. See Julia Kristeva, "Word, Dialogue, Novel," in *Desire in Language*, and Ross Chambers, "Narrative and Textual Functions," in *Room for Maneuver*.

3. In this regard see James Phelan's rebuttal to Robert Scholes's structuralist theory of character in "Thematic Functioning and Interpreting by Cultural Codes," in *Reading People, Reading Plots*.

4. For a discussion of this example and of the phenomenon it illustrates, see David Freedberg, *The Power of Images: Studies in the History and Theory of Response* (Chicago: University of Chicago Press, 1989).

5. Jay Cantor, "Death and the Image," in *On Giving Birth to One's Own Mother*, 145.

6. Another reference to dogs in connection with literary value occurs in the preface to *What Maisie Knew:* "Once 'out,' like a house-dog of a temper above confinement, [the theme] defies the mere whistle, it roams, it hunts, it seeks out and 'sees' life; it can be brought back but by hand and then only to take its futile thrashing. It wasn't at any rate for an idea seen in the light I here glance at not to have due warrant of its value—how could the value of a scheme so finely workable *not* be great?" (*AN*, 144). Here, by contrast, value is dog-gedly alive, but needs the hand of the artist, in a telling gesture of "discipline and punish," to leash it in from its forays into life.

7. I'm thinking here of Peter Sloterdijk's analysis of cynicism as a culture's transparency to itself in the midst of the false consciousness it maintains. See *The Critique of Cynical Reason*, trans. Michael Eldred (Minneapolis: University of Minnesota Press, 1988).

8. Henry James, *Notes and Reviews*. (Salem, Mass.: Ayer, 1968), 18.

9. Henry James, "The Real Thing," in *The Aspern Papers and Other Stories* (Harmondsworth, Eng., Penguin, 1976), 113. Further references are to this edition.

10. See Levenson, *Modernism and the Fate of Individuality*, 29. Levenson conducts a brilliant analysis of the play of figural forces in *The Ambassadors* and James's fiction generally. I refer to it in the last section of this chapter.

11. In his study *The Fantastic*, Todorov explains the dual function of allegory in Gogol's "The Nose": "On the one hand, it shows that one may produce the impression that there is an allegorical meaning when there is, in fact, no allegorical meaning present. On the other hand, in describing the metamorphoses of a nose, it narrates the adventures of allegory itself" (73).

12. I quote from Mary Doyle Springer, *A Rhetoric of Literary Character: Some Women of Henry James* (Chicago: University of Chicago Press, 1978), 162.

13. Marx defines variable capital as the portion of capital which reproduces itself together with a surplus value during the process of production. Ironically, however, for the Monarchs, their use-value ultimately disappears as they strive to realize it through establishing its exchange-value. As commodities, they presumably already possess use-value, but instead of proving it upon circulation, they lose it. See Karl Marx, *Capital: A Critique of Political Economy*, trans. Eden Paul and Cedar Paul (London: J. M. Dent, 1930), 205.

14. On James and the economic forces of production, see Ahearn, *Marx and Modern Fiction*, and Porter, *Seeing and Being*.

15. Instead of minting the "authorized coinage" of characters drawn from real life, according to Miller, Trollope freely invents his characters without recourse to reality. Thus does he "print counterfeit money," and thus does he produce an "imperceptible inflation in the general currency" for his readership. Compare James's own comments on Trollope in "The Art of Fiction."

16. In his book on Hawthorne's story "The Minister's Black Veil," Hillis Miller remarks, "The face is a defacing, as the *pro* ('in front of, before') in *prosopon* or *prosopopoeia* suggests. *Prosopon* means face *or* mask. . . . The figure of the face as that which is 'in front' of something behind is present still in all our English words in 'front': 'confront,' 'affront,' 'frontal,' and 'front' itself" (*HH*, 99). I discuss this text again in Chapter 5. (Another, brilliant working out of this idea can be seen in John Frankenheimer's 1966 film *Seconds*. An appropriately serviceable alternate for "the real thing," the title connotes both used goods and falsified self-doubling, as the film traces its protagonist's ultimately fatal attempt to circulate the exchange value of frontage. In allowing himself to be made over (a surgically altered face substitutes for his own), he merely engineers his own death and defacement in order to make way for someone else's "adventure in allegory.")

17. Levenson, *Modernism and the Fate of Individuality*, 161.

18. For example, *The Portrait of a Lady* (through the figures of Gilbert Osmond and Madame Merle) restricts the costs of aestheticizing others primarily to those incurred by characters; "fine embossed vaults and painted arches" (as James himself puts it in his preface) come to represent intersubjective spaces as well as architectural ones. Although the same might be said for "The Real Thing," I believe its greater importance—as representational ethics—lies in its minimizing the substantiality of character, and etching in sharper relief the hand of both narrator and author.

19. Elaine Scarry, *The Body in Pain: The Making and Unmaking of the World* (New York: Oxford University Press, 1985), 244.

20. Compare, however, Mary Doyle Springer's more optimistic reading of this dénouement: "If, by being presented, [Miss Churm] is 'lost' to the real world, 'it was only as the dead who go to heaven are lost—in the gain of an angel the more.' To call her an angel is to praise her for having become a

truth-giver by very reason of departing this world to become an artefact, and a type" (*A Rhetoric of Literary Character*, 211).

21. Compare, however, similar moments in the fiction of James's contemporary Edith Wharton, where neither author nor character has any compunction in using a tag like "dingy" to sum up the essence of another character, and thus "fit the case" so completely.

22. See, in this context, James's own essay on Hawthorne and Hillis Miller's discussion of it in *HH*.

23. I quote from Italo Calvino's *The Uses of Literature* (New York: Harcourt Brace Jovanovich, 1986), 113.

24. See James's prefaces to "The Lesson of the Master," "The Author of Beltraffio," and "Daisy Miller."

25. Henry James, "The Art of Fiction," in *The Art of Criticism: Henry James on the Theory and Practice of Fiction* (Chicago: University of Chicago Press, 1986), 182.

26. See Freedberg, *The Power of Images*.

27. Cantor, *On Giving Birth to One's Own Mother*, 144. Compare Carolyn Porter's view: "Not only is the objectified surface of rationalization torn, revealing the irrational void lying beyond the limit of the thing-in-itself, but once admit that observation of the world constitutes a form of participation in its activity, and you experience a curious modern version of the Fall, for you become at least theoretically implicated and complicit in events which you presume merely to watch, analyze, and interpret" (*Seeing and Being*, 33–34).

28. The work of Pierre Bourdieu on symbolic economies has great relevance for all the texts I read in this chapter. See especially his *Language and Symbolic Power* (Cambridge: Harvard University Press, 1991).

29. In her essay "A Literary Postscript," *in The Identity of Persons*, 301–323, Amelie Rorty explains the shift in cultural self-understanding which replaces "persons" with "selves"; the person is an actionable or legal entity, while the self is economic and political. Persons inhabit the world of Jane Austen and the Bordereaus; selves, by contrast, represent the narrator's element, a mercantile world of inalienable property—which includes belles-lettres. More palpably than "The Real Thing," then, *The Aspern Papers* illustrates a transition between different concepts of personhood and also gives a deeper account of literary personality.

30. Henry James, *The Aspern Papers and Other Stories* (Harmondsworth, Eng.: Penguin, 1976), 11. Further references are to this edition.

31. See Max Weber's discussion of charisma in *Economy and Society: An Outline of Interpretive Sociology*, ed. Guenther Roth and Claus Wittich (New York: Bedminster Press, 1968), and the chapter on transference in Ernest Becker's *The Denial of Death* (New York: Free Press, 1973).

32. Barbara Herrnstein Smith, *On the Margins of Discourse: The Relation of Literature to Language* (Chicago: University of Chicago Press, 1978), 79.

33. "[Narrator:] I look at you but I don't see you. [Juliana:] I want to watch

you" (75). Her "frontage" is hidden Gyges-like by muslin or a green shade, so "that she might scrutinize me without being scrutinized herself. . . . The old woman remained impenetrable and her attitude bothered me by suggesting that she had a fuller vision of me than I had of her" (25). In her adamant refusal to withdraw from hiddenness, Juliana looks back, we might say, to the self-allegorizers and sign functions of Hawthorne's *The Blithedale Romance* and "The Minister's Black Veil," and perhaps ultimately, given the story's inspiration, to Shelley's poem "The Witch of Atlas" (James wrote the story after reading a similar anecdote about one of Shelley's still living ex-lovers).

34. See, for example, pp. 48, 56, and 73.

35. See Karl Marx, "Money and the Circulation of Commodities," in *Capital*, and *The Economic and Philosophic Manuscripts of 1844*, (New York: International Publishers, 1964).

36. Wayne Booth, *The Rhetoric of Fiction* (Chicago: University of Chicago Press, 1983). All references are to this edition.

37. Superficially, James's concept of unimpeded remembrance echoes Proust's. In fact, however, they diverge quite sharply. Jamesian memory conforms to what Walter Benjamin, in discussing Proust, called *memoire volontaire*, a conscious expression of the subjective will. Unlike Bakhtin's construct, it proceeds from and returns to egological desire. It likewise differs from Levinasian memory, whose structure perhaps more closely approximates Proust's *memoire involontaire*, a transpersonal, nondeliberative act, or more precisely, a summons.

38. See Emmanuel Levinas, *Time and the Other*, trans. Richard Cohen (Pittsburgh: Duquesne University Press, 1987), and "The Trace of the Other," in *Deconstruction in Context*, ed. Mark C. Taylor (Chicago: University of Chicago Press, 1987), 345–359. Walter Benjamin, in "Theses on the Philosophy of History," in *Illuminations*, supplies a cultural, trans-historical horizon for a model of ethically constrained memory by insisting on the *burden of possession* with which the Past—as other—saddles the Present: "For every image of the past that is not recognized by the present as one of its own concerns threatens to disappear irretrievably" (Thesis V). See also Theunissen's *The Other* for an incisive discussion of phenomenology's limiting reliance on intentionality, which bases intersubjective relation on a model of subjective *memoire volontaire*.

39. Rorty, *The Identity of Persons*, 314.

40. See Rabinowitz's explanation of this term in *Before Reading*, 29–36, and also Phelan's *Reading People, Reading Plots*.

41. See J. Hillis Miller, *ER*, and "Is There an Ethics of Reading?" in *Reading Narrative: Form, Ethics, and Ideology*, (Columbus: Ohio State University Press, 1988).

42. *ER*, 114.

43. Aside from Pierre Bourdieu's work on symbolic capital in *Language and Symbolic Thought*, see Jean-Joseph Goux, *Symbolic Economies: After Marx and Freud* (Ithaca: Cornell University Press, 1990), and Marc Shell, *Money, Lan-*

guage, Thought: Literary and Philosophical Economies from the Medieval to the Modern Era (Berkeley: University of California Press, 1982), for important studies of this conversion process.

44. In Freud's *Civilization and Its Discontents*, the ego is obliged to forgo acting on its desires, but is still punished by the superego for manifesting those desires in the first place, the very double bind imposed on the protagonist of *In the Cage*.

45. In *The Sovereignty of Good* (New York: Schocken, 1974), Iris Murdoch formulates a notion of contextual privacy which grants an interior and unrepresentable space to the substantial self; one can name this space perhaps, she claims, but not exhaust it.

46. Henry James, *In the Cage*, in *Eight Tales from the Major Phase* (New York: Norton, 1969), 177. Further references are to this edition.

47. In Henri Lefebvre's terms, she engineers the "production of space": "social relations . . . have a social existence to the extent that they have a spatial existence; they project themselves into a space, becoming inscribed there, and in the process producing that space itself." *The Production of Space*, trans. Donald-Nicholson-Smith (Oxford: Blackwell, 1991), 129.

48. The description is by Thomas Pavel in *Fictional Worlds*, 85.

49. See Erving Goffman, *The Presentation of Self in Everyday Life* (New York: Overlook Press, 1974). Emile Benveniste's description of the third person as a potential nonperson applies here as well; see the essay "The Nature of Pronouns," in *Problems in General Linguistics*.

50. See Peter Brooks, *Reading For the Plot*, and Frank Kermode, *The Sense of an Ending: Studies in the Theory of Fiction* (New York: Oxford University Press, 1987), for detailed explanations of these concepts.

51. See Levinas, "The Trace of the Other," in *Deconstruction in Context*, 351.

52. Levenson, *Modernism and the Fate of Individuality*, 69–70.

53. Levinas, "The Trace of the Other," in *Deconstruction in Context*, 357.

54. Sören Kierkegaard, *The Point of View from My Work as an Author*, trans W. Lowrie (New York: Harper and Row, 1962), 40. Compare Blanchot's use of Valéry's notion of "interruption as if on a Riemann surface") in his essay "Interruptions."

55. Levinas, "The Trace of the Other," in *Deconstruction in Context*, 357.

56. For these terms, see Dorrit Cohn, *Transparent Minds*. For a good summary on methods of representing consciousness in fiction, also see Wallace Martin, *Recent Theories of Narrative* (Ithaca: Cornell University Press, 1986).

57. See Carolyn Porter's discussion of narratorial stance in *Seeing and Being*, especially relevant for the moral and epistemological implications it traces in a presumed detachment of observation. If the third-person subject lens in *The Ambassadors*, *The Portrait of a Lady*, and *The Golden Bowl* corrects for the compositional dilemma posed by *The Sacred Fount*—"the liability of the 'I' who speaks and thereby . . . forfeits the position outside the world constituted by

[his] discourse" (*AN*, 124)—*In the Cage* resituates this problem between the narrator and his mimetic apprentice, the telegraph girl.

58. In this respect, James's novella bears comparison perhaps with George Eliot's "The Lifted Veil," where the protagonist-narrator's first-person omniscience allegorizes the authorial command of perspective.

59. Levinas, "Reality and Its Shadow," in *Collected Philosophical Papers*, 6.

5. Creating the Uncreated Features of His Face

1. "Impasse" is Critchley's word *(ED)*, and is central to his important analysis of the way politics "works" in deconstruction. I agree with him that the flaw here is not apoliticism at all, but rather a certain failure of nerve to thematize politics as "a place of contestation." Compare Benhabib's discussion of agonal, associational, and discursive models of public space in *Situating the Self*.

2. See, for instance, Vincent Pecora's formulation of politics versus ethics in "Ethics, Politics, and the Middle Voice," in *Reading Narrative: Form, Ethics, Ideology* (Athens: Ohio Universisty Press, 1989), 217.

3. Levinas, *Face to Face with Levinas*, 29–30. See also "The Ethical Relation and Time" in *TI*.

4. See Critchley's discussion, *ED*, 219. Critchley further emphasizes Levinas' idea that there is a simultaneity of ethics and politics which doubles all discourse, such that "the relation to the Other, my Saying, is at the same time the setting forth of a common world."

5. The trope of the veil, for instance, can be found as early as Jefferson's *Notes on Virginia*—the "immovable veil of blackness which covers [the Negro's] emotions"—before its seminal application by W. E. B. Du Bois in *The Souls of Black Folk*. But the image of the unveiled face, as either a misconceived threat or a target for defacement, is perhaps even more common in African-American texts. See the chapter on self-veiling in Michael Cooke's *Afro-American Literature in the Twentieth Century: The Achievement of Intimacy* (New Haven: Yale University Press, 1984). See also my "Incognito Ergo Sum; The Value of Ethnic '-' in Cahan, Johnson, Larsen, and Yezierska," in *Ethnicity, Modernism, and Modernity*, ed. Henry Louis Gates, Jr. (New York: Oxford University Press, 1995).

6. Compare Edward Said's argument that history only becomes legible through human presence; see his essay "On Repetition," in *The World, the Text, and the Critic* (Cambridge: Harvard University Press, 1983). "Never mind," he writes, "if epistemologically the status of repetition itself is uncertain: repetition is useful as a way of showing that history and actuality are all about *human persistence*" (113).

7. Frantz Fanon, *The Wretched of the Earth* (New York: Grove Press, 1968), 27; further references are to this edition. Ralph Ellison, *Shadow and Act* (New York: Random House, 1964), 28. See also Charles Johnson's "The Primeval

Mitosis: A Phenomenology of the Black Body," in *Being and Race* (Bloomington: Indiana University Press, 1988), and Sander Gilman's *Difference and Pathology: Stereotypes of Sexuality, Race, and Madness* (Ithaca: Cornell University Press, 1985) and *The Jew's Body* (New York: Routledge, 1991) for relevant work on physicality and cultural marginalization.

8. In Levinas' view, unmediated vision does not constitute the *summum bonum* of ethical encounter anyway, nor can it really, since the face represents primarily an aural, not a visual phenomenon—the site of language. Not surprisingly, given Levinas' negative opinion of "disclosure" (which I described in Chapter 3), the ethical face to face breathes less the air of Greek *apokalypsis* than that of Hebrew *gala* ("bodily uncovering") with its uncanny echo of biblical proscriptions against uncovering nakedness or of the Lord's injunction to Moses not to let Himself be beheld directly.

9. Frantz Fanon, *Black Skin, White Masks*, trans. C. L. Markmann (New York: Grove Press, 1967), 218. Further references are to this edition.

10. William Boelhower's *Through a Glass Darkly: Ethnic Semiosis in American Literature* (New York: Oxford, 1987) opposes to such universalism an equally defective model which he calls "facework," a kind of ethnic shape-shifting by which one effaces, by displacing, one's ethnic identity.

11. See Geoffrey Hartman, *Criticism in the Wilderness: The Study of Literature Today* (New Haven: Yale University Press, 1980). Hillis Miller's view of history as uncanniness does not answer to the special conditions of black-American history as worked out in novels like Ralph Ellison's *Invisible Man*, Toni Morrison's *Beloved*, and David Bradley's *The Chaneysville Incident*, where historical events must ultimately signify and be assimilated beyond the uncanny.

12. Ellison, *Shadow and Act*, 75.

13. Twice in *The Monster*, thinghood substitutes for personhood. When Dr. Trescott saves Henry in section 8, he is described as bringing forth "a thing which he laid on the grass" (141), and in section 16, a scene evocative of Shelley's *Frankenstein*, a girl traumatized by Henry's appearance at her window is asked, "Was it a man? She didn't know. It was simply a thing, a dreadful thing" (163).

14. What Fried thus calls a "thematics" or "metaphorics" of writing—a will-to-see which is alternately fascinated and excruciated—functions rather like the textual corollary to the rhetorical effect which Miller ascribes to prosopopoeia, except that instead of sublating latent into manifest content, it places the two in equipoise or, more precisely, in permanent tension. See Michael Fried, *Realism, Writing, and Disfiguration: On Thomas Eakins and Stephen Crane* (Chicago: University of Chicago Press, 1987).

15. Fried, *Realism, Writing, and Disfiguration*, 132. For similar oppositions, see Warner Berthoff's *The Ferment of Realism: American Literature, 1884–1919* (New York: Free Press, 1965); Michael Warner's "Value, Agency, and Stephen Crane's *The Monster*," *Nineteenth-Century Fiction*, 40 (June 1985), 76–93; and Donald Pease's "Fear, Rage, and the Mistrials of Representation in *The Red*

Badge of Courage," American Realism: New Essays, ed. Eric Sundquist (Baltimore: Johns Hopkins University Press, 1982), 155–174.

16. For this interpretation, see James Hafley, "'The Monster' and the "Art of Stephen Crane," *Accent*, 19 (1959), 159–165, and Max Westbrook's more sophisticated "Whilomville: The Coherence of Radical Language," in *Stephen Crane in Transition: Centenary Essays*, ed. Joseph Katz (Dekalb: Northern Illinois University Press, 1972), 86–105.

17. Lee Clark Mitchell, "Face, Race, and Disfiguration in Stephen Crane's *The Monster*," *Critical Inquiry*, 17, no. 3 (Fall, 1991), 175. Further page references are given in the text.

18. All references are to Stephen Crane, *The Monster*, in *"The Red Badge of Courage" and Selected Prose and Poetry* (New York: Rinehart, 1959).

19. James Weldon Johnson, *The Autobiography of an Ex-Coloured Man* (New York: Vintage, 1989). Further references are to this edition.

20. See Patricia Williams, *The Alchemy of Race and Rights: The Diary of a Law Professor* (Cambridge: Harvard University Press, 1991), 119.

21. See Eric Sundquist's discussion of the tragic paradox of minstrelsy for blacks (a fate Twain described as "imitation nigger") in the North's post-Reconstruction nostalgia for the Old South in the chapter "Mark Twain and Homer Plessy," from *To Wake the Nations: Race in the Making of American Literature* (Cambridge: Harvard University Press, 1993).

22. See Richard Cohen's illuminating discussion of this point in "God in Levinas," *Journal of Jewish Thought and Philosophy*, 1 (1992), 197–221.

23. See Levinas' discussion of murder in *TI*, 198.

24. Charles Chesnutt, "The Web of Circumstance," in *"The Wife of His Youth" and Other Stories of the Color Line* (Ann Arbor: University of Michigan Press, 1986), 293. Further references are to this edition.

25. Levinas, *Face to Face with Levinas*, 29.

26. See Houston Baker, *Blues, Ideology, and Afro-American Literatuare: A Vernacular Theory* (Chicago: University of Chicago Press, 1984), 151.

27. Michael Warner, "Value, Agency, and Stephen Crane's *The Monster*," 82.

28. Henry's response merits attention. He speaks coherently, albeit somewhat outlandishly, though the narrator calls it "gabbling": "I jes' drap in ter ax you 'bout er daince, Miss Fa'gut. I ax you if I kin have the magnificent gratitude of you' company on that 'casion, Miss Fa'gut." This can be read, like Henry's expostulations to Trescott on the buggy in section 12, as irony: I will be the same person I was even if you cannot allow me continuous identity. But the "blackface" context militates against such an interpretation; Henry, through the narrator's eyes, cannot possess the subversive power of the anti-minstrel minstrel.

29. Warner, "Value, Agency, and Stephen Crane's *The Monster*," 89.

30. As Jill Robbins points out, Levinas rarely uses the word "man." *Visage* is man in his infinite alterity; it is a description added not onto the conception

of "man" but, rather, prior to it. See "Visage, Figure: Reading Levinas' *Totality and Infinity*," *Yale French Studies* 79 (1991), 140.

31. Levinas, "Freedom and Command," in *Collected Philosophical Papers*, 21.

32. In "Value, Agency, and Stephen Crane's *The Monster*," Michael Warner points to the fact that Henry "dies" twice in section 10—once when he, as "thing," is laid on the grass and carried away on a covered stretcher, and once again when the newspaper announces his death. And certainly for Whilomville, after the fire, he effectively dies as Henry Johnson and, like Frankenstein's creation, becomes "a monster" restored to life.

33. Derrida first made a connection between Levinas' concept of the face and the trope of prosopopoeia in "Violence and Metaphysics," in *Writing and Difference*, trans. A. Bass (Chicago: University of Chicago Press, 1978). But as Jill Robbins correctly notes, this "is tempting particularly for literary critics because when Levinas gives the face as *voice* here, he in a sense defaces it, gives it a *figure*. . . . Yet while this seems tropological, prosopopoeia or any other rhetorical term is inapplicable here, again because of the level of Levinas' description, which is written both within and against the tradition of Husserlian phenomenology and Heideggerian ontology, and because, in short, of the *founding* status of the encounter involved." "Visage, Figure," 139.

34. See Sander Gilman, *Difference and Pathology* and *Jewish Self-Hatred: The Hidden Language of the Jews* (Baltimore: Johns Hopkins University Press, 1986).

35. Fanon, *Black Skin, White Masks*, 161.

36. Ralph Ellison, *Invisible Man* (New York: Vintage, 1972), 14. Further references are to this edition.

37. Compare *Benito Cereno*: "the negro Babo asked [Don Benito] whose skeleton that was and whether, from its whiteness, he should not think it a white's." Herman Melville, *"Billy Budd, Sailor," and Other Stories* (Harmondsworth: Penguin, 1976), 295. Further references are to this edition.

38. This is a common theme in Melville's later fiction, from *The Piazza Tales* to the final prose work published in Melville's lifetime, *The Confidence Man*, a deeply skeptical turn which followed in the wake of the commercial failure of *Moby-Dick*.

39. Ellison himself raised the issue at mid-century by suggesting that a writer like Twain, perhaps more than twentieth-century writers like Hemingway or Faulkner, knew how useful for white America was a mask of blackness: "Whatever else the Negro stereotype might be as a social instrumentality, it is also a key figure in a magic rite by which the white American seeks to resolve the dilemma arising between his democratic beliefs and certain antidemocratic practices" (*Shadow and Act*, 44).

40. *Putnam's Monthly*, in which *Benito Cereno* first appeared in 1855, was the first national magazine to come out against slavery, its editor being the free-soil journalist Frederick Law Olmstead. As Jean Fagan Yellin points out, "In addition to Melville's tale, the last three numbers for 1855 included articles on the threat of slavery in Kansas, a review of Frederick Douglass' autobiography

and an announcement of *Putnam's* new radicalism, which concludes, 'The nigger is no joke, and no baboon; he is simply a blackman, and I say: Give him fair play and let us see what he will come to.'" "Black Masks: *Benito Cereno*," *American Quarterly*, 22 (1970), 679.

41. See Philip Fisher, "Democratic Social Space: Whitman, Melville, and the Promise of American Transparency," *Representations* 24 (Fall 1988), 60–101.

42. See Eric Sundquist, "Suspense and Tautology in *Benito Cereno*," *Glyph*, 8 (1981), 103–126, and the greatly expanded version in *To Wake the Nations*.

43. Among the many comparisons of Amasa Delano's *Narrative of Voyages and Travels* with *Benito Cereno*, see particularly Max Putzel, "The Source and Symbols of *Benito Cereno*," *American Literature*, 34 (1962), 191–206, and Robert J. Ward, "From Source to Achievement in *Benito Cereno*," *Anglo-American Studies*, 2 (1982). Thomas D. Zlatic suggests as the probable source for Melville's addition a description by Delano elsewhere in his text of a woman's beheading after being placed on an ass. See "*Benito Cereno*: Melville's 'Back-Handed-Well-Knot,'" *Arizona Quarterly*, 34 (1978) 327–343. Melville almost certainly knew the grisly aftermath of both Nat Turner's rebellion in 1831 and Toussaint L'Ouverture's Santo Domingan insurrection in 1791, in which slaves' heads were stuck on pikes in retribution. The latter very probably influenced Melville's decision to change the name of the original Spanish ship in Delano's account from *Tryal* to *San Dominick*; we should see in the same light the insurrectionists' substitution of a white slaveowner's skeleton for the figurehead of Christopher Columbus, whose first port of call in his New World "discoveries" was the island of Santo Domingo.

44. Yellin suggests a precedent for it in black insurrectionists' determination to "die silent" and notes that not Nat Turner himself but his captors wrote *The Confessions*. As she says, "Legally, a black man's speech did not exist: his testimony inadmissable, his literacy forbidden by law, quite literally he stood mute." "Black Masks: *Benito Cereno*," 688. See also Sundquist's observations on silence as both an act of subversion and a subvocalized speech "hidden within the veil of black life" in *To Wake the Nations*.

45. See Fisher's analysis in "Democratic Social Space."

46. See Catherine Juanita Starke's *Black Portraiture in American Fiction: Stock Characters, Archetypes, and Individuals* (New York: Basic Books, 1971), for a discussion of such alter-ego figures.

47. Three varieties of metaphor attend Delano's reading for the plot: fairly crude comparisons used by him, such as "unsophisticated as leopardesses; loving as doves" (251); those which the narrator attributes to him but which underscore his obtuseness, like the "one sinister eye" which I quoted above; and last what should be seen as authorially intended, for example, the knot a sailor hands Delano to untie or the revelation of Aranda's skeleton over the motto "Follow your leader" (a pertinaciously floating signifier throughout the text). In all three cases, however, the reliance on simile and metaphor, either

extravagant or conventional, conforms entirely to the story's internal critique of hermeneutic invention, indeed to its play with allegory and symbolism generally.

48. Sundquist, "Suspense and Tautology," 121.

49. See Charles E. Nnolim, *Melville's "Benito Cereno": A Study in the Meaning of Name Symbolism* (New York: New Voices, 1974).

50. I draw the phrase from John Samson's *White Lies: Melville's Narrative of Facts* (Ithaca: Cornell University Press, 1989), a study of Melville's conflation of fact and fiction.

51. In "Man in the Mirror," in *Notes of a Hanging Judge: Essays and Reviews, 1979–1989* (New York: Oxford University Press, 1990), 210–214, Stanley Crouch prefers masquerade over vitiligo as the key to Jackson's idiosyncrasies. Crouch makes the case for his improvised identity and "look" as both quintessentially American and quintessentially African.

52. Richard Wright, *Native Son* (New York: Library of America, 1991), 538. Further references are to this edition, which restores important passages deleted by Wright's publishers and missing in all subsequent printings. Chief among these are explicitly sexual descriptions, which widen our frame of reference for Bigger's actions, and equally "brazen" social commentary from Max's defense, such as additional mention of the lawyer's Jewishness or the repeated references to institutionalized racism in the United States.

53. See Dan McCall, *The Example of Richard Wright* (New York: Harcourt Brace and Jovanovich, 1969).

54. Fisher, "Democratic Social Space," 96.

55. Jean Toomer, *Cane* (New York: Norton, 1987), 81. Further references are to this edition.

56. "Face" and recognition are dominant tropes in *Cane*.

57. McCall, *The Example of Richard Wright*. Compare the famous dream passage after Mary's murder, where Bigger falls asleep while looking out onto a curtain of white snow: "he had a big package in his arms so wet and slippery and heavy that he could scarcely hold onto it and he wanted to know what was in the package and he stopped near an alley corner and unwrapped it and the paper fell away and he saw—it was his own head—his own head lying with black face and half-closed eyes and lips parted with white teeth showing . . . and when the people closed in he hurled the bloody head squarely into their faces" (599): Bigger as Babo / Henry Johnson.

58. In her essay on *Cane* Barbara Bowen notes, "In the lines of narration between the lines of the song, Toomer gives us the process by which the slaves invested the spirituals with veiled messages." Kabnis' "Rock-a-by-Baby" dramatizes the creation of a literary form which allows words to subvert themselves and a calm linguistic surface to express violent meanings. See "Untroubled Voice: Call and Response in *Cane*," in *Black Literature and Literary Theory*, ed. Henry Louis Gates, Jr. (New York: Methuen, 1984), 200.

59. See Roger Rosenblatt, *Black Fiction* (Cambridge: Harvard University Press, 1974), and also McCall, *The Example of Richard Wright.*

60. See Henry Louis Gates, Jr., *The Signifying Monkey: A Theory of Afro-American Literary Criticism* (New York: Oxford University Press, 1988), 52; Gates, *Figures in Black: Words, Signs, and the "Racial" Self* (New York: Oxford University Press, 1987); Claudia Mitchell-Kernan, "Signifying, Loud-Talking, and Marking," in *Rappin' and Stylin Out: Communication in Urban Black America,* ed. Thomas Kochman (Urbana: University of Illinois Press, 1972); Roger Abrahams, *Deep Down in the Jungle: Negro Narrative Folklore from the Streets of Philadelphia* (New York: Aldine, 1970).

61. Roger Rosenblatt's caveat is important, however: "Richard Wright's conception of horror is not Brockden Brown's or Poe's, nor is his naturalism that of Norris or Dreiser. . . . The families which disintegrate in Ann Petry and Zora Neale Hurston are unlike their counterparts in Cable or Faulkner. . . . Ralph Ellison's Rinehart and William Kelley's Cooley are con-men as shifty as Melville's or Twain's, but they pull different tricks for different reasons." *Black Fiction,* 4.

62. For a related argument about the almost autonomous life which mass culture leads in Wright's novel (partly a legacy of Dreiserian narrative materialism and partly a force impinging on author and protagonist alike), see Ross Pudaloff, "*Native Son* and Mass Culture," *Studies in American Fiction,* 11, no. 1 (Spring 1983).

63. Valerie Smith, *Self-Discovery and Authority in Afro-American Narrative* (Cambridge: Harvard University Press, 1987).

64. Ellison, *Shadow and Act,* 29.

65. For an excellent treatment of the modes of narration in *Native Son,* see Laura Tanner, "The Narrative Presence in Richard Wright's *Native Son,*" *Texas Studies in Language and Literature,* 29, no. 4 (Winter 1987), 412–431. She notes, for example (much as in *Benito Cereno*), that "the effect of the narrative reading is not to increase our understanding of and sympathy for Bigger but to distort our perception of his existence by framing it within a highly metaphorical context" (413). In a review of Nathan McCall's memoir, *Makes Me Wanna Holler,* which emphasizes its *Native-Son-ship,* Henry Louis Gates, Jr., makes the related point that the burden of representativeness obliges even black autobiography to "communicate a tale that is never completely your own." See "Bad Influence," *The New Yorker,* March 7, 1994, 94.

66. In *The Grotesque in Negro American Fiction: Jean Toomer, Richard Wright, and Ralph Ellison* (Basel: Francke Verlag Bern, 1975), Fritz Gysin explains that Bigger arrives at the plot of *Native Son* already distorted by cultural symbolism and metaphor, and thus the novel's grotesqueness derives more from realistic description in the service of plot than from figurative language. One might plausibly argue that Wright inserts Bigger's rape and murder of Bessie entirely in order to bolster Buckley's charge that Bigger must have raped Mary Dalton

as well. Bigger's "act of creation" is thus qualified by a gratuitous and displaced act of authorial creation, Wright amplifying and then serving up Bigger's monstrousness to feed the appetite of, in Irving Howe's words, "white fantasy and white contempt." Irving Howe, "Black Boys and Native Sons," in *A World More Attractive: A View of Modern Literature and Politics* (New York: Horizon, 1983), 102.

67. Johnson, *Being and Race*, 12.

68. Sartre asks the question in the section "For Whom Does One Write" in the essay "What Is Literature?" in *"What Is Literature" and Other Essays.*

69. Dorothy S. Redden's "Richard Wright and *Native Son:* Not Guilty," *Black American Literature Forum*, 10, no. 4 (Winter 1976), 111–116, reviews the divergence of opinion on Wright and brings it up to date.

70. James Baldwin, *Notes of a Native Son* (Boston: Beacon Press, 1990), 24. Further references are to this edition.

71. Irving Howe, *A World More Attractive*, 100.

72. It is with this idea in mind, I would argue, that Chester Himes crams his fiction with a gallery-ful of Dickensian grotesques. Here, the world is almost uniformly a black world; that everyone is grotesque, that black faces show forth in the most lurid and extravagant terms, "carnivalizes" the very fact of a racist image-repertoire. Or, to take another example, from John A. Williams' *The Man Who Cried I Am*, the cameo appearance of Moses Boatwright—cannibal-murderer—signifies with transparent satire on both Wright, whose name the character "incorporates," and the whole belabored trope of "black monsters."

73. Henry Louis Gates, Jr., *Black Literature and Literary Theory* (New York: Routledge, 1984), 6.

74. The phrase is from Ellison's *Invisible Man.*

75. The commercial was devised not by Roger Ailes but by Larry McCarthy, who worked for an independent organization called Americans for Bush. Not having enough money to purchase network time for his commercial, McCarthy offered it first to cable TV in two versions, one with the mug shot and one without; the networks opted for the former. The ad then received free air time on commercial television when a videotape was aired and discussed on PBS's *The McLaughlin Group*. In short order, the commercial began appearing in feature stories on all the major networks. See Martin Schram, "The Making of Willie Horton," *The New Republic*, May 28, 1990, 17–18. (Compare *Time*'s shading of O. J. Simpson's mug shot, June 27, 1994.)

76. Needless to say, I am not exculpating Willie Horton here, but rather teasing out a culpability which lies in the dynamics of representation. Horton makes the following pertinent statement himself in an interview: "The fact is, my name is not 'Willie.' It's part of the myth of the case. The name irks me. It was created to play on racial stereotypes: big, ugly, dumb, violent, black—'Willie.' I resent that. They created a fictional character—who seemed believable but who did not exist." Quoted in Jeffrey M. Elliot, "The 'Willie' Horton

Nobody Knows" (interview with William Horton, Jr.), *The Nation*, August 23, 1993, 201–206.

6. Telling Others

1. Cavell, *Disowning Knowledge*, 335.

2. Philip Roth, *The Facts: A Novelist's Autobiography* (New York: Farrar, Straus, and Giroux, 1988), 172.

3. The question of fictionality and generic boundaries haunts most recent theoretical approaches to autobiography, though clearly it is first raised by literary texts themselves, such as *Sartor Resartus*. For the restrictive position, see Dorrit Cohn, "Fictional *versus* Historical Lives: Borderlines and Borderline Cases," *Journal of Narrative Technique*, 19, no. 1 (Winter 1989), 3–24; for the opposite view, see Louis A. Renza, "The Veto of the Imagination: A Theory of Autobiography," *New Literary History*, 9 (1977), 1–26.

4. John Stuart Mill, *Autobiography*, ed. John M. Robson (New York: Penguin, 1989), 25.

5. See Phyllis Grosskurth, "Where Was Rousseau?" in *Approaches to Victorian Autobiography*, ed. George Landow (Athens: Ohio University Press, 1979), 26–38, on the expectations which a Victorian readership had for its autobiographers.

6. Miller, *The Novel and the Police*, 200. Further references are given in the text.

7. George Steiner, *After Babel: Aspects of Language and Translation* (Oxford: Oxford University Press, 1975), 175.

8. See Sissela Bok's *Secrecy: On the Ethics of Concealment and Revelation* (New York: Pantheon, 1982) on this and other aspects of private versus public worlds.

9. Predictably, the critical approach one finds most often applied to *Bleak House* concentrates primarily on *récit*. The novel leaves us in the position of its characters: we await only more facts, more truth. When studies of the novel turn to the realm of voice, of character, of person, they actually follow Dickens' lead, tending either to descant morally upon it or to expose its flagrant textuality. Both approaches reify character at the level of representation, in the same way that readings "for the plot" collapse the narrational and hermenuetic properties of character into the restrictive interplay of story/discourse.

10. Charles Dickens, *Bleak House*, ed. George Ford and Sylvere Monod (New York: Norton, 1975), 128. Unless otherwise indicated, all references are to this edition.

11. Bok, *Secrecy*, 21 (my italics).

12. See Barry Westburg, *The Confessional Fictions of Charles Dickens* (Dekalb: Northern Illinois University Press, 1977), for a discussion of how Dickens chose to distribute details of his own life among his fictions.

13. On split subjectivity in the novel of education, see Bakhtin's essay "The

Bildungsroman and Its Significance in the History of Realism," in *Speech Genres and Other Later Essays*, trans. Vern W. McGee (Austin: University of Texas Press, 1987), and Georg Lukács' famous analysis in *The Theory of the Novel*, trans. Anna Bostwick (Cambridge: MIT Press, 1971).

14. In structural *dédoublement*, only James Hogg's *Confessions of a Justified Sinner* (1824) compares with *Bleak House* in nineteenth-century British fiction, Martin Amis' *Success* being, I think, its only modern British counterpart. Dramatic monologues like Browning's *The Ring and the Book* and Clough's *Amours de Voyage* should perhaps also be mentioned in this context.

15. De Man, "Excuses," in *Allegories of Reading*, 279.

16. Henry James, *What Maisie Knew* (New York: Doubleday Anchor, 1965), 41.

17. Compare Rilke's essay on dolls, "An die Puppe." "We took our bearings from the doll . . . through it to keep the world, which was entering into us on all sides, at a distance," he observes, noting how dolls permit a child to split its personality into "part and counterpart." *Rodin and Other Prose Pieces*, trans. G. C. Houston (London: Quartet, 1986), 73.

18. See *DI*, 342–346.

19. See Robert Garis, *The Dickens Theater* (Oxford: Oxford University Press, 1965), and W. J. Harvey, *Character and the Novel* (Ithaca: Cornell University Press, 1965). Harvey notes rather incredibly that "we do not, so to speak, look at Esther; we look *through* her at the teeming Dickensian world," when it is in fact her facial disfigurement which absolutely magnetizes our attention to her as surface.

20. As Harvey correctly observes of Esther, "she must seem to be living in the dramatic present." The complementarity of narrators is borne out on the text's surface in other crucial ways. The two converge early (if only momentarily) at the level of discourse, Esther in her reference to her "portion of these pages" (13) hinting at the knowledge that she shares them with another, the anonymous narrator implicitly doing likewise when he picks up the story "while Esther sleeps, while Esther wakes" (76). They flow together at several points in the plot; they describe identical scenes; finally, they converge according to frequent likenesses of style. All of these likenesses point not only to the narrators' overall mutuality but to the author's commanding presence behind them, and his perhaps deliberately imperfect attempt at split focalization.

21. See Bakhtin's discussion of *Little Dorrit* in "Discourse and the Novel," in *DI*, for an extensive treatment of heteroglossia in Dickens.

22. See Hilllis Miller's introduction to *Bleak House* (New York: Penguin, 1981), 34.

23. Terence Cave uses the term "cynegetic model" to describe recognition plots like *Bleak House*'s, which depend on the hunting and tracking of persons and the signs which may give them away—signs such as the novel's unmistakable signals about its own predilections, the chapters entitled "Signs and Tokens" and "The Track." See *Recognitions*, 251–255.

24. This is, incidentally, a conspicuously gendered machinery. For the

women in the novel, such "visual aids" combine distinct but related themes of motherhood, death, duplicity, and self-division; the handkerchief-veil which passes from Esther to Lady Dedlock to Hortense to Jenny's dead infant perfectly symbolizes the mobility of this mechanism within the text.

25. Cave, *Recognitions*, 499.

26. De Man, "Autobiography as De-Facement," in *RT*, 81.

27. Structurally, it can be argued that *Bleak House* has almost as much in common with epistolary as with multiplot novel forms, as witness the preponderance of actual letters within the text. The multiplicity of letters sent and received in the novel sends its own clear signal about the damaged and defective conditions under which ordinary social discourse must operate within the novel, and indicates why secrecy has become its defining trait.

28. In this second, static set of characters, one notes the motivating ideology behind authoritative discourse. Despite class differences, families like the Dedlocks, Bagnets, Jarndyces, and Rouncewells, as well as solitaries like Phil Squod or Boythorn, all rely on some notion of "natural" social relations and common law utterly at odds with the newer, legislative model of law and polity which had been firmly established by the mid nineteenth century. It is not by accident, then, that Tulkinghorn, Smallweed, and others all traffic (after one fashion or another) in the instrumentalizing, codifying, and reifying procedures of legal positivism. In his essay "On the Jewish Question," Marx uses the phrase "allegorical" to describe the formalized, empty, and abstract subjectivity which the legal revolution in England had fashioned; it formed the utilitarian counterpart to Kant's model of self-legislating rational agency. By one of those remarkable yet telling historical coincidences, Dickens, writing ten years after Marx, places in Tulkinghorn's office, above his desk, the pointing figure of Allegory, taken by most readers for a symbol of Justice—abstract, yet ultimately unfathomable and meaningless. It can just as plausibly be seen, I would suggest, as a symbol of pure instrumentality; the logic of pointing, of moving without moving, thus conveys the manipulatory and self-regulating ethos for which Tulkinghorn stands as the ideal "repository." See Marx's essay in *Karl Marx: The Essential Writings*, ed. Frederic Bender (New York: Harper and Row, 1972), and the chapter "Surplus Values" in Vincent Pecora's *Self and Form in Modern Narrative*.

29. Very different from these are the "third-person" stories either elicited from or cunningly narrated to Lady Dedlock, Jo, and Mr. George (by Grandfather Smallweed), and the demonstration of narrative hegemony (or blackmail) staged by Tulkinghorn for the Dedlocks (505–511).

30. Bucket relates to Esther the fact that Skimpole had given away the whereabouts of Jo for a bribe. Liz discloses to both of them that Lady Dedlock travels incognito, although "there's something kept back" (685). George Rouncewell explains his reasons for secrecy to Sir Leicester; yet in the same chapter, the narrator conspires in keeping a secret from him—Lady Dedlock's death.

31. Bok, *Secrecy*, 21.

32. Julian Barnes, *Flaubert's Parrot* (New York: Knopf, 1985), 102. Further references are to this edition.

33. Robert Unger, *Passion: An Essay on Personality* (New York: Free Press, 1986), 235. The entire passage is illuminating.

34. James J. Gibson, *The Senses Considered as Perceptual Systems* (Boston: Houghton Mifflin, 1965), 204.

35. Kazuo Ishiguro, *The Remains of the Day* (New York: Knopf, 1988), 67. Further references are to this edition.

36. See Elizabeth Bruss's excellent *Autobiographical Acts: The Changing Situation of a Literary Genre* (Baltimore: Johns Hopkins University Press, 1976) for a theory of autobiography as performative langauge.

37. Gibson, *The Senses*, 204.

38. The terms are Philip Roth's, from *The Facts*.

39. Bakhtin views such openness in another way. "My own word about myself is in principle incapable of being the last word, the word that consummates me." To want to confess at all opens up a space for another; it testifies "that I am not alone in my self-accounting, that someone is interested in me" (*AA*, 144). Hence, of course, with a logic that is pure pathos, the need for hedging in Braithwaite's and Stevens' cases in the first place.

40. The second moment occurs when Stevens meets Miss Kenton at the end of his journey, to find his hopes for her return to Darlington Hall unfounded. The third, more devastating one follows shortly thereafter, when Stevens confesses to a stranger that his slavish, uncritical regard for Lord Darlington actually compromised rather than exemplified "dignity." Significantly, each of these moments transpires as narrative revelation, as confession in the presence of a witness.

41. Compare Robert Langbaum's treatment of Browning's dramatic monologues in terms of "sympathy and judgment" (judgment in Browning's case being very close to irony as Braithwaite defines it) in *The Poetry of Experience: The Dramatic Monologue in Modern Literary Tradition* (New York: Norton, 1957).

42. See the introduction to *Nine Talmudic Readings*, trans. Annette Aronowicz (Bloomington: Indiana University Press, 1991).

43. Gadamer, *Truth and Method*, 16–17.

44. See the important article by Henry Louis Gates, Jr., "'Authenticity': Or the Lesson of Little Tree," *New York Times Book Review*, November 24, 1991. However apt a term for Ishiguro's astonishing performance, "impersonation" can perhaps be more precisely described as the alignment of two compatible sensibilities—the *japonaise* and the ceremonial English.

45. Philip Roth, *The Counterlife* (New York: Farrar, Straus, and Giroux, 1987), 210.

46. Richard Poirier, *The Performing Self: Compositions and Decompositions in the Languages of Everyday Life* (New York: Oxford University Press, 1971).

47. Compare Mill's "accidental" (he uses that very word) double exposure of self in his account in the *Autobiography* of reading Marmontel's *Memoirs*.

48. For these concepts, see Bernard Williams, *Moral Luck* (Cambridge: Cambridge University Press, 1982); John Rawls, *A Theory of Justice* (Cambridge: Harvard University Press, 1971), especially chap. 7; and Thomas Nagel, *The Concept of Altruism* (Oxford: Oxford University Press, 1970).

49. Stevens is caught crying twice in the novel: once, at the end, when he confesses his desolation on a seaside pier (243) and once while he is attending to dignitaries after his father has just died upstairs (105). The involuntary act of crying links the latter event to the former (his explanation in both cases is identical: "the strains of a hard day"), and associates the purgation that comes with confession with, in this instance, the not wholly successful "looking away" that follows in the wake of death.

50. Given the affinity the novel shares in form and tone with Ford Madox Ford's *The Good Soldier* (the recent purchaser of Darlington Hall and Stevens' new employer is American), the significance of the car's being a Ford is tantalizing (one of the many elements tied to this novel's discourse, incidentally, not present in the film version, where the car becomes a Daimler). Also similar to Ford's novel is the allegorical significance of the text's topographical "markers": a high, clear, morning vista as the journey begins, a narrow passageway overgrown with high foliage on either side in the afternoon, an unplanned detour to the perch of a lonely hill at nightfall, "dark all around, the mist growing thicker" (162).

51. Blanchot, "Interruptions," in *The Sin of the Book: Edmond Jabès*, 44.

Conclusion

1. See Benjamin, "The Storyteller," in *Illuminations*, 90. Further references are given in the text.

2. See Bakhtin's essay "The Problem of Speech Genres," in *Speech Genres and Other Later Essays*.

3. Bruno Schultz, "Tailors' Dummies," from *The Street of Crocodiles* (New York: Penguin, 1989), 64.

4. See A. R. Luria, *The Mind of a Mnemonist: A Little Book about a Vast Memory* (Cambridge: Harvard University Press, 1987) and *The Man with a Shattered World* (Cambridge: Harvard University Press, 1987); and Oliver Sacks, *The Man Who Mistook His Wife for a Hat* (New York: Harper and Row, 1987) and "The Last Hippie," *New York Review of Books*, March 26, 1992.

5. Edmond Jabès, *The Book of Questions: Yael*, trans. Rosemarie Waldrop (Middletown: Wesleyan University Press, 1986), 115.

Index

Adorno, Theodor, 21, 30, 54, 55, 298n30
Altieri, Charles, 64, 67, 300n46, 304n31, 308n63
Amis, Martin, 326n14
Anderson, Sherwood, 14, 15, 20, 21, 22, 32, 57, 58, 290; "Adventure," 118; anagnorisis in, 120; force in, 108; "The Form of Things Concealed," 76–78; fragment in, 104; "Godliness," 111–112; "Hands," 110–111; "Loneliness," 14–18, 19–22, 45, 66, 95, 200, 298n31; "Mother," 113–114; "The Philosopher," 118–121; "Queer," 116–117; "Respectability," 115–116; "Sophistication," 234; "Teacher," 108, 112, 240; *Winesburg, Ohio*, 23, 24, 169, 174, 104–121 passim, 210, 247, 249, 279, 292, 311n31
Arendt, Hannah, 299n39
Aristotle, 9, 12, 57, 62, 305n37, 306n45
Arnold, Matthew, 9, 117
Artaud, Antonin, 66
Auerbach, Eric, *Mimesis*, 266
Augustine, Saint, 22, 249

Baker, Houston, 195
Bakhtin, Mikhail, 12, 23–24, 30, 78, 79, 84, 88, 138, 153, 245, 326nn13,21; on authoritative/inner persuasive discourse; 252, 253–264, 260–261; on confession, 328n39; on death, 116; and de Man, 46–50, 104, 302n4, 305n10; dialogism in, 47; on face, 145; hero in, 23, 145, 156; and Kant, 47, 303nn19,22; live-entering (*vzhivanie*), 79, 85–86, 111, 148, 149, 161, 298n34; living aesthetically, 82; mem-

ory in, 153; and the novel, 246; on "outsideness," 148, 309n7; penetrative word in, 95, 116; phenomenalism in, 46; reflection in, 90; representation in, 138; on split subjectivity, 57, 326n13; on unfinalizability, 88, 96
Bal, Mieke, 52
Baldwin, James: *Notes of a Native Son*, 232–233, 235; "Sonny's Blues," 63
Balzac, Honoré de, "Sarrasine," 55
Barnes, Julian, *Flaubert's Parrot*, 26, 247, 267, 268–269, 270, 271–273, 274–275, 277–279, 280, 284
Barthes, Roland, 27, 55, 100, 108; and narrative codes, 300n43, 310n22
Baudelaire, Charles, 125, 127, 146, 297n22
Beckett, Samuel, 63
Benhabib, Seyla, 179, 296n16, 299n39, 301n47
Benjamin, Walter, 47, 116, 123, 176, 290, 292; on Proust, 306n40, 315n37
Benveniste, Emile, 298n31, 302n8, 316n49
Blanchot, Maurice, 6, 36, 38, 39, 49, 96, 285, 287, 290
Boelhower, William, 318n10
Bok, Sissela, 267, 325n8
Booth, Wayne: *The Company We Keep*, 10, 61, 64–65, 67, 129–130; on friendship, 308n58; *Rhetoric of Fiction*, 152–153, 154
Bourdieu, Pierre, 314n28
Brecht, Bertolt, 67
Brooks, Peter, *Reading for the Plot*, 98–99, 306n48, 307n49

331

Browning, Robert, 295n5, 326n14, 328n41
Broyard, Anatole, 94
Brudney, Richard, on *The Golden Bowl*, 67–68, 276
Bruss, Elizabeth, 328n36
Bunyan, John, 195
Burke, Edmund, 309n2

Calvino, Italo, 314n23
Camus, Albert, 7
Cantor, Jay, 128, 146
Cave, Terence, on anagnorisis, 99, 258, 284, 326n23
Cavell, Stanley, 4, 5, 6, 28, 40, 42, 43–44, 74, 144, 292; on acknowledgment, 28, 43, 149, 219, 250, 303n11; on claim, 11; on contract, 307n51; and Derrida, 300n44; on fiction, 129, 142, 169, 298n35; on first vs. third person, 85, 152, 243, 309n6; on *King Lear*, 66, 152, 198; on Othello, 59–60; on paraphrase, 295n2; on skepticism, 4–5, 56, 295n2; on theater, 298n35
Cervantes, Miguel de, 59
Cézanne, Paul, 128
Chambers, Ross, 27, 58–60, 307n50
Chaucer, Geoffrey, 295n5
Chesnutt, Charles, 187; "The Web of Circumstance," 184, 193–196 passim, 212
Ciamarelli, Fabio, on Levinas, 12
Clough, Arthur, 326n14
Cohen, Richard, 28, 300n45, 319n22
Cohn, Dorrit, 171, 305n38, 325n3
Coleridge, Samuel Taylor, 272; *The Rime of the Ancient Mariner*, 3–7 passim, 11, 14, 16, 17, 18, 28, 58, 66, 73, 114, 116, 121, 124, 279, 290, 291, 299n36
Conrad, Joseph: anagnorisis in, 99; essay on James, 28; *Heart of Darkness*, 98–99; *Lord Jim*, 19–20, 32, 51, 59, 72, 73–76, 78, 79, 80–104 passim, 122, 123, 124, 143, 161, 190, 201, 210, 211, 247, 292, 299n36, 310n20; narration in, 83–85, 88–89, 192; *Nigger of the "Narcissus,"* 169; perception in, 81–83, 90–91; therapeutics in, 93–97
Cortazar, Julio, 63

Cowper, William, "The Castaway," 213
Crane, Stephen, 26; *The Monster*, 58, 176, 179, 182, 184, 184–206 passim, 210, 219, 221, 222, 224, 225, 227, 233, 247, 291, 300n43, 318n13, 319n28, 320n32
Critchley, Simon, 178, 303n12, 317nn1,4
Croce, Benedetto, 128
Crouch, Stanley, 322n51

Dällenbach, Lucian, 22
Dallmayr, Fred, 296n13
Davis, Miles, 63
Defoe, Daniel, 31
de Man, Paul, 28, 39, 40, 42, 44, 45, 52, 74, 122, 250; on autobiography, 258; and Bakhtin, 47–49, 104, 304n27; and Benjamin, 47, 123, 259, 304n27; and Heidegger, 47, 302n4; on history, 311n36; and Kant, 50, 302n6; on prosopopeia, 203, 258, 266; "The Resistance to Theory," 40–41, 44
de Quincey, Thomas, 175, 192
Derrida, Jacques, 28, 39, 49, 109, 300n44; and Cavell, 310n2; and Levinas, 28, 201, 301n2, 301n47, 308n58, 320n33
Descartes, René, 3, 296n13
Dickens, Charles, 32, 63, 275; and Bakhtin, 326n21; *Bleak House*, 26, 58, 244, 247, 248–267 passim, 272, 290, 326, 327; *David Copperfield*, 248, 325n12; *Dombey and Son*, 9; *Great Expectations*, 25, 113, 230; *Hard Times*, 244
Dostoevsky, Fyodor, *Notes from Underground*, 16
Du Bois, W. E. B., 189, 317n5
Dunbar, Paul Laurence, 227

Eldridge, Richard, 32
Eliot, George, 26, 32; *The Lifted Veil*, 241, 317n58; *Middlemarch*, 32, 63, 104
Ellison, Ralph, 183, 185, 206, 207, 208, 229, 232, 235, 238, 320n39, 323n61; *Invisible Man*, 195, 207, 227, 300n43, 324n74; *Shadow and Act*, 320n39
Emerson, Ralph Waldo, 238
Evans, Walker, 140

Fanon, Frantz: *Black Skin, White Masks*, 183, 184, 188, 202, 205, 207, 233; *Wretched of the Earth*, 208, 209, 211, 218, 227
Faulkner, William, 111; *Absalom, Absalom!* 25; *Light in August*, 221, 234, 320n49
Felman, Shoshana, on de Man, 301n3
Fielding, Henry, 9
Fischer, Michael, 35, 38
Fish, Stanley, 17
Fisher, Philip, on *Benito Cereno*, 208, 224
Flaubert, Gustave, 244, 269, 270, 271, 273, 278, 279
Fogel, Aaron, on Conrad, 96, 114
Ford, Ford Madox, 268, 328n50
Foucault, Michel, on Velásquez, 21–22
Frankenheimer, John, 313n16
Freud, Sigmund, 156, 307n49, 316n14
Fried, Michael, on Stephen Crane, 186, 187, 199, 203, 318n14
Frost, Robert, 51; "All Revelation," 87; "Figure in a Doorway," 126, 127; "The Most of It," 87, 170
Frye, Northrop, 10, 296n11

Gadamer, Hans-Georg, on "tact," 276, 297n17
Gates, Henry Louis, Jr., 227, 228, 232, 236, 322n58, 328n44
Genesis, 112, 331n27
Genette, Gérard, 8, 21, 52, 53, 305n37
Gibson, James J., 269
Giddens, Anthony, 301n49
Gilman, Sander, 204, 320n34
Girard, René, 307n49
Godzich, Wlad, 52, 54, 61, 303n22
Goffman, Erving, 159
Goodman, Nelson, 308n60
Greimas, Algirdas, 53
Gyges, 143, 159, 198, 262, 315n33

Habermas, Jürgen, 11, 12, 62, 301n47
Hacking, Ian, 297n21
Halliwell, Stephen, on Aristotle, 306n45
Hardy, Thomas, 26
Hartman, Geoffrey, on history, 185
Hawthorne, Nathaniel, 53, 144, 227, 297n22; "The Minister's Black Veil," 180, 182, 186; *The Scarlet Letter*, 55

Hegel, G. W. F., 11, 41, 202, 208
Heidegger, Martin, 11, 46, 47, 302n4, 303n23
Hemingway, Ernest, 320n39
Himes, Chester, 324n72
Hoffmann, E. T. A., 6
Hogg, James, 326n14
Hölderlin, Friedrich, 42
Holiday, Billie, 192
Holquist, Michael, on Bakhtin, 46, 303n19
Horton, William, 238–239, 324n76
Howe, Irving, on Wright, 232, 234–235
Hulme, T. E., 65
Hume, David, 9, 12
Husserl, Edmund, 81, 82, 127

Ingres, Jean-Auguste-Dominique, 268, 274, 284
Iser, Wolfgang, 297n25, 301n49
Ishiguro, Kazuo, 32; *The Remains of the Day*, 26, 247, 267, 268, 269, 270, 272, 273, 275–277, 279, 281–284, 292

Jabès, Edmond, 35, 45, 72, 103, 121, 122, 123, 329
Jackson, Michael, 221–222, 322n51
Jakobson, Roman, 56, 159, 302n8
James, Henry, 9, 16, 26, 32, 53, 214, 224, 227, 271, 290; *The Ambassadors*, 132, 167, 171, 172, 316n57; *The Aspern Papers*, 144, 146–155 passim, 156, 159, 160, 162, 165, 171, 172, 314nn29,31; "The Beast in the Jungle," 172; "The Figure in the Carpet," 59; *The Golden Bowl*, 10, 62, 63, 67, 68, 134, 139, 154, 316n57; indexicals in, 167; *In the Cage*, 144, 155–172, 251, 317n57; memory in, 315; *The Portrait of a Lady*, 126, 146, 156, 171, 313n18, 316n57; "The Real Thing," 129, 130–146 passim, 154, 155, 156, 162, 165, 171, 172; *Roderick Hudson*, 129; *The Sacred Fount*, 144, 171, 316n57; *The Spoils of Poynton*, 130, 132; *What Maisie Knew*, 154, 156, 171, 251; *The Wings of the Dove*, 26, 146
Jameson, Fredric, 27
Jauss, Hans-Robert, 10

Johnson, Charles, 231
Johnson, James Weldon, 187, 189, 195
Johnson, Samuel, 43

Kafka, Franz, 36, 55, 107
Kant, Immanuel, 4, 12, 23, 29, 30, 41,
    47, 50–51, 297n26, 302n6, 303n22,
    304n31, 305n34, 308n63, 309n2,
    327n28
Kierkegaard, Sören, 170
Kleist, Heinrich von, 38
Krafft-Ebing, Richard von, 14
Kristeva, Julia, 299n37

Lacan, Jacques, 57, 139, 306n46
Laclos, Choderlos de, 59
Langbaum, Robert, on Browning,
    328n41
Lanzmann, Claude, 181, 308n61
Lardner, Ring, 22, 190
Lefebvre, Henri, 316n47
Lentricchia, Frank, 10
Levenson, Michael: on Conrad, 309n4;
    on James, 167, 312n10
Levi, Primo, 71, 123–124, 302n3
Levinas, Emmanuel, 12, 33, 35, 50, 69,
    79, 105, 110, 127, 131, 142, 165, 201,
    217, 302n3; on allegory, 19; answer-
    ability in, 227; and Bakhtin, 86; and
    de Man, 39; and Derrida, 177, 301n2,
    320n33; on disclosure, 88, 92; on exte-
    riority, 199; on face, 18, 86, 114, 120,
    175, 180, 181, 191, 200, 203, 215,
    232, 318n8; on figuration, 291; on his-
    tory, 181; on interruption, 38; on jus-
    tice, 183; on language, 109, 111, 166;
    *Otherwise Than Being, or beyond Es-
    sence*, 179; on Poe, 53; on politics,
    178–179, 183, 204, 317n4; on repre-
    sentation, 305n40; "rubbing the text,"
    246; on Saying and the Said, 5–6,
    105, 166; on Signification, 164, 228;
    on skepticism, 42; on *sollicitation*, 248;
    on temporality, 153; on the third
    party, 179, 261; *Totality and Infinity*,
    179, 199; on the trace, 170–171; on
    violence, 76; on voice, 320n33
Luria, A. R., *The Man with a Shattered
    World*, 24, 25, 292
Lyotard, Jean-François, 62, 201, 299n37

Macmillan, Harold, 268
Marx, Karl, 134, 151, 156, 307n55,
    313n13, 327n28
Mauriac, François, 277
McCall, Dan, on *Native Son*, 225
Mead, George Herbert, 30
Melville, Herman, 26, 323n61; *Bartleby
    the Scrivener*, 180, 182, 297n22; *Benito
    Cereno*, 179, 207–222 passim, 223,
    225, 227, 233, 234, 236; *Billy Budd*,
    220
Merleau-Ponty, Maurice, 128, 241
Mill, John Stuart, *Autobiography*, 26, 243–
    246, 248, 253, 260, 267, 269, 275,
    277, 283, 284, 328n47
Miller, D. A.: on narratability, 308n57;
    The Novel and the Police, 32, 244, 249,
    252, 265, 272, 300n41
Miller, J. Hillis: on *Bleak House*, 326n22;
    The Ethics of Reading, 10, 67; *Haw-
    thorne and History*, 180–181, 182, 203,
    206, 235, 236, 318nn11,16; on James,
    154–155; on *Lord Jim*, 19–20, 91; on
    Trollope, 134, 163, 303n12, 313n15
Mingus, Charles, 63
Mitchell, Lee Clark, on *The Monster*,
    187, 203
Montaigne, Michel de, 245
Morrison, Toni, *Beloved*, 48, 122, 195,
    235
Mosley, Oswald, 282
Murdoch, Iris, 316n45

Nagel, Thomas, 329n48
Norris, Christopher, on de Man, 51,
    302n6
Nussbaum, Martha, 61–62, 63, 65, 68,
    305n35, 307n55

Ozick, Cynthia, 305n40

Pascal, Blaise, 244, 277
Pater, Walter, 89
Patterson, Orlando, 189
Pecora, Vincent, 31–32, 317n2
Peperzak, Adrian, on Levinas, 298n33
Perkins, David, 301n48
Phelan, James, 101, 311n25, 312n3
Picasso, Pablo, 268, 274, 284
Plessy v. Ferguson, 186, 191

Poe, Edgar Allan, 53, 227, 230, 323n63
Porter, Carolyn, on James, 308n55,
    316n57
Poulet, Georges, 303n14
Prendergast, Christopher, 58
Prince, Gerald, 52
Proust, Marcel, 42, 195, 280, 315n37

Rabinowitz, Peter, 315n40
Rawls, John, 329n48
Richardson, Mary, 128, 146
Richardson, Samuel, 59
Ricoeur, Paul, 55, 56, 299n39, 305n34
Rilke, Rainer Maria, 42, 326n17
Rimmon-Kenan, Shlomith, 55
Robbe-Grillet, Alain, 278
Robbins, Jill, on Levinas, 319n30
Rorty, Amelie, 136, 154, 314n29
Rosenblatt, Roger, 323n63
Rosenzweig, Franz, 175
Roth, Philip, 3, 8, 243, 276, 278, 328n38
Rousseau, Jean Jacques, 9, 41, 42, 193,
    325n5
Ruskin, John, 120

Sacks, Oliver, on Luria, 24, 329n4
Said, Edward, on history, 317n6
Sapir, Edward, 52
Sartre, Jean-Paul, 19, 20, 22, 23, 44, 45,
    184, 244, 292, 297n26; on Fanon,
    208; on Wright, 232
Scarry, Elaine, 141
Schiller, Friedrich von, 41
Schultz, Bruno, 291
Searle, John, 49
Shakespeare, William: King Lear, 66, 67,
    198; Othello, 43, 59–60, 220
Shelley, Mary, Frankenstein, 6, 55, 190,
    195, 196
Siebers, Tobin, 50, 61
Simpson, O. J., 324n75
Sloterdijk, Peter, on cynicism, 312n7
Stein, Gertrude, 55

Steiner, George, 245
Stowe, Harriet Beecher, Uncle Tom's
    Cabin, 9, 66, 186
Sundquist, Eric, on Benito Cereno, 210,
    211, 216

Taylor, Charles, 61, 64
Thoreau, Henry David, 22, 152
Thousand and One Nights, The, 7
Todorov, Tzvetan, 10, 311n33, 312n11
Tolstoy, Leo, 65, 66, 68
Toomer, Jean, Cane, 224–226, 322n58
Turgenev, Ivan, 7
Twain, Mark, 22, 319n20, 323n61

Valéry, Paul, 304n25, 316n54
Velásquez, Diego Rodríguez Silva y: Las
    Meninas, 20–21; Rokeby Venus, 128,
    144, 146
Vygotsky, Lev, 303n21

Warner, Michael, on The Monster, 196
Watt, Ian, 296n9, 310n12
Weber, Max, on charisma, 314n31
Weiskel, Thomas, 309n2
West, Nathanael, 297n19
Wharton, Edith, 314n21
Whitman, Walt, 86
Williams, Bernard, 62, 329n48
Williams, John A., 324n72
Williams, Raymond, 309n11
Woolf, Virginia, 55
Wordsworth, William, 42, 287, 289,
    290, 295n5
Wright, Richard, 32; "The Man who
    Lived Underground," 195, 234; Na-
    tive Son, 185, 222–238 passim, 323;
    oeuvre, 234

Yeats, William Butler, 42
Yehoshua, A. B., Mr. Mani, 7, 292,
    311n27